Knowledge-based
systems for
industrial control.

IEE CONTROL ENGINEERING SERIES   43

Series Editors: Professor P. J. Antsaklis
Professor D. P. Atherton
Professor K. Warwick

KNOWLEDGE-BASED SYSTEMS FOR INDUSTRIAL CONTROL

Other volumes in this series:

KNOWLEDGE-BASED SYSTEMS FOR INDUSTRIAL CONTROL

Edited by
J. McGhee,
M. J. Grimble,
& P. Mowforth

Peter Peregrinus Ltd. on behalf of the Institution of Electrical Engineers

Published by: Peter Peregrinus Ltd., London, United Kingdom

© 1990: Peter Peregrinus Ltd.

Peter Peregrinus Ltd.,
Michael Faraday House,
Six Hills Way, Stevenage,
Herts. SG1 2AY, United Kingdom

A CIP catalogue record for this book
is available from the British Library

ISBN 0 86341 221 1

Printed in England by Short Run Press Ltd., Exeter

Contents

List of Contributors

J. McGhee and M. J. Grimble
Dept. of Electrical and Electronic Eng.
University of Strathclyde
Level 7, Marland House
50 George Street
Glasgow G1 1QE

H. J. Efstathiou
The Oxford Trust
S.T.E.P. Centre
Osney Mead, Oxford OX2 0ES

J. L. Alty, D. Michie, M. Bain,
J. Hayes-Michie
Turing Institute
George Street
36 North Hanover Street
Glasgow G1 2AD

R. R. Leitch
Dept. of Electrical and Electronic Eng.
Heriot-Watt University
Edinburgh EH1 2HT

P. J. Fleming
School of Electronic Eng. Science
University College of North Wales
Dean Street, Bangor
Gwynedd LL57 2DG

T. P. Williams
British Gas
Research and Technol. Division
Midlands Research Station
Wharf Lane, Solihull
West Midlands

D. H. Owens and F. Ahmed
School of Engineering
University of Exeter

P. W. H. Chung, R. Aylett, D. Bental
R. Inder, T. Lydiard
Artificial Intelligence Applications
Institute
University of Edinburgh
80 South Bridge
Edinburgh EH1 1HN

K. Hunt and G. R. Worship
Dept. of Mechanical Eng.
James Watt Building
The University
Glasgow G12 8QQ

R. Milne
Intelligent Applications Ltd.
Kirkton Business Centre
Kirk Lane, Livingston Village
West Lothian EH54 7AY

R. Shaw
SD
Pembroke House
Pembroke Broadway
Camberley, Surrey GU15 3XD

M. J. Willis, C. De Massimo
G. A. Montague, M. T. Tham
A. J. Morris, M. Aynsley, D. Peel
A. G. Hofland
Dept. of Chemical and Process Eng.
Merz Court, The University
Newcastle upon Tyne NE1 7RU

B. Postlethwaite
Dept. of Chemical and Process Eng.
University of Strathclyde
James Weir Building
75 Montrose Street, Glasgow G1 1XJ

Chapter 1

Holistic approaches in knowledge-based process control

J. McGhee

Abstract

A consideration of the nature and scope of knowledge based process control (KBPC), leads to the proposal that Artificial Intelligence, Systems Engineering and Information Technology are three core elements of the discipline. Some aspects of all three are described. Systems Engineering methods are based upon whole life whole system considerations which are argued to be fundamental to KBPC. Applying the principles of taxonomy, or classification science, leads to a hierarchical perspective of control instrumentation systems which helps to gain breadth of comprehension of information machines. By first introducing the Systems Engineering approach and the methods of taxonomy, the chapter allows further development of the core theoretical elements in automatic control systems in general but especially in process control. Highlighting of the cardinal elements in the technology of knowledge based process control systems is also allowed using these methods.

1.   Introduction

Control of the states of equilibrium and motion of solids liquids, gases and the systems they constitue, which is of fundamental importance in industrial manufacturing, is dominated by a well developed and important body of theoretical material. Application of this theory using computers is described by Astrom and Wittenmark (1984, [1]). Astrom and others (1986, [2]) have considered expert control. When considering the technology of knowledge based process control, or KBPC, a question arises as to what elements are central to this technology. It is proposed that there are three key elements in KBPC. Each of these elements is briefly described in the chapter.

2.   The nature and scope of KBPC

Knowledge, as informed learning, requires the acquisition and elicitation of information. Consequently the concepts and theory of information are essential to any theory of knowledge. From another point of view, as knowledge may also imply cognition, comprehension, consciousness, discernment, judgment, recognition, understanding and wisdom it also implies intelligence. In the present context this intelligence is captured within a type of information machine which can store and process both objective and fuzzy information. Objective and fuzzy information are defined later. This body of information handling is economically described by the title Artificial Intelligence or AI.

Since the earliest times men and machines have been linked in the pursuit or achievement of aims. This link between men and machines provides the key to a deeper awarenes of the basis for KBPC. A primary aim in this cooperation is the drive for men to control not only their environment or other biological systems but also the systems they have developed to assist in achieving their technological goals. As machines for control purposes may be regarded as systems, it is proposed that Systems Science and Systems Engineering are essential elements in KBPC. The holistic or "whole life, whole system", concepts of this science with their associated sub-division or reticulation of systems by their function and structure is described in this chapter. A basis for the systematic ordering required by such a sub-division is seen to be an adaptation of the science of classification or taxonomy used in the life sciences. Such a theory of ordering exposes the need to introduce the concept of a machine kingdom by analogy with the animal and plant kingdoms of the super-kingdom of living things and the kingdom of materials of the super-kingdom of inanimate things. It provides a perspective from which the context of KBPC can be clearly visualised.

The pervasive nature of Information Technology has caused attention to be focused upon that class of machines now commonly referred to as information machines. Machines for control purposes, members of the class of information machine (McGhee and others, 1986 [3]), are high fidelity executers of commands generated from processed information feedback. The information, which is processed, is normally obtained from the states of the system to be controlled, whilst the executed commands normally regulate some, possibly various, kinds of energy flows within the process. Consequently control instruments may be properly regarded as systems in their own right, quite apart from the fact that they are embedded in some other wider system. For this reason the control machine cannot be regarded in isolation. It must always be considered from the point of view of the impact which it exerts upon its suspersystem as well as from the impact it undergoes from this suspersystem. The supersystem is merely the system within which the control system is embedded. Because of the systems context of control machines it is proper to argue that the theory and concepts of Systems Engineering underly the theory of control systems. Because control machines are members of the class of information machine, the science of Information Technology is inextricably bound up with KBPC. With the aid of taxonomy, the breaking-down or sub-division of Information Technology into its main divisions, is a principal factor in determining the constitution of KBPC.

It can now be concluded that there are three main groups of principles which constitute KBPC. A diagram which represents these three, as well as other contributory sub-divisions, is given in Fig. 1. The three main groups of priciples are thus:-

ARTIFICIAL INTELLIGENCE may defined as the acquisition, elicitation, storage, processing and utilisation of knowledge, using information machines.

SYSTEMS ENGINEERING, which is primarily concerned with the interdependent effects between interconnected elements, contains a holistic or total approach to the analysis, design and utilisation of all kinds of systems. It is based upon the functions performed by systems and the structures possessed by them.

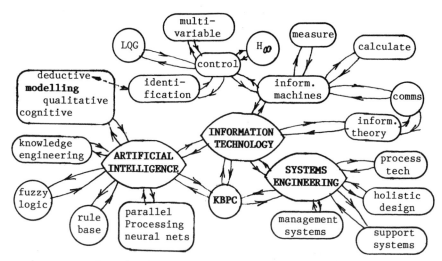

Fig. 1. the constituent disciplines of KBPC

INFORMATION TECHNOLOGY is concerned with the analysis design and utilisation of all forms of information and information machines. The information machines in KBPC are of course the computer and the control machine.

3. Artificial intelligence for KBPC

Deduction is a process where numerical algebra, mathematical equalities and identities and logical reasoning are combined to produce a unique inexorable numerical value as a solution. Thus deduction leads to a sharp specific conclusion. The theories which constitute classical control systems are almost all exclusively deductive in nature. Sometimes the mathematical formalism obscures breadth of understanding. Later, the grouping of adaptive controllers will be used to illustrate how breadth of understanding may be assisted by taxonomy without knowing the complete theory in detail.

It is increasingly apparent that many situations exist where conventional deductive methods of analysis place a severe limitation upon the possibility of solving a range of problems which can arise not only in process control systems, but also in other types of automatic control systems as well as in areas not related to control.

Human reasoning, which is principally inductive and heuristic, handles information using symbolic interpretations. Imprecisely, or fuzzily, defined concepts are inductively processed in a rule-based manner. By this process a fuzzy general conclusion is reached. For this reason, it is possible to acquire machine based intelligence (Astrom and others, 1986 [2]; Inst MC, 1986 [4]; Rodd and Suski, 1989 [5]; Opie, 1986 [6]). The algorithms, which are built around a framework of applied inductive or reasoning analysis, may also describe the rules used in reaching a given conclusion. It is possible to distinguish between two main forms of reasoning (Simmonds, 1985 [7]). Thus analytical reasoning is primarily concerned with assessing the operational status of a plant. Contrastingly, formative reasoning is

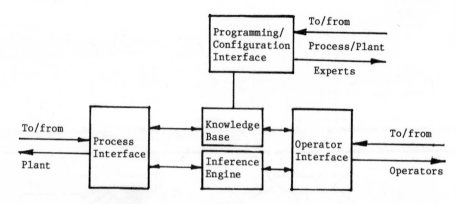

Fig. 2. A structure for AI in knowledge based process control

elementally about planning. This is especially true in determining appropriate courses of action as occur, for example, in design. A combination of deductive and expert analysis has been successfully applied in response analysing self-tuners (Cheshire, 1986, [8]). A measure for fuzzy information will be introduced later.

In the case of process control systems, a typical block structure for applying artificial intelligence is shown in Fig. 2. Three interfaces may be identified. The system must provide the means by which operators may assess plant status as a result of acquiring information from the operational states of the process, the knowledge base and the rule base or inference engine. Initially more emphasis is placed upon what the plant is meant to do rather than how it does it. Another interface, called the Programming/Configuration Interface, elicits knowledge from process/plant experts which is stored in the form of facts and rules. Aiding operator perception through succinct but meaningful communication of information is the primary function of the Operator Interface. Artificial Intelligence is dealt with in more detail in later chapters.

4.   Man-machine systems: a context for KBPC

4.1.   Boundary impacts and sub-structure of man-machine systems

Between men and machines there is ever a relation whose manifestattion alone does not constitute a system. Systems are understood to have an opaqueness and obscurity of structure, characteristic of complexity. For the purposes of analysis sytems are decomposed into an assembly of simpler interacting components. All of these components as well as the system are analysed first on the basis of the functions they perform and subsequently on the structures they possess. Thus functional and structural reticulation, or sub-division, is the main technique for system analysis whilst functional and structural synthesis is the principal technique for system design.

On this basis, a proposal by McGhee and others (1986, [3]) argues that the milieu of Systems Engineering is a relevant context within which instruments, instrument systems and thus KBPC may be incisively

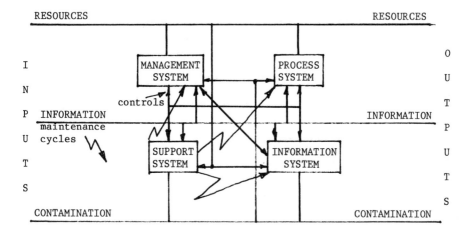

Fig. 3. Structure/boundaries of man-machine system

analysed and studied. A main benefit accrued by this systems approach is the holistic or total attitude which it encourages. As taxonomy also encourages the total or universal view it may be considered as a fundamental means for the analysis of systems. The primary feature of the Systems Engineering method [3] applies an underlying technique of analysis called reticulation. It is concerned with the process of simplifying problems, perhaps also using recursive methods, by breaking them down into simpler elements. For the general purpose of system analysis, this sub-division classifies systems by the functions they perform and the structures they possess. This manner of grouping, which allows a top-down classification of information systems from sub-system to component level, provides an aid to deeper perception of the role and function of information systems within a wider system.

A boundary and structural model of a man-machine system is given in Fig. 3. Boundary impacts may belong to the resource, contamination or information class. **RESOURCES,** which consist of men, money machines and materials, are often referred to as the 4Ms of systems. **CONTAMINATION,** implying impurity and interference, may be due to disruptions, social factors and resource failure. **INFORMATION** is probably the most important impact in KBPC. For this reason it will be considered in more detail in Section **5**.3.

A man-machine system has an internal sub-structure consisting of four discernible sub-systems. Through the **PROCESS** system the man-machine system realises its aim or goal, which is to produce a useful resource output. Organisation and co-ordination of all system functions is the responsibility of a **MANAGEMENT** system with the assistance of an **INFORMATION** system. This sub-system is the most important for the present consideration. It acquires, processes, communicates and distributes all relevant data which is necessary for proper, efficient, smooth and optimal execution of all system functions including the management function. As systems are subject to mal-function due to various forms of external and internal contaminations and failures, a **SUPPORT** system is required for adequate maintenance and resource scheduling. Further details may be found in McGhee and others (1986,

[3]), M'Pherson (1980, [9]; 1981, [10]) and Sandquist (1985, [11]).

4.2. Taxonomy or classification science in KBPC

In the short description of the structure and boundary impacts, given above as features of man-machine systems, the need for a theory of ordering or grouping is required for engineering systems. Taxonomy, which is a science of classification, is a term first proposed by the botanist De Candolle for the theory of plant classification. From the original classification of living things by Aristotle, has grown the contemporary view of classification due to Linnaeus [12, 13]. In this classifying approach entities are ordered first by kingdom. Kingdoms are then split into divisions (for plants) or phyla (for animals), then subdivisions or sub-phyla, class, order, family, genus and species. A first proposal to adapt this classical taxonomy to systems, particularly instrument systems, by McGhee and Henderson (1989, [14]), has been developed further by Henderson and McGhee (1990, [15]). The machine kingdom which they propose, should be sub-divided in the same way as for the plant kingdom. Criteria of classification should depend upon the function or functions performed by the machine (or system) and the structure(s) possessed by them [3, 14] but may also be based upon energy form [15].

Six aspects of taxonomy may be differentiated. These correspond to the objectives and functions of the method, its materials and activities together with methods of discrimination and hierarchical descriptive ordering. As details are given elsewhere [12, 13, 14] only the briefest description will be given here.

The objectives of classification allow a discrimination between different classes of objects so that other different objects may be uniquely identified. Reticulation possesses this primary property of discrimination. In control systems, whilst it is necessary to specify their primary features of function and structure, it may also be necessary to identify those parameters which determine their dynamic behaviour. To avoid confusion, the methods of description must be agreed and standardised. The knowledge acquired by taxonomy must be of an organised nature beefore it can fairly be called a science.

Taxonomy is characterised by three main functions. The systemic approach to the analysis and synthesis of systems reveals that a diversity of systems is possible from a more limited number of functional elements and interconnections. Although there is diversity the number of possibilities is not of the same order as the myriad forms of animal and plant life. Nevertheless, there is still a large enough variety of physical systems to bring order into the means of communication and retrieval of information of each type. It is also important to allow the acquisition of new information so that the characteristics of other unfamiliar systems may be predicted. Thus, taxonomy may be viewed as a short-hand which permits concise description. Classification finally shows the unifying features of the different variety of systems without in any way diminishing the important differences existing among them.

The basic materials of classification in KBPC are the various forms of individual system. It is essential for holistic understanding to bring order into the apparent chaos typical of such large numbers. The elements of taxonomy in engineering and technology are those entities which constitute systems and which give them the labyrinthine property of complexity.

Assembling the various taxonomic materials is the main activity in the science of classification. This implies the formation of collections for further study and analysis. By this means as yet unknown, or newly proposed system functions and structures may be objectively identified as unique. When seen as a contributory element in the study of systems, such collections will generally appear in graphical or iconic forms and theoretical descriptions.

Other activities are concerned with the grouping of systems into progressively larger taxa in such a manner that a hierarchical ordering becomes possible. Assistance with this task is allowed by discriminational criteria using reticulation. These criteria are based upon two main approaches. In the life sciences the approaches are based upon evolutionary factors, called phyletic criteria, and upon physical appearance or structure, phenetic criteria. For the purposes of a theory for classifying systems the same names may be adopted. Thus a phyletic approach, based upon genetic considerations in the life sciences, when adapted for physical systems must concentrate upon the construction of family trees forming a functional hierarchy. This functional hierarchy may also include details of energy form. On the other hand, the phenetic approach of the life sciences, used in the classification of physical systems, should group by division or taxa through the differentiation of similarities and comparison of differences in structural features.

5.   Information Technology

5.1.   The four information machines

A view of Finkelstein (1985, [16]), elaborated by McGhee and Henderson (1989, [14]), proposed that there are five main interrelated groups of concepts and principles which constitute the science of information technology. Although these same principles contribute to control engineering, the emphasis placed upon them is slightly different.

The theory of classification for physical systems [14, 15] is regarded as an essential tool in all technology not just Information Technology. As scientific knowledge must be organised a theory of ordering is essential. Taxonomy, or classification science, briefly introduced earlier, provides an analytical approach which allows such grouping by order. The idea of information and its underlying theory are obviously of central importance. The basis of information theory for hard sets, sometimes called Boolean sets, and soft sets, known as Fuzzy sets [17], is described later.

Contrivances for handling information, which have a long history, constitute the core elements in Information Technology. It is generally accepted that four instrumentation contrivances, constituting the group of information machines, perform primary information handling operations. Instruments are systems which enhance and refine the human faculties of

(a) sensing, by information acquisition   .the **measuring**   machine,

(b) perception, by data reduction/processing .the <u>calculating</u>   machine,
(c) distribution, by data communication   .the <u>communicating</u> machine,
(d) utilisation, by command execution   .the <u>control</u>   machine.

A close symbiosis between machines for measurement, calculation communication and control, which is manifested in their many similarities [3, 14, 15], indicates that they constitute this group of information machines. The predominant similarity is the manner in which all of them except the control machine, transform information inputs to information outputs. By contrast the control machine regulates energy flow by executing commands in the form of information. As these machines constitute the technical instrumentation sub-systems embedded within a man-machine system, they form the cardinal constituents in KBPC.

5.2.   Function and Structure of Technical Instruments

The holistic features of the systems engineering method highlights the placing of information, information systems and thus KBPC within the structure of man-machine systems. This location is indicated in the classification tree of Fig. 4. Thus, the functions and boundary structure of information machines may be linked to the hierarchical structure of the complete system.

Technical instrumentation systems, performing four primary functions, which are also shown in Fig. 4, distinguish between instruments for measuring, calculating, communicating and controlling. Bearing in mind the essential support provided by the calculating function, it is possible to distinguish the main secondary functions performed by technical instruments.

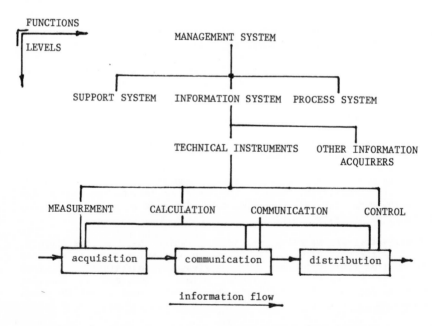

Fig. 4. Instruments in a systems and functions hierarchy

Before any data can be processed, it must be acquired. Within the context of KBPC the information may be process measurements or knowledge expertise. Further sub-division by function is possible. Hence, a separation of the functions of sensing and transduction in a measuring system, from those performed by any conditioning of the sensor output, is apparent. Communication and data distribution, which includes control instrumentation systems, are important from the broader view of KBPC. Some subsidiary functions, which may be highlighted through a phenetic and phyletic analysis of the complete information system are given elsewhere [3, 14]. Once more the holistic benefits, which are gained using the methods of taxonomy in conjunction with the systems engineering approach, are difficult to exaggerate. This point will be further reinforced in a later section, where classification in control system implementations will be considered.

5.3.   Information and Its Quantification

Due attention must be paid to the theory of information, since the context of KBPC lies within the general field of Information Technology. Applying the ideas of grouping theory or taxonomy reveals that three main classes of information may be distinguished.

SUBJECTIVE information is the most nebulous since it is embodied in those human perceptions resulting from intuitions, opinions and feelings. Although it is difficult to justify, it may sometimes be correct. Hence, it should be assessed properly and not dismissed out-of-hand.

Those technical instruments, which support and extend the human faculties of sensing and perception, enable humans to acquire **OBJECTIVE** information about the physical universe. Objective information may be quantified by means of the theory of information (Shannon and Weaver, 1972 [19]). In this theory, information is regarded as the removal of uncertainty. Thus, the occurrence of a more likely event conveys less information than that of a less likely event. Consider an alphabet consisting of k symbols having the probability of occurrence, p_j, for the j-th symbol. The self information (in bits) of the j-th symbol is defined as

$$I_j = -\log_2 p_j \tag{1}$$

Additionally, the average information per symbol or the entropy of the alphabet is

$$H = -\sum_{j=1}^{k} p_j \log_2 p_j \tag{2}$$

This quantification of information, allowed by the Shannon and Weaver theory, has far reaching implications. Information machines and information handling processes may be studied more generally because the theory allows a higher level of abstraction from particular cases. Fundamental limits in Information Theory, beyond which improvement is impossible, are discussed at length by Wyner (1981 [20]).

Natural language has developed many semantic overtones so that there exists a number of possible interpretations for the same group of symbols. A means of quantifying these possible meanings into more likely or less likely possibilities is provided by the notion of **FUZZY** information, which was first formulated by Zadeh (1965, [17]). As this fuzzy imprecision is quite distinct from stochastic imprecision, the theory is sometimes referred to as possibility theory. The concepts of the Shannon Theory of self-information and entropy of ordinary or hard sets may be applied to fuzzy sets with specified membership grades (Xie and Bedrosian, 1984 [21]). It is concluded that the average amount of information possessed by fuzzy data has two components. One component is the entropy associated with the randomness of the two events in a binary alphabet. The other specifies the average information which results from the fuzziness of the fuzzy set relative to its ordinary set. If H_S is the entropy of the binary alphabet and H_F is the entropy of the fuzzy alphabet then the total entropy of the fuzzy set is

$$H_{tot} = H_S + H_F \tag{3}$$

For the binary alphabet, the binary entropy is

$$H_S = -p_0 \log_2 p_0 - p_1 \log_2 p_1 \tag{4}$$

whilst, the fuzziness in the fuzzy set is

$$H_F = 1/N \sum_{i=1}^{N} H_f(u_i) \tag{5}$$

The self information in a single fuzzy event is $H_f(u_i)$ and is defined as

$$H_f(u_i) = -u(x_i)\log_2[u(x_i)] - [1 - u(x_i)]\log_2[1 - u(x_i)] \tag{6}$$

in which $u(x_i)$ is the grade of membership of the fuzzy event, x_i. Thus, the self information in a fuzzy event is defined in an identical manner to the Shannon self information of a binary Shannon information source. The N fuzzy events, x_i, are treated as N independent "fuzzy Shannon sources".

5.4.   Data Flow Rate in information handling channels

Another salient measure in information handling processes is the rate at which information may be handled by the process. This measure is defined as follows.

Definition 1. The rate of data flow in an information handling (communication) channel is the rate of handling information (communicating) in number of information operations (messages)/unit time times the resolvable bits per information operation (message).

Thus:
       C = channel capacity = rate of data flow
         = $n\log_2 m$ (7)
where
       n = number of information operations (messages) per unit time
       m = number of resolvable information operations (messages).

A question now arises. How many information handling operations (messages) per unit time can an information (communicating) machine handle? The answer to this question relies upon the signalling rate of the machine. Combining the concept of energy bandwidth for real networks with the response of ideal filters allows the definition of a maximum signalling rate. This rate and data flow rate, or channel capacity, are cardinal properties of information machines. McGhee and Henderson (1989, [18]) have shown that they have implications which are as important in control systems as they have in communication systems. The concepts were first proposed in the field of communication systems.

Consider a second order system with the natural frequency, w_n, the normalised damping coefficient, ξ, and elastance S. If this system has the maximum displacement, ϑ_{max}, and the ambient temperature is T K then it has been concluded [18] that the rate of data flow or the information capacity, of the machine channel to within x% of pulse settling error is given by

$$C_{tx} = \text{data channel capacity to x\% pulse settling}$$
$$= n\log_2 m \propto (xw_n/\xi)\log_2[1 + \vartheta_{max}(S/kT)] \tag{8}$$

This relation is of fundamental importance in the theory of information for KBPC. It clearly demonstrates that the ability of **any** physical system to handle information is closely related to the physical elements from which the system is made.

6.   Taxonomy of deductive adaptive control systems

Adaptive control has become important because some of the knowledge based controllers which are commercially available make use of adaptive control algorithms. As these algorithms require estimates of system behaviour they employ identification algorithms. The present section will apply the methods of grouping to both adaptive controllers and identification algorithms.

6.1.   Classification of Adaptive Controllers

A clear overall view of contemporary control is sometimes difficult because of the complexity of the algebra used to derive the resulting deductive algorithm for control purposes. McGhee and Henderson (1989 [14]) have expressed the opinion that higher motivation for detailed study may be given through the application of functional and structural reticulation. This may be applied not only to the physical elements of the control instrumentation system but also to control algorithms upon which effective control depends. In this manner, it is possible to impart incisiveness and breadth of understanding as well as detailed theory.

An illustration of the method of taxonomy applied to the classification of adaptive controllers [14] confirms the above opinion. One of the important objectives of taxonomy is the agreement and standardisation of terminology. It is apparent that the range of terms which has been developed in academia to describe the approaches to adaptive control are generally different from those used by manufacturers. Consequently some confusion arises from this lack of terminological standardisation. For this reason those involved in both

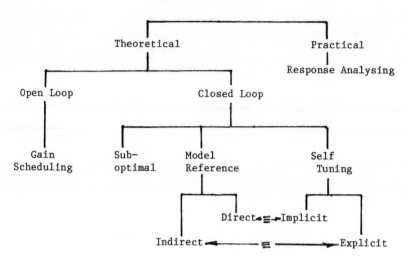

Fig. 5. Adaptive controllers classified

the manufacture and theoretical development of control should take care to avoid this fundamental violation of taxonomic standardisation.

From this classification [14]) an "adaptive control tree" may be formed as shown in Fig. 5. It is clear that the two main groups of adaptive controllers use either a theoretical or practical approach. Theoretical methods may be based upon open or closed loop structures. This important distinction, which is not made by Epton (1986, [22]), appears in Astrom and Wittenmark (1984, [1]) for a gain scheduling implementation. As there is no feedback to compensate for an incorrect schedule, this controller uses an essentially open loop algorithm. Epton's (1986, [22]) tree obscures the similarity between Model Reference Adaptive Systems and the implicit and explicit Self Tuning Regulators. These similarities are considered by Astrom and Wittenmark (1984, [1]). Fenney (1990, [23]) describes how adaptive control algorithms may be combined with knowledge expertise to deal with non-linearities and varying process conditions.

6.2.   Recursive Identification

Adaptive controllers require estimates of system behaviour in the form of models [24, 25] in either parametric or non-parametric form. Identification, which is a general measurement problem with specific relevance to control implementations, is the branch of instrument science and technology which is concerned with these problems. As it is characterised by the variety and complexity of its means and theories (Eykhoff, 1984 [26]), a functional and structural division of identification methods provides an important aid to understanding. Although there is full justification for applying the science of taxonomy to this important field of endeavour, it is impossible to be comprehensive in this chapter. For further details see Eykhoff (1984, [26]).

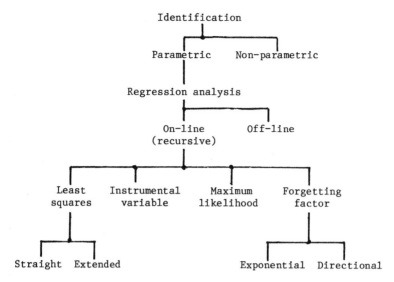

Fig. 6. Classification in recursive identification

Recursive algorithms have been reviewed by Hunt (1986, [27]). They provide not only a topical example to illuminate the application of taxonomy but also the opportunity for emphasising their importance in KBPC. On-line adaptive control demands information on those parameters, which determine system behaviour, evaluated in real-time. Because of the effects of inherent and measurement noise, it is necessary to acquire regressive statistical estimates and modify them by up-dating them with time. This is allowed by recursive algorithms which can take one of the four main forms given in Fig. 6. As the present purpose is only to illustrate the application of classification science to recursive identification, further explanation of the differences and similarities of the various methods will not be considered here. The theories of these algorithms are well covered in many other sources. However it is worthwhile observing that all four algorithms possess striking similarities. Summaries of the differences appear in Hunt (1986, [27]).

An important adaptation of these methods to time- varying systems is worth mentioning. This time-variation may be either in respect of a varying parameter of the system or in a non-stationarity of the corrupting noise. A forgetting factor, which attaches more importance to present data than to past data, can be proposed. In order to speed up the calculations it is appropriate to use parallel computing architectures (Chisci and Mosca, 1987 [28]).

7. Conclusions

In this chapter constituent elements of KBPC have been proposed and described. Systems Engineering was offered as a suitable context for KBPC. Important benefits of this method are the holistic, or total attitudes which it encourages. An essential ingredient in this body of concepts is the theory of taxonomy, a science of classification. Thus, the principles of classification science have been shown to form an important underlying technique in the analysis not only of KBPC but the engineering sciences in general.

Functional and structural reticulation, the essential basis of engineering taxonomy for the Systems Engineering approach, have been shown to be powerful methods of analysis through illustrative examples in Systems Engineering and Information technology. These examples were taken from the fields of information theory, instrument science, adaptive control and identification.

Although no comprehensive application of taxonomy has been made to the field of Artificial Intelligence it is now known that AI should also be analysed on the basis of the functions or tasks to be performed and the software structures to realise these functions.

8.   References

[1] Astrom, K.J. and Wittenmark, B. 1984. Computer controlled systems : theory and design. Prentice-Hall, Englewood Cliffs.
[2] Astrom, K. J., Anton, J. J. and Arzen, K.-E. (1986). Expert control. Automatica, **22**, 3, pp. 277–286.
[3] McGhee, J., Henderson, I.A. and Sankowski, D. (1986). Functions and structures in measuring systems: A Systems Engineering context for instrumentation. Measurement, **4**, pp. 111–119.
[4] InstMC. (1986). Measurement and Control. Special issue on AI and Expert Systems, **19**, 9.
[5] Rodd, M. G. and Suski, G. J. (Editors) (1989). Artificial intelligence in real time control. IFAC Proc Series May 1989.
[6] Opie, R. (Oct 1986). Expert systems developing applications. Cont. and Instrum., p. 57 and p. 59.
[7] Simmonds, W. (Sept 1985). Expert systems in instrumentation. Cont. and Instrum., pp. 58–60
[8] Cheshire, K. (Dec. 1986). Expert systems aid temperature unit self tuning. Cont. and Instrum., pp. 42–43.
[9] M'Pherson, P.K. (1980). Systems Engineering: An approach to whole-system design. Radio and Electronic Eng., **50**, pp. 545–558.
[10] M'Pherson, P.K. (1981). A framework for systems engineering design, Radio and Electronic Eng., **51**, pp. 59–93.
[11] Sandquist, G.M. (1985). Introduction to system science. Prentice-Hall, Englewood Cliffs.
[12] Daly, H.V. and Linsley, E.G. (1970). Taxonomy. In Gray, P. (Ed.) (1970). Encyclopaedia of the biological sciences. (2nd Ed.). Van Nostrand Reinhold, New York.
[13] Martin, E., Larkin, S. and Bernbaum, L. (Editors) (1976). The penguin book of the natural world. Penguin Books Ltd., Middlesex.
[14] McGhee, J. and Henderson, I.A. (1989). Holistic perception in measurement and control: applying keys adapted from classical taxonomy. In Linkens, D. A. and Atherton, D. P. (Editors). Trends in control and measurement education. IFAC Proc Series, 1989, No 5, pp. 31–36.
[15] Henderson, I. A. and McGhee, J. (1990). A taxonomy for temperature measuring instruments. To be presented at TEMPMEKO 90, Helsinki.
[16] Finkelstein, L. (1985). State and advances of general principles of measurement and instrumentation science. Measurement, **3**, pp. 2–6.
[17] Zadeh, L.A. (1965). Fuzzy sets. Infor. Control, **8**, pp. 338–353.
[18] McGhee, J. and Henderson, I.A. (1989). Introducing information capacity as a figure of merit for instrument systems using the concepts of energy bandwidth. In Linkens, D. A. and Atherton, D. P.

(Editors). Trends in control and measurement education. IFAC Proc Series, 1989, No 5. pp. 95-100.

[19] Shannon, C.E. and Weaver, W. (1972). A mathematical theory of communication. University of Illinois Press, Illinois.

[20] Wyner, A.D. (1981). Fundamental limits in information theory. Proc. IEEE., **69**, pp. 239-251.

[21] Xie, W.X., and Bedrosian, S.D. (1984). An information measure for fuzzy sets. IEEE Trans. Sys. Man and Cyber., **SMC-14**, pp. 151-156.

[22] Epton, J. (1986). Intelligent self tuners under the microscope. Cont. and Instrum., **18**, No 5, pp. 85-89.

[23] Fenney, L. (April 1990). Calling the tune in temperature control. Processing, pp. 35-36.

[24] Finkelstein, L., and Watts, R.D. (1983). Fundamentals of transducers: description by mathematical models. In Sydenham, P.H. (1983). Handbook of measurement science : Vol 2 practical fundamentals. John Wiley and Sons, New York. Chapter 18.

[25] MacFarlane, A.G.J. (1970). Dynamical systems models. Harrap.

[26] Eykhoff, P. (1984). Identification theory: Practical impli- cations and limitations. Measurement, **2**, pp. 75-84.

[27] Hunt, K. J. (1986). A survey of recursive identification algorithms. Trans Inst MC, **8**, No 5, pp. 273-278.

[28] Chisci, L. and Mosca, E. (1987). Parallel architectures for RLS with directional forgetting. Int J Adaptive Cont. Sig. Proc., **1**, pp. 69-88.

Chapter 2

Introduction to knowledge-based systems for process control

H. J. Efstathiou

1. INTRODUCTION

Expert systems began as a branch of Artificial Intelligence, but have evolved to fill many different technological niches, in financial planning and management, medical and health care and process control, among others. As a result of this evolution, expert systems are taking on quite different forms and functions, characteristic of any evolving species. At the same time, they are acquiring a separate identity, distinct from their forebears in Artificial Intelligence.

This paper will give an introduction to expert systems as they have been and are likely to be applied to the domain of process control. The evolutionary context of expert systems will be discussed, so as to pick out those features of process control expert systems which make them different from expert systems in other domains and artificial intelligence in general.

Section 2 introduces the broad field of Artificial Intelligence, but Section 3 focuses quickly on the sub-field of expert systems and their derivatives. The evolution of the field is described, from the early medical applications to the more complex and demanding present day systems. The basic concepts of the field, such as inference, knowledge representation and expert systems shells are introduced. Section 4 concentrates on the special requirements of process control and describes the roles expert systems may play in process control and their special requirements. Section 5 describes and discusses briefly some examples of expert systems in process control. Section 6 ends the paper with some concluding remarks.

2. WHAT IS ARTIFICIAL INTELLIGENCE?

This question is more often asked than answered. Part of the reason it is so hard to answer has to do with our lack of a satisfactory definition of intelligence. It is possible to take an ostensive approach to defining intelligence, and point to examples of objects that display greater or lesser degrees of some quality which is denoted by 'intelligence'. That approach to defining intelligence leaves us with a definition of intelligent behaviour along the lines of "Intelligent behaviour is what animate beings, but especially humans, do."

This definition is not very good for producing a scale or scales for measuring intelligence, but it is a start. We can proceed from there to say that "Artificial Intelligence is making machines carry out the intelligent actions which humans do." This definition accommodates two approaches to the study of artificial intelligence:

1) the study of psychology and cognition through the simulation of behaviour,
2) an improvement in automation of intelligent processes hitherto performed by humans.

The two forms of study of artificial intelligence are not completely separate and learn much from each other. The study of machine vision, for example, benefits from an understanding of how the brain processes images, so that more effective artificial vision systems may be devised.

The development of expert systems has benefited from the influence of parallel psychological developments, which have indicated why some approaches to knowledge representation or knowledge acquisition have been disappointing. But a body of experience is growing up which is sufficiently well understood to be useful for the would-be practitioner of expert systems.

To return to the question posed at the start of this section, let us take an ostensive approach to defining Artificial Intelligence (AI). AI is (or includes):
- the simulation of behaviour,
- making computers behave like people,
- the ability to learn from unstructured data,
- a collection of scientific principles and techniques for applying knowledge flexibly,
- symbolic computation,
- applying non-quantitative mathematics,
- the next stage in automation.

And AI is not necessarily:
- programming in Lisp/Prolog/Poplog,
- using an AI workstation,
- Fortran IF statements.

Artificial Intelligence studies humans' capability to perform various tasks, such as understanding natural language, reasoning with incomplete and uncertain data, understanding pictures, planning courses of action, moving around in a changing world etc. Many of these topics have little relevance to process control today, but as technology and culture continue to evolve, these topics will become more important in the design of user interfaces and will extend the scope of computers to tackle more tasks and improve the overall control and management of the plant.

3. EXPERT SYSTEMS, KNOWLEDGE BASED SYSTEMS AND IKBS

3.1 The early applications of expert systems

Expert systems, Knowledge Based Systems and IKBS (Intelligent Knowledge Based Systems) are names used to describe systems which possess both the following characteristics:

1) The representation of a human expert's skill in a particular domain,

2) The representation of that expertise in a knowledge base, separate from the inference software.

Expert systems began in the sixties at Stanford University with the MYCIN program (Ref. 1). This oft-cited example modeled medical expertise on the diagnosis of bacterial infections. The expert's knowledge was represented as IF..THEN rules, with a certainty factor associated with each rule to accommodate the numerous possibilities that could account for the symptoms observed.

This paradigm example possessed both the characteristics mentioned above. The interesting and novel feature of MYCIN was that the program (called the inference engine) that manipulated the knowledge-base had no 'knowledge' of medical diagnosis. All the knowledge was separate in the knowledge base. Hence, in principle, it would have been possible to replace the original knowledge base on bacterial infection with some-

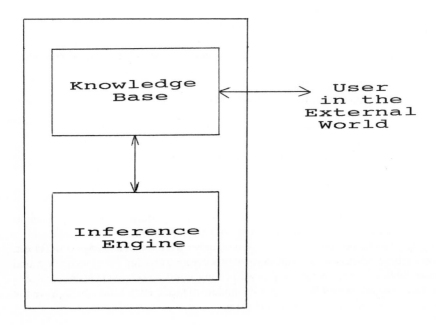

Fig 1. Structure of a simple expert system.

thing different, such as the diagnosis of rheumatological diseases.

This was an important milestone in the development of AI, although it is consistent with the way software engineering was evolving at the time. Greater emphasis was being placed on independence in programming, with databases developing logical and data independence, and other software tools striving to become independent of their operating environment so as to improve portability between systems. See Fig 1.

MYCIN's distinction between the inference program and the knowledge gave rise to the idea of the expert system shell. The shell was the empty husk of the expert system, protecting the knowledge base inside, and interacting with the outside world. The shell manipulates the knowledge to set up chains of inference. It accepts input from the user to commence the consultation and questions the user when more data are needed to proceed with the reasoning. The user is the eyes, ears and hands of the expert system shell.

3.2 Evolution begins

One of the first points of evolution of expert systems was in the 'control strategy'. This referred to strategy for executing rules. Some systems would scan through the whole rule-base and execute all the rules that could be fulfilled. Other systems might scan until they found one rule only which could be executed. (Clearly, this had implications for the way in which rules appeared in the rule-base.) Other systems could scan the rule base several times until no more rules could be fired. Some systems were based on forward chaining only, some on backward chaining and some used both where appropriate (e.g. Muse, (Ref. 2)). A control strategy was needed here to govern when and how to swop from one inference mechanism to another. However, as expert systems and knowledge-based systems became more and more complex, so did the control strategies.

The original expert system program was fairly simple in structure, consisting of the knowledge base and the shell. Several different shells began to appear and it was soon clear that there was no single universal shell which would be able to accommodate every kind of expertise-based problem. For example, the representation of uncertainty was important in MYCIN, but for expert systems which were used for diagnosing faults on process plant, the experts did not always have a need for uncertainty and sometimes preferred to express their knowledge in straightforward black and white decision trees.

So, as other and more complex expert systems and their shells appeared, the original term "expert system" was no longer adequate. The knowledge that could be represented in an expert system shell was criticised for being "shallow" and "superficial". Experts knew much more about their domain than could be represented as IF..THEN rules. They could produce some IF..THEN rules when asked, but some at least seemed to have a model of how their domain worked. Doctors knew about how parts of the body interacted and affected each other. Fitters in a factory did not understand the plant entirely as a collection of IF..THEN rules - they understood how material flowed around the plant and how changes in temperature, viscosity, ingredient mix etc could affect the behaviour of the plant, together with some IF..THEN rules of thumb.

3.3 Model-based IKBS

An obvious way to improve the performance of the expert system was to include some of this so-called "deep" knowledge. It could be represented as a mathematical simulation of the plant, which could be run by the expert system program to test the validity of some of its hypotheses. Mathematical simulations were not always available because models could not be derived or were too complex to process, so qualitative simulation techniques were developed to reason about processes and plants where a mathematical model could not be developed or where its execution would take too long (Refs. 3,4,5). These more complex systems became known as Intelligent Knowledge-based Systems or IKBS.

An IKBS is not a well-defined creature either, but it is likely to possess some or all of the following characteristics:
1) One or more knowledge bases,
2) More than one inference mechanism,
3) More than one knowledge representation format,
4) A model of the domain,
5) Not all the knowledge bases need be 'expert',
6) Other tools to manipulate, acquire and present knowledge,
7) May be used to derive knowledge not before known to humans.
The IKBS will retain the distinction between knowledge and inference mechanism as far as possible, but that too may begin to blur.

The reason for the lessening of the distinction between knowledge and inference programs was introduced earlier. As more and more expert system shells began to appear, it was realised that different domains demanded different kinds of reasoning and expertise, and consequently different styles of knowledge representation and inference. Hence, an inappropriate choice of expert system shell would lead to an unsatisfactory expert system, because the experts' knowledge could not be represented or manipulated as required. So, while still striving to keep knowledge and inference separate, the strong interdependence between knowledge style and its representation and manipulation meant that expert system shells evolved to fill their chosen niches. As a result of their specialisation, they became less likely to be used for complex and very specific projects, since they could not offer the range of tools that might be needed.

Before proceeding to study expert systems relevant to process control in more detail, it is worth saying a little more about the characteristics mentioned above.

3.4 Characteristics of a knowledge-based system

This section will consider the seven characteristics listed above.

3.4.1 One or more knowledge bases
The original expert system was conceived as holding one knowledge base only, usually containing rules elicited from an expert. Later KBSs needed more to accommodate the different kinds of knowledge they required, such as a map of the plant, general properties of plant components, properties of individual components (instances), histories of components, plots of plant variables and, of course, operators' heuristics, often expressed as rules. Some examples will be described briefly

in Section 5.

3.4.2 <u>Inference Mechanisms</u> The simplest form of inference associated with IF..THEN rules is forward chaining. For example, if we have the rules:

> A implies B
> B implies C

then forward chaining would lead to the inference A implies C. Other forms of inference are possible, with IF..THEN rules, such as backward chaining and induction. Referring again to the two-line example above, backward chaining would be used in circumstances where we knew C to be true and wanted to find out what caused it. The second rule would suggest that B could be the cause. Checking through the database of known facts does not confirm B, but the first rule indicates that if A is true, then B would follow. If A in turn cannot be established from the known facts, then the system could generate a question and ask the expert system user if they know whether A is true. If another rule were added

> X implies B

then the backward chaining algorithm would have to cope with the possibility that either X or A would prove B.

Forward chaining is preferred when quite a lot of data has been assembled and the inference procedure is required to produce a conclusion which could explain the observations. Backward chaining is used when less data is on hand and the inference procedure is required to check whether a single hypothesis is true. Backward chaining can generate the right questions to establish or rule out the hypothesis.

Induction is a quite different procedure. It accepts as input a collection of rules, linking observations with conclusions and generates an efficient decision tree to associate observations with conclusions. It can be used to compress a rule-base, although the rules so generated are not guaranteed to contain any of the causal knowledge which the expert may have used in formulating them.

3.4.3 <u>Knowledge representation formats</u> IF..THEN rules are a knowledge representation format which is easily understood and simple to represent in a computer. Its basic associated inference mechanisms are also simple to implement. Other knowledge representation formats may be used, such as extended versions of rules which allow for the simple rules to be qualified by uncertainty measures. These complicate the inference mechanism by requiring the calculation of certainty factors and the selection between competing hypotheses based on their performance with respect to the certainty of their outcome. Clearly, as the number of knowledge representation formats is also expanded, then more inference mechanisms are called in to exercise the knowledge.

Apart from extended rules, the other knowledge representation format which has found favour in complex engineering applications is the frame. Frames are best represented in object-oriented programming languages, since frames share many of the same properties on inheritance and classes. Frames 'chunk' knowledge together, so that all the properties and behaviour of, say, tanks can be represented as a unit, rather than being scattered around the knowledge base. Furthermore, different types of tanks can be defined as subclasses of the main tank class, inheriting properties from the main tank class and adding extra properties which distinguish the use and behaviour of other tank types. Tanks with different temperature tolerances or different shapes would be represented as different sister classes, with their own distinguishing properties, but inheriting common properties from their parent tank class.

The frame can be seen in its evolutionary context by examining the behaviour of rules as the knowledge base grew larger and the execution time became too long. Part of the original joy of rule-based programming was the alleged fact that the order in which the rules were added to the knowledge base did not matter. The inference programs would take care of all that. However, it did matter. There had been nothing to prevent rules being added which contradicted those already there. More general rules (i.e. those with fewer conditions in the IF.. part of the rule) might not be triggered if a less general rule were encountered in the rule-base first. A higgledy-piggledy rule-base was very difficult to maintain. Some discipline was needed on the source of the rules, their ordering within the rule-base and their credibility. Rule-bases could not be allowed to grow unchecked. Structure was introduced, and the frame evolved to solve those problems.

3.4.4 Sources of knowledge

The proliferation of knowledge representation formats and knowledge types accommodated different kinds and sources of knowledge. Some of the knowledge may still be based on the experts' heuristics, but as already mentioned knowledge from other sources may be used, such as commonsense, text-books, manuals, simulations, databases etc. The knowledge bases need not all contain 'expert' knowledge, based on the experts' heuristics or rules of thumb. Some of them might contain 'deeper' knowledge, perhaps mapping out the layout of the plant or system to be diagnosed, or expressing commonsense knowledge about the behaviour of plant components or material when subjected to abnormal conditions of temperature or pressure. Some of this knowledge could be in the form of a model of the plant and its processes.

Obtaining the knowledge from the multitude of sources is known as knowledge acquisition. The term knowledge elicitation is often reserved for the more specialised task of eliciting knowledge from the expert. Many psychological tools have been devised to assist knowledge elicitation, some of which are being computerised (Refs. 6,7).

3.4.5 Other knowledge manipulation tools

Apart from the several inference mechanisms that might need to be accommodated, there is interest in other tools to perform tasks such as data acquisition, consistency checking or induction, and to help in knowledge acquisition and elicitation. Report generation and the presentation of knowledge through graphs and diagrams are also likely to be needed.

3.4.6 New knowledge

The importance of these extra tools, and the reason for dubbing IKBS as "Intelligent", may be in their capacity to derive knowledge not before known to humans. Induction programs have been successful in simplifying a collection of rules down to a much smaller number of more insightful and widely applicable rules. This has been demonstrated in chess most noticeably, where the complex knowledge of grand master chess players on the chess end game has been reduced, to their surprise, to a small number of rules (Ref. 8).

Similarly, expert systems which rely solely on human expertise to supply rules covering the failure modes of a plant are prone to failure, because the human expert cannot be relied upon to have encountered and remembered every possible mode of failure. In such systems, failures can occur where more than one component or material is at fault. Such complex faults are likely to be outside the domain of human expertise and so IKBS assistance is invaluable under the stressful and alarming conditions associated with such rare and difficult faults.

3.4.7 Model-based reasoning Knowledge representation formats proliferated under two quite separate pressures - the need to represent adequately human knowledge and the need to perform well in practice. Rules and simple chaining inference mechanisms were soon seen as not being adequate to represent human expertise, except in straightforward domains. But they also had drawbacks in coping with the complexity of their domains and the kinds of problems they were asked to solve.

This was especially true in problems involving the diagnosis of faults on a complex plant with many sensors. The expert system's rules needed to be able to verify the readings it received from the sensor by comparing results with other sensors in the vicinity. This increased the number of rules that were required and increased their complexity, with more clauses in the antecedent of the rule (IF.. part). All this caused more computation and slowed down the execution speed of the expert system. According to some estimates, up to three-quarter of industrial expert system rules are concerned with verifying sensor accuracy (Ref. 9).

Even if sensor verification is handled adequately, there is still the problem of ensuring that the expert system is complete. Experts cannot be relied upon to recall every possible failure mode of a complex system, or to give the best advice on how to cope with it when it has been identified. The approach taken to solve this is to generate a model of the system, introduce faults and observe the effects. Koukoulis (Ref. 5) was one of the earliest to demonstrate this approach for a quasi-industrial application.

Once the model has been created, it could be used in either of two ways. One way would be to introduce every possible fault, run the model and observe the effects. These observations could then be used to create a rule linking observations to fault. Clearly this procedure will only be feasible in very small systems with little complexity, since the number of possible faults can quickly grow very large, especially if more than one fault is present at the same time.

The other way to use the model is to keep it on-line and use it to test hypotheses about the behaviour of the plant. Some initial rules or knowledge could be used to generate a list of possible hypotheses, which could then be tried on the model, running faster than real time. In this way, a combination of rules and models could be used. The rules can suggest the list of hypotheses and the model run to test them out against observations.

The paragraphs above refer to fault diagnosis expert systems, and highlight the increasing complexity of control systems. The earliest industrial expert systems were

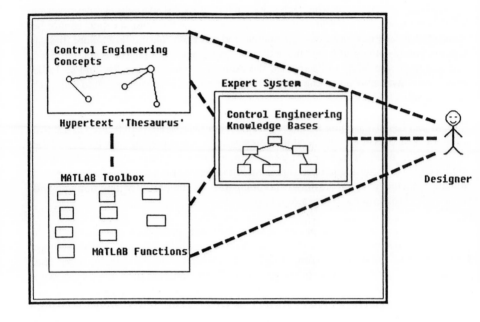

Fig 2. Structure of a knowledge-based system for control enginering design.

The second way of using expert systems involves much greater interaction between the expert system and the plant, with the expert system controlling the plant directly, although remaining under the supervision and responsibility of the human operator. Although the former method of using expert systems has many interesting problems and specialities, it is similar in many ways to applications of expert systems in other domains. However, the direct control of plant by expert systems raises other problems, which are peculiar to process control and worth examining in more detail.

The main features of process control expert systems which will be discussed here are:
type of problem,
real time expert systems, and
user interface.

See Table 1 for a summary of the features of process control expert systems.

applied in domains analogous to those of the medical forebears, so fault diagnosis was an obvious choice. Expert systems for low level process control were being developed in the UK, based on fuzzy logic (Ref.10). Expert systems for fault diagnosis have obvious links with expert systems for process control, since one should be able to pass data to the other in an integrated factory control network.

4. EXPERT SYSTEMS FOR PROCESS CONTROL

The previous sections have looked at expert systems in a broad context, examining their role within AI and in domains of application which have little directly to do with process control. Now that the evolutionary context expert of systems has been established, it is appropriate now to look at the application of expert systems to process control.

Expert systems may be used in process control in two main ways:
1) in assisting the control engineer in the design of a conventional controller, or
2) in taking over the control of a process previously controlled by a human operator.

In the first way, the control engineer uses the expert system as an assistant or guide, which can help with strategies on guiding the selection of the design, setting up the controller, choosing values for the settings and helping with the calculations. Once the controller is designed and tested, the expert system's task is complete, so that the expert system does not come in contact with the process or plant at all.

Expert systems are potentially very useful for the interactive design of control systems for the following reasons:
* They can help a designer handle the complex trade-offs and uncertainties involved in the design process.
* They can provide a high level design environment for non-expert users, offering "expert-like" help at each stage of a design process.
* They can give explanations of the design process in terms of the procedures known bu the expert system and by displaying the theory (or concepts) on which those procedures are based.
* They can help a user to drive a design package in which a model (e.g. state space) of the system under design is stored.

The resulting knowledge-based design environment integrates a knowledge base of procedures, a thesaurus of concepts (that form the theory behind the thesaurus) and a toolbox of functions (or numerical algorithms) that manipulate a plant model during the design process. The design process is controlled by the user who follows procedures and looks at explanations of concepts in order to complete (with understanding) a design. This environment and the interactions between the parts are shown in Fig 2.

Table 1. Summary of Features of Process Control posing special requirements for Expert Systems

Processes operate continuously.

There may be many experts, operating at different shifts.

Changes propagate and amplify through the system.

Input materials may not be consistent in their quality.

The process itself may change gradually over time.

The structure of the plant may be very complex.

Many sensors may be reading data from the plant.

The sensors themselves are prone to error and failure.

Different levels of description of the plant may be appropriate for different control and management tasks.

The models of the plant may be in many different forms, involving thermodynamics, chemical dynamics, spatial organization of the plant and operating procedures.

The models may be approximate and incomplete, not covering all operating regimes.

4.1 Type of Problem

Expert systems and IKBS may be applied to many different kinds of problem, but one of the most important means of classification is according to whether a problem involves synthesis or interpretation (Ref. 11). Synthesis problems involve constructing a solution subject to constraints, such as planning a route from one point to another, designing a circuit board or designing a controller. Interpretation problems involve taking input data from the world and interpreting these to understand what state of the world pertains. Interpretation problems include diagnosis of disease or faults on plant and process control.

An expert system which helps design a controller is involved with synthesis, while the expert system which takes over the task of the human operator is involved with interpretation. It is making an interpretation of the state of the plant and recommending a suitable change in order to hold or restore the plant back to the desired state. So these two kinds of expert systems are quite different. The synthesis expert system could potentially consider many thousand solutions to a problem, depending on the constraints, whereas the interpretation expert system is trying to discover the one true state of the world, subject to the data it may acquire.

Expert systems for controlling plant and process need a taxonomy based on the kinds of task they perform (Refs. 12, 13). Process control expert systems require short chains of forward reasoning. These may be enhanced with alarm monitoring and fault detection facilities, but for fault diagnosis to be accomplished, more complex reasoning will be required, involving at least backward chaining by more recently there has been emphasis on model-based reasoning too. Once the faults have been diagnosed, then there is interest in generating tests to check these hypotheses, involving direct intervention with the configuration of the plant. From here, it is a small step to scheduling, which is a synthesis problem. Fault diagnosis and control are interpretation problems, but test generation and scheduling are synthesis problems. Test generation may be so highly constrained that it can still be done with model-based reasoning, but it falls at the boundary between interpretation and synthesis. Ultimately, planning and plant design are synthesis problems, but they require little or no direct access to real-time plant data.

4.2 Real Time Expert Systems

Real time expert systems are different from other forms of interpretive expert systems, such as medical diagnosis systems in the obvious respect that they must operate in real time. This provides the constraint that the system must reach its conclusion faster than the plant would. It's no good if the system figures out that a major catastrophe is about to occur two minutes after the explosion has happened!

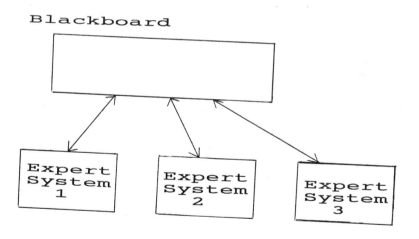

Fig 3. Structure of a blackboard expert system.

Medical diagnosis systems are not usually subject to such a formidable constraint. The condition of a patient presenting himself at a GP's surgery is unlikely to change during the consultation. Most patients in hospital are unlikely to worsen appreciably even if the consultation takes half an hour or more. After all, many diagnostic tests themselves take of the order of days to yield a result.

The real time constraint means that the expert system should be adapted to suit the process under control, and not have any of the extra features desirable in other applications which might clutter up the interface and slow down the speed of execution. If the process has relatively long time constants, say of the order of minutes, then it should not be too great a problem to execute an expert system consultation in that time. Rule-based process control expert systems can run in few microseconds and diagnostic expert systems can run in much less than a minute. This would give the human operator plenty of time to consider the state of the process and the expert system's recommendation, should the system be in supervised control.

Special techniques are employed to speed up the execution of the real time expert system, such as writing some of the critical rules in a lower level language, such as C or Assembler. Demons are used in some software packages. These are special procedures which execute when specified data values are received or specific inferences are drawn. The knowledge base may be partitioned so that different parts of it execute on separate processors, known as the "blackboard" technique. Each separate processor is viewed as a stand-alone expert, and they communicate with each other by placing the results of their inference procedures on a "blackboard", where another expert system can take that result and apply it (Ref. 14).

4.3 User Interface

Expert systems and IKBS can appear in many guises, appropriate to their many roles and the different kinds of knowledge which they use. Users might not even need to be aware that the software tool they are using is or contains an expert system. For example, how many users of spreadsheets are aware of the fact that AI algorithms are used to speed up their execution?

The interface between the user and the expert system may take many different forms, depending on the task that the expert system is performing and the manner in which it complements the work of the expert. Skilled professionals, such as doctors, would want an expert system to take over some of the time-consuming and 'drudge' tasks, such as identifying comparable cases, recommending therapies, critiquing alternative diagnoses and assessing other therapy plans. The process operator might require the system to make its recommended control action first, with the option available to display the reasoning which led to that conclusion.

The plant operator is accustomed to having many kinds of data available on the values of operating parameters, so the software should be able to display these in the formats expected. The expert system part of the control software might only form a small part of the complete set of information displayed to the user.

As expert systems become more widely accepted and understood, then they will disappear into the whole toolkit of tools and techniques available to the control engineer and control operator. The novelty value will eventually disappear. They will no longer be sold to the customer as incorporating AI features, but as tools for improving quality and increasing profitability.

An expert system is in rather a special position, nevertheless, because it is taking on some of the skills previously employed only by humans. If the human operators rely completely on the expert system, to the extent that they cease exercising their own skill and judgment, then these skills will be lost to the human operators. Should a situation occur where the expert system is no longer able to operate because of some hardware or software failure, then it would be desirable for the human operator to retain enough expertise to be able to operate the plant safely, if not at quite the optimum level of efficiency.

This problem is being addressed by designating some of the tasks as only done by the computer, some as done only by the human and some which may be done by either. When the plant is in a steady state and operating efficiently and safely, some of the borderline tasks are handed over to the operators who can practice and maintain their level of skill. Tutoring, critiquing and what-if tools could be available to help the operator understand how the system would behave under different control regimes. If the behaviour of the plant should deviate beyond the safe state, with hazard warnings starting to appear, the system would take over more of the cognitive effort, interpreting the signals so that the operator is not burdened with understanding a large number of alarm signals at the same time as trying to diagnose the fault or faults which gave rise to the cascade of alarms. This is particularly important in military applications, but this kind of research is being supported by large manufacturing organizations too.

The original expert systems had little interaction with the outside world, relying upon a user to act as their eyes, ears and hands. This will remain the case for some systems, but systems are becoming embedded in the corpus of software so that they can derive data from a number of sources. The user might still be required to act as the senses for some expert systems, but for others, the user is becoming a partner in the cognitive effort of understanding and interpreting the world.

5. EXAMPLES OF PROCESS CONTROL EXPERT SYSTEMS

This section will use the earlier discussion to point out the interesting features of applications of expert systems and knowledge based systems to process control. The review makes no attempt to be comprehensive, but merely indicative.

5.1. Rescu

Rescu was a real-time expert system for production plants which was developed under the Alvey programme with the support of a club of 25 users (Ref. 15). The preparation of the Rescu expert system began in mid-1985. The system was built on the ethoxylates detergent plant at ICI Wilton.

The Rescu expert system needed to know the configuration of the plant it is intended to control. It understood how the instrumentation performed minute by minute. Not only did it have access to the formally laid down rules for operating the plant, it also had the informal rules of thumb which the operators used. It accessed the static data about the process and linked to the existing plant control computer for on-line data.

Shaw (Ref. 15) states that although the system builders tries to make the software application-independent, the nature of the expert system's knowledge base meant that some content was included specific to the plant they were working on. As mentioned in Section 3, it is almost impossible to keep domain knowledge and inference programs completely independent of each other.

Shaw also mentions the importance of the the control strategy, "reasoning about how best to reason (meta-knowledge)". He also emphasises the importance of the correct structure of the knowledge base, pointing out that this is vital for reasoning to be efficient. These constraints were not considered in the early medical expert systems, indeed at first expert systems were hailed as avoiding the need to be concerned with structure. By contrast, real-time expert systems demand attention be paid to the need for structure and ordering in the knowledge base.

5.2. Escort

Escort was written by PActel to demonstrate how expert systems could reduce the 'cognitive overload' on the process operator (Ref 16). The application was fault diagnosis on an oil rig.

Escort used several knowledge representation formats. It had rules about fault diagnosis and a causal graph on how faults propagated around the rig. It also had general knowledge about the behaviour of classes of components, as well as knowledge of specific instances (i.e. actual plant components).

Escort used two computers. A MicroVAX maintained the data base of plant values and identified the first symptoms of the problem. A special purpose AI workstation, a Symbolics, was used to carry out the reasoning which would lead to a diagnosis of the fault.

5.3. G2

G2 is the most powerful of the process control knowledge-based systems available. It covers a range of control activities, from process control, computer integrated manufacturing, monitoring and automatic testing. It can run on many familiar machines as well as the AI workstations.

G2 makes use of many knowledge representation schemes, such as dynamic models, objects and heuristics. the models may be either heuristic or analytic, and can be used on-line to compare expected with observed behaviour. Historical data is also available.

The user interface of G2 has been carefully designed so that knowledge can be entered easily and that the running system can be configured to suit the needs of the control engineer. Processing can be distributed over a network of computers, so that lower level tasks, such as scanning and testing, can be delegated to lower level machines.

5.4. LINKman

The design of LINKman is focused on process control, without the other features that are required for fault diagnosis etc (Refs. 13,17). LINKman grew from a project at Blue Circle cement to control cement kilns automatically. Shifts of human operators were controlling the kilns, but it was known that they were non-optimal in their strategies, and there were variations in the performance of operators. In particular the operators tended to keep the burning zone temperature in the kiln too high, which caused excess fuel consumption, extra wear and tear on the refractory lining of the kiln, which lead to more frequent spells of downtime and expense while the lining was replaced.

LINKman uses rules to represent knowledge about kiln control. It uses forward chaining only and short chains of inference. This means it can reason quickly, much faster than required for the original application to cement manufacture. As well as displaying the conclusions from its reasoning, LINKman presents the operator in the control room with graphs of process inputs and outputs. The operator has information available in a familiar form and can choose to override LINKman's recommendation.

However, this rarely happens in practice. LINKman has been very successful in operation, with a pay back period of only 3 to 6 months. Blue Circle are now converting most of their UK cement kilns to control by expert system. LINKman is now being sold world-wide by Sira Ltd. Some of the sales are still in kiln control, but other processes are now seeing the benefits of expert system control.

5.5. Extase

Extase was developed to find the cause of an alarm signal and to relate alarms having the same cause, so this is a diagnostic rather than a simple control application (Ref. 18). The application was in the diagnosis of faults on a heating system, fed by two fuels. It heated a feed of material which was then passed through a column. It covered 24 control loops, about 140 sensors and 50 alarm signals.

Extase was programmed in an object-oriented language and it followed the causal model used in Escort. Extase was designed to explain unit functioning based on known relationships between represented elements. This knowledge was represented in a causal graph. When an alarm signal was triggered, the causal graph was searched to build up a hypothesis graph, which holds currently known data and represents the status of the reasoning process. One of Extase's main features is in the generation of explanations which may then be presented to the user, i.e. the plant operator.

The system works with a propagate-and-check cycle. Extase is activated when a process alarm signal is fired. This generates a first hypothesis. They hypothesis checks its own validity by checking the expected data against the real process data measured. If the hypothesis fails the test, then the changes in the data in the meantime are observed and a new hypothesis generated. If a hypothesis does not lead to a successful diagnosis, the system can backtrack to generate other hypotheses. Extase generates explanations for the user and can give partial explanations based on its failed hypotheses.

6. CONCLUDING REMARKS

This paper on expert systems for process control has taken an evolutionary view of the field, examining how expert systems have evolved from their roots in Artificial Intelligence to become something quite distinct from the medical expert systems from which they sprang. However, they are not so separate that there is no more to be learnt from the applications in the medical domain. While the experts in process control and medicine may not discuss the intricacies of their knowledge-based systems, the designers and academics remain in communication.

The evolution of process control expert systems is not yet over. Expert systems are being applied to more and more domains, each with their own characteristics and problems. As expert systems become more price effective, so they will be applied ever more widely, posing yet more new challenges and continuing the evolutionary pressures.

Pressures on industry to curb waste, reduce emissions and use energy more efficiently will increase the need for industry to become better managed and controlled. The potential for disaster in complex plant with hazardous materials is matter of public concern. The development of complex control systems to manage and control these plants and processes will need to be tackled in the next decade.

Expert systems for process control have moved on enormously in the past decade. I see yet more changes and challenges in the next decade as expert systems for process control move on to colonise yet more industrial habitats.

7. REFERENCES

1   SHORTLIFFE, E.H.: 'Computer Based Medical Consultations: MYCIN' (American Elsevier, 1976)
2   Muse, Cambridge Consultants Ltd., Science Park, Milton Road, Cambridge CB4 4DW.
3   FORBUS, K.D.: 'Qualitative process theory', *Artificial Intelligence*, 1984, 24, pp.85-168
4   KUIPERS, B.J.:'Commonsense reasoning about causality:deriving behaviour from structure', ibid., 1984, 24, pp.169-204
5   KOUKOULIS, C.G.: 'The application of knowledge-based techniques to industrial maintenance problems'. Ph.D. Thesis, Queen Mary and Westfield College, London, England, Feb., 1986

6   DAVIES, D., and HAKIEL, S.:'Knowledge harvesting: A practical guide to interviewing', *Expert Systems*, Feb 1988, 5, 1, pp.42-49

7   BURTON, A.M., SHADBOLT, N.R., HEDGECOCK, A.P., and RUGG, G.:'A formal evaluation of knowledge elicitation techniques for expert systems' in MORALEE, D.S., 'Research and Development in Expert Systems', (Cambridge University Press, 1987), pp.136-145

8   BRATKO, I., and MULEC, P.: 'An experiment in automatic learning of diagnostic rules', *Informatica*, 1980, 4, pp.18-25

9   FULTON, S.L., and PEPE, C.O.:'An introduction to model-based reasoning', *AI Expert*, January 1990, 5, 1, pp.48-55

10   MAMDANI, E.H.:'Advances in the linguistic synthesis of fuzzy controllers', *International Journal of Man-Machine Studies*, 1976, 8, pp.669-678

11   CLANCEY, W.J.:'Heuristic Classification', *Artificial Intelligence*, 27,pp.289-350, 1985

12   EFSTATHIOU, J.:'Knowledge-based systems for industrial control', *Computer-Aided Engineering Journal*, 1987, 4, 1, pp. 7-28.

13   EFSTATHIOU, J.:'Expert Systems in Process Control', (Longman, 1989)

14   SKAPURA, D.M.:'A faster embedded inference engine', *AI Expert*, 1989, November, pp.42-49

15   SHAW, R.:'RESCU - on-line real-time artificial intelligence', *Computer-Aided Engineering Journal*, 1987, 4, 1, pp.29-30

16   SACHS, P.A., PATERSON, A.M., and TURNET, M.H.M.:'Escort - an expert system for complex operations in real time', *Expert Systems*, 1986, 3, (1), pp.22-29.

17   HASPEL, D.:'Application of rule-based control in the cement industry', in MAMDANI, A., and EFSTATHIOU, H.J. (Eds.):'Expert systems and optimisation in process control' (Technical Press, 1986)

18   JAKOB, F., and SULENSCHIC, P.:'Situation Assessment for Process Control', *IEEE Expert*, April 1990, 5, 2, pp.49-59

Chapter 3

Basic theory and algorithms for fuzzy sets and logic

B. Postlethwaite

1. INTRODUCTION

In the following chapter I have tried to explain the foundations of fuzzy
set and fuzzy logic theory in a fairly straightforward manner. I have
simplified notation where possible and can make no claims of theoretical
completeness. It is my hope that, after reading the chapter, someone
who is new to the field will have developed a 'feel' for the subject and
will go on to study more complete works.

Fuzzy sets were first introduced by Zadeh[1] as a method of handling
'real-world' classes of objects. Ambiguities abound in these real-world
sets, examples given by Zadeh include the 'class of all real numbers
which are much greater than 1, and the 'class of tall men'. Examples of
these ambiguous sets are easily found in the process control field,
where operators may talk about 'very high temperatures' or a 'slight
increase in flowrate'.

Conventional set theory is clearly inadequate to handle these ambiguous
concepts since set members either do, or do not, belong to a set. For
example, consider the set 'tall men' - a man who is seven feet tall will
clearly belong to the set and one who is four feet tall will not, but
what about someone who measures five feet ten inches? Zadeh's solution
to this problem was to create the fuzzy set, in which members could have
a continuous range of membership ranging from zero, or not belonging, to
one indicating definite belonging.

2. FUZZY SETS

2.1 Definition

Let X be an interval containing the possible values of a variable, with
an individual value in X denoted by x. Thus X is the set of all possible
values of x, i.e. $X = \{ x \}$.
A fuzzy set F defined in interval X is characterised by a membership
function $\mu_F(x)$ which associated each value in X to a real number in
the interval [0,1]. The particular value of $\mu_F(x)$ at x is known as the
'grade of membership' of x in F, and the closer this value is to one,
the higher the grade of membership of x in F. If F was a conventional
set, the membership function could only take on the values 0 and 1, with
a value of zero indicating that an element does not belong to the set
and value of one indicating that it does. Thus, fuzzy sets can be
thought of as extensions to conventional set theory and, as shall be

shown later, obey many of the conventional set identities.

Taking the previous example a little further, a fuzzy set representing 'tall men' would assign a grade of membership of zero to a man four feet tall, and an intermediate grade of membership, perhaps 0.8, to a man who was five feet ten iches in height. The choice of membership function for a particular fuzzy set is completely subjective, and most certainly is not made statistically. Although the membership function of a fuzzy set appears superficially to resemble a cumulative probability distribution, there are important differences between the two concepts. Considering the 'tall men' example, if we gather together a group of men belonging to the set 'tall men', it would be incorrect to say that the probability of a given man being less than five feet ten inches in height is 0.8. Conversely, it makes no sense to say that the probability of someone less than five feet ten inches tall belonging to the set 'tall men' is 0.8, since the probability of membership is, in fact, one.

2.2   TYPES OF MEMBERSHIP FUNCTION

Figure 1 illustrates, graphically, three common types of membership function. Figure 1a shows a quaantised membership function, where the range of a variables value is divided into a number of sub-ranges and the membership function of the fuzzy set consists of a set of grades of membership for each sub-range. Quantised membership functions are usually represented in tabular form, and may, sometimes, offer computational advantages.

Figure 1b shows a bell-shaped, continuous, membership function. Several authors have used membership functions of this sort, and although there must be some difficulty in deciding an appropriate shape and spread for the function, they do have the capability of including a wide range of values at low grades of membership. Some of the mathematical functions used to generate membership functions of this sort are given in Table 1.

A triangular membership function is shown in Figure 1c. This is a semi-continuous function which has the major advantage of being completely specified by just three values.

3.   SIMPLE OPERATIONS WITH FUZZY SETS

<u>3.1</u>   A fuzzy set can be said to be empty if, and only if, its membership function is zero for all values of x.

<u>3.2</u>   The complement of a fuzzy set F is denoted by F' and defined by

$$\mu_{F'}(x) = 1 - \mu_F(x)$$

Linguistically, the complement can be represented as the operator NOT, e.g. the complement of the set of tall men, is the set of men who are not tall.

<u>3.3</u>   A fuzzy set F is a subset of fuzzy set G if, and only if, $\mu_F(x) \leqslant \mu_G(x)$ for all x, or

$$F \subset G \Leftrightarrow \mu_F(x) \leqslant \mu_G(x) \text{ for all } x$$

3.4   Two fuzzy sets, F and G, are equal (F=G) if, and only if,

$$\mu_F(x) = \mu_G(x) \text{ for all } x.$$

3.5   The union of two fuzzy sets F and G is a third fuzzy set H, written as H = F∪G, with the membership function

$$\mu_H(x) = \text{Max } [\mu_F(x), \mu_G(x)], \; x \in X$$

or, in a more usual, abbreviated form

$$\mu_H = \mu_F \vee \mu_G$$

Linguistically, the union of fuzzy sets can be interpreted as the operator OR, e.g. if F is the set of high temperatures and G is the set of medium temperatures the union of the sets is the set of temperatures which are high or medium. This is illustrated graphically in Figure 2.

3.6   The intersection of two fuzzy sets F and G is a third fuzzy set H, written as H = F∩G, with the membership function given by

$$\mu_H(x) = \text{Min}[\mu_F(x), \mu_G(x)], \; x \in X$$

or, in abbreviated form

$$\mu_H = \mu_F \wedge \mu_G$$

Linguistically, the interesection of fuzzy sets can be interpreted as the logical operation AND, e.g. if F is the set of high temperatures and G is the set of medium temperatures, then the intersection of F and G is the set of temperatures which are both medium and high. The fuzzy intersection operation is illustrated graphically in Figure 3.

3.7   Many of the basic ordinary-set identities hold for fuzzy sets when the complementation, union and intersection operators are defined as above, for example

A∪ (B∪C) = (A∪B)∪C	) associative laws
A∩ (B∩C) = (A∩B)∩C	)
(A∪B)' = A'∩ B'	)De Morgan's laws
(A∩B)' = A'∪ B'	)
C∩(A∪B) = (C∩A)∪(C∩B)	)Distributive laws
C∪(A∩B) = (C∪A)∩(C∪B)	)

4.   FUZZY LOGIC

Fuzzy logic is an extension of fuzzy set theory. Conventional set theory is based around Boolean logic where set membership is either true or false, but in fuzzy set theory membership is defined over a continuous range of grades of membership, which is equivalent to grades of truth in a logical sense. Conventional logic would allow the statement:

'The temperature is high'

to be either true or false, dependent on whether or not the current numerical value of temperature belonged to the set 'high temperature'. This is true regardless of whether 'high temperature' is, or is not, a fuzzy set. Fuzzy logic, however, allows intermediate grades of truth to exist between true (logic 1) and false (logic 0), and thus it makes sense to say that the statement is true with a grade of truth equal to, say, 0.7.

4.1   Logical operations based on fuzzy set theory

Many authors make use of fuzzy logical operators (NOT, AND, OR) based on the definitions produced from fuzzy set theory. The definitions for the compound operators are intuitively defensible, but cannot be said to be theoretically correct since many compound conditions will be defined on different spaces.

4.1.1 Logical NOT

Let γ_A = degree of truth of the proposition, x is A

then $\gamma_{NOT\ A}$ = degree of truth of the proposition, x is NOT A

$$= 1 - \gamma_A$$

This definition comes directly from fuzzy set theory since γ_A represents the membership of the value of the variable in A, and $\gamma_{NOT\ A}$ represents the membership of the value of the variable in the set NOT A.

i.e.   if the variables value is x

$$\gamma_A = \mu_A (x)$$

$$\gamma_{NOT\ A} = \mu_{NOT\ A} (x) = 1 - \mu_A(x) = 1 - \gamma_A$$

4.1.2   Logical AND

Let γ_A = degree of truth of the proposition, x is A

γ_B = degree of truth of the proposition, y is B

Then $\gamma_{A\ AND\ B}$ = degree of truth of the proposition, x is A AND y is B

$$= \min (\gamma_A, \gamma_B)$$

Note that this definition does not come directly from fuzzy intersection since the two conditions may be defined in different spaces, e.g. high temperature and low pressure.

Example: if γ_T = the degree of truth that the temperature is high

= 0.6

γ_P = the degree of truth that the pressure is low

= 0.4

Then the degree of truth of the compound condition

'the temperature is high and the pressure is low'

is $\gamma_{T\ AND\ P}$ = min (0.6,0.4) = 0.4

4.1.3 Logical OR

Let γ_A = degree of truth of the proposition, x is A

γ_B = degree of truth of the proposition, y is B

Then $\gamma_{A\ OR\ B}$ = degree of truth of the proposition, x is A OR y is B

$$= max\ (\gamma_A,\ \gamma_B)$$

Example: using the degrees of truth from the previous examples, the truth of condition

'the temperature is high OR the pressure is low'

is $\gamma_{T\ OR\ P}$ = max (0.6,0.4) = 0.6

4.2   Fuzzy logical operators based on probablistic expressions

Several investigators have discovered that systems using the fuzzy-set based logical operators exhibit discontinuities, an undesirable characteristic for a controller. Alternative means of implementing the logical operators, based on probablistic expressions, have therefore been produced which seem to improve the characteristics of fuzzy-logic systems which use them. I know of no real justification for these definitions other than the purely pragmatic reason that they seem to work.

4.2.1 Logical NOT

The expressions given in 4.1.1 is used.

4.2.2 Logical AND

Using the nomenclature of 4.1.2

$$\gamma_{A\ AND\ B} = \gamma_A \cdot \gamma_B$$

and using the same example as 4.1.2

$$\gamma_{T\ AND\ P} = 0.6 \cdot 0.4 = 0.24$$

4.2.3 Logical OR

Using the nomenclature of 4.1.3

$$\gamma_{A\ OR\ B} = \gamma_A + \gamma_B - \gamma_A \cdot \gamma_B$$

and using 4.1.3's example

$$\gamma_{T\ OR\ P} = 0.6 + 0.4 - 0.24 = 0.76$$

5. FUZZY SETS AND FUZZY LOGIC FOR CONTROL

5.1 Reference sets

The parameters and solutions for control problems are usually expressed in crisp, measurable, values such as 60°C, 10^5N m^{-2} etc, but systems which operate using fuzzy logic make use of qualitative concepts like low temperature or high pressure. A means of associating crisp values with qualitative terms is therefore required. This is often achieved by defining several reference fuzzy sets for each of the variables of interest. These reference sets provide a quantitative description of the qualitative terms which are used in the fuzzy system. A particular crisp numerical value of a variable can, and often does, belong to several of the fuzzy reference sets defined for the variable, and the assignment of set grades of membership to a particular value is known as fuzzification. An example of fuzzification is given in Figure 4. In this example, three fuzzy sets have been defined to represent qualitative values of temperature. The crisp value (70°C) belongs to the fuzzy set 'low temperature' (is low) with a grade of membership of 0.3, and belongs to 'medium' and 'high' temperatures with memberships of 0.9 and 0.2 respectively.

The definition of appropriate reference sets always has to be the first step in constructing any type of fuzzy control system. The choice of reference sets is an important one, since a poor choice will result in a system with a poor performance. Unfortunately, as yet, no systematic method of making this choice has been developed which out-performs inspired guesswork. On the other hand, with most problems, it is usually not too difficult to produce reference sets which lead to reasonably performing systems.

5.2 Rule-based Systems

The rule-based system is the most common, current, application of fuzzy logic and fuzzy sets to control problems. As its name implies, the rule-based system is constructed around a set of rules which describe, in qualitative terms, how an output behaves when subjected to various inputs. In the case of a rule-based controller, the inputs may be the change and rate of change in error measurement and the output may be the change in control action. A rule-based process model would use process inputs as input values and return an estimated process output.

The rules which make up a rule-based system are usually expressed in the form of IF... THEN... statements. The conditional part of the statement can make full use of the fuzzy logical operators to produce quite complicated conditions. The consequent part of a particular rule always assigns, to some degree, a particular qualitative value to the output. The qualitative value assigned is an output reference set and the degree of assignment is the overall degree of truth of the conditional expression. The degree of assignment modifies the membership function of the assigned reference set by putting a 'cap' on to the function's maximum values, i.e.

$$\mu_{RULE}(x) = Min(\gamma_{RULE}, \mu_{OUT}(x))$$

where $\mu_{out}(x)$ = membership function of the assigned reference set

γ_{RULE} = overall degree of truth of the conditional part of the rule

$\mu_{RULE}(x)$ = membership function of the rules output set

Each rule will thus produce its own fuzzy output set and, since all of these sets are defined in the same space, the overall output from all these rules can be arrived at by carrying out a fuzzy union.

A simple exaple may make the procedure clearer. Consider a rule-based controller described by three rules:

(a)   IF ε IS LARGE AND $\Delta\varepsilon$ IS LARGE THEN ΔCa IS LARGE
(b)   IF ε IS MEDIUM THEN ΔCa IS MEDIUM
(c)   IF $\Delta\varepsilon$ IS MEDIUM THEN ΔCa IS MEDIUM

If we assume that fuzzification gives the following truth values for the inputs

$$\gamma_{\varepsilon\ IS\ LARGE} = 0.3 \qquad \gamma_{\varepsilon\ IS\ MEDIUM} = 0.5$$

$$\gamma_{\Delta\varepsilon\ IS\ LARGE} = 0.6 \qquad \gamma_{\Delta\varepsilon\ IS\ MEDIUM} = 0.2$$

then the overall degrees of truth of the three rules are (using the logical operators described in 4.1)

(a) γ_a = min(0.3,0.6) = 0.3 → ΔCa IS LARGE
(b) γ_b = 0.5 → ΔCa IS MEDIUM
(c) γ_c = 0.2 → ΔCa IS MEDIUM

Figure 5 shows the resulting output sets from each of the rules and the resultant overall output from the rule-base, achieved by carrying out a fuzzy union.

Some authors take advantage of the limited number of allowable input values obtained when quantised fuzzy sets are used, to pre-calculate all of the possible outcomes of a rule-base. This has some advantages in that the on-line calculations for a large rule-base are reduced since most of the work is done off-line, and also that self-modification algorithms have been developed for this form of fuzzy controller[2]. The method has the disadvantage of all quantised systems, that is, loss of resolution.

Regardless of the form of rule-based system, the biggest problem is in obtaining appropriate rules. The traditional methods involve interviewing and/or observing 'experts' in the field of interest, and obtaining a set of rules which is further refined by a process of trial and error. This is obviously a lengthy and expensive process which must limit the applications of the rule-based tehniques to problems where the potential savings are fairly large. New techniques are, however,

being developed which will allow rule-based systems to self-modify and
even to self-generate, and if these prove successful the range of
applicability of the rule-based system may increase.

5.3   Relational systems

Another way that fuzzy logic can be applied to control problems is
through fuzzy relational equations. Basically, when expressed in terms
of reference sets, a fuzzy relational equation is a way of representing
relationships which may exist between qualitative input and qualitative
output states. The core of a relational model is the relational array,
which is a matrix made up of values which represent the degrees of truth
of all the possible cause-and-effect relationships between the input and
output reference sets. The principle advantage of relational systems
over rule-based systems is that several techniques exist which allow
relational array entries, and hence the relational model, to be
identified directly from input-output data.

Although it should be possible to produce a fuzzy relational controller
directly from observations of manual control, most workers have looked
at producing a model of the process to be controlled with a view to
incorporating the model in a model-based control scheme. This approach
has the advantage that the resultant controller is not constrained to
the imitation of manual control but instead can, perhaps, improve on
this.

5.3.1 Algorithms for relational models

A fuzzy relational equation is represented by

$$y = R \ o \ x$$

where y =   array of degrees of truth of output sets
         x =   array of degrees of truth of input sets
         R =   fuzzy relational array

Given an input, the fuzzy relational equation is resolved to produce an
output by using

$$\gamma_{y(i)} = \max_{j \in x} \left[\min(\gamma_R(i,j), \ \gamma_x(j)) \right]$$

where $\gamma_{y(i)}$ = degree of truth that the ith output set applies

$\gamma_{x(j)}$ = degree of truth that the input belongs to the jth
                     input set

$\gamma_R(i,j)$= relational array entry representing the degree of
                  truth of a cause and effect relationship between the
                  j^{th} input set and the ith output set

Example

A system has been modelled using a relational equation with the output
and input described by two fuzzy reference sets. The resultant
relational array produced by identification is:

$$R = \begin{bmatrix} 0.2 & 0.7 \\ 0 & 0.1 \end{bmatrix}$$

Given that an input to the system, described in terms of its reference sets, is x = [0.8,0.2] what is the output?

$$y = \begin{bmatrix} \delta_{y(1)} \\ \delta_{y(2)} \end{bmatrix} = \begin{bmatrix} \max(\min(0.2\ ,0.8),\min(0.2,0.7)) \\ \max(\min(0,0.8),\min(0.1,0.2)) \end{bmatrix} = \begin{bmatrix} 0.2 \\ 0.1 \end{bmatrix}$$

A discussion of the various identification algorithms for relational systems is beyond the scope of this work and the interested reader is referred to the literature.

5.4   Defuzzification

The output from both rule-based and relational fuzzy systems is a fuzzy set, which usually must be converted back into a single 'crisp' value before it is of use to a control system. The procedure for doing this is called defuzzification, and there are three popular types of defuzzification - mean of maxima, centre of area and fuzzy mean. Figure 6 illustrates an output defuzzified by each of the three methods.

5.4.1 Mean of maxima defuzzification

With this method of defuzzification,if there is a single maximum in the output membership function, then the value of the output at this point is taken as the defuzzified output. Where there are several points at which the membership function is at its maximum (i.e. if the function is multi-modal) then the defuzzified value is taken to be the mean of all the output values where the membership function is at its maximum.

The disadvantage of this method is that quite small changes in the systems inputs can cause very large shifts in the defuzzified output.

5.4.2   Centre of area method

As its name implies, the centre of area method of defuzzification involves finding the value of output which bisects the area under the membership function curve. This method has considerable advantages over the mean of maxima method in that changes in the crisp output value take place smoothly. The method suffers from the disadvantages of high computational requirements and proneness to problems with 'edge-effects'. The 'edge-effect' problem occurs when a reference set at one end of the output variables range extends to very high values, or even infinity. In such a case, this reference set, even when triggered at very low grades of truth, pulls the centre of area towards itself. Since it is often necessary for relational identification to use output reference sets with these characteristics, the centre of area method is particularly unsuitable for relational systems.

5.4.3. Fuzzy Mean Method

With this method of defuzzification each output reference set is
assigned a characteristic output value. With triangular reference sets
this value is usually taken to be the centre point, and with other
types of reference set the value where the membership function is
largest is normally taken. To generate a duffuzzified output a weighted
mean of the characteristic values is taken, where the weighting factors
are the degrees of truth for the relevant reference sets.

i.e.

$$y = \sum_{i=1}^{n} y_i . \gamma_i \bigg/ \sum_{i=1}^{n} \gamma_i$$

y_i = characteristic value of set i

γ_i = degree of truth that set i applied

y = defuzzified output

This method of defuzzification produces a smooth output, which is easy
to calculate and is not subject to end effects.

6.1 Further Reading

As explained in the introduction, the intention of this chapter was to
give the reader a basic grounding in fuzzy set and logic theory. For
those readers who wish to study the subject in more depth, the
following short list of books and papers may be of some use.

6.1.1 Books

Fuzzy Control and Fuzzy Systems. W. Pedrycz, Research Studies Press,
1989.
This book is aimed mainly at relational systems. Good theoretical
coverage.

Expert Systems in Process Control. H.J. Efstathiou, Longman 1989.
I have not read this book yet, but from the contents list it looks very
interesting!

6.1.2 Papers

'A restrospective view of fuzzy control systems'. R.M. Tong, Fuzzy
Sets & Systems, 14 (1984), pp 199-210.

'A control engineering review of fuzzy systems'. R.M. Tong,
Automatica, 13 (1977), pp 559-569.

Two good review papers covering different periods.

'An experiment in linguistic synthesis with a fuzzy logic controller'.
E.H. Mamdani & S. Assilan, Int. J. Man-Machine Studies, 7 (1975), pp 1-13.
A good example of the early work done on rule-based controllers by
Mamdani and his co-workers.

'On identification in fuzzy systems and its applications in control problems'.   E. Czogola & W. Pedrycz, Fuzzy Sets and Systems, 6 (1981), pp 73-83.

'An identification algorith, in fuzzy relational systems'.   W. Pedrycz, Fuzzy Sets and Systems, 13 (1984), pp 153-167.

Good descriptions of methods of identifying relational fuzzy models.

REFERENCES

1.   Zadeh, L.A. 'Fuzzy Sets', Information & Control, vol 8 (1965), pp 338-353.

2.   Efstathion, J.   'Rule-based Process control', from Expert Systems and Optimisation in Process Control, Mamdani, A. and Efstathion,J. (eds).   Technical Press, 1986   (ISBN 0-291-39710-7)

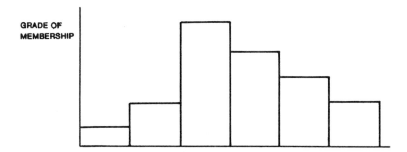

FIG 1a   QUANTISED MEMBERSHIP FUNCTION

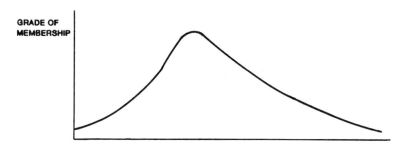

FIG 1b   CONTINUOUS MEMBERSHIP FUNCTION

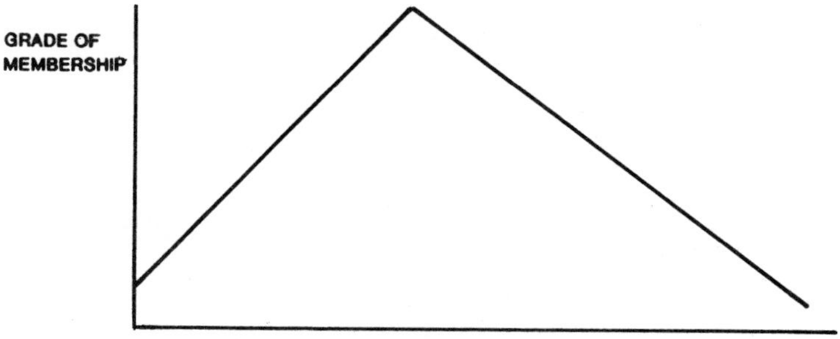

FIG 1   FUZZY MEMBERSHIP FUNCTIONS

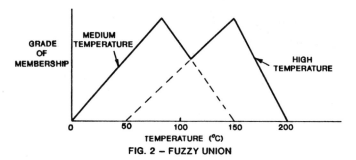

FIG. 2 – FUZZY UNION

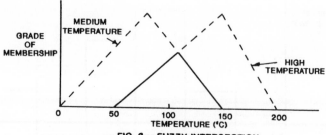

FIG. 3 — FUZZY INTERSECTION

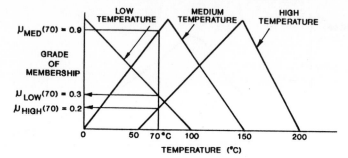

FIG. 4 — FUZZIFICATION

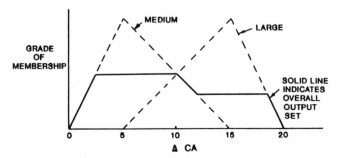

FIG. 5 - OUTPUT FROM A FUZZY RULE - BASE

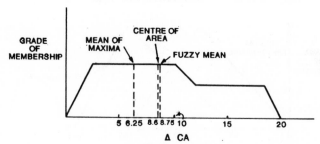

FIG. 6   - DEFUZZIFICATION

Chapter 4

Knowledge engineering and process control

J. L. Alty

1. INTRODUCTION

Knowledge engineering is the term used to describe the process of building knowledge based systems. When the knowledge is derived from a human expert such systems are often called "expert systems". The processes involved in knowledge engineering have some similarities with those of systems analysis. In both cases the system designer is trying to extract knowledge from human beings and processes in order to produce an automated system. It is therefore not surprising that some of the ideas of software engineering have been borrowed and adapted for knowledge engineering. However there are some important differences. The traditional software life cycle places great emphasis on a written statement of requirements, a detailed specification, a step-wise refinement approach to the design process, an implementation schedule, a testing strategy and maintenance. In knowledge engineering, precise requirements analysis is usually very difficult and thus clear specification is not possible. Additionally, the knowledge engineer is trying to explicate the experts knowledge (i.e. make it visible) and any derived explicit representation must be preserved, as far as possible, in the finished system in order to provide good explanation facilities. Finally, the step-wise refinement process makes some assumptions about the nature of the control strategy which will almost certainly not be valid for knowledge based systems. The classical Von Neumann instructional approach lacks the ability to distinguish context dependent situations and is far too linear.

The nature of the knowledge captured in knowledge based systems also tends to differ to that captured in more conventional systems. One can categorise knowledge along a number of dimensions (Wolfgram et al, 1987):

> definitional versus empirical
> imperative versus declarative
> algorithmic versus heuristic
> theoretic versus pragmatic
> general versus specific
> prescriptive versus descriptive
> certain versus uncertain.

Knowledge based systems tend to congregate to the right hand side of the above dimensions. For example, it is generally recognised that problems which involve general prescriptive knowledge are not good candidates for the expert systems approach. The last three dimensions in the list have been used by Hayes-Roth (1984) to develop a taxonomy in which he termed these dimensions scope, purpose and validity.

The process of building an expert system consists of two main activities which often overlap - acquiring the knowledge and implementing the system. This overlap, which usually involves rapid prototyping and iteration, has been the subject of much debate in recent years and has resulted in two main, contrasting approaches to expert system building - the modelling approach and the rapid prototyping approach. These will be discussed in more detail later. The acquisition activity involves the collection of knowledge about facts and reasoning strategies from the domain experts. Usually, such knowledge is elicited from the experts by so-called knowledge engineers, using interviewing techniques or observational protocols. However, machine induction, which automatically generates more elaborate knowledge from an initial set of basic knowledge (usually in the form of examples), has also been extensively used (Michie and Johnston, 1985). In the system construction process, the system builders (i. e., knowledge engineers), the domain experts and the users work together during all stages of the process.

To automate the problem solving process, the relevant task knowledge in the domain of interest needs to be understood in great detail but acquiring the knowledge for expert system building is generally regarded as a hard problem. It is well-known that experts, like all human beings, have faulty memories or harbour inconsistencies. Human beings generally have difficulty in estimating probabilities, (Tversky and Kahnemann, 1974), experience difficulty in dealing with disjunction, have problems with understanding negation and rarely argue consistently when dealing with everyday problems. All of us at one time or another have promoted illusory correlations or supported fallacies such as the "gamblers fallacy". Thus the knowledge which an expert provides as part of the knowledge elicitation process must be treated with caution and separate validation of the expertise elicited from experts is usually essential (Chignell and Peterson, 1988). Experts also exhibit cognitive biases such as overconfidence, simplification, and a low preference for abstract, relative and conflicting evidence. It is not uncommon for human beings to totally ignore key evidence which conflicts with their current problem hypothesis. It is therefore important to test and validate expert systems both by analysing the expertise in the knowledge base and by examining failures in actual performance. As far as possible, cognitive biases should be filtered out during the elicitation process.

Knowledge based systems have a wide area of applicability   in industrial control. Hayes-Roth and others (1983), for example, have identified ten generic categories of knowledge engineering applications. These are :

> interpretation and prediction,
> diagnosis and control,
> designing and planning,
> monitoring and debugging,
> instruction and repair

Such systems normally comprise two main components (Davies, 1982), the inference mechanism (the problem solving component) and the knowledge base (which may actually comprise a number of knowledge bases).

From a process control point of view, the classification by Madni (1988) has provided a useful hierarchical classification of expert systems. One level of his classification distinguishes between expert systems with respect to different purposes:
- perform a task
- assist in a task,
- teach a task.

The first category deals with autonomous expert systems such as those found in autonomous robots or automation systems. The second category largely comprises expert consultation systems. Teaching systems have more granular uncompiled knowledge and access a pedagogical knowledge base in addition to domain knowledge bases. In industrial systems, expert systems of the first category are always embedded within the technical system whereas those in the second category can be either stand-alone, embedded or loosely connected. At present in process control it is unusual to have expert systems directly in control of plant. Engineers normally insist that the operator is still in the control loop. Thus, an expert system will often occupy a place in the whole system as characterised by Figure 1.

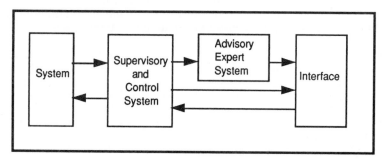

Figure 1 Typical Advisory role of an Expert System in Process Control

The operator can interact with the supervisory and control system independently of the advisory module which can be invoked by the operator, when needed, for advice. An example of a typical system in this category is the GRADIENT system which advises operators controlling power generation stations or telecommunications networks (Alty and Johannsen, 1989)).

Expert systems have had a rather chequered history. The initial expectations were too high and have resulted in disappointment. As a result few systems have progressed beyond the research or prototype phase and this has often been attributed to inherent difficulties in the knowledge acquisition process (Breuker and Wielinga, 1987) though a lack of good tools and a limited understanding of what constituted a good application area, also contributed to this situation. Recently, however there have been encouraging signs that expert systems are "coming of age". The tools are greatly improved, the knowledge acquisition process is a little better understood and there is now a general awareness of the critical factors involved in choosing an area for expert systems exploitation.

2. WHAT IS KNOWLEDGE ENGINEERING ?

There are a number of terms used to describe the expert system building process which are not well defined and appear to overlap. Such terms include knowledge elicitation, knowledge acquisition, system implementation, machine induction and even the term knowledge engineering itself. Buchanan and others (1983) define knowledge acquisition as "the transfer and transformation of problem-solving expertise from some knowledge source to a program". The definition covers the whole process including identification of the problem, its conceptualisation, formalisation, implementation, testing and prototype revision. This seems to be an overstretched use of the term "acquisition" as it would seem reasonable to distinguish between the capturing of knowledge and its implementation in an expert system. Ideally one would like some form of intermediate representation (i.e a Knowledge Representation Language) which would capture the knowledge of the expert. Such a language would be independent of any implementation strategy or technique.

Knowledge elicitation has been described as "the process of extracting domain expertise which includes facts, explanations, justifications, rules of thumb and procedures given by a recognised domain expert" (Greenwell, 1990). Diederich and Linster (1989) actually subdivide knowledge acquisition into knowledge elicitation and an operational phase. Motta and others (1989) term the whole process knowledge engineering but subdivide it into knowledge acquisition, knowledge representation and implementation. They further break down knowledge acquisition into knowledge elicitation and data interpretation. This approach seems to be the most sensible one and is encapsulated in Figure 2. (taken from Johannsen and Alty,1990).

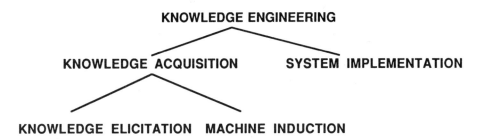

Figure 2 Relationship between Terms in Knowledge Engineering

The general term of knowledge engineering appears to have a common meaning across many authors. The above taxonomy separates the knowledge acquisition process from the system implementation process (like Motta and others). Although the two intertwine if one uses the prototyping approach there are good reasons for separating them out, at least conceptually. We have also separated out elicitation (either manual or automatic) from machine induction since these acquisition techniques are quite distinct and have followed different development paths.

As Motta and others state "The separation of acquisition from implementation leads to a view of knowledge acquisition as the production of an abstract architecture distinct from the implementation of the system". However, they accept that such a characterisation is also problematic since the only way of testing the knowledge is to run it so that the boundaries between acquistion and implementation can be blurred.

3. KNOWLEDGE ENGINEERING AND PROCESS CONTROL

Recently, serious mismatches have become evident between the view of a process as seen by the operator and that seen by the designer. This in part arises from the distinction which has been observed between an operator's view of the dynamic interaction and that of the system designer. The terms "knowledge of utilisation" and "knowledge of functioning" have been introduced (De Montmollin and De Keyser, 1986) to illustrate this distinction. Operators need to build internal models to enable them to successfully control dynamic systems and the competence of the operator derives from the successful internal cohesion of such images (De Keyser, 1986). However such models are rarely of the Engineering, Mathematical or Physical type. They are based on the common everyday experience of the operator.There is therefore often a mismatch between designer models and operator models. Furthermore, current control systems are designed on the basis of an analytical model of the process being controlled but it is difficult to define precise models which account for all behaviour. This has led to the Theory-Practice Gap (Leitch and Francis, 1986) and the inevitability of unforseen occurrences.

The situation is worsening as the reliability of systems increases. Operators develop images about the system from their familiarity in dealing with normal and abnormal situations. As systems are progressively automated there is a reduction in abnormal situations and a loss of such experience. Yet, when unforseen problems do occur and the operators demand full knowledge about the dynamic parameters involved they are frequently overloaded with information often presented in an unstructured form. One important need therefore is for intelligent knowledge-based assistance. Such advisory systems should be able to reason about the system and present their reasoning to the operator in a meaningful way (Alty and Johannsen, 1989). Dialogues need to be at a much higher level and must employ knowledge about the communication process itself as well as knowledge about the domain.

These points suggest that the next generation of dynamic control system interfaces will require a design philosophy based upon a human-centred design approach rather than the more traditional technology-centred approach. The human-centred approach concentrates upon the capabilities and limitations of the human operators with respect to information processing and the tasks which have to be performed.   Recently a number of systems have taken a more human-centred approach and some have utilised techniques from artificial intelligence (Monta et al, 1985, Ogino et al, 1983, Gallenti and Guida, 1986).

Expert systems can be introduced into process control systems to provide support for different classes of people such as designers, operators and maintenance personnel. In general such systems will be off-line (for designers and maintenance personnel) and on-line (for operators). The knowledge engineering task will be different for each of these applications since the tasks involved will comprise different knowledge sources and structures. Off-line knowledge-based systems are not time critical. They may utilise several knowledge sources including technical documents, reference literature, handbooks, ergonomic knowledge, and knowledge about operator personnel. Whilst their operation is not time critical they may still have to take into account operator time constraints.

Generally, designer activity in industrial systems ranges from the computer aided design of subsystems and components to picture design for control rooms (Rouse 1986; Elzer and Johannsen, 1988). Thus for designer support, knowledge about the application domain in addition to that concerned with design procedures is needed for all these tasks (Borys, 1988).

The most critical and challenging industrial expert systems are those developed for system operation. They may encompass support for the automatic system as well as support for the operators and may provide heuristic control, fault diagnosis, consequence prediction, and procedural support (Johannsen, 1990). The latter is particularly suitable for consistency checking of input sequences or for operator intent recognition (Hollnagel, 1988; Shalin and others, 1988). All these support expert systems work under time constraints because they are running in parallel with the dynamic industrial process. Like off-line systems, these expert systems will depend upon a number of knowledge sources related to knowledge of functioning and knowledge of utilisation. Additional knowledge such as that of senior engineers will be required.

It is also important to realise that in the industrial environment not all applications are suitable for the application of knowledge-based techniques. For example, existing numerical supervision and control systems are based upon thorough engineering methodologies and replacement by knowledge-based techniques would in most cases lead to performance degradation.

Most industrial applications are very complex and this makes the problems of acquiring and assembling the knowledge in the industrial environment much more severe than in traditional computing domains. The full process is likely to take years rather than months. In the absence of a powerful methodology, we will have to work with inadequate tools for some time to come.

4. COMPETING METHODOLOGIES FOR KNOWLEDGE ACQUISITION

There are two competing methodologies for building expert systems which might be described as bottom-up and top-down. The bottom-up practicioners aim to prise data and concepts out of the expert and then iteratively refine it. Feigenbaum for example has described knowledge acquisition as "mining those jewels of knowledge out of their (*the experts*) minds one by one" (Feigenbaum and McCorduck, 1983) and the implication is that deeper mining will reveal more and more relevant knowledge. However, this assumes that there is a simple relationship between what is verbalised by experts and what is actually going on in their minds. The bottom-up philosophy, exemplified by Hayes-Roth and others (1983) is based upon the view that the building of expert systems "is inherently experimental" and is therefore characterised by rapid prototyping which is essentially a bottom-up process. The basic assumption underlying this bottom-up approach is that an expert system is based upon a large body of domain specific knowledge and that there are few general principles underlying the organisation of the domain knowledge in an expert's mind.

However, the existence of underlying principles and causal relationships (Davies, 1983) may be an indication that expert knowledge is more domain independent than was assumed by Feigenbaum (1979). Breuker and Wielinga (1987), for example state that "In our experience over the past three years in analysing eight widely different domains a number of concepts have invariably recurred, such as 'procedure', 'process', 'quantification object'... and 'identification object'...... Such concepts are abstractions of real world knowledge". So "expert behaviour that is seemingly domain-specific may originate from higher level problem solving methods which are well-structured and have some degree of domain independence".

The alternative methodology strongly put forward by Breuker and Wielinga is based upon a top-down approach. They claim that there is a crucial step missing in the prototyping approach between the identification of the relevant characteristics of the domain and selection of solution methods, that of "the interpretation of the data into some coherent framework, a model, schema or canonical form". They equate it to the knowledge level of Newell (1980) or the "missing level" of Brachman (1979) in semantic network analysis. Breuker and Wielinga propose five levels of knowledge analysis - identification, conceptualisation, epistemological, logical and implementational, and have developed these ideas into a knowledge acquisition methodology called KADS (Knowledge Acquisition and Documentation Structuring, Breuker and Wielinga, 1985). Note that the epistemological level is totally missing from the bottom-up approach. An example of the application of the technique to insurance underwriting is given in Hayward and others, 1988.

The KADS system is both a methodology and a tool which supports the methodology. The procedure begins with an analysis of the problem solving behaviour itself. Complex problems are broken down into less complex sub-problems. Furthermore, the problem is analysed as far as possible before any possible solutions are attempted. This is in complete contrast to the prototyping approach. Knowledge is acquired in such a way that an interpretive framework is built up. This interpretive model is the core of the methodology and is used to make sense of the data acquired during knowledge acquisition. The methodology is not yet really suitable for large scale knowledge acquisition, but it has been tested in a limited number of commercial domains and will, no doubt, be eventually honed down into a really useful methodology.

The bottom-up methodology has been criticised severely during the past decade and has often been identified as one of the major causes of failures in expert systems. Roth and Woods (1989), for example, identify "failing to appreciate the demands of the task" as a major reason for the failure in current expert systems developments. They identify the iterative refinement approach of Hayes-Roth, used almost universally during the knowledge acquisition phase as the main cause. From a small prototype, the full system is developed through iterative refinements until the final delivery system is produced. They claim that "the amount of time and resources typically available for systems development in industry does not allow for the long term evolution of systems entailed in the iterative refinement approach" and point out that "architectures which are built based on consideration of a core set of examples will often not have the necessary structural hooks and processing mechanisms to deal with new cases that have complex aspects that had not been represented in the original set" (Bachant and McDermott, 1984). The correct handling of new cases then requires major restructuring of the knowledge rather than fine tuning. Experts often state rules to which there are exceptions, which are not usually revealed until much later.

They further point out that systems designed from a core set of examples often result in oversimplified representation of goals and constraints and this results in the optimisation of one dimension of the user's problem at the expense of ignoring other goals.

5. TECHNIQUES FOR KNOWLEDGE ELICITATION

A number of techniques for knowledge elicitation are now in use though there has been little done by way of an analysis of the effectiveness of the various techniques. Ideally one would like to know how effective each technique is in different situations. Many of the techniques are borrowed from traditional psychology. They usually involve the collection of information from the domain expert either explicitly or implicitly. Originally, reports written by the experts were used but this technique is now out of favour since such reports tend to have a high degree of bias and reflective thought. Current techniques include interviews (both structured and unstructured), questionnaires, or observational techniques such as protocol analyses and walkthroughs. The success of a particular technique is probably best judged by the expert.

It is important to document the whole elicitation process carefully. Some authors have suggested the use of a Knowledge Handbook (Wolfgram et al 1987), since the process can take place over many months. Such a Handbook would contain

- general problem description
- user expectations
- breakdown into sub-problems
- domain selected for prototype (and why)
- vocabulary
- list of relevant experts
- reasonable performance standards
- typical reasoning scenarios

Overall, in the elicitation phase the knowledge engineers tread a delicate path between knowing too little and appearing to know too much. It is important to do a great deal of preparatory reading before talking with the expert so that some basic ideas in the domain are understood. However it is dangerous to appear to know too much since this will come over as arrogance and will irritate. The best approach is one of "informed humbleness".

5.1 Interviews

In a structured interview, the knowledge engineer is in control. Such interviews are useful for obtaining an overall sense of the domain. They tend to involve highly directed questions such as "what are the most important tasks ?", "How do you decide ?".   In an unstructured interview, the domain expert is usually in control. They are useful for the introduction of vocabulary, ideas and general principles. However, such interviews can, as the name implies, yield a somewhat incoherent collection of domain knowledge - in the extreme form a "brain dump" of the experts knowledge. The result can be a very unstructured set of raw data that needs to be analysed and conceptualised. Group interviews can be useful particularly for cognitive bias filtering since small groups of experts tend to exhibit better judgement than individuals. There are a number of useful group techniques (McGraw and Seale (1988).

It is important to realise that experts will tend to use a narrative style and will usually provide many anecdotal examples. Such "informal" knowledge is more difficult to analyse.

Team interviewing is strongly recommended by some workers in the field. A two-to-one technique suggested by Walters and Neilson (1987) involves a pair of knowledge engineers, one acting as questioner and the other as scribe. The roles are periodically reversed. Switching might typically happen about every 5 to 10 minutes. Although this can at first be intimidating for the domain expert, the gain in accuracy usually outweighs any adverse effects.

5.2 Questionnaires and Rating Scales

Questionnaires can be used instead or in addition with interviews. The interviews can be standardised in question-answer categories or questionnaires can be applied in a more formal way. However, the latter should be handled in most cases in a relaxed manner for reasons of building up an atmosphere of confidence and not disturbing the expert too much when applied in actual work situations (Borys and others, 1987).

Rating scales are formal techniques for evaluating single items of interest by asking the expert to cross-mark a scale. Verbal descriptions along the scale such as from "very low" to "very high" or from "very simple" to "very difficult" are used as a reference for the expert. The construction, use and evaluation of rating scales is described very well in the psychological and social science literature. Rating scales can also be combined with interviews or questionnaires.

5.3 Observations

Observations are another technique used in the knowledge elicitation process. All actions and activities of the expert are observed as accurately as possible by the knowledge engineer who records the observed information. A special mixture of interview and observation techniques are the observation interviews (Matern, 1984; Johannsen, 1989). Sequences of activities are observed and questions about causes, reasons, and consequences asked by the knowledge engineer during these observations. The combined technique is very powerful because the sequence of activities is observable whereas decision criteria, rules, plans etc. are elicited in addition through what-, how- and why-questions.

5.4 Protocol Analysis

The recording and analysis of "think-aloud" data has been carried out for many years. Such protocol analyses are useful for obtaining detailed knowledge about the domain. It must be remembered however that such activities produce huge amounts of data which involve many hours of analysis. The main concern of such techniques is by how far the object of measurement is distorted by the technique. In such protocols, the expert should not be allowed to include retrospective utterances. He or she should avoid theorising about their behaviour and should "only report information and intentions within the current sphere of conscious awareness" (Newell and Simon, 1972). Newell and Simon conclude that self-reporting need not interfere with the task and may even be helpful by allowing the reporter to concentrate on reasoning. Incompleteness is more likely than lack of validity.

Protocol analysis can involve verbal protocols in which the expert thinks aloud whilst carrying out the task, or motor protocols in which the physical performance of the expert is observed and recorded (often on video tape). Eye movement analysis is an example of a very specialised version of this technique. Motor protocols, however, are usually only useful when used in conjunction with verbal protocols.

In a verbal protocol, the expert thinks aloud and a time-stamped recording is made of his utterances (Ericsson and Simon, 1984). As a verbal protocol is transcribed, it is broken down into short lines corresponding roughly to meaningful phrases (see Kuipers and Kassirer, 1987 for examples of the technique). The technique can collect the basic objects and relations in the domain and establish causal relationships. From these a domain model can be built. The experience with the use of verbal protocols from the analysis of trouble-shooting in maintenance work of technicians is described by Rasmussen (1984).

It is important when using the transcription method not to allow any proposed expert systems technology (i.e., rule-based approach) to influence the selection of items. Fox, when examining failures in the performance of an expert system designed to diagnose Leukemia, noted that the expert systems technology used (in this case EMYCIN) strongly influenced the method used to "identify" useful information in the verbal protocols (Fox and others, 1987). He also comments "we are even less confident about knowledge that may be implicit or distributed in the structure of the protocols rather than concentrated in identifiable fragments".

5.5 Walkthroughs

Walkthroughs are more detailed than protocol analysis. They are often better than protocol analysis because they can be done in actual environment which gives better memory cues. They need not, however, be carried out in real time. Indeed, such techniques are useful in a simulated environment where states of the system can be frozen and additional questions pursued.

5.6 Teachback Interviewing

Another technique used in knowledge elicitation is "teachback interviewing". In this technique, the expert first describes a procedure to the knowledge engineer, who then teaches it back to the expert in the expert's terms until the expert is completely satisfied with the explanation. Johnson and Johnson (1987) describe this technique and illustrate its use in two case studies. Their approach is guided by Conversation Theory (Pask, 1974), in which interaction takes place at two levels - specific and general. The paper gives a useful set of guidelines on the strengths and weaknesses of the technique.

5.7 More Formal Techniques

Formal techniques include multidimensional scaling, repertory grids and hierarchical clustering. Such techniques tend to elicit declarative knowledge. The most commonly used is the repertory grid technique (Kelly, 1955) based on personal construct theory. It is used in ETS (Boose, 1986) which assists in the elicitation of knowledge for classification type problems, and PLANET (Shaw and Gaines, 1986). In personal construct theory the basic unit is the construct or dichotomous distinction. The expert is interviewed to obtain elements of the domain. Relationships are then established by presenting triads of elements and asking the expert to identify two traits which distinguish the elements (these are the constructs). They are then classified into larger groups called constellations. Various techniques such as statistical, clustering and multidimensional scaling are then used to establish classification rules which generate conclusion rules and intermediate rules together with certainty factors. The experts are interviewed again to refine the knowledge. ETS, which uses the technique, is said to save between 2 and 5 months over conventional interviewing techniques. The system has been modified and improved and is now called AQUINAS (Boose and Bradshaw, 1988).

6.   MACHINE INDUCTION

The machine induction approach to knowledge acquisition has some similarities with the way in which many human beings may learn. Human beings are accomplished pattern matchers. They can quickly discern patterns in example sets of data provided the data sets are not too large. The resultant patterns are usually in the form of rules. If, once a pattern is established, an exception is found, the pattern match (or rule) is modified to take into account the errant example. Hence learning takes place. The interesting point about knowledge learned in this way is that the learner need not understand the reasons behind the knowledge. It is a common observation that experts have great difficulty in explaining the procedures which they use in making decisions and this is possibly because much of their knowledge has been acquired using inductive techniques. Experts often make use of assumptions and beliefs which they do not explicitly state and are surprised when the consequences of these hidden assumptions are pointed out (Jackson, 1985).

The inductive approach relies on the fact that experts can usually supply examples of their expertise even if they do not understand their own reasoning mechanisms. This is because creating an example set does not require any understanding of how different evidence is assessed or what conflicts were resolved to reach a decision. Sets of such examples are then analysed by an inductive algorithm (one of the most popular being the ID3 algorithm of Quinlan, 1979) and rules are generated automatically from these examples. The inductive technique is used in the following way:

- a set of result classes is chosen (the set of possible outcomes)
- a set of attributes which might contribute to the outcome is chosen
- sets of possible values for the various attributes are selected
- example sets are then constructed across all the examples
- a machine algorithm is then used to derive rules (say ID3)
- the resultant rules are then examined by the domain expert
- as a result attributes may be added or deleted and additional examples created.
- the cycle is repeated until the expert is satisfied with the result.
- the rules are then tested on new data.

The rules induced depend both upon the example set chosen and the inductive algorithm used so there is no guarantee that the rules induced will be valid knowledge. This is why checking with the expert to see if the induced rules are reasonable is very important in the process. It is not uncommon to cycle a number of times through the induction process refining the knowledge base with the domain expert. Bratko (1989) gives a useful account of the techniques and the application of the ID3 algorithm.

The inductive approach has another use in process control - in cases where a large body of data exists about a process but the underlying rules are not known. The technique can therefore be used on large collections of historical process data (i.e. log data) about industrial plants in order to induce the rules of their operation. Once the rules are known the process can often be optimised. A well-known example of the use of this technique was at the Westinghouse Corporation where over $10,000,000 was saved (Westinghouse, 1984). By using inductive techniques on historical plant performance data, the rules of operation were derived. When these were examined, improved operational performance levels became possible and resulted in the savings. The technique has also been used successfully on large bodies of financial and insurance data.

6.1 Use of Induction for Acquiring Engineering Knowledge

The inductive technique seems particularly appropriate for extracting engineering knowledge. An example of this is the design of a gas-oil system (called Gas-oil) for British Petroleum to assist engineers in designing gas-oil separators. The underlying hydrocarbon production separation process is quite complicated relying on a variety of knowledge sources such as that in manuals, codes of practice, space limitations, and by the crude oil quantity and the gas quality required. Gas-oil is a large system - containing over 2,500 rules and it is expected to grow in size to 100,000 rules eventually. The remarkable fact about the system is that it took one year of effort to create and now requires about one month per year of maintenance effort. Much of this reduced development and maintenance cost is claimed to result from the use of inductive techniques (Guilfoyle, 1986). One interesting feature of the system is that the induced rules are in FORTRAN, which makes interfacing to other, more conventional parts of the system much easier.

Slocombe of British Petroleum (Slocombe and others, 1986) claims that the inductive technique is ideally suited to the engineering temperament. "The expert is invited to suggest a possible set of solutions to a particular problem. Then he thinks of the factors which are involved in deciding which choice to make. For example, in choosing a type of vessel for use in a refinery, the expert would take into account the quality of output needed, the throughput of material, the size of the site available and so on. The last stage of this process involves the expert providing a few examples of real cases. The software then induces the rule. At this stage, the expert's interest is caught. The rule may be over simple, so the expert thinks up another example to illustrate the difference between the two cases. Or the rule may separate two factors which are later decided to be the same. This technique concentrates on: Homing in on the psychological problems".

An important point here is that the domain experts were able to interact directly with the knowledge acquisition process with minimum assistance from a knowledge engineer. This has often been suggested as one of the main goals of the development of knowledge acquisition tools - to eliminate the need for a knowledge engineer. As Moore points out (Slocombe and others, 1986), "The academic approach... requires a knowledge engineer with no expertise in the engineering domain to approach the expert and say " I know nothing about your area, but would like you to tell me everything you know, and preferably in the form of explicit rules". Our best experts are long experienced individuals with a wealth of heuristics and rules of thumb. They find it very difficult to articulate their knowledge explicitly but can reel off any number of examples and outcomes under particular circumstances".   BP   combine   this   inductive   approach   with sophisticated system building facilities and are now using the inductive techniques in a number of application areas.

5.2 Satellite Power System Diagnosis

Another interesting use of inductive techniques which will have a wide application in process control is their use in conjunction with a qualitative model of the process. The technique was first carried out in the analysis of electro-cardiograms (Lavrac and others, 1985) where a qualitative model of the heart was built (in Prolog) and this was then used to generate examples of failure caused by sets of arrhythmias. These examples were then fed into an inductive algorithm to produce the rules for interpreting electrocardiograms. The technique is particularly amenable to solving problems in process control because the models underlying the process are well-known.

A more directly relevant example of the use of the qualitative model/induction technique is an application which involved the construction of a prototype on-board expert system for dealing with power failures in a satellite. The work was carried out at the Turing Institute, Glasgow, and has been reported by Pearce (1988).

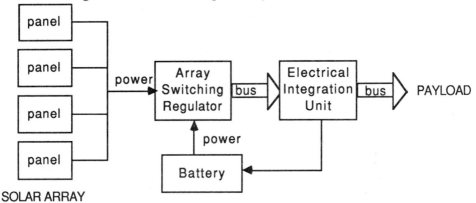

Figure 3   The Satellite Power System

The area of application was the electrical power sub-system of a satellite. This consisted of a set of solar arrays, switching circuits, two batteries and an electrical bus for connecting with the payload as shown in Figure 3. When the satellite is in sunlight, power is generated in the solar array panels and this power is used to drive the payload and recharge the batteries. In the eclipse phase, the battery maintains the payload. The Array Switch Regulator (ASR) contains switches to enable or disable solar panels. A comparator detects a rise or fall in bus voltage and automatically opens or closes ASR switches to restore the bus voltage. The Electrical Integration Unit contains switches for main charging or trickle charging the two batteries. Thirty seven telemetry points provided information for ground control and from such information the ground based operators had to determine faults and suggest error correction procedures.

A model of the subsystem was constructed in PROLOG. It consisted of a set of predicates which defined the interconnectability of the constituent components and their initial states. Behaviour rules were then specified for each component to define how a change of state of one particular component affected another. By running these heuristic behaviour rules the performance of the satellite can be simulated. In particular, its behaviour (and the corresponding values of the thirty seven telemetry points) when one or more components fail can be generated.

The procedure for deriving the rules for diagnosing failure is as follows:

- a component is failed.
- the model is run until it reaches a steady state.
- all the possible measuring points (in the satellite's case the set of telemetry points relayed to ground control) are read-off. These together with the introduced fault form an example of failure, the result being the introduced fault and the telemetry points being the attributes.
- a second component is then failed and the above process is repeated yielding a second example.
- the process is repeated until all components have been individually failed. At this point an induction algorithm is applied to induce a set of rules which summarise the complete set of behaviour represented by the example set.
- these rules can then be used for diagnosing all single faults in the subsystem.

The above process can be repeated for all combinations of two faults to give the rules for two-component failure and so on.

The important point about the above process is that the induction is carried out over a complete set of examples and thus avoids the usual problems of completeness when inducing rules from an incomplete set of examples. Thus if our original model is correct our rules should be correct so the validity problem reduces to ensuring that the model itself is correct.

In the case reported by Pearce, an expert system had already been constructed for the power subsystem by traditional means. This had been constructed using the Expert System Shell "Envisage", had taken about 6 man-months to construct and had resulted in a 110-rule system. By comparison, the induction approach yielded 75 rules and required only 3 to 4 man-months to construct. When both sets of rules were tested on a real-time simulator the induced rules achieved a 100% success rate as compared with 75% for the Envisage rules. The superiority of the qualitative modelling approach is clearly evident in this particular example. It is also interesting to note that Pearce also ran both sets of rules (the Envisage rules and the induced rules) through a Knowledge Integrity Checker. Whilst the induced rules

passed without any identified error, six faults were found in the rules derived by conventional knowledge engineering techniques.

The qualitative model was constructed in the language PROLOG. The model consists of definitions of each component and its relationship to other components (upstream and downstream of it). Behaviour rules specify how each component affects any neighbouring components. All that is then needed is an initial state and the model can be executed. The model is a qualitative one in that it does not deal with precise values of voltages or currents over time. Rather it deals with values such as low, medium and high. Although, at first sight, this seems very restrictive it corresponds closely to domain expert descriptions when reasoning about the operation of devices, and it is able to give more meaningful explanations than a quantitative model. Of course, it is also computationally less complex.

In order to understand why the qualitative modelling approach yields superior results it is necessary to examine how each rule set was created. In the envisage case, standard Knowledge Engineering techniques were used to extract the rules from the engineers. This is a difficult process and checking the validity of a set of 110 rules is problematic. In the qualitative modelling case the model was developed from discussions with the engineers and a key feature of the process was the construction of a visual simulation of the model. The PROLOG model was used to drive a schematic representation on a colour SUN workstation using the HYPERNEWS graphics interface software (Van Hoff,1989). Engineers were therefore able to play with the model and verify (by experience) its "correctness". Whilst this is no guarantee of its validity it is certainly much easier to do than verify a set of rules. Thus we have pushed back the validation problem into one of validating a visual model (a much easier process).

Because example creation involves the systematic failing of each component in turn it might be said that the above approach will be similarly limited by the combinatorial explosion problem. In particular two- and three- simultaneous component failure will involve large amounts of computation. Furthermore, the satellite problem described above only had 61 functional components under 8 payload conditions and 3 solar phases. A complete example set therefore covered 1464 examples in all. A justifiable criticism would be that such an approach would not scale-up for "real" problems.

In fact, the induction process is reasonably fast and the time taken for the ID3 algorithm to induce rules is roughly linear with respect to the number of examples. The above example required about 20 seconds on a SUN/3 workstation so increasing the number of components to, say, 2,000 or 3,000 would not be serious particularly as the induction process only has to be done once and so could be left running overnight if necessary.

A more serious problem, however, is the generation of the examples. To generate each example the model has to be run until it reaches a steady state. In the 1464 example mentioned earlier, this took nearly one hour. Although this process is effectively linear with respect to the number of components, a 2,000 or 3,000 component model might require 30 to 40 hours. Although, once again this is a one-off process, it does suggest that such a size of model might pose a real upper limit for the technique.

There are two other ways of reducing the combinatorial complexity - by introducing real world constraints in order to limit the number of examples, and by decomposing the problem hierarchically and solving each subsystem separately. In the heart modelling case (Mozetic et al) some faults simply could not exist simultaneously so that the number of possible examples was considerably reduced. Whilst it is undoubtedly true that some faults will be mutually exclusive in the electric circuit case it is unlikely that there will be a significant reduction in problem complexity, so this is not an option in our case. We are therefore examining the possibility of using the hierarchical nature of collections of components to reduce problem complexity.

This example shows the power of the approach. Furthermore, it can deal with multiple error situations - one simply creates examples of multiple error situations. Although this is computationally intensive it only has to be done once. For complex systems, the system can be broken down into lower level subsets and solved individually. Then, the interactions between these subsets can be treated separately. The approach is ideally suited to diagnostic problems in process control systems where validation is important.

7. KNOWLEDGE ACQUISITION TOOLS

A number of tools for supporting the knowledge acquisition process have been developed in the academic environment and some of these have been mentioned already. The general aim of all these tools is to minimise the number of iterations needed for the whole knowledge engineering process by bridging the gap between the problem domain and the implementation. Boose and Gaines (1988) give a brief summary of the main tools under development and provide a summary.

Some tools endeavour to make the process fully automatic (e.g. KRITON Diederich and others, 1987). Other tools (for example KADS and ACQUIST) merely provide a set of tools to aid a more methodological approach. Thus, KADS aims only to produce a document describing the structure of the problem in the form of a documentation handbook. KRITON supports only bottom-up knowledge acquisition but KADS supports both top-down and bottom-up approaches.

8. CONCLUSIONS

The lack of well-tried and reliable knowledge engineering techniques has been a limiting factor in the development of expert systems. The initial successes of early systems resulted in too much emphasis being placed upon the bottom-up strategy for knowledge acquisition. More recently the importance of differentiating between the acquisition task and the implementation level has been highlighted with more emphasis being placed upon the modelling approach. It is clear that the cognitive behaviour and knowledge structures in human problem solving tasks have to be understood and formalised by appropriate knowledge acquisition techniques, before any systems implementation makes sense. Ideally, we need a better understanding of the cognitive processes which take place in the minds of experts. These factors, however, are not well understood at the present time.

At the present time the technology used for implementing knowledge based systems tends to exert too great an influence on the acquisition process itself. We should be striving to develop some form of intermediate knowledge representation formalism or language, (for example Matsumura and others, 1989) but we are still a long way from achieving this objective. This fact, together with the requirement for several iterations over the knowledge acquisition process will inevitably mean that knowledge acquisition will be a skilled and time consuming activity for the foreseeable future.

There is an urgent need for better tools to aid the knowledge acquisition process. Can tools be provided which allow domain experts to play a more direct role in the knowledge acquisition activity ? Is this even desirable ? A good intermediate knowledge representation tool might at least enable us to allow domain experts to create representations of their knowledge which could then be implemented by more traditional systems designers. The answer will probably be decided by domain expert availability. Perhaps scarce experts will always be too busy to become involved on their own initiative in the knowledge acquisition process.

In the process control area we need better tools for creating models of the process and relating these to operator actions and cognitive processes. There is also a need for tools to assist in validating expert systems since progress will almost certainly be limited by safety considerations. The qualitative modelling approach (when coupled with inductive techniques) has shown some promise in at least pushing back the validation process away from direct rule validation towards model validation which is somewhat easier to do.

We have come a long way using ad-hoc methods. Further significant advances will probably only be possible through concentration on more rigourous approaches.

9. REFERENCES

Alty, J.L., and Johannsen, G., (1989), "Knowledge Based Dialogue for Dynamic Systems", Automatica (to appear), also in Proc. IFAC 10th World Congress on Automatic Control (Isermann, R., (ed.)), (Preprints, 1987, Vol 7, pp 358 - 367).

Bachant, J.A., and McDermott, J., (1984), "R1 Revisited: Four Years in the Trenches", The AI Magazine, Vol 4, Fall 1984, pp 21 - 32.

Boose, J.H., (1986), "Expertise Transfer for Expert Systems Design", Elsevier, New York,

Boose, J.H., and Bradshaw, J.M., (1988), "Expertise Transfer and Complex Problems: using AQUINAS as a Knowledge-Acquisition Workbench for Knowledge-Based Systems", Int. J. Man-Machine studies, Vol 2, pp 39 - 64.

Boose, J.H., and Gaines, B., (1988), "Knowledge Acquisition Tools for Expert Systems", in Knowledge Acquisition Tools for Expert Systems, Boose, J.H., and Gaines, B., (eds.), Academic Press, London, pp xiii - xvi.

Borys, B,-B., (1988), "Ways of Supporting Ergonomically and Technically Correct Display Design", Proc. Workshop Human Computer Interaction and Complex Systems, Alexandria, Scotland.

Borys, B. -B., Johannsen, G., Hansel, H, -G., and Schmidt, J., (1987), "Task and Knowledge Analysis in Coal Fired Power Plants", IEEE Control Systems Magazine, Vol 7, pp 26 - 30.

Brachman, R.J., (1979), "A Structured Paradigm for Representing Knowledge", BBN Technical Report, Bolt, Beranek and Newman, Cambridge, Mass.

Bratko, I., (1989), "Machine Learning", In Human and Machine Problem Solving, Gilhooly, K.J., (ed.), Plenum Press, New York, pp 265 - 286.

Breuker, J.A., and Wielinga, B., (1985), "KADS: Structured Knowledge Acquisition for Expert Systems", Proc. 5th Int.Workshop on Expert Systems and their Applications, Avignon, France.

Breuker, J.A., and Wielinga, B., (1987), "Use of Models in the Interpretation of Verbal Data", in Knowledge Acquisition for Expert Systems (Kidd, A.L., ed.) Plenum Press, New York, pp 17 - 44.

Buchanan, B.G., Barstow, D., Bechtal, R., Bennett, J., Clancey, W., Kulikowski, C., Mitchell, T., and Waterman, D.A., (1983), "Constructing an Expert System", in Building Expert Systems (Hayes-Roth, F., Waterman, D.A., and Lenat, D.B., eds.), Addison-Wesley, Reading, Mass., Chapter 5.

Chignell, M.H., and Peterson, J.G., (1988), "Strategic Issues in Knowledge Engineering", Human Factors, Vol 30, pp 381 - 394.

Davies, R., (1982), "Expert Systems: Where are we ? and Where do we go from here ?", AI Memo No. 665, MIT AI Laboratory.

Davies, R., (1983), "Reasoning From First Principles in Electronic Trouble Shooting", Int. J. of Man-Machine Studies, Vol 19, pp 403-423.

De Montmollin, M., and DeKeyser, V., (1986), "Expert Logic versus Operator Logic", in Analysis, Design and Evaluation of Man-Machine Systems (Johannsen, G., Mancini, G., and Martenssen, L, (eds.), Proc 2nd IFAC/IFIP/IFORS/IEA Conf., Pergammon Press, Oxford, pp 43 - 49.

Diederich, J., and Linster, M., (1989), "Knowledge Based Knowledge Elicitation", in Topics in Expert Systems Design, Guida, G., and Tasso, C., (eds.), North Holland, Amsterdam, pp 325.

Diederich, J., Ruhmann, I., and May, M, (1987), " KRITON, a Knowledge Acquisition Tool for Expert Systems", Int. J. Man-Machine Studies, Vol 26.

Elzer, P., and Johannsen, G., (eds.), (1988), "Concepts, Design and Implementations for an Intelligent Graphical Editor (IGE1)", ESPRIT GRADIENT P857 Report No. 6, Labor. Man-Machine Systems, University of Kassel (GhK).

Ericsson, K., and Simon, H.A., (1984), "Protocol Analysis: Verbal Reports as Data", MIT Press, Cambridge, Mass.

Feigenbaum, E.A., (1979), "Themes and Case Studies in Knowledge Engineering", in Expert Systems in the Microelectronic Age, Michie, D., (ed.), Edinburgh University Press, Edinburgh.

Feigenbaum, E.A., and McCorduck, P., (1983), "The Fifth Generation", Addison-Wesley, New York.

Fox, J., Myers, C.D., Greaves, M.F., and Pegram, S., (1987), "A Systematic study of Knowledge Base Refinement in the Diagnosis of Leukemia", in Knowledge Acquisition for Expert Systems: A Practical Handbook, (Kidd A.L., ed.), Plenum Press, New York, pp 73 - 90.

Gallenti, M., and Guida, G., "Intelligent Decision Aids for Process Environments: An Expert System Approach ", in E. Hollnagel, G. Mancini and D.D. Woods, (eds.), Intelligent Decision Support in Process Environments, Springer-Verlag, Berlin, (1986), pp 373 - 394

Greenwell, M., (1990), "Knowledge Elicitation: Principles and Practice", in Understanding Knowledge Engineering (McTear, M.F., and Anderson, T.J., eds.), Ellis Horwood, Chichester, pp 44 - 68.

Guilfoyle, C., (1986), "Ten Minutes to Lay the Foundations", Expert System User, August 1986, pp 16 - 19.

Hayes-Roth, F., Waterman, D.A., and Lenat, D.B., (1983), "Technowledge Series in Knowledge Engineering, Vol 1, Building Expert Systems, Addison-Wesley, Reading, Mass

Hayes-Roth, F., (1984), "Knowledge-based Expert Systems", IEEE Computer, pp 263 - 273.

Hayward, S.A., Wielinga, B.,and Breuker, J.A., (1988), "Structured Analysis of Knowledge", in Knowledge Acquisition Tools for Expert Systems, Boose, J., and Gaines, B., (eds.), Academic Press, London, pp 140 -160.

Hollnagel, E., (1987), "Plan Recognition in Modelling of Users", Reliability Engineering and System Safety, Vol 22, pp 129 - 136.

Jackson, P., (1985), "Reasoning about Belief in the Context of Advice-giving Systems", in Research and Development in Expert Systems, Bramer, M., (ed.), Cambridge University Press.

Johannsen, G., (1990), "Towards a New Quality of Automation in Complex Man-Machine Systems", IFAC 11th World Congress Automatic Control, Tallinn, (to appear).

Johannsen, G., and Alty, J.L., (1990), "Knowledge Engineering for Industrial Expert Systems", to appear in Automatica, Dec. 1990.

Johnson L.E., and Johnson, N.E., (1987), "Knowledge Elicitation Involving Teachback Interviewing", in Knowledge Acquisition for Expert Systems: A Practical Handbook, (Kidd., A.L., ed.), Plenum Press, New York, pp 91 - 108.

Kelly, G.A., (1955), "The Psychology of Personal Constructs", Norton, New York.

De Keyser, V., "Technical Assistance to the Operator in Case of Incident: Some Lines of Thought", In E. Hollnagel, G. Mancini, and D.D. Woods, (eds.), Intelligent Decision Support in Process Environments, Springer-Verlag, Berlin, (1986), pp 229 - 253.

Kuipers B., and Kassirer, J.P., (1987), "Knowledge Acquisition by Analysis of Verbal Protocols", in Knowledge Acquisition for Expert Systems (Kidd, A.L., ed.) Plenum Press, New York, pp 45 - 71..

Lavrac, N., Bratko, I., Mozatec, I., Cercek, B., Horvat, M., and Grad, D., (1985), "KARDIO-E: An Expert System for Electrocardiographic Diagnosis of Cardiac Arrhythmias", Expert Systems, Vol. 2, No. 1, pp 46 - 50.

Leitch, R., and Francis, J., "Towards Intelligent Control Systems", in A. Mamdani and J. Efstathiou, (eds.), Expert Systems and Optimisation in Process Control, Unicom Seminars Ltd., Gower Technical Press, England, (1986).

McGraw, K.L., and Searle, M.R., (1988), "Knowledge Elicitation with Multiple Experts: Considerations and Techniques", AI Review, Vol 2, (1).

Madni, A.M., (1988), "The Role of Human Factors in System Design and Acceptance", Human Factors, Vol 30, pp 395 - 414.

Matern, B., (1984), "Psychologische Arbeitsanalyse", Springer-Verlag, Berlin.

Matsumura, S., Kawai, K., Kamiya, A., Koi, T., and Momoeda, K., (1989), "User Friendly Expert System for Turbine-Generator Vibration Diagnosis", 4th IFAC/IFIP/IFORS/IEA Conf. Man-Machine Systems, Xi'an, China,

Michie, D., and Johnston, R., (1985), "The Creative Computer", Pelican, London, England.

Monta, K., Fukutomi, S., Itoh, M., and Tai, I., "Development of a Computerised Operator Support System for BWR Power Plants", International Topical Meeting on Computer Applications for Nuclear Power Plant Operation and Control, Pasco, Wash., USA (1985).

Motta, E., Eisenstadt, M., Pitman, K., and West, M., (1988), "Knowledge Acquisition in KEATS: The Knowledge Engineers Assistant", Expert Systems, Vol 5, No 2.

Mozetic, I., Bratko, I., and Lavrac, N., "Automatic synthesis and compression of cardiological knowledge", Machine Intelligence 11, (1988).

Newell, A., (1980), "Physical Symbol Systems", Cognitive Science, Vol 4, pp 333 - 361.

Newell, A., and Simon, H.A., (1972),   "Human Problem Solving", Englewood Cliffs, N. J., Prentice-Hall.

Ogino, T., Fujita, Y., and Morimoto, H., "Intelligent Man-Machine Communication System for Nuclear Power Plants", IAEA Seminar on Operating Procedures for Abnormal Conditions in Nuclear Power Plants, Munchen, West Germany, (1986).

Pask, G., (1974), "Conversation, Cognition and Learning: A Cybernetic Theory and Methodology", Elsevier, London.

Pearce, D.A., (1988), "The Induction of Fault Diagnosis Systems from Qualitative Models", Turing Institute Report No. TIRM-88-029, available from the Turing Institute, Glasgow, UK.

Quinlan, R., (1979), "Discovering Rules from Large Collections of Examples: A Case Study", in Expert Systems in the Microelectronic Age, Michie, D., (ed.), Edinburgh Univ. Press.

Rasmussen, J., (1984), "Strategies for State Identification and Diagnosis in Supervisory Control Tasks, and Design of Computer Based Support Systems", in Advances in Man-Machine Systems Research, Rouse, W.B., (ed.), JAI Press, Greenwich, Conn., Vol 1, pp 139 - 193.

Roth, E.M., and Woods, D.D., (1989), "Cognitive Task Analysis: An Approach to Knowledge Acquisition for Intelligent System Design", in Topics in Expert System Design (Guida, G., and Tasso, C., eds.), North Holland, Amsterdam, pp 233 - 264.

Rouse, W.B., (1986), "On the Value of Information in System Design: A Framework for Understanding and Aiding Designers", Information Processing and Management, Vol 22, pp 217 - 228.

Shallin, V.L., Perschbacher, D.L., and Jamar, P.G., (1988)," Intent Recognition: An Emerging Technology", Proc. Int. Conf. Human Machine Interaction and Artificial Intelligence in Aeronautics and Space, Toulouse, pp 139 - 149.

Shaw, M.L.G., and Gaines, B.R., (1986), "Techniques for Knowledge Acquisition and Transfer", Proc. Knowledge Acquisition for KBS Workshop, Banff, Canada.

Slocombe, S., Moore, K.D.M., and Zelouf, M., (1986), "Engineering Expert System Applications", Offprint. Available from the Turing Institute, Glasgow, UK.

Tversky, A., and Kahnemann, D., (1974), "Judgement under Uncertainty: Heuristics and Biases", Science, Vol 125, pp 1124 - 1131.

Van Hoff, A., "HyperNeWS 1.3 User Manual", available from the Turing Institute, Glasgow, UK., (1989)

Walters, J.R., and Nielsen, N.R., (1988), "Crafting Knowledge Based Systems", Chapter 3, Wiley, New York.

Westinghouse, (1984), Press Release.

Wolfgram, D.D., Dear, T.J., and Galbraith, C.S., (1987), "Expert Systems for the Technical Professional", Wiley, New York.

Chapter 5

Cognitive models from subcognitive skills

D. Michie, M. Bain and J. Hayes-Michie

> It is a profoundly erroneous truism ... that we should cultivate
> the habit of thinking what we are doing. The precise opposite is
> the case. Civilisation advances by extending the number of
> important operations which we can perform without thinking
> about them.
>
> A.N. Whitehead, *An Introduction to Mathematics*, 1911.

Introduction

We consider the acquisition of skill in dynamical control tasks for
which the "recognise-act" cycle is relatively fast, as in piloting a
helicopter. Human pilots commonly receive their initial training
on computer simulations. From such trial-and-error learning they
acquire cognitive capabilities which they cannot articulate. As
observed by Dennett (1987), "... the cognitive psychologist
marshals experimental evidence, models and theories to show that
people are engaged in surprisingly sophisticated reasoning
processes of which they can give no introspective account at all.
Not only are minds accessible to outsiders; some mental activities
are more accessible to outsiders than to the very 'owners' of those
minds!"

Over the past 15 years, machine learning methods have been
developed (see Michie 1986 and review papers in Quinlan 1987,
1989) by which computer-executable models of such capabilities
can be extracted from recorded traces of skilled behaviour.
Moreover, Shapiro and Michie (1986) among others have
demonstrated that by a straightforward programming trick the

models which are inductively inferred from such human-generated decision data can automatically be endowed with a self-explanation facility, and thus rendered articulate. The end-products can justly be described as articulate models of inarticulate ("subcognitive" skills).

Laboratory development and commercial exploitation have been restricted to problem-solving domains where the recognise-act cycle is of the order of minutes or longer, as for example in assessing a loan application, diagnosing an electronic fault or predicting a severe thunderstorm. In this paper we report preliminary laboratory studies using dynamical control tasks based on the inverted pendulum, where the decision-cycle is of the order of a second or less. Evidence was obtained that:

(1)   at least partial reconstruction from behavioural traces of the trainee's "silent" decision-rules is possible, and

(2)   computer execution of rules extracted in this way can generate skilled behaviours which are in some respects more reliable than the same skills as executed by the trainee's own nervous system.

We conclude that the new methods may hold promise when it is not feasible to provide a fledgling pilot with a more experienced human co-pilot as safety back-up. This infeasibility applies, for example, to the piloting of small one-man aircraft such as helicopters. Instead, we propose providing a computer "co-autopilot" which has been trained on the pilot's own behavioural traces, but to a higher level of run-time consistency. The need and possibility for over-designing in this way flow from the interfering effects of "noise" and inattention errors in the human nervous system. These are smoothed out by inductive inference to construct an optimised model of what the trained pilot does as a general rule. The effects of the human's intermittent lapses of attention and consistency are thus eliminated.

Learning by imitation using pole-balancing

In 1960 Donaldson demonstrated a machine which learned to balance a rigid pole by imitation of the actions of a skilled human controller. Actions took a graded form on a scale of positive and negative applied force, and varied continuously. Donaldson's method of "error decorrelation", rather as today's neural net approaches to learning, resulted in a solution in the form of lists of numerical co-efficients. The same applies to a successful exercise in imitative learning of pole-balancing reported by Widrow and Smith (1964) based on their Perceptron-like ADALINE device. The latter authors used "bang-bang" control in place of continuous, there being only two states of the motor in their system, namely full force left and full force right. They also placed a number of numerical thresholds on each of the monitored state variables, thus partitioning the total state-space into a number of discrete local regions. These corresponded to the basic sensory inputs of the ADALINE architecture.

Influenced by this work, Chambers and Michie (1969) developed an algorithm, BOXES, capable of learning the task autonomously by trial-and-error, without need to imitate a tutor. Their work, as the present work, used computer simulations of the task, rather than physical apparatus. BOXES also supported a co-operative mode in which human "pilot" and computer "co-pilot" could learn together, an opportunistic combination of trial-and-error and mutual imitation. An unexpected discovery was that the cycle-time was sufficiently fast to disable any assistance which human learners might otherwise have derived from their intuitive understanding of how such objects as poles and carts actually behave. Learning was thus confined to the acquisition of heuristic, or "shallow", models of the task without involving causal, or "deep", models. Experimental subjects were divided into two groups. One group saw an animated picture on the screen similar to that of **Figure 1**. For the second group this was replaced by an animated image of four horizontal lines of fixed length, along each of which a pointer wandered back and forth. The subjects were unaware that the pointers corresponded to the current values of the four sensed state variables, cart-position, velocity, pole angle and angular velocity (see **Figure 1**). Whenever any of the pointers ran off the end of its line in either direction, the FAIL message appeared and a new trial was initiated. In all other respects, the subjects in the two groups faced identical learning situations. They used a light-pen to administer LEFT and RIGHT decisions to the computer simulation, regardless of which of the two graphical representations was employed. The learning curves of the two groups were found to be indistinguishable. Thus Chambers and Michie had isolated a pure "seat-of-the-pants" skill, divorced from complications arising from the subjects' powers of cause-and-effect interpretation.

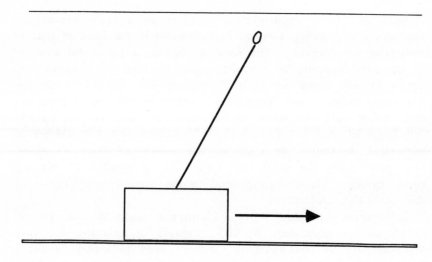

Arrow indicates current direction of motor

The following variables	x	position of cart on track;	
are monitored	xdot	cart velocity	This task is called
	theta	angle of pole	**STATION-**
	thetadot	angular velocity	**HOLDING**

Figure 1. A pole is to be kept balanced on a motor-driven cart which must not be allowed to run off either end of a track of fixed length.

In the work reported here, we were accordingly concerned to establish a similar separation so as to focus on procedural learning in isolation from relational learning. We initially tried two alternative cycle-times. We opted for the faster when it appeared that the slower rate introduced issues of planning as well as of learning. We saw these as extraneous to the immediate objectives.

Statement of objectives

Our experimental aims are as follows.

With the co-operation of a simulator-trained human, we seek to demonstrate the inductive inference from behavioural traces of an an effective computational model of the human's acquired skill, with a view to installing this in the form of a control program. By applying inductive learning tools to automatically logged traces of simulator-trainees' skilled behaviours, the hidden rules stored in the "silent" regions of trained central nervous systems are to be rendered explicit. We wish to test the conjecture that such computer-executable models, after validation, can then be installed to reproduce a "cleaned-up" version of the original behaviour.

Phrased in more specific terms, we aim to provide the following laboratory demonstrations:

(1) that a computer can learn by imitation of a control activity demonstrated by a trained human controller, then reproduce the learned skill when subsequently performing on its own, *and finally deliver an articulate account of the given acquired skill in the form of a rule-structured expression*;

(2) that in learning by imitation such a computer can improve on the observed performance by automatically filtering out human errors and inconsistencies from the sequence of behavioural snapshots from which it infers control rules.

Task-grades

Three grades of task were developed in simulation on a Compaq 386 PC.

1. <u>One-pole station-holding</u>. The simulated apparatus (on the Compaq PC) was as in **Figure 1**. The task was simply to avoid failure ("crash"), defined as either excursion of the mid-point of the cart beyond the end of the track, or excursion of the pole angle outside the range from -12° to +12°. A real-time inset display recorded current state-variable values and cumulative crash scores.

2. <u>One-pole line-crossing</u>. Using the same one-pole simulation the task was to achieve as many mid-line crossings as possible, without crashes, within the test period. The real-time score-board was extended to include the cumulative point-score for line-crossings.

3. <u>One-pole goal-seeking</u>. Using one-pole simulation the cart was to be driven without crashes alternately to the two ends of the track, scoring a goal each time a pre-terminal line was crossed. The simulator was modified to display at each successive moment a coloured square to indicate the location of the goal, and a further extension of the real-time score-board kept track of the current status of a more complex system of points-scoring.

Human learns from simulator

20 psychology student volunteers from the University of Strathclyde learned by trial and error to control with a joystick the pole-and-cart system displayed in dynamic simulation on a PC screen.   The object was (1) to get an idea of the human learnability of the easiest, and of the hardest of the three human-learnable grades of task, and (2) to find at least one subject capable of being trained to the level of full mastery, analogous to the pre-selection procedures applied before the simulator-training of airplane pilots. He or she would then become the subject of more intensive study of machine learning by imitation. The investigation was motivated both by a scientific perspective, concerned with human learning, and by the technological perspective of automated transfer of human-learned skills into computer-based industrial controllers.
    Cognitive psychology distinguishes between "cognitive" and "motor" skills, while placing emphasis on commonalities of underlying mechanism.   The following is taken from J.R.

Anderson's (1980) summary introduction to his chapter on "Cognitive Skills".

1. Our knowledge can be categorised as declarative knowledge and procedural knowledge. Declarative knowledge comprises the facts we know: procedural knowledge comprises the skills we know how to perform.

2. Skill learning occurs in three steps: (1) cognitive stage, in which a description of the procedure is learned; (2) an associative stage, in which a method for performing the skill is worked out, and (3) an autonomous stage, in which the skill becomes more and more rapid and automatic.

3. As a skill becomes more automatic, it requires less attention and we may lose our ability to describe the skill verbally.

4. Skills can be represented by sets of productions. Each production consists of a condition and an action. The condition is a general description of the circumstances under which the production should apply. The action consists of both the external behaviour and the changes to be made in memory if the production applies.

5. One of the dynamic properties of procedures is that they can be held in a short-term memory state and that they undergo generalization and discrimination.

Anderson's original point 5 also addressed facilitation and interference. Not being concerned with these effects we have here shortened it. We further distinguish two forms of "discrimination". A production can become more accurate (i) through numerical tuning of its applicability condition, or (ii) through partial overlap of its condition by that of a newly acquired production (i.e. "if ... then ... except when ...").
We add the further observation that procedures are executed fallibly. Even the autonomous stage remains susceptible to inattention, inconsistency and error. We picture on the one hand a set of production-rules building in long-term memory, and on the other hand a noisy channel intervening between these structures and their manifestation as skilled performance. A goal of the work was to discover whether modern induction algorithms can filter out the noise and lay bare the underlying structures. In this paper we refer to such structures as "subcognitive", reserving "cognitive" for those mental processes of which the subject can give an explicit account.

Experiment 1:   station-holding

In the first experiment, each subject was available for two experimental sessions, separated by a week.   Each session was divided into two seven-minute learning tests, designated T1 and T2 in Week 1 and T3 and T4 in Week 2.   Of the twenty subjects, the first ten to be signed up were provided with a slower-running version of the simulator and the remaining group of ten with a faster version.   Subjectively the slower version appeared to the experimenters to have more the character of a planning task for the learner, while the faster version seemed subjectively more of a pure trial-and-error sensorimotor learning task.

At the start of a subject's first session, he or she was shown the action of the joystick and given an information sheet to read.   The subject's view of the screen was as pictured in **Figure 1** except for the addition of the real-time inset display of numerical information, already mentioned.   The simulated apparatus was assumed rigid and frictionless, with the following parameters.

mass of cart	1.0 kg	mass of pole	0.1 kg
length of pole	1.0 m	length of track	4.8 m

other assumptions: mass is evenly distributed along pole; acceleration due to gravity is 32 cm/sec./sec.

However, the animated diagram of the physical apparatus modelled by the simulator was not drawn to scale, so that the physical parameters of the task as perceived would be somewhat different from those given above.   But the perceived task, although difficult, was accepted by subjects as a "natural" one in terms of their physical intuitions about how such real-world objects would behave.   The "cycle-time" of the simulator places a lower bound on the time between sensing a pole-cart state and the earliest opportunity to signal a new decision to the motor. This was of the   order of 0.5 and 0.4 seconds respectively for the "SLOW" and "FAST" variants diagrammed in **Figure 2.**

A statistical analysis by Dr Chris Robertson of the University of Strathclyde confirmed that learning takes place, mainly from T1 to T2 during the first week, but probably with some further real improvement, and that fast-trained subjects do better than slow-trained.   This led to a closer look at the records of the fast-trained ten, to distinguish among their crashes the two variant forms i.e.

"theta-crashes" (dropping the pole) and "x-crashes" (running off the edge). Pooling all four sessions shows an average of 4.5 crashes per 7-minute session, distributed as 3.0 theta-crashes and 1.5 x-crashes. It was noticeable, however, that learning effects in these beginners were concentrated in the reduction of the theta-crash rates: 4.2, 2.8, 3.0, 2.0, with x-crash rate holding fairly steady: 2.0, 1.4, 1.2, 1.6. Control over the latter appeared to us as observers to be a mark of experience. At first a subject worries only about the pole.

Experiment 2:   goal-seeking

The best five of the slow-trained and the best five of the fast-trained were selected for the subsequent goal-seeking training sessions, all conducted with the fast cycle time. The same experimental regime was followed as before, except that the session lasted 10 minutes instead of seven. Scoring was according to the following calculation.

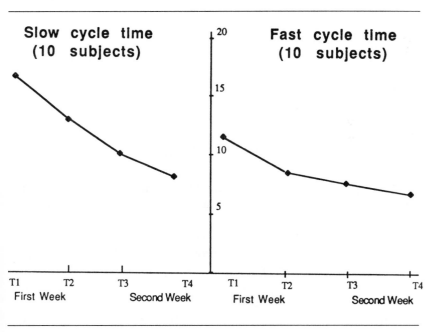

Figure 2. Number of crashes in five-minute tests with station-holding.

1.   Crashes are separately counted and recorded, as before. Each crash, however, adversely affects a subject's progress in accumulating bonus points, as will appear below.

2.   Crossing the pre-terminal line on the current "goal" end of the track gains one point.   If a crash occurs before successful return from the edge over this line, then a restart occurs from the cumulative score reached so far.   If the cart returns over the line, then the single point is converted into a five-point goal score.

3.   Successive goals with no intervening crashes accumulate bonus points according to the following:

		cumulative bonus
1st goal in sequence	0 bonus points	0
2nd goal in sequence	5 bonus points	5
3rd goal in sequence	10 bonus points	15
4th goal in sequence	15 bonus points	30
5th goal in sequence	20 bonus points	50
6th goal in sequence	25 bonus points	75
7th goal in sequence	30 bonus points	105
8th goal in sequence	35 bonus points	140
9th goal in sequence	40 bonus points	180
10th goal in sequence	45 bonus points	225

Thus, the record run shown later at the top of **Figure 3** consists of 10 goals within ten minutes without crashes.   The goal component of the score is 10 x 5 = 50.   Add to this 225 cumulative bonus points (see above tabulation) to get 275.

Ability to learn and perform this task was found to be significantly worse among the five who had earlier been slow-trained than among the fast trained five.   The latter's records were analysed further (see **Figure 3**).   In general the *goal-seeking* task proved beyond most subjects' ability to attain convincing performance, although two of the ten acquired some skill.   Of these, Mr Wyndham Davies (S18 in the experimental record), was outstandingly the better.   The full statistical analysis confirmed this impression and identified S18's record as an outlier.   S18 was accordingly selected for further study with goal-seeking.

	Score	Plot
	271-275	O
	276-270	
	261-265	
	256-260	
	251-255	
	246-250	
	236-240	
	231-235	
	226-230	
	221-225	
	216-220	
	211-215	
	206-210	
	201-205	
	196-200	
	191-195	
	186-190	
S	176-180	X
	171-175	
C	166-170	
	161-165	
O	156-160	
	151-155	
R	146-150	
	141-145	
E	136-140	
	131-135	
S	126-130	
	121-125	
	116-120	
	111-115	
	106-110	
	101-105	
	96-100	
	91-95	
	86-90	
	81-85	
	76-80	X
	71-75	X
	66-70	
	61-65	
	56-60	
	51-55	
	46-50	
	41-45	X
	36-40	
	31-35	x
	36-36	x x
	21-25	x x x x
	16-20	x x x x x x x
	11-15	x x x x x x x x x x
	6-10	x x x x x x x x
	1-5	x x x x

Figure 3. Of the 20 subjects trained on station-holding, the ten with the most promising performance records were selected to go on to goal-seeking trials. As before, there were four successive test sessions making 40 in all. These are shown as a frequency plot against points-score. The four X's in larger type are all from S18. The O at the top is the same subject's subsequent record score achieved after several further practice sessions.

We earlier made the generalisation that beginners, and (we would add) chronic poor performers, make most of their crashes through theta-failures, while the trained expert increasingly reverses this pattern. Results with goal-seeking strongly confirms this. Of the five fast-trained subjects who went through the goal-seeking series of four test sessions (ten minutes each session), the worst performer averaged 12.0 theta-crashes per session and 2.0 x-crashes, while the star performer S18 averaged 0.75 and 2.25 respectively.

Summary of human learning experiments

The main objective of the above-described exercise arose from the need to make a realistic laboratory model of learning by imitation applicable to the control industry. Can this variant of machine learning be used to generate controllers for tasks which are only marginally tractable by training humans to perform them operationally, e.g. as pilots? In **Figure 3** we see a representation of S18's performance on the four test sessions of goal-seeking, in comparison with that of the other nine subjects in the group (also four-test-sessions each) who had been positively selected for training. It is evident that the trawl for a suitable subject has been successful. The next step is to investigate the transferrability to machines of such acquired skill. This requires that we first validate the purported ability of the rule-learning algorithms proposed. We have to find some way of verifying that the representations which these algorithms construct from the behavioural traces of a trained human are logically similar to the representations in his CNS which encode the same skill. Our approach to this question is now described.

Construction and performance of an "artificial" subject

The first requirement is to establish that the chosen software tool, Quinlan's C4.5 induction program (a derivative of C4, see Quinlan 1987) can be trusted reliably to recover all, and only, the rules concealed within behavioural traces. This step is thus one of calibration. Specifically, calibration trials start by generating behavioural data from "artificial subjects" by running a rule interpreter supplied with concocted rule-sets. Situation-action records are collected and processed exactly as with natural subjects, and the extracted rules are compared with those which generated the artificial subject's behaviour. In the case of discrepancies, user-controlled parameters of C4.5 are varied in search of settings which result in reconstruction of the original rule-sets.

Cycle-times and delays of response

To two decimal places of accuracy, the simulator cycle is subdivided as follows:

signal-to-input = 0.00 secs (i.e. instantaneous effect of joystick on left/right status of simulated motor):

input-to-output = 0.07 secs (i.e. delay before re-drawing the screen graphic with the new state from simulation of motor action).

"Signal" denotes the emission of a message ("left" or "right") from the subject to the simulator, which, be it noted, simply repeats the previous signal unless the subject has meanwhile switched the direction of the joystick. "Input" denotes the arrival of the signal to update the simulation program's input variable. "Output" denotes a message from the simulator to the subject, conveyed as a screen graphic corresponding to the newly computed values of x and theta. In terms of the simulated physical system, we picture the input-to-output period as being in effect occupied by continuous application of a constant motor force.

When a controlling agent is inserted into the loop, the control cycle now in reality consists of two cycles, each with its own IN-OUT delay, coupled to each other only to the extent that each makes a regular inspection (at its own characteristic frequency) of the other's latest update (of the screen and of the joystick respectively), as depicted below.

Simulator's cycle	Controller's cycle
	(total of all delays in the cycle adds up to "reaction time")
signal-to-input	
input-to-output	output-to-decision
signal-to-input	recognition and matching
input-to-output	decision-to-signal
signal-to-input	motor system transmission
etc., etc.	etc., etc.

If and only if there were no central delay associated with interpreting the input and matching it with a stored decision-generating strategy or rule, then for young adult subjects, reaction times would be expected to lie in the region of 200-300 milliseconds. In designing an "artificial pilot" we assumed a slower total cycle time, for reasons which we shall now discuss.

According to the usual tests from which quoted reaction times are derived, an ultra-simple stimulus is presented to the subject (a light goes on, a buzzer sounds, etc.) who must respond as fast as possible with a single choice-free action. The conditions of eliciting a skilled real-time stream of reactive choices are very different, and insert additional delays into the stimulus-response cycle. The latter now comprises (i) the time taken visually to interpret a new configuration of a complex animated stimulus; (ii) the time taken to find a matching rule in the stored rule-set; (iii) the time taken to read off the corresponding action-choice and to deliver the result to the centre from which the action command is issued to the neuromuscular motor system; and (iv) the time taken as before for the appropriate motor impulses to travel down the spinal cord and thence along the peripheral motor nerves to activate the muscles.

For choice-free responses the neuropsychologist and science writer Rodney Cotterill (1989, p. 266) reports rather slow times: "My own students working in psychophysics routinely measure reaction times by exploiting the internal timing devices in personal computers. (The subject sits with a finger poised on one of the keys and depresses it as soon as a coloured disc appears on the screen.) They have now made so many measurements of this kind that their statistics are quite reliable. And the measured reaction times are typically 350 milliseconds..." Unfortunately, Professor Cotterill does not say whether these times are stable from the outset or whether they become shorter over time with repetition. But he adds an item of information which is directly relevant to item (ii) of our above-listed components of a subject's cycle: "When a decision is built into the test, such as asking the subject to depress the G key if a green circle is shown, and the R key if it is red, the reaction time jumps to 650 milliseconds". *Prima facie* we can conclude that the time consumed in (ii) for discriminating a single attribute to execute a rule delivering one bit of decision-information is of the order of 300 (i.e. 650 minus 350) milliseconds. We can picture the first and second rules symbolically as in **Figure 4**.

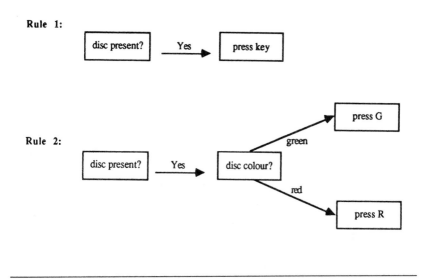

Rule 1:

Rule 2:

Figure 4. Schematic representation of Cotterill's response-time tests.

For more complex, multi-attribute stimuli, such as must be discriminated in the pole-balancing tasks, yet longer delays must be anticipated. We adopted an assumption of time-lags in the region of 400-450 milliseconds. In the light of our present knowledge of the role of multi-attribute complexity in tasks involving discrimination, we now see this as too short, as noted in the **Discussion**.

We should now return to the main qualitative features of the interactions which occur between two loosely coupled input-output cycles — the subject's and the simulator's. As soon as the simulator has completed the input-to-output transition it immediately reads the next signal from the joystick and recycles, being unconcerned with the subject's sensing of its last output and conversion into a new input signal. The simulator will pick up the result of this conversion at the signal-to-input phase of a subsequent cycle. As for the subject, after launching the signal from motor centres in the CNS, he or she will not wait to see its effect or even wait for its delivery *via* the joystick before returning attention to the screen.   Therefore a sequence of records from a trained subject written to memory by the present hardware-software set-up has the following properties.

> The value entered in the decision part of a given record represents a human subject's decision in response to the situation part of a record or records occurring one or more recording-cycles earlier in the sequence.   This same decision's effect is first visible in the situation part of a later record.

Realistically, rule induction from records collected from human subjects should be based on some assumption that each decision is a response to the subject's integration of earlier records, — i.e. the means of two or three earlier x values, of two or three earlier theta values, etc.   A human's perception of theta-dot would probably be more realistically mimicked if an artificial subject had to form the difference between successive theta values, instead of being presented with first derivatives directly.   But numerically it comes to much the same thing.

An artificial subject consists essentially of a rule interpreter together with a supplied rule-set and appropriate timing delays in its I/O.   But to create a complete "artificial subject" with the right pattern of delays is a more complex matter than at first appears. We assumed that as soon as a decision is handed to the motor nervous system the subject is again free to process the current output on the screen.   Can we even perhaps suppose that in some sense he or she can watch the screen virtually all the time, delegating the remainder of the recognise-act cycle to concurrent and unconscious processes which occasion only momentary interruptions to his or her perceptual attention?   In the event we settled on a procedure which worked well enough for the immediate purpose.   When interpreting records taken from our artificial subject the delays were such that the analysis program matched the situation part of each given record with the decision field found in the record located five steps ahead, corresponding to a delay of about four tenths of a second.   The same lag was imposed when analysing records from skilled humans, with acceptable results.   There is no doubt that much remains to be done in the way of refining this model, and that sharper results would have been obtained had we standardised on a longer lag. Rectifying this must be left for the future.

Incorporating random error in the artificial subject

Human subjects performing a skilled task are subject to errors of perception, of matching and of acting on decisions. The first category is too complex to try to cater for at this phase of the project. The last two categories can be lumped into a single random disturbance intervening between what the rule prescribes and what signal is finally given to the simulator. We decided that after the rule interpreter has emitted a decision, this should be subjected to a chance, p, of being reversed before being input to the simulator, with p tried at values of 0.0, 0.05, 0.10, 0.15, 0.20. Expressed in terms of percentage corruption by noise, these are 0.00, 0.10, 0.20, 0.30, 0.40. With more noise, the "artificial subject" explores a more variegated and widely representative sample of the state-space, thus resulting in a more tutorially effective training set. It is important that when generating data in this mode both the rule's prescription and the actual decision should be included in the recorded trace, in order to preserve the option in later analysis of comparing rule-recovery from such a file under the two alternative "oracle" regimes. We finally settled for an error rate in the region of 20 per cent, corresponding to corruption of the output channel with a relatively heavy noise overlay of about 40 per cent. The way in which this was done was to set p = 0.05, but to cause its effect to propagate by a global constraint requiring that no change of action (left-to-right or right-to-left) be reversed during the ensuing five cycles. This largely mimics the marked persistence of switching actions which we observe in our human trained subjects. Time has not allowed exact comparison of this parameter as between natural and artificial expert, but inspection suggested that a further strengthening of the damper on rapid switching is probably indicated.

This has subsequently been confirmed by an independent analysis made by Dr Chris Robertson of the University of Strathclyde's Statistics Department (see also the **Discussion**). He had been given four behavioural traces from expert performances of the line-crossing task. Unknown to him, one of these (Trace 4) had been generated, not by a human trainee, but by the artificial subject. In his written report his comments on this trace included the following: "My impression of Trace 4 is that the subject used a strategy which involved rapid switching from left to right. The subjects in the other three data files tended to stay in the same [decision] state for longer."

Dr. Robertson's report also indicated that setting the noise level at 40 per cent was too high: "Trace 4 is very different from the other three" he remarked, commenting on its low predictivity under the fitted multiple regression model.   That is, a relatively low proportion of the total variance was assignable to dependency of decision outputs on past sensed inputs, the remainder consisting largely of (artificially introduced) "error" variance.

Installing a known rule with a view to its later recovery

On the platform thus defined we installed a rule based on that of Makarovic (1990).   The latter was known to give good performance when mounted on an "ideal platform" devoid of human-like errors and lags.   The results were satisfactory.   Test runs exhibited behaviour which was superficially, at least, human-like and corresponded to a high, but not impeccable, level of performance.   Objective performance measures on line-crossing are reproduced in **Figure 5**.

When watching this non-learning artificial subject performing on the screen one is made aware of the existence of marked human variation in control "styles".   Through casual opportunities to practice, two of the experimenters (MB and DM) have attained a fair competence at line-crossing.   It is not clear which of the two would be expected to score higher if subjected to formal experimental conditions of test, and as a line-crosser the artificial subject was also at roughly the same performance level.   Yet if misinformed that an artificial-subject sequence which one was watching was either sampled from MB or from DM, one would have little hesitation in plumping for the latter, mainly because of greater perceived sloppiness, risk-taking and fluctuations of approach.   Differences of temperament and of age may both enter into it: it is well known that decision and control processes in the human CNS become increasingly slow and "noisy" in older subjects.

In the final step of calibration the rules hidden in an artificial subject were shown to be partially reconstructible by the C4.5 algorithm as will now be described.

Figure 6 contains the particulars of what was found.   The rule reconstructed from the artificial subject's trace produced similar performance to that of the original rule mounted on the artificial subject.   More significant was the approximate logical reconstruction that it was possible to obtain, although errors of

RULE + ERRORS + TIME-LAGS = ARTIFICIAL SUBJECT

LAGS = 0.35 seconds

ERRORS = 20%

In this framework we instal a **known rule**
(theta and theta-dot expressed in radians)

i f theta-dot <-0.50	t h e n	LEFT	i f theta-dot>0.50	t h e n	RIGHT
i f theta <-0.07	t h e n	LEFT	i f theta >0.07		t h e n RIGHT
i f xdot <-0.40	t h e n	LEFT	i f xdot >0.40		t h e n RIGHT
i f x =<0.00	t h e n	LEFT	i f x >0.00		t h e n RIGHT

ARTIFICIAL SUBJECT'S PERFORMANCE:

LINE-CROSSINGS IN FIVE MINUTES =   1 1

CRASHES IN FIVE MINUTES =   0

Figure 5. An 'artificial subject' does line-crossing. A computer program simulates the kinds of error-variability, time-lags etc., which characterise a human. The first trial on "line-crossing" is shown.

The inductively reconstructed rule was:

i f theta-dot =<-0.50 t h e n LEFT   i f theta-dot >0.50t h e n RIGHT

i f theta=<-0.08   t h e n LEFT   i f xdot =>0.49
                                   a n d   theta=<0.08 t h e n RIGHT

i f theta>0.08   t h e n RIGHT i f x >0.00   t h e n RIGHT

i f xdot >0.29   t h e n RIGHT i f xdot=<0.29   t h e n LEFT

with LAGS = 0.35 seconds and ERRORS = 0%

LINE CROSSINGS IN FIVE MINUTES = 10

CRASHES IN FIVE MINUTES = 0

Figure 6. Reconstruction experiment on a behavioural trace recorded from an 'artificial subject'. Performance of rule induced from the trace is shown for "line-crossing".

RULE + ERRORS + TIME-LAGS = ARTIFICIAL SUBJECT

LAGS = 0.35 seconds

ERRORS = 20%

In this framework we instal a known rule
(theta and theta-dot expressed in radians)

if theta-dot<-0.50 then LEFT   if theta-dot>0.50 then RIGHT

if theta <-0.07 then LEFT   if theta >0.07   then RIGHT

if xdot <-0.40 then LEFT   if xdot >0.40   then RIGHT

if x =<0.00   then LEFT   if x >0.00   then RIGHT

ARTIFICIAL SUBJECT'S PERFORMANCE:

LINE-CROSSINGS IN FIVE MINUTES = 11

CRASHES IN FIVE MINUTES = 0

Figure 5. An 'artificial subject' does line-crossing. A computer program simulates the kinds of error-variability, time-lags etc., which characterise a human. The first trial on "line-crossing" is shown.

The inductively reconstructed rule was:

if theta-dot =<-0.50 then LEFT   if theta-dot >0.50 then RIGHT

if theta=<-0.08   then LEFT   if xdot =>0.49
                                   and theta=<0.08   then RIGHT

if theta>0.08   then RIGHT   if x >0.00   then RIGHT

if xdot >0.29   then RIGHT   if xdot=<0.29   then LEFT

with LAGS = 0.35 seconds and ERRORS = 0%

LINE CROSSINGS IN FIVE MINUTES = 10

CRASHES IN FIVE MINUTES = 0

Figure 6. Reconstruction experiment on a behavioural trace recorded from an 'artificial subject'. Performance of rule induced from the trace is shown for "line-crossing".

estimation in the presence of noise inevitably results in discrepancies in the numerical parts of the rule (values of decision thresholds) from the "ideal" original.

We feel safe in concluding that the reconstructions obtained from human-generated traces *prima facie* show the logical structure of hidden representations stored in the trained subject's skill-memory. Brain localisations for pure decision-skills are not known (*see* e.g. Popper and Eccles, 1977, p. 507).

Machine learns by imitating an expert human "pilot"

Tasks at two levels of complexity are considered. The first is *line-crossing*. The second is goal-seeking.

At the time of finalising this report we have been able only to make a pilot investigation along the needed lines (a sort of "dress rehearsal") using one of the experimenters (MB, *see* above) as a skilled subject on line-crossing. It was possible to run this pilot study through to completion, including extraction of rules and use of extracted rules to control the simulator. Statistical evaluation, as mentioned earlier, of the extracted rules was also carried out with respect to the looked-for property of enhanced reliability. Comparison was with the original human control behaviour from which learning by imitation had been achieved.

Validation of rules

Five-minute samples of line-crossing yielded training sets of approximately 3500 records. Decision rules induced by C4.5 from these samples were assessed on two criteria:

(i) the ability of an induced set of rules correctly to describe other recorded behaviour from the same skilled human source,

and

(ii) task-performance of the rule-set when run as an automatic controller in substitution for the trained human.

In respect of (i), predictive ability against test sets of new data from the same human source was somewhat better than the equivalent ability of induced rules from traces generated by the artificial subject, i.e. about 70 per cent correct prediction, on average, of each move (random guessing would give 50%). We are inclined to attribute this (*see* earlier) to our having set the artificial subject's noise level at the very high level of 40 per cent. In future trials we propose to reset the level to, at most, 20 per cent. This would also be more in line with known neurobiology.

In respect of (ii) performance was as shown in **Figure 7**. In terms of line-crossings and crashes performance is similar to the performance of the original author of the trace, any differences being small relative to sampling variation. There is, additionally, an encouraging suggestion from these data of an effect that we have referred to as "clean-up", — that is to say, the total range of excursion of all four state variables has a tendency to be constrained within a smaller interval as compared to the behaviour originally recorded from the subject. This effect was the original suggestion of Mr Bain, who also carried out the critical experiments. When watching the performance on the screen as it is generated by the machine-learned rule-set, one is struck by a "gestalt" impression of almost superhuman precision and stability. A simple descriptive statistic, namely range, was used to quantify this effect. By range we mean the difference between the maximum and minimum observed values of a variable. The measure of clean-up was based on the difference in ranges of the system variables between the human performance and that of the rules induced from the recorded trace. Taking this range-difference as a percentage of the original range, we arrive at a measure of clean-up. For instance, we found a mean clean-up over the four system variables of 69% in the case of the subject whose rules and score are given in **Figure 7**. The actual values were as follows.

	Ranges		
	x	xdot	theta	theta-dot
Human trainer	2.79	4.85	0.562	5.021
Induced rule	0.46	1.83	0.134	2.276
Range differences	2.33	3.02	0.428	2.745
% "clean-up"	83	62	76	55

Time and resources have permitted us to investigate the clean-up effect only to this preliminary stage. But the potential significance to problems of controller synthesis has not escaped our notice.

MACHINE LEARNS LINE CROSSING FROM TRAINED HUMAN

A trained human subject recorded 16 line-crossings in five minutes with 0 crashes. From this machine-monitored performance 3574 successive records were automatically recorded (about 12 per second). This behavioural trace was stored as the basis for machine-inferring a cleaned-up, rule-structured model of the subject's strategy ('noise' etc., filtered out), as follows:

if theta <=-0.07   **then**   LEFT   **if** theta >0.13   **then**   RIGHT

if theta-dot=< -0.07 **and**   theta=< 0.06   **and**   x=<-0.08 **then** LEFT

if theta-dot=< 0.00 **and**   theta=< 0.00   **and**   x>-0.08 **then** LEFT

if theta-dot=< -0.56 **and**   theta=< 0.06   **and**   theta>0.0   **then** LEFT

if theta-dot>-0.56   **and**   theta-dot=<0.00 **and**   theta=< 0.06
                                                    and   theta>0.00 **then** RIGHT

if theta-dot >   0.00   **and**   theta > 0.00   **then** RIGHT

if theta-dot >   0.78   **and**   theta =< 0.0   **then** RIGHT

if theta-dot=<0.78   **and**   theta-dot>0.00 **and**   xdot-<-0.13 **then** LEFT

                                                          else   RIGHT

This rule produced 11 line-crossings in five minutes with 0 crashes.

Figure 7. The rule-generated behaviour scored acceptably relative to that of the original, and also showed smaller overall ranges of excursion for each of the four state-variables (see text).

Discussion

The work conducted so far is preliminary and the results incomplete. Work planned and in progress includes the following:

(1) A multivariate statistical and time-sequence analysis by Dr Chris Robertson of the University of Strathclyde Statistics Department is seeking improved estimates of the duration of the recognise-act cycle in this family of skilled tasks.

(2) First results confirm other indications that the currently assumed duration should be substantially lengthened. Corresponding changes are be introduced to the methodology both of artificial-subject design and inductive analysis of human traces.

(3) Using the revised basis a new artificial subject is to be constructed and tested on the goal-seeking task.

(4) Analyses made of human records on the line-crossing task, are to be extended to include a full inductive analysis of the behaviour of subject S18 (the "star" subject) on goal-seeking.

(5) The effects of sample sizes on the attainable fidelity of inductive reconstruction is to be explored.

Engineering considerations and directions

The new design philosophy indicated by this work can, we believe, offer an approach to certain goals of recognised importance. We have in mind that class of problem in which it is desired to exercise dependable and fault-tolerant control of seemingly "intractable" systems, i.e. those which are in principle controllable but which face impassable blocks to *both* (1) classical automatic control and (2) use of a trained human pilot.

Block no. (1) Owing to the complexity and ill-structured nature of some tasks it is not always possible to develop a comprehensive and exact mathematical model of a system sufficient for classical automatic control to figure as a feasible option.

Block no. (2) For some given tasks, humans may prove to be trainable only to moderate, but not crash-proof levels of performance.   Hence the strategy of training human **pilots** is in this case not a safe and complete solution.

The scenario sketched above represents an apparent double bind. On the one hand complexity puts the task beyond reach of classical methods.   On the other hand, although complexity can up to a point be penetrated by simulator-trained humans, the pilot's nervous system is too slow and approximate an instrument to translate its learned strategies into the real-time performance demanded by operational conditions.

Pressure of need, in particular in military applications, has recently been steering developments towards a hybrid approach. Incremental automation of lower-level sensing and corrective action can transform the initial intractable task into a simplified perceived task which is more tractable ("carefree handling"). Tactical adjustments are automated out of the pilot's way, leaving him free to concentrate on decisions at a more strategic level. This combined modelling of the mechanics of instability and of human factors points a promising direction in which much modern advanced automation is moving today — namely the use of information technology to build bridges between these two widely disparate systems, the computer and the brain.   AI-oriented Human-Computer Interface techniques can seek to create dynamic partnerships in which each covers for the deficiencies of the other.

There remains, however, a class of task where a third road-block bars the way even to the hybrid approach.

Block no. (3)   For reasons of vehicle size (e.g. certain instrument-bearing radio-controlled model helicopters used in inspection and survey), or restricted payload (e.g. shuttle-type space-craft), or hazards of task environments (radioactivity, smoke and fumes etc.), operational use of human pilots is ruled out.   *But they could in principle be trained to a certain level on simulators.*

The motive for italicising the preceding sentence will become apparent.   If we possessed magical powers we could first simulator-train and then physically shrink the pilot, or render him or her impervious to radioactivity, toxic fumes or other relevant hazard.   Then we could proceed as before with hybrid solutions.   Since we do not possess such powers, we have to explore a possibility which at first sight seemed fanciful.   Our results have, however, indicated that it may not be.   On the contrary, it appears to be a serious option with the co-operation of a simulator-trained human pilot, to build an effective computer-based model of his or her cognitive skill, with a view to installing *this* as a control program. The method is not that of "dialogue acquisition", since such skills are intuitive, and cannot dependably be elicited in this way. Instead we apply modern inductive learning tools to automatically logged behavioural traces of simulator-trainees' skilled behaviours. The reconstructed computer-executable model, after validation, is then installed in the vehicle to act as a simulated pilot. A result will be to unblock the road to the "carefree handling" approach. This time the "carefree handling" is made the basis of training human pilots, as before, but subsequent performance in the vehicle is not that of the trainees but of their (cleaned-up) functional copies. Instead of grafting the simulator-trained pilot's body into the vehicle, we graft his/her disembodied skill.

In these studies we have found evidence that in suitable circumstances a skill-grafting exercise may be possible. If so, it offers a way round all three road blocks. The key idea is that if we could look inside the head of a pilot who has been simulator-trained on an "intractable" task, we might see an encoding of a fully sufficient skill — degraded in real-time execution by sensorimotor lags and errors. Recovery of the postulated rule structure and its transplantation to an error-free device — i.e. a control computer — then yields a source of enhanced machine performance. We see prospects of developing "skill grafting" into a systematic technology, as follows:

Step 1. Train the human on a simulator, automatically capturing and recording a trace of the state-vector —> decision —> state-vector sequence.

Step 2. Using an automated inductive learning package, extract from the trained subject a rule-based model of his acquired skill, automatically generating a run-time version runnable on the intended control computer.

Step 3. Mount the run-time controller so obtained, and validate on the simulator for all regions of the state space over which fault-free performance is regarded as mandatory.

Step 4. If not fully validated use classical methods to patch local gaps, or combine the fruits of Steps 1 — 3 from several subjects.

Note once more in conclusion that when the human executes his/her own mental rule-base, performance is inescapably degraded by various combinations of time-lags and errors, both (as is well known) in the sensorimotor loop itself and also (to an as-yet-unknown degree) in the internal scanning and matching of memory stored rules. Preliminary support is to hand for the expectation that the run-time performance of induced rule-bases will be found consistently more reliable (the "clean-up effect") than the performance of the trained human from whose behavioural trace it was extracted.

Acknowledgements

This project owes a debt to the engineering insights, conceptual overview and patient attention to our needs and problems which have been contributed to Dr Andrew Hay of the National Engineering Laboratory, East Kilbride, and also to the stimulus of interaction with Dr Robert Parkinson's simulator-based group at British Aerospace, Stevenage. Guidance and substantial statistical data analysis is acknowledged from Dr Chris Robertson, Department of Statistics, University of Strathclyde, and we also record our thanks to Professor Ross Quinlan, University of Sydney, for generously making available for our use his C4.5 rule induction program.

References

Anderson, J.R. (1980) *Cognitive Psychology and its Implications*, Freeman & Co.

Chambers, R. A. and Michie, D. (1969) Man-machine co-operation on a learning task. In *Computer Graphics: Techniques and Applications* (eds. R. Parslow, R. Prowse and R. Elliot-Green), London: Plenum.

Cotterill, R. (1989) *No Ghost in the Machine*, London: William Heinemann

Dennett, D.C. (1987) Consciousness. In *The Oxford Companion to the Mind* (ed. R.L. Gregory), Oxford: Oxford University Press, pp. 160-164.

Makarovic, A. (1990)   A qualitative way of solving the pole-balancing problem. In *Machine Intelligence* 12 (eds. J.E. Hayes, D. Michie and E. Tyugu), Oxford: Oxford University Press.

Michie, D. (1986) The superarticulacy phenomenon in the context of software manufacture. *Proc. Royal Soc., London.* A, *405*, 185-212; also reproduced in *The Foundations of Artificial Intelligence* (eds. D. Partridge and Y. Wilks), Cambridge University Press, 1990

Popper, K.R. and Eccles, J.C. (1977) *The Self and its Brain.* London and New York: Routledge & Kegan Paul.

Quinlan, J.R. (1987) Generating production rules from decision trees. In Proc. *Internat. Joint Conf. on Artificial Intelligence,* Milan, 304-307.

Quinlan, J. R. (ed. 1987) *Applications of Expert Systems 1*, Turing Institute Press in association with Addison-Wesley.

Quinlan, J.R. (ed. 1989) *Applications of Expert Systems 2,* Turing Institute Press in association with Addison-Wesley.

Shapiro, A.D. and Michie, D. (1986) A self-commenting facililty for inductively synthesised endgame expertise. In: *Advances in Computer Chess* 4 (ed. D.F. Beal), Oxford; Pergamon Press.

Widrow, B. and Smith,. F. W. (1964) Pattern recognising control systems. In *Computer and Information Sciences* (eds. J.T. Tou and R.H. Wilcox). Clever-Hume Press.

Chapter 6

A review of the approaches to the qualitative modelling of complex systems

R. R. Leitch

1. INTRODUCTION

The development of qualitative models of physical systems is currently attracting much interest from the Artificial Intelligence research community. It consists of a set of eclectic techniques designed to generate a qualitative description of the behaviour of physical systems from a description of its structure and some initial 'disturbance'. The term "qualitative" has been used in many ways and generally to mean "non- numerical" models. However, the whole field of Artificial Intelligence utilises non-numeric symbolic models. We will, therefore, use the term "qualitative modelling" to mean reasoning about systems characterised by continuously changing variables (of time) by discrete abstractions of the value of such variables. Most of the work on qualitative modelling concerns identifying appropriate 'abstractions' that allows the important distinctions, or landmarks, in the behaviour to be computed. This requires quantisation of the real-number line into a finite set of distinctions; the goal of qualitative modelling research is to identify useful discretisations for particular generic tasks.

Abstract descriptions of state make it possible to have more concise representations of behaviour. However, the generation of the behaviour from such descriptions tends not to produce a *unique* solution. This, of course, is to be expected, as the information required to produce a unique description has been eliminated in the intentional abstraction. Therefore, qualitative models produce ambiguous descriptions of behaviour. However, such ambiguous behaviour can still contain useful information for some tasks. For example, if it is required to predict whether the current state can lead to a critical or faulty condition, it may be sufficient to show that *none* of the possible behaviours leads to a critical situation. It is important to show, therefore, that the set of possible behaviours includes the 'actual' behaviour of the system. In this way, a task can be satisfied even with incomplete descriptions. Whereas in traditional methods, all of the information needs to be available, and it needs to be precisely and uniquely characterised before any inference can be made.

2. MOTIVATION

Reflecting the various backgrounds, skills and goals of the research workers, there exists a diverse set of motivations for people interested in the development of techniques for qualitative modelling. In fact, this work is characterised by an unusually large range of contributing disciplines: mathematicians, physicists, engineers, computer scientists, economists, psychologists, cognitive scientists and philosophers, all of which are currently playing a role in developing the

Roy LEITCH is with the Intelligent Automation Labotatory, Department of Electrical and Electronic Engineering, Heriot-Watt University, Edinburgh EHI 2HT. e-mail: rrl@ee.hw.ac.uk.

various theories or refining the theories to particular application domains. However, a common aspect is that the system to be modelled is somehow too *complex* for the effective or efficient utilisation of traditional approaches. The degree of complexity at which the traditional methods become suspect, of course, depends upon the task for which the model is to be used and also the characteristics of the underlying system. Such differences in motivation have led to very distinct developments of the area, confusing and contradictory terminology, and a mutual lack of understanding and appreciation of the motivation of other groups. This has resulted in significant duplication of effort and in some cases re-discovery of some basic concepts from other disciplines. However, in many cases, it is just this fresh look at old problems without any preconceptions that has generated the new approaches and insights that now form the main techniques within qualitative modelling.

The motivation for the initial work in qualitative reasoning [de Kleer and Brown 84] came from the development of an Intelligent Tutorial System for troubleshooting electronic circuits, called Sophie III. There the need was to represent 'simpler' or more abstract models of electronic circuits such that a student could obtain an understanding of the function of the device without requiring a precise description of the detailed behaviour. In this case, a detailed description in the form of a conventional mathematical model is available and reliable. However, a qualitative description should support a simpler computational mechanism than the detailed model (in practice, this has not yet been achieved) and permit a conceptual understanding of the operation to be gained without the clutter of unnecessary detail.

In other cases, however, a reliable mathematical model, usually in terms of numerical differential or difference equations, is either not available or the expense, in time and effort, of generating one is not justified for the particular application the model is to be used for. For these applications, a qualitative model may be all that can be reliably used to generate a behavioural description.

We can, therefore, identify four (non-distinct) motivations for developing qualitative models of physical systems:

(i) To provide simpler computational mechanisms than those already existing, implying that a conventional model already exists, and is well-posed, but that the computation on this model is complex and prohibitive. This is usually the motivation of people working in the domain of astronomy, for example.

(ii) To provide a description for systems where traditional methods are ineffective, either due to lack of knowledge of the system description or the development costs are prohibitive. This is often the case in the chemical or process industries, where chemical reactors, flow processes and thermal systems are more difficult to characterise than say mechanical systems of the aerospace industry or robotics.

(iii) To provide modelling paradigms that accord more closely with our "common sense" intuition of the operation of physical systems. Such descriptions do not require that the modeller, or the person utilising the model, have a knowledge of physics in order to understand the way a system behaves. This motivation is based on the premise that people interact with the physical world based on their experience and intuition and not on an understanding of the 'principles' of physical laws.

(iv) To develop modelling methods based on the principles of Knowledge Based Systems. This includes, representing the model in a declarative format such that the same description can be used for a number of different purposes or tasks, and reasoning with partial, uncertain or incomplete information. Additionally, this motivation includes the goal of providing effective explanation facilities. This aspect is, of course, vitally important for real-time applications where the need to be able to 'justify' a given decision is crucial to its acceptance and verification.

These motivations are not independent and any application domain will exhibit a mixture of these. However, the developers of the qualitative modelling techniques to be discussed usually have one of the above motivations as their primary goal.

Broadly speaking there are three main approaches to qualitative modelling, each providing its own set of representation primitives reflecting a particular ontology of the physical world, and stemming from one of the motivations of the previous section. The first of these approaches, and the most highly developed, is the Qualitative Simulation (QSIM) technique developed by [Kuipers 84, 86]. This is based on the so-called *constraint centred* ontology, that provides a structural description derived from an abstraction of a conventional differential equation representation. The second approach, and the earliest, utilises the identification of primitive subsystems or components of the systems. This establishes a *component-centred* ontology [de Kleer and Brown 84, Williams 84]. Models are instantiated from a library of generic components and connected together through terminals. The third approach derives from the motivation to represent a "common sense" description of the world. This utilises the notion of a process acting on various parts of the system and provides a *process-centred* view of the world [Forbus 84].

The following three sections outlines the main ingredients of each of the above mentioned approaches to qualitative modelling, followed by a discussion on the temporal issues involved in each method. A short review of current developments is then presented and finally a comparison of the approaches is attempted and criteria for selecting the most appropriate technique for a particular application is given.

The area of qualitative modelling is still comparatively young, with the significant developments occurring within the last six years (since 1983). This is manifested in conflicting terminology and a lack of formality in some of the methods. In what follows, I will attempt to concentrate on the main features of each system under the topics of *ontology*, the representation of variables, called the *quantity space*, the set of *modelling primitives* provided, and the inference mechanism or *simulation algorithm*.

3. CONSTRAINT-CENTRED APPROACH

This approach is typified by the Qualitative Simulation (QSIM) algorithm of Ben Kuipers [Kuipers 86]. It has been extensively discussed and experimented with due to Kuipers' enlightened policy of distributing his software for a minimal handling charge.

3.1. Ontology

This approach starts from a mathematical description of the system in terms of a conventional differential equation model. As such, it makes no attempt to model "common sense" knowledge of the process. Rather, it abstracts a conventional description, derived from formal physical theories, to obtain a 'weaker' description of the system that may be more consistent with the available knowledge, but still based on formal theories. This reliance on mathematical descriptions has led some workers to discount this ontology as providing a method for qualitative (common sense) reasoning. However, if the full range of motivations discussed in the previous section is considered the constraint-based view can be seen as a technique for overcoming limitations in the conventional approach, without disregarding scientific theories.

In fact, the constraints used in QSIM can be obtained by viewing the system as a set of primitive energy storage mechanisms. Each storage mechanism represents a differential relationship between the input and output depending upon whether it has inductive storage and capacitive storage. That is, whether the through variable is proportional to the rate-of-change of the across variable (capacitative storage) or the across variable is proportional to the rate-of-change of the through variable (inductive storage). Analogues of physical systems in most domains exist in terms of these two types of storage. The structural description then comes from interconnecting these primitive energy storage devices. However, this 'pre- processing' of the differential equation is not part of the QSIM approach. The ontology adopted by QSIM is best illustrated by Figure 1 [Kuipers 86] which clearly shows the relationships between the actual system, the conventional mathematical model and the qualitative description.

3.2. Quantity Space

A quantity space is the set of values that a continuous variable can take as the result of its evolution over time. In QSIM these values are termed *landmarks* and are totally ordered points on the real line. Landmarks may be either numeric or symbolic with an ordinal relationship between them. The quantity space is, therefore, an alternating sequence of points and intervals on the real line. A quantity space always includes the landmarks {inf, 0, minf} where inf and minf represent plus and minus infinity respectively. An important feature of the QSIM algorithm is that it can 'create' landmarks as the behaviour evolves (e.g. at the min or max of some variable). This significantly increases the complexity of the algorithm, but allows more distinctions on the behaviour to be generated. Forbus [Forbus 88] terms these as *temporally specific* landmarks and argues that they are only relevant to a particular behaviour, and therefore only relevant to determining properties of that behaviour, e.g. oscillations.

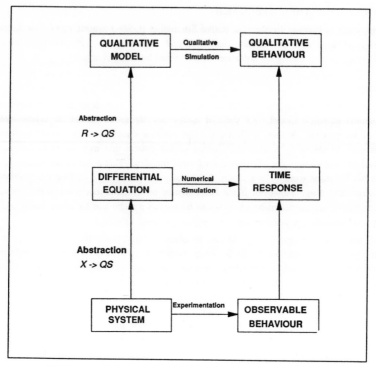

Figure 1 Qualitative Simulation as an Abstraction of a Conventional Model

At a given time the qualitative state QS of a variable V is described by the pair < qval, qdir >. The value *qval* represents the magnitude of the variable and can be a particular landmark or an interval between two landmarks, i.e.

$$QS(v, t) = < qval(v, t), qdir(v, t) >$$

where

$qval(v, t) = l_j$ if $v(t) = l_j \; \varepsilon \; L$

$qval = (l_j, l_{j+1})$ if $v(t) \; \varepsilon \; (l_j, l_{j+1})$

L is the set of landmarks and (l_j, l_{j+1}) represents an open interval.

The value *qdir* represents the direction of change of v with respect to time and can take one of three values {dec, std, inc} standing for decreasing, steady or increasing respectively.

$$qdir\ (v,\ t) = \begin{cases} inc & \text{if } v'(t) > 0 \\ std & \text{if } v'(t) = 0 \\ dec & \text{if } v'(t) < 0 \end{cases}$$

Therefore, the qualitative state of a variable is represented by two values: a qualitative magnitude of a finite, but variable, resolution and a qualitative derivative with a fixed resolution of three elements.

3.3. Modelling Primitives

QSIM defines a variety of constraint primitives allowing ordinary differential equations to be "mapped onto" qualitative descriptions. These constraints are in three categories: arithmetic, derivative and functional.

Arithmetic constraint, at a particular time t

$$ADD\ (x,\ y,\ z)\ :\ x(t) + y(t) = z(t)$$

$$MULT\ (x,\ y,\ z)\ :\ x(t) * y(t) = z(t)$$

$$MINUS\ (x,\ y)\ :\ x(t) = -\ y(t)$$

Derivative constraint

$$DERIV\ (x,\ y)\ :\ x'(t) = y(t)$$

Functional constraints

QSIM provides weak functional constraints between the values of the variables. This allows the partial or lack of detailed knowledge of the relationship between variables to be represented. Specifically, monotonic functional dependencies are allowed, indicating that some variable is monotonically dependent on the rate of change of another:

$$M^+(x, y) \quad : \quad y(t) = H(x(t)) \cap H'(x) > 0$$

$$M_0^+(x, y) \quad : \quad M^+(x, y) \cap H(0) = 0$$

$$M^-(x, y) \quad : \quad y(t) = H(x(t)) \cap H'(x) < 0$$

$$M_0^-(x, y) \quad : \quad M^-(x, y) \cap H(0) = 0$$

Additionally, the functional dependencies can have *correspondences* specified. A correspondence is a pair of landmarks l_1 and l_2 such that x is l_1 when y is l_2. For example, M_0^+ and M_0^- have a correspondence <0, 0>. More generally, correspondence can be used to relate a priori known values.

3.4. Simulation Algorithm

QSIM takes as input a set of variables (parameters in QSIM terminology), a set of constraints relating the variables, and a set of initial qualitative values for the variables. As output, QSIM produces a tree of states with each path representing a possible behaviour of the system.

The behaviour is represented by a sequence of the state of the system at a set of *distinguished time-points*. That is, those points in the quantity space where each variable takes a distinguished or critical value, e.g. an extrenum or landmark. The set of distinguished time-points of a complete system is the union of the distinguished time-points of all the variables comprising the system state description. We can then define the Qualitative State for an interval (t_i, t_{i61}) where t_i ε finite set of distinguished time-points as

$$QS (v, t_i, t_{i+1}) = QS (v, t) \quad t \, ε \, (t_i, t_{i+1})$$

The qualitative behaviour of a variable v(t) is, therefore, a sequence of qualitative states at distinguished time-points and the intervals between them.

$$QS(v, t_0), QS (v, t_0, t_1), QS (v, t_1) ..... QS (v, t_n).$$

Time is, therefore, represented, in QSIM by an alternating sequence of points and open intervals determined by the value of *any* variable changing its qualitative state. In general, the qualitative state of the *system* is the union of the qualitative states of each variable, and represents a complete 'snapshot' or *state* of the system at a distinguished time-point. The simulation algorithm of QSIM differs substantially from conventional simulation routines. From a given set of initial conditions (states), the set of possible next state transitions are determined, by using versions of the intermediate value and mean value theorems based on the assumption of continuous and differential functions as the variables of the system. These form a set of transition 'rules' depending upon whether the system is currently at a distinguished time-point or an open interval between time-points. When transitioning from a point to an interval the set of P-transition shown in Table 2(a) applies (taken from [Kuipers 86]). Similarly, when transitioning from an interval to a time- point the set of I-transitions of Table 2(b) applies. A variable may be at either a landmark or an interval for each time-point or time-interval. The initial state is always given at a time-point corresponding to a landmark value.

From the table we can see that in some cases the next state is uniquely defined, e.g. P4 and P6: if a function is increasing (decreasing) at a time-point then it must transition into the next region depending upon the direction of change. Similarly, if a variable is between landmarks at a time-point it must continue in the same interval during the following time- point, as the variable cannot attain the endpoint of the internal instantaneously. In other cases, multiple possible next states exist, and it is not possible to discriminate between these on the basis of the propagation rules alone. For example, when a variable is decreasing during an interval there are four possible next states I5, I6, I7 and I9, corresponding to whether it hits a landmark and continues to decrease (I6) or stay steady (I5) or it continues to decrease but between landmarks (I7). The case of the variable becoming steady between landmarks (I9) is catered for by creating a new landmark which splits the open interval into two. This ability of QSIM to dynamically create new landmark values significantly extends the 'resolution' of the variable at the expense of complicating the simulation algorithm.

Once the possible next states are generated the constraints representing the relationships between the variables are applied to further restrict the set of next states. For each constraint, a set of value/derivative pairs is generated by computing the cross product of the possible next states and eliminating those pairs inconsistent with the definition of the constraint. Consistency between constraints, that share a variable, is then checked by using a Waltz filtering algorithm to further eliminate inconsistent states. Complete state descriptions are now generated from the remaining pairs and become the *successor* states i.e. the consistent state transitions. At this stage the set of next states is non-unique and may contain multiple next states from one predecessor states. This ambiguity leads to the generation of 'spurious' behaviours that do not correspond to any feasible behaviour of the actual system. Some of these behaviours can be eliminated by applying *global filters* derived from system theoretic properties of the behaviour or from other (external) sources. Common global filters include checking for no-change or divergence of a variable to infinity. Filters can also be used to check for periodic oscillation by checking for cycles of the state values.

Point to Interval

$P1$ $\langle l_j, std \rangle$ $\langle l_j, std \rangle$

$P2$ $\langle l_j, std \rangle$ $\langle (l_j, l_{j+1}), inc \rangle$

$P3$ $\langle l_j, std \rangle$ $\langle (l_{j-1}, l_j), dec \rangle$

$P4$ $\langle l_j, inc \rangle$ $\langle (l_j, l_{j+1}), inc \rangle$

$P5$ $\langle (l_j, l_{j+1}), inc \rangle$ $\langle (l_j, l_{j+1}), inc \rangle$

$P6$ $\langle l_j, dec \rangle$ $\langle (l_{j-1}, l_j), dec \rangle$

$P7$ $\langle (l_j, l_{j+1}), dec \rangle$ $\langle (l_j, l_{j+1}), dec \rangle$

Interval to Point

$I1$ $\langle l_j, std \rangle$ $\langle l_j, std \rangle$

$I2$ $\langle (l_j, l_{j+1}), inc \rangle$ $\langle l_{j+1}, std \rangle$

$I3$ $\langle (l_j, l_{j+1}), inc \rangle$ $\langle l_{j+1}, inc \rangle$

$I4$ $\langle (l_j, l_{j+1}), inc \rangle$ $\langle (l_j, l_{j+1}), inc \rangle$

$I5$ $\langle (l_j, l_{j+1}), dec \rangle$ $\langle l_j, std \rangle$

$I6$ $\langle (l_j, l_{j+1}), dec \rangle$ $\langle l_j, dec \rangle$

$I7$ $\langle (l_j, l_{j+1}), dec \rangle$ $\langle (l_j, l_{j+1}), dec \rangle$

$I8$ $\langle (l_j, l_{j+1}), inc \rangle$ $\langle l^*, std \rangle$

$I9$ $\langle (l_j, l_{j+1}), dec \rangle$ $\langle l^*, std \rangle$

Figure 2 Tables of a) P - Transitions and b) I - Transitions

A lot of work has recently been done to develop further methods of eliminating spurious behaviours. These include: applying global energy constraints [Chui and Kuipers 87] i.e. that the system is assumed to be dissipative, non-intersecting constraint [Struss 88] which utilises the uniqueness property of continuous systems, and other empirical filters based on parameter correspondences. Other methods of reducing these unwanted behaviours have been proposed. Kuipers [Kuipers 88a, 88b] suggests using 'temporal abstraction' to produce a model with a reduced set of variables that can be used to constrain the original description. However, the most recent interest has been in developing other representation for the quantity space that can minimise the ambiguity problem at source [Raiman 86, Weld 88] rather than eliminating it once it is generated. This is currently the major focus of Qualitative Simulation and will be further discussed in later sections.

The QSIM algorithm has been subjected to a number of mathematical analyses [Kuipers 86, Struss 88]. Kuipers has shown that although QSIM produces spurious behaviours i.e. behaviours that do not correspond to any actual behaviour of the system, it does include the 'real' behaviour. Unfortunately, for a realistic size of problem the number of spurious behaviours tends to obscure the real behaviour, making the use of 'problem specific' global filters mandatory for practical use.

4. COMPONENT-CENTERED APPROACH

This is the original approach to developing qualitative models and has been pioneered by [de Kleer and Brown 84, Williams 84]. It has explored and exposed some of the basic properties of qualitative reasoning and has resulted in qualitative modelling techniques being used in a range of different problem solving situations e.g. fault diagnosis and explanation.

4.1. Ontology

The basic view of the physical world, adopted by the component-centred approach, is of a 'complex' system composed of a number of identifiable sub- systems or *components*. The assumption is that the behaviour of the complete system can be determined from the behaviour of its components. For this to be possible, an assumption of 'nearly' decomposable is required: that the subsystems interact in a minimal way and that this interaction does not affect the individual description of the behaviour of the component. This modelling paradigm is widely used in Systems Engineering and is fundamental to coping with the complexity found in industrial applications. The goal of the component-centred approach is to formalise this method for the use of qualitative descriptions, and hence allow generic 'component- libraries' to be developed providing quantative model instantiation.

There are three basic entities: *materials* (such as air, water, electricity) that pass information or energy between components; *components* (such as valve, pump, transistor) which operate on materials to alter their form; and *conduits* which passively transport material between components.

4.2. Quantity Space

The most commonly occurring representation for quantity used in this approach is the simple three-valued system {-, 0, +}, where the only qualitative distinction is made on the strict sign of the variable, denoted [·]. Variables are also often represented by their temporal derivative, i.e. ∂v, $\partial^2 v$ etc. This is because the use of such models has, so far, been restricted to reasoning with static models of systems in equilibrium. The use of the derivative of the variable determines the direction of change from this equilibrium position. This is a very simple quantity space. However, it does have the important property that associativity is preserved [Struss 88] with respect to an underlying real-valued differential equation model. Unfortunately, it produces a large number of ambiguities in the inference process due to the extremely weak representation of the value of variables.

4.3. Modelling Primitives

The fundamental modelling primitive of the component-centred approach is the *confluence*. This is a 'qualitative differential equation' representation of the behavioural description of each component, e.g. (Bernoulli's equation).

$$Q = C_d \ a \ P \ \sqrt{2|P|}/\rho \ |P|$$

where C_d, a, ρ > 0, is described by the confluence

$$[Q] = [P]$$

or, equivalently

$$\partial Q = \partial P$$

Clearly, this is a gross simplification. However, useful information can still be extracted from such models.

A set of confluences may be insufficient to represent a system over a wide range of operating conditions. In which case de Kleer and Brown introduced the concept of 'qualitative state' to represent the set of confluences that are applicable under a particular operating condition. A precondition determines when to activate a given set of confluences. In this way a value can have the 'qualitative states' open, working and closed with the corresponding behavioural descriptions. Unfortunately, this use of the term 'state' conflicts with the usage in the previous section on constraint- centred approaches. There the state is used to define the values of the variables, at a given time, rather than the particular operating condition that the system is in.

Conduits are used as a set of *terminals* through which components are connected and form the basic structure of a system consisting of a given set of components. They are represented by a restricted set of confluences : the *continuity* confluence ($\partial p_1 = \partial p_2$) where p_1 and p_2 are the input and output variables respectively, and the *compatibility* confluence where two conduits can be connected together

$$\partial p_1 + \partial p_2 = \partial p_3 \ : \ \text{flow is conserved.}$$

4.4. Simulation Algorithm

Within the component-centred ontology the term *envisioning* is used to describe the process of generating the behaviour of a system from its structural description. A change is made to the value of one of the state variables and the envisionment consists of the possible transitions between component states. If this is done for each of the state variables a complete envisionment, also known as the qualitative state diagram, is generated consisting of all the possible combinations of states for the system (described by the structural model). The envisionment thus represents a complete description of all possible *interstate* behaviours of the generic system. From such a diagram, such global properties as cyclic behaviour or 'uncontrollability' and 'observability' can be determined. An envisionment diagram can also be used for explanation purposes and to answer questions about 'what if' a change is made to a particular variable. This aspect is potentially very useful in design tasks where changes in system parameter or relations can be made to see if it results in a desired behavioural description.

The determination of a particular state of the component is done by a process of constraint propagation. In fact, this was the application for which constraint propagation techniques were developed. This process is called *intrastate* determination in order to distinguish it from the transitions between behaviour determined by the interstate propagation. However, it is often the case that the state cannot be uniquely determined, i.e. to obtain a consistent set of values for the asserted confluences. This is usually due to the necessary ambiguity in the qualitative calculus, where the 'addition' and 'subtraction' operators are incomplete and result in ambiguous results for certain values, e.g.

MULTIPLICATION				ADDITION			
$\otimes$	-	0	+	$\oplus$	-	0	+
-	+	0	-	-	-	-	
0	0	0	0	0	-	0	+
+	-	0	+	+		+	+

Figure 3 Propagation of values under (a) Addition and (b) Multiplication

Constraint propagation can also become 'stuck' due to simultaneous equations resulting from algebraic 'loops' in the equations representing the confluences. In both cases a mixture of constraint propagation, generate and test and component heuristics is used in an attempt to overcome these problems and determine a consistent set of values for the variables within a given state.

The interstate behaviour is determined by assuming that the variables, or more accurately the functions, describing the state are continuous and differentiable. In which case, *transition analysis* [de Kleer 84, Williams 84] can be undertaken to determine which next states are possible under the continuity assumption. These rules are determined from the intermediate value theorem of infintesimal calculus which (informally) states that a variable must cross a boundary when changing from one 'qualitative' state to another and cannot make arbitrary discrete jumps. Rather, the mean value theorem of calculus can be used to further restrict the possible next states by taking into account the value of a variable and its rate of change. For example, a variable, x, with values $[x] = \text{'}0\text{'}$ and $\partial x = \text{'}+\text{'}$ must transition to $[+] = \text{'}+\text{'}$. This corresponds to a qualitative 'integration rule' [Williams 84a]. Once the set of possible transitions has been determined, further information on the limits of variables and use of the constraints within the confluences can be used to 'order' the transitions in terms of which will occur first. If a unique transition of a variable is determinate, this is asserted as the next state and the process of constraint propagation and transition analysis is repeated until an equilibrium state, where all derivatives are zero, is attained.

As previously stated, one of the main motivations for the development of the envisionment technique was to produce 'causal' explanations of system operation. The sequence of state changes, resulting from an initial disturbance from equilibrium, until the system again returned to an equilibrium condition was assumed to be the result of 'mythical causality'. That is, each state in the envisionment is 'caused' by the previous state. It is termed 'mythical causality' because, in fact, the changes occur in an infinitesimal amount of time - also known as 'mythical time'. De Kleer and Brown argued [de Kleer and Brown 86] that mythical causality 'explained' the operation of a system even although the behavioural description was non- unique. In fact, this notion of causality is very suspect in that no use of the actual time elapsed between equilibria is used. Further, the state transitions do not correspond to the transient behaviour of the actual system, but rather to the computational mechanism used in determining a consistent set of values corresponding to the new equilibrium state. Attempting to characterise this computation as reflecting causality is very dubious.

An alternative methodology for determining a causal account from the solution of a set of (qualitative) equations was given by Iwasaki [Iwasaki and Simon, 86]. They introduce the notion of *exogeneous* and *endogeneous* variables representing variables external and internal to the model, respectively. Exogeneous variables are not influenced by any of the endogeneous variables and are determined by mechanisms external to the part of the system being being modelled. Endogeneous variables, on the other hand, are influenced by both other endogeneous (internal) variables and by the exogeneous variables. Their technique, called Causal Ordering, determines necessary conditions for a set of equations to be 'self contained' by identifying a sequence of minimally complete subsets; the number of variables required to make the equations self contained is determined and these must be assigned before hand, i.e. assumed to be exogeneous. Under these conditions a unique 'causal' ordering is determined, without generating simultaneous equations reflecting feedback loops. De Kleer and Brown responded, however, by asserting that their method coped with feedback loops via their component, confluence and conduit heuristics. No consensus was reached: Iwasaki and Sinon sticking to their position that feedback loops were inherent in such systems and could not be avoided. A limitation in the causal ordering technique is that it could sometimes produce causal ordering graphs that did not accord with our intuition about causal interactions.

Recently, Iwasaki [Iwasaki, 88] has extended the causal ordering technique to include dynamic equations, i.e. equations including derivative operators. In this case, the causal network obtained produces intuitively correct orderings and, hence, has removed many of the objections to the original version.

5. PROCESS-CENTRED APPROACH

This approach, developed by Forbus [Forbus 84a], directly stems from the motivation to represent our everyday "common sense" notion of physics and to develop a reasoning mechanism based on such concepts. In this way, it represents an attempt to automate the Naive Physics of Hayes [Hayes 79]. The basic ontology is of *processes* acting on objects to modify them. Processes can correspond to everyday notions such as "boiling", "freezing", "stretching" etc. Processes can be dynamically activated by satisfying their preconditions and quantity conditions. Forbus makes a closed world assumption in that he assumes that all changes are caused by processes, what he calls the sole mechanism assumption. This allows reasoning by mutual exclusion to determine the activation of processes.

5.1. Quantity Space

Like the other methods, Qualitative Process Theory, QPT, [Forbus 84a] assumes continuous variables, however, QPT's quantity space is considerably more complicated than the others. A quantity is represented by an *amount* A(v) and a *derivative* D(v). These are in turn composed of:-

$$\text{sign } s[A], s[D], \quad \varepsilon \{-1, 0, 1\}$$

$$\text{magnitude } m[A], m[D], \quad \varepsilon \ R_0^+,$$

The magnitudes are represented by a partial ordering to real valued (landmark) elements of the quantity space. Although more complicated, this partial ordering of the quantity space allows the ambiguity of the qualitative calculus of de Kleer to be resolved. The real-valued landmarks of the quantity space corresponds to physically meaningful values if the variables, such as top and bottom of tanks, maximum pressure etc.

5.2. Modelling Primitives

The basic modelling primitive within QPT is the *individual view* that describes portions of the world in terms of collections of objects and relations between them. For example, flow may have two views corresponding to turbulent or laminar flow conditions. Views have four parts:

* *individuals* - consisting of the objects within the view;
* *quantity conditions* - inequalities between individuals and other external views;
* *pre-conditions* - conditions for the activation of an individual view;
* *relations* - valid relationships between objects when a view is active.

An individual view instance is created for every collection of objects satisfying the "individuals" description: it will be active whenever its quantity and pre-conditions are satisfied. This allows different views of an overall system to be dynamically activated as the simulation is running.

Processes are individual views with additional *influences* specified. An influence is the mechanism by which variables affect each other. For example $I_+(v, A[w])$ specifies that the variable v is positively "influenced" by the amount of variable w.

The functional relationships that may hold between objects is represented by the relations field. In particular, *qualitative proportionalities* is used to state that two variables are monotonically related, written $v\ \alpha_{q+}w$, to mean the v is monotonically increasing with respect to w. This is similar to QSIMs monotonic operator, however, QPT allows dependence on more than one variable through the use of indirect influences.

5.3. Simulation Algorithm

The generation of a qualitative description of behaviour from a QPT model is obtained by instantiating the processes and views that satisfy the individuals specification. The activation of process and view instances is then made according to their quantity conditions and pre-conditions. This results in the *process structure* for a given situation. This structure is resolved to determine the derivatives of all the quantities. These derivatives are then related to the inequalities in the quantity space to determine possible changes in the relations. This procedure continues until a limiting condition is attained.

QPT includes two types of histories, that is, alternative descriptions of behaviour: parameter histories and process histories. Parameter histories correspond to the evolution of the variables in the quantity space as the simulation procedes. As such, it corresponds to the behaviour description of the other methods. Process histories, consists of "episodes" where a process remains active. This allows segments of parameter histories to be aggregated into process histories, thereby reducing the detail. This offers the prospect of separately computing "nonintersecting" process histories, thereby avoiding the need to compute a global state. However, examples given so far do not show this advantage.

Although QPT provides a sophisticated modelling environment for common sense reasoning, it lacks a formal base. The ontological status of many of the concepts is vague and the envisionment procedure is complex and difficult to control. However, it is the first real attempt to provide a methodology for representing and reasoning with common sense knowledge and, as such, has attracted much interest.

6. CONCLUSION

Much work has been done in developing basic representational paradigms for the qualitative representation of complex systems. This work, however, is just the begining. Much more needs to be done in determining the relationship between the various approaches so that the systems modeller can select the most appropriate method for the particular problem under study. Also, further work on developing other quantity spaces that reduce the qualitative ambiguity and hence result in less spurious behaviors needs to be done. Finally, realistic applications need to be tackled to determined whether these techniques will 'scale-up' to real size practical applications.

REFERENCES

[Brown 76]
  Brown, A.
  *Qualitative Knowledge, Causal Reasoning, and the Localisation of
  Failures*
  M.I.T. AI-TR-362, 1976
[Bobrow 84]
  Bobrow, D.G.
  Qualitative Reasoning about Physical Structures
  Artificial Intelligence, Vol. 24, Nos. 1-3, 1984
[Chiu]
  Chiu, C.
  *Abstracting Qualitative Behaviours from Quantitative Simulation
  Models, Draft*
  University of Texas at Austin, September 4, 1987
[Davis 84]
  Davis, R.
  Diagnostic Reasoning Based on Structure and Behaviour
  Artificial Intelligence, Vol. 24, Nos. 1-3, 1984
[Davis 87]
  Davis, E.
  *Order of Magnitude Reasoning in Qualitative Differential
  Equations*
  New York Univ. Tech. Report #312, 1987
[de Kleer 77]
  de Kleer, J.
  *Multiple Representations of Knowledge in a Mechanics Problem-
  Solver*
  IJCAI-77, 1977
[de Kleer 79]
  Causal and Teleological Reasoning in Circuit Recognition
  MIT AI-TR-529, 1979.
[de Kleer, Brown 81]
  de Kleer, J. and Brown, J.S.
  Mental Models of Physical Mechanisms and their Acquisition
  in: Anderson, J. (ed.), Cognitive Skills and their Acquisition,
      Hillsdale N.J., 1981
[de Kleer 82]
  de Kleer, J.
  Foundations of Envisioning

AAAI-82, 1982
[de Kleer, Brown 83]
de Kleer, J. and Brown, J.S.
Assumptions and Ambiguities in Mechanistic Mental Models
in: Gentner, D. and Stevens, A.S. (eds.), Mental Models,
Hillsdale N.J., 1983
[de Kleer, Brown 84]
de Kleer, J. and Brown, J.S.
A Qualitative Physics Based on Confluences
Artificial Intelligence 24, (1-3), 1984
[de Kleer 86a]
de Kleer, J.
An Assumption-Based Truth Maintenance System
Artificial Intelligence, Vol. 28, No. 2, 1986
[de Kleer 86b]
de Kleer, J.
Problem Solving with the ATMS
Artificial Intelligence, Vol. 28, No. 2, 1986
[de Kleer 87]
de Kleer, J.
Qualitative Physics
In: Shapiro, Eckroth (eds.), Encyclopedia of Artificial Intelligence,
New York, 1987
[de Kleer, Sussman 78]
de Kleer, J. and Sussman, G.J.
Propagation of Constraints Applied to Circuit Synthesis
MIT AI-TR-485, 1978
[de Kleer, Williams 86]
de Kleer, J. and Williams, B.
Diagnosing Multiple Faults
Proceedings of the AAAI 1986
[Forbus 81]
Forbus, K.D.
Qualitative Reasoning about Physical Processes
IJCAI-81, 1981
[Forbus 82]
Forbus, K.D.
Qualitative Process Theory
MIT AI Lab. Memor. No. 664, 1982
[Forbus 84]
Forbus, K.D.

Qualitative Process Theory
Artificial Intelligence, Vol. 24, Nos. 1-3, 1984
[Forbus 84a]
    Forbus, K.D.
    Qualitative Process Theory
    MIT AI-TR-789
[Hayes 78]
    Hayes, P.
    The Naive Physics Manifesto
    in: Michie, D. (ed.), Expert Systems in the Micro-Electronic Age,
        Edinburgh, 1978
[Hayes 85a]
    Hayes, P.
    The Second Naive Physics Manifesto
    in: Hobbs, J. and Moore, R. (eds.), Formal Theories of the
        Commonsense World, Norwood, 1985
[Hayes 85b]
    Hayes, P.
    Naive Physics 1: Onotology for Liquids
    in: Hobbs, J. and Moore, R. (eds.), Formal Theories of the
        Commonsense World, Norwood, 1985
[Kuipers 85]
    Kuipers, B.
    Commonsense Reasoning about Causality: Deriving Behaviour from Structure
    Artificial Intelligence 24 (1-3), 1984
[Kuipers 85]
    Kuipers, B.
    The Limits of Qualitative Simulation
    IJCAI-85, 1985
[Kuipers 86]
    Kuipers, B.
    Qualitative Simulation
    Artificial Intelligence 29, (3), 1986
[Kuipers 87]
    Kuipers, B.
    Abstraction by Time-Scale in Qualitative Simulation
    AAAI 1987
[Kuipers 87a]
    Kuipers, B.
    A Reply to Peter Struss

Draft, University of Texas at Austin, July 8, 1987

[McDermott]
McDermott, D.
Flexibility and Efficiency in a Computer Program for Designing Circuits
MIT AI-TR-402, 1976

[Moore 66]
Moore, R.E.
Interval Analysis
Englewood Cliffs, N.J., 1966

[Nickel 75]
Nickel, K. (ed.)
Interval Mathematics
Proceedings of the International Symposium, Karlsruhe 1975, Berlin 1975

[Raiman 86]
Raiman, O.
Order of Magnitude Reasoning
Proceedings of the AAAI, Philadelphia, 1986

[Rieger, Grinberg 77]
Rieger, C. and Grinberg, M.
The Declarative Representation and Procedural Simulation of Causality in Physical Mechanisms
IJCAI-77

[Rieger, Grinberg 77b]
Rieger, C. and Grinberg, M.
The Causal Representation and Simulation of Physical Mechanisms
University of Maryland, TR 495, 1976

[Rieger, Grinberg 78]
Rieger, C. and Grinberg, M.
A System of Cause-Effect Representation and Simulation for Computer-Aided Design
in: Latombe (ed), Artificial Intelligence and Pattern Recognition in Computer-Aided Design, Amsterdam, 1978

[Sacks 87]
Sacks, E.
Piecewise Linear Reasoning
AAAI 1987

[Schmid 87]
Schmid, L.
Impediments to a Qualitative Physics Based on Confluences

in: Fruchtenicht et al. (eds.), Technisch Expertensysteme -
Wissensreprasentation und Schlussfolgerungsverfahren, Munich 1988
[Simmons 86]
Simmons, R.
'Commonsense' Arithmetic Reasoning
Proceedings of the AAAI, Philadelphia, 1986
[Stallman-Sussman 77]
Stallman, R.M. and Sussman, G.J.
Forward Reasoning and Dependency - Directed Backtracking in a
System for Computer-Aided Circuit Analysis
Artificial Intelligence, Vol. 9, No. 2, 1977
[Struss 88]
Struss, P.
Problems of Interval-Based Qualitative Reasoning
in: Fruchtenicht et al. (eds.), Technische Expertensysteme -
Wissensreprasentation und Schlussfolgerungsverfahren, Munich 1988
also SIEMENS Tech. Rep. INF 2 ARM-1-87
[Struss 88a]
Struss, P.
Mathematical Aspects of Qualitative Reasoning
in: Int. J. for Artificial Intelligence in Engineering, July 1988
[Struss 88b]
Struss, P.
Reasons and Filters for Spurious Behaviours
Second Workshop on Qualitative Physics, Paris, July 1988
[Struss 88c]
Struss, P.
Extensions to ATMS-Based Diagnosis
in: Gero, J. (ed.), Artificial Intelligence in Engineering: Diagnosis
and Learning, Amsterdam 1988
[Struss 88d]
Struss, P.
Global Filters for Spurious Behaviours
Proceeding of the AAAI, St. Paul 1988
[Struss 88e]
Struss, P.
Mathematical Aspects of Qualitative Reasoning - Part 2:
Differential Equations
SIEMENS Tech. Rep. INF 2 ARM-10-88, Munich 1988
[Sussman, Stallman 75]
Sussman, G.J. and Stallman, R.M.

Heuristic Techniques in Computer-Aided Circuit Analysis
IEEE Transactions on Circuits and Systems CAS-22 (11), 1975

[Sussman, Steele 80]
Sussman, G.J. and Steele, G.L.
CONSTRAINTS - A Language for Expressing Almost-Hierarchial Descriptions
Artificial Intelligence 14 (1), 1980

[Weld 87]
Weld, D.
Comparative Analysis
IJCAI 1987

[Williams 86]
Williams, B.
Doing Time: Putting Qualitative Reasoning on Firmer Ground
AAAI 1986

[de Kleer and Brown 83]
The Origin, Form and Logic of Qualitative Physical Laws
8th IJCAI, 1983.

[Iwasaki and Simon 85]
Causality in Device Behaviour
Artificial Intelligence, Vol. 29, No. 1, 1986.

[de Kleer and Brown 86]
Theories of Causal Ordering
Artificial Intelligence, Vol. 29, No. 1, 1986.

[Williams 84]
The Use of Continuity in a Qualitative Physics
NCAI (AAAI), 1984.

[de Kleer and Bobrow 84b]
Qualitative Reasoning with Higher-Order Derivatives
NCAI (AAAI), 1984.

[Kuipers 86]
Qualitative Simulation as Causal Explanation
TR86-24 (MIT).

[Weld 88]
Theories of Comparative Analysis
Technical Report 1035, MIT AI Lab,1988.

[Leitch 87]
Modelling of Complex Dynamic Systems
Proc. IEE, PartD, Vol.134,1987.

[Kuipers 87]
Taming Intractible Branching in Qualitative Simulation

Proc. IJCAI,1987
[Iwasaki 88]
    Causality in Mixed Stuctures
    Proc. IJCAI, 1988
[Leitch and Stefanini 88]
    QUIC: A Development Environment for Knowledge Base Systems for Industrial Automation Applications
    Proc. 3rd. ESPRIT Technical Conf.,1988.

Chapter 7
Solving process engineering problems using artificial neural networks
M. J. Willis, C. De Massimo, G. A. Montague, M. T. Tham and A. J. Morris

Summary. Artificial neural networks are made up of highly inter-connected layers of simple 'neuron' like nodes. The neurons act as nonlinear processing elements within the network. An attractive property of artificial neural networks is that given the appropriate network topology, they are capable of characterising nonlinear functional relationships. Furthermore, the structure of the resulting neural network based process model may be considered generic, in the sense that little prior process knowledge is required in its determination. The methodology therefore provides a cost efficient and reliable process modelling technique.

This contribution introduces the concepts involved in the formulation of artificial neural networks. Their suitability for solving some process engineering problems is discussed, and illustrated using results obtained from both simulation studies and recent applications to industrial process data. In the latter, neural network models were used to provide estimates of biomass concentration in industrial fermentation systems and of top product composition of an industrial distillation tower. Measurements from established instruments such as off-gas carbon dioxide in the fermenter and overheads temperature in the distillation column were used as the secondary variables for the respective processes. The advantage of using these estimates for feedback control is demonstrated. The range of applications is an indication of the utility of artificial neural network methodologies within a process engineering environment.

1. INTRODUCTION

The idea of using artificial neural networks (ANNs) as a potential solution strategy for problems which require complex data analysis is not new. Over the last 40 to 50 years, scientists have been attempting to realise the 'real' neural structure of the human brain, and to develop an algorithmic equivalent of the human learning process. The principal motivation behind this research is the desire to achieve the sophisticated level of information processing that the brain is capable of. However, the structure of the human brain is extremely complex, with approximately 10^{11} neurons and between 10^{14} to 10^{15} synapses (the connections between neurons). Whilst the function of single neurons is relatively well understood, their collective role within the conglomeration of cerebrum elements is less clear and a subject of avid postulations. Consequently, the architecture of an ANN is based upon a primitive understanding of the functions of the biological neural system. Even if neuro-physiology could untangle the complexities of the brain, due to the limitations of current hardware technology, it will be extremely difficult, if not impossible, to emulate exactly its immensely distributed structure. Thus, rather than accurately model the intricacies of the human cerebral functions, ANNs attempt to capture and utilise the connectionist philosophy on a more modest and manageable scale.

Within the area of process engineering, process design and simulation; process supervision, control and estimation; process fault detection and diagnosis rely upon the effective processing of unpredictable and imprecise information. To tackle such tasks, current approaches tend to be based upon some 'model' of the process in question. The model can either be qualitative knowledge derived from experience; quantified in terms of an analytical (usually linear) process model, or a loosely integrated combination of both. Although the resultant procedures can provide acceptable solutions, there are many situations in which they are prone to failure because of the uncertainties and the nonlinearities intrinsic to many process systems. These are, however, exactly the problems that a well trained human decision process excels in solving. Thus, if ANNs fulfil their projected promise, they may form the basis of improved alternatives to current engineering practice. Indeed, applications of artificial neural networks to solve process engineering problems have already been reported.

One of the major obstacles to the widespread use of advanced modelling and control techniques is the cost of model development and validation. The utility of neural networks in providing viable process models was demonstrated in Bhat et al (1989a,b), where the technique was used to successfully characterise two non-linear chemical systems as well as interpret biosensor data. The application of ANNs to provide cost efficient and reliable process models therefore appears to be highly promising.

In an adjunct area, the use of neural network based models (NNMs) for the on-line estimation of process variables was considered by Montague et al (1989). Lant et al (1990) further discussed the relative merits of process estimation using an adaptive linear estimator (Guilandoust et al, 1987), and an estimator based on an NNM. In addition, the applicability of neural networks for improving process operability was investigated by Di Massimo et al (1990). In some situations, techniques based on the use of an NNM may offer significant advantages over conventional model based techniques. For instance, if the NNM is sufficiently accurate, it could theoretically be used in place of an on-line analyser. Indeed, such a philosophy may be used to provide more frequent measurements than could be achieved by hardware instrumentation. This is advantageous from the control viewpoint as the feedback signals will be not be subject to measurement delays. Consequently, significant improvements in control performance can be expected. A tentative exposition of a neural model based inferential controller was also presented in Montague et al (1989). Here, an NNM was used to provide estimates of 'difficult-to-measure' controlled variables by inference from other easily measured outputs. These estimates were then used for feedback control.

If an accurate NNM is available, then it could obviously also be directly applicable within a model based control strategy. The particularly attractive feature is the potential to handle nonlinear systems. Psaltis et al (1988) investigated the use of a multi-layered neural network processor for plant control. A novel learning architecture was proposed to ensure that the inputs to the plant gave the desired response. Willis (1990), on the other hand, proposed the use of NNMs in the synthesis of cost-function based controllers. Here, an on-line optimisation algorithm is used to determine the future inputs that will minimise the deviations between setpoints and the predicted outputs obtained from an NNM.

Another promising area for ANNs is in fault diagnosis and the development of intelligent control systems (Bavarian, 1988). Here, a robust control system must be designed to accommodate highly complex, unquantifiable data. Hoskins and Himmelblau (1988) described the desirable characteristics of neural networks for knowledge representation in chemical engineering processes. Their paper illustrated how an artificial neural network could be used to learn and discriminate successfully amongst faults. Birky and McAvoy (1989) presented an application of a neural network to learn the design of control configurations for distillation columns. They were able to demonstrate that their approach was an effective and efficient means to extract process knowledge.

2. PROCESS MODELLING VIA THE USE OF ARTIFICIAL NEURAL NETWORKS

As would have been noted, in almost all of the work cited above, an NNM is used in place of conventional models. The accuracy of the NNM model may be influenced by altering the topology (structure) of the network. It is the topology of the network, together with the neuron processing function, which impart to an ANN, its powerful signal processing capabilities. Although a number of ANN architectures have been proposed (see Lippmann, 1987), the 'feedforward' ANN (FANN) is by far the most widely applied. Indeed, Cybenko (1989) has recently claimed that any continuous function can be approximated arbitrarily well on a compact set by a FANN, comprising two hidden layers and a fixed continuous non-linearity. This result essentially states that a FANN could be confidently used to model a wide range of non-linear relationships. From previous discussions, the implications of this statement are therefore considerable. In view of this, subsequent discussions will therefore be restricted to FANNs.

2.1 Feedforward Artificial Neural Networks

The architecture of a typical FANN is shown in Fig.1. The nodes in the different layers of the network represent 'neuron-like' processing elements. There is always an input and an output layer. The number of neurons in both these layers depends on the respective number of inputs and outputs being considered. In contrast, hidden layers may vary from zero to any finite number, depending on specification. The number of neurons in each hidden layer is also a user specification. It is the hidden layer structures which essentially defines the topology of a FANN.

The neurons in the input layer do not perform data processing functions. They merely provide a means by which scaled data is introduced into the network. These signals are then 'fed forward' through the network via the connections, through hidden layers, and eventually to the final output layer. Each interconnection has associated with it, a weight which modifies the strength of the signal flowing along that path. Thus, with the exception of the neurons in the input layer, inputs to each neuron is a weighted sum of the outputs from neurons in the previous layer.

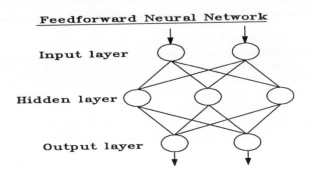

Fig. 1. Schematic of Feedforward Neural Network Arcitecture

For example, if the information from the ith neuron in the $j-1^{th}$ layer, to the kth neuron in the jth layer is $I_{j-1,i}$, then the total input to the kth neuron in the jth layer is given by:

$$\alpha_{j,k} = d_{j,k} + \sum_{i=1}^{n} w_{j-1,i,k} I_{j-1,i} \qquad (1)$$

where $d_{j,k}$ is a bias term which is associated with each interconnection. The output of each node is obtained by passing the weighted sum, $\alpha_{j,k}$, through a nonlinear operator. This is typically a sigmoidal function, the simplest of which has the mathematical description:

$$I_{j,k} = 1/(1+\exp(-\alpha_{j,k})) \qquad (2)$$

and response characteristics shown in Fig. 2. Although the function given by Eq.(2) has been widely adopted, in principle, any function with a bounded derivative could be employed (Rumelhart et al, 1986). It is, however, interesting to note that a sigmoidal nonlinearity has also been observed in human neuron behaviour, (Holden, 1976). Within an ANN, this function provides the network with the ability to represent nonlinear relationships. Additionally, note that the magnitude of bias term in Eq. (1) effectively determines the co-ordinate space of the nonlinearity. This implies that the network is also capable of characterising the structure of the nonlinearities: a highly desirable feature.

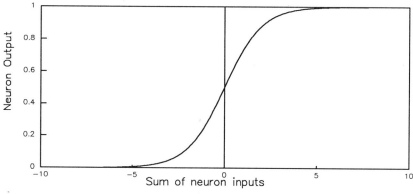

Fig. 2. Sigmoidal function

To develop a process model using the neural network approach, the topology of the network must first be declared. The convention used in referring to a network with a specific topology follows that adopted by Bremmerman and Anderson (1989). For example, a FANN with 3 input neurons, 2 hidden layers with 5 and 9 neurons respectively, and 2 neurons in the output layer will referred to as a (3-5-9-2) network. A (2-10-1) network, thus refers to a FANN with 2 neurons in the input layer, 10 neurons in 1 hidden layer, and 1 neuron in the output layer.

2.2 Algorithms for Network Training (Weight Selection)

On having specified the network topology, a set of input-output data is used to 'train' the network, ie. determine appropriate values for the weights (including the bias terms) associated with each interconnection. The data is propagated forward through the network to produce an output which is compared with the corresponding output in the data set, hence generating an error. This error is minimised by making changes to the weights, and may involve many passes through the training data set. When no further decrease in error is possible, the network is said to have 'converged', and the last set of weights retained as the parameters of the NNM. Process modelling using ANNs is therefore very similar to identifying the coefficients of a parametric model of specified order. Loosely speaking, specifying the topology of an ANN is similar to specifying the 'order' of the process model. For a given topology, the magnitudes of the weights define the characteristics of the network. However, unlike conventional parameteric model forms, which have an *a priori* assigned structure, the weights of an ANN also define the structural properties of the model. Thus, an ANN has the capability to represent complex systems whose structural properties are unknown.

A numerical search technique is usually applied to determine the weights as this task is usually not amenable to analytical solution. Clearly, determining the weights of the network can be regarded as a nonlinear optimisation problem. The objective function for the optimisation is written as:

$$V(\Theta,t) = \tfrac{1}{2} \Sigma\, E(\Theta,t)^2 \qquad\qquad (3)$$

where 'Θ' is a vector of network weights, 'E' is the output prediction error and 't' i time. The simplest optimisation technique makes use of the Jacobian of the objective function to determine the search direction, and can be generalised by:

$$\Theta^{t+1} = \Theta^t + \delta^t \, S\nabla V(\Theta,t) \qquad (4)$$

where δ^t is the 'learn' rate which influences the rate of weight adjustments, and S i the identity matrix. Eq. (4) was used by Rumelhart and McClelland (1986) as th basis for their 'back-error propagation' algorithm, which is a distributed gradien descent technique. In this approach, weights in the jth layer are adjusted by makin use of locally available information, and a quantity which is 'back-propagated' fron neurons in the $j+1^{th}$ layer. However, it is well known that steepest descent method may be inefficient, especially when the search approaches the minima. Therefore, i most neural network applications, a 'momentum' term is added to Eq. (4):

$$\Theta^{t+1} = \Theta^t + \delta^t \, S\nabla V(\Theta,t) + \beta(\Theta^t \text{-} \Theta^{t-1}) \quad 0 < \beta < 1 \qquad (5)$$

ie. the current change in weight is forced to be dependent upon the previous weigh change. Here, 'β' is a factor which is used to influence the degree of this dependence Although this modification does yield improved performances, in training network where there are numerous weights, gradient methods have to perform exhaustiv searches and are also rather prone to failure. A potentially more appealing metho would be a Newton-like algorithm which includes second derivative information. I this case, the S matrix in Eq.(4) would be the inverse of the Hessian. Recently Sbarbo (1989) approximated the Hessian using an approach similar to that utilised i 'classical' recursive system identification algorithms (eg. Ljung and Soderstron 1983), and showed that faster network convergence could be achieved. The increas in computational overheads, due to the matrix inversion, is balanced by improve convergence speeds.

An alternative approach was proposed by Bremermann and Anderson (1989) Postulating that weight adjustments occur in a random manner, and that weigh changes follow a multivariate Gaussian distribution with zero-mean, their algorithn adjusts weights by adding Gaussian distributed random values to old weights. Th new weights are accepted if the resulting prediction error is smaller than tha recorded using the previous set of weights. This procedure is repeated until th reduction in error is negligible. They claimed that the proposed technique wa 'neurobiologically more plausible'. Indeed, parallels have been drawn to bacteria 'chemotaxis', and thus the procedure is referred to as the chemotaxis algorithm.

In this contribution, attention will be confined to the back error propagation and th chemotaxis algorithm: the former because of its popularity, and the latter because o its flexibility and ease of use. The respective techniques are summarised below:

The Back-error Propagation (Rumelhart and McClelland, 1986)

Step I   Initialise weights with small random values.
Step II   Set δ (the learn rate) and β (the momentum term) in Eq. (5).

Step III Present a single set of inputs, and propagate data forward to obtain the predicted outputs.

Step IV Update the weights according to Eq. (5). For hidden to output weights, $\nabla V(\Theta,t)$ is given by:

$$\nabla V(\Theta,t)_{ok} = I_{o,k}(1-I_{ok})(y_k - I_{o,j})$$

where y_k is the actual process output and the subscript 'o' denotes an output layer. For input to hidden weights, $V(\Theta,t)$ is given by:

$$\nabla V(\Theta,t)_{jk} = \sigma^{t+1}_{j,k}I_{j-1,k}$$

where: $\sigma^{t+1}_{j,k} = I_{j,k}(1 - I_{j,k})\Gamma^{t+1}_{j,k}$

$$\Gamma^{t+1}_{j,k} = \sum_{k=1}^{n} \Gamma^{t}_{j+1,k}w_{j,k,i}$$

Step V Return to step III and proceed with the next data record.

Steps III to V are repeated for successive sweeps through the data set until convergence is deemed to have been achieved. Whilst an orderly sequence of input/output presentation is usually successful, in some cases, superior results may be achieved by random choice of the data sequence (McAvoy, 1990).

The Chemotaxis Algorithm (Bremmermann and Anderson, 1989)

Step I   Initialise weights with small random values

Step II   Present the inputs, and propagate data forward to obtain the predicted outputs

Step III Determine the cost of the objective function, E_1, over the whole data set.

Step IV   Generate a Gaussian distributed random vector.

Step V   Increment the weights with random vector.

Step VI   Calculate the objective function, E_2, based on the new weights.

Step VII If E_2 is smaller than E_1, then retain the modified weights, set E_1 equal to E_2, and go to Step V. If E_2 is larger than E_1, then goto Step IV.

Note that during the minimisation, the allowable variance of the increments may be adjusted to assist network convergence.

2.3 Comparison of Back-error Propagation and the Chemotaxis Algorithm

The complexity of the weight adjustment 'rule' has been a major criticism of the back-error propagation philosophy (Crick, 1989). On the other hand, the chemotaxis algorithm which was proposed as an alternative learning mechanism, appears to adjust network weights in an arbitrary manner. However, algorithms that are formulated within a 'random walk' framework have long been preferred in particle physics (eg. see Metropolis et al, 1953; Kirkpatrick et al, 1983). In the latter citation, it was shown that there was a useful connection between multivariable optimisation and statistical mechanics (the behaviour of systems with many degrees of freedom in thermal equilibrium at a finite temperature). Indeed, this analogy provided the basis for an increasingly popular optimisation technique known as 'simulated-annealing' (Kirkpatrick et al, 1983). In applications to very large scale problems, this method has been found to be faster and more accurate than other combinatorial minimisation procedures.

The chemotaxis approach is analogous to the simulated-annealing technique, and should therefore possess similar accelerated convergence properties. In fact, modifying the chemotaxis algorithm to that of simulated-annealing is relatively easy. The basic differences between the two is that simulated-annealing generates changes in search directions according to the Boltzmann probability distribution, and has the ability to accept values that cause an increase in the objective function. Whilst this algorithm is marginally more complex, it has a greater potential for achieving global minimum. Although Bremermann and Anderson (1989) did attempt to incorporated the essence of simulated annealing within their chemotaxis approach, they concluded that the modification was detrimental to their algorithm.

As may be appreciated, it is in the application to complex systems where ANNs are likely to achieve their maximum benefits. Under these circumstances, it is possible that a complex network architecture is also necessary, and it here that the back-error propagation becomes extremely cumbersome. Since the chemotaxis algorithm presents a more efficient method for determining the weights of large networks, it is potentially a more viable technique. To compare the two approaches, a (1-2-1) and a (1-10-10-1) network with known weights were used to generate 2 sets of 'standard' test data. These sets were then used to train corresponding 'empty' networks using both the chemotaxis algorithm and the back-error propagation. The ideal technique would result in a set of weights equivalent to those used to generate the data in the respective networks.

The performance of the two network paradigms were quantified in terms of the Integral of Squared Error (ISE). Figs.3 and 4 show the ISE, recorded as a function of the number of iterations in the training circuit, for the (1-2-1) and (1-10-10-1) networks respectively. In both figures, the ISE recorded using the back-error propagation showed a smoother trajectory. The 'erratic' ISE traces relate to the chemotaxis approach, and is a direct consequence of the random manner in which the weights of the network were being adjusted. In this comparison, an attempt was made to achieve the best possible results from both techniques, ie. to achieved minimum ISE using the least number of iterations.

From Figs.3 and 4, the chemotaxis approach appears to produce superior results. For the (1-2-1) network, this contradicts the results of Bremmerman and Anderson (1989), who showed that back-error propagation approach was superior for simple network structures, whereas the chemotaxis method would be better for larger networks. Nevertheless, the objective of this study was not to prove the superiority of one technique over the other. Indeed, it is possible that given the correct choice of experimental conditions, back-error propagation could be shown to be superior for all cases. The issue here is to demonstrate that the chemotaxis algorithm is not only a feasible approach, it is also a more alluring technique due to its neurobiological appeal; ease of computation and its implementation flexibility. A good example of the latter feature, is the ease with which dynamics may be incorporated into a FANN.

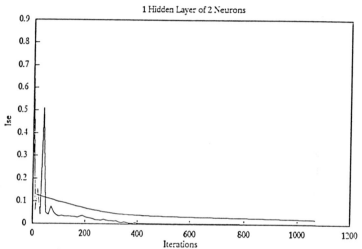

Fig.3 ISE versus Iterations using a (1-2-1) Network

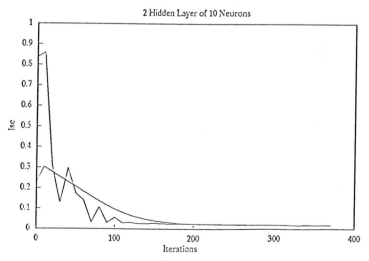

Fig.4 ISE versus Iterations using a (1-10-10-1) Network

2.4 Dynamic Neural Networks

The ANNs discussed above, merely perform a non-linear mapping between inputs and outputs. Dynamics are not inherently included within their structures, whilst in many practical situations, dynamic relationships exist between inputs and outputs. As such, the ANNs will fail to capture the essential characteristics of the system. Although, dynamics can be introduced in a rather inelegant manner by making use of time histories of the data, a rather more attractive approach is inspired by analogies with biological systems. Studies by Holden (1976) suggest that dynamic behaviour is an essential element of the neural processing function. It has also been suggested that a first-order low-pass filter may provide the appropriate representation of the dynamic characteristics (Terzuolo et al, 1969). The introduction of these filters is relatively straightforward, with the output of the neuron being transformed in the following manner:

$$y^f(t) = \Omega y^f(t-1) + (1-\Omega)y(t) \qquad 0 \le \Omega \le 1 \qquad (6)$$

Suitable values of filter time constants cannot be specified a priori, and thus the problem becomes one of determining 'Ω' in conjunction with the network weights. Unfortunately, back-error propagation does not lend itself easily to this task. However, an appealing feature of the chemotaxis approach is that the algorithm does not require modification to enable incorporation of filter dynamics: the filter time constants are determined in the same manner as network weights.

A particular instance where the use of a time history would still be appropriate is when uncertainty can exist over system time delays. The use of input data over the range of expected dead-times could serve to compensate for this uncertainty. In this situation a 'limited' time history together with neuron dynamics may be appropriate.

3. POTENTIAL APPLICATION AREAS

3.1 Inferential Estimation

There are many industrial situations where infrequent sampling of the 'controlled' process output can present potential operability problems. Linear adaptive estimators have been employed to provide 'fast' inferences of variables that are 'difficult to measure' (Tham et al, 1989). Although results from industrial evaluations have been promising, it is suggested that, due to their ability to capture nonlinear characteristics, the use of NNMs may provide improved estimation performances. The following sections present the results of some evaluation studies.

3.1.1 Biomass estimation in continuous mycelial fermentation. Due to industrial confidentiality, a thorough description of the fermentation process is not permissible. Nevertheless, note that biomass concentration within the fermenter is the primary control variable. However, with existing sensor technology, on-line measurements are not possible. In this example, biomass concentrations are determined from laboratory analysis and only made available to the process operators at four hourly intervals. However, this frequency is inadequate for effective control. The control problem

would be alleviated if the process operators were provided with more frequent information. Fortunately, a number of other (secondary) process measurements such as dilution rate (the manipulative input), carbon dioxide evolution rate (CER), oxygen uptake rate (OUR), and alkali addition rate, provide useful information pertaining to biomass concentration in the fermenter. If the complex relationships between these variables and biomass concentration can be established via an ANN, then the resulting NNM could be used to infer biomass concentrations at a frequency suitable for control purposes. Although other variables, eg. pH, temperature etc., affect the nonlinear relationship, tight environmental regulation maintains these at an approximate steady state.

These preliminary neural network studies considered a time history of inputs in order to incorporate dynamics. To model the process, a (6-4-4-1) network was specified, and 'trained' on appropriate process data. Although a number of input variables could be used to train the ANN, any duplication of information in the network could be detrimental to the quality of estimates. This problem is similar to that due to multi-collinearities in multivariate regression. Inputs to the network should therefore be chosen with care. Two variables have already been identified as being 'critical' in previous estimation work (Montague et al, 1989), viz. CER and fermenter dilution rate. Thus, at each pass of the training circuit, inputs to the network were the current values of CER and dilution rate values in the data base. Additionally, two previous respective data pairs were also used. The data for comparison with network output for weight adjustment purposes, was the biomass concentration corresponding to the first input data pair. Therefore, 6 neurons were specified in the input layer, and 1 in the output layer. This serves to demonstrate the use of the time histories of the data can be used to incorporate dynamics. However, the use of dynamic neural networks as described in section 2.4, is a more elegant technique and will therefore be demonstrated in later examples.

Two sets of fermentation data were used to assess the goodness of fit produced by the neural net model. Fig.5 demonstrates the ability of the neural network to fit the first data set, even when there was a major change in operating conditions. Here, a step change in the fermenter dilution rate has been applied at approximately 200 hrs. The performance of the NNM when applied to the second data set is shown in Fig.6. It should be noted that at around 400 and 500 hrs., the CO_2 analyser failed resulting in poor biomass estimates. Nevertheless, the overall ability of the neural network to fit the fermentation data in the presence of significant process disturbances was not compromised. The integrity of networks in the presence of such sensor failures is a subject of current study.

3.1.2 Biomass estimation in fed-batch penicillin fermentation. The measurement difficulties encountered in the control of penicillin fermentation are similar to those experienced in the continuous fermentation system described above. The growth rate of the biomass has to be controlled to a low level in order to optimise penicillin production. Whilst the growth rate can be influenced by manipulating the rate of substrate (feed) addition, it is not possible to measure the rate of growth on-line. The aim is, therefore, to develop a model which relates an on-line measurement to the rate of biomass growth. In this case, the OUR was used as the on-line measured

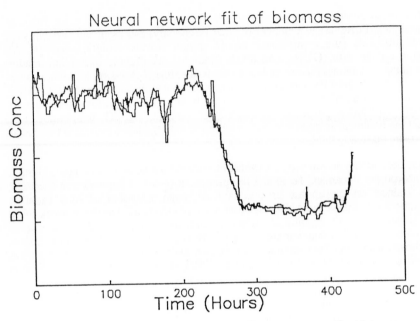

Fig.5 Application of Neural Network Estimator to a Continuous
       Mycelial Fermentation (Data set 1)

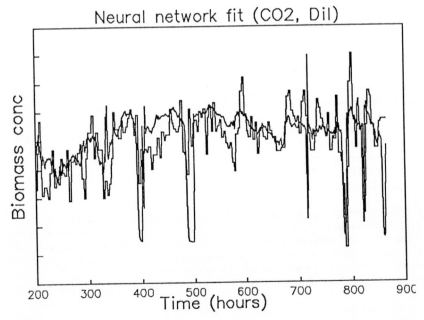

Fig.6 Application of Neural Network Estimator to a Continuous
       Mycelial Fermentation (Data set 2)

variable, although the CER could have provided the same information. This is because the ratio of CER to OUR, known as the respiratory quotient (RQ), remains constant after approximately 20 hrs. into the fermentation.

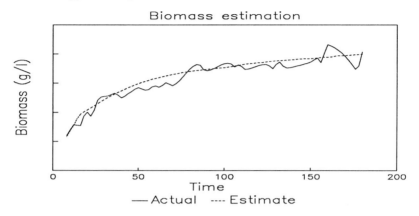

Fig.7. Biomass Estimation of Penicillin Process (Data Set 1)

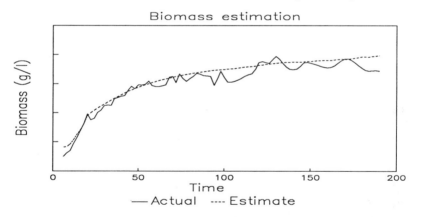

Fig.8. Biomass Estimation of Penicillin Process (Data Set 2)

The continuous fermentation process considered previously normally operates around a steady state. Thus a linear estimator may prove sufficient in the vicinity of normal process operating conditions. On the other hand, the fed-batch penicillin fermentation presents a more difficult modelling problem since the system passes through a wide spectrum of dynamic characteristics, never achieving a steady state. The results of applying a NNM to predict fermentation behaviour should therefore provide an indication of the viability of the technique for modelling complex processes. Data from two fermentation batches were used to train the neural network. The current on-line measurement of OUR, was one of the inputs to the neural network. Unlike the previous case, fermenter feed rate was not used as an input variable since it is essentially constant from batch to batch at any point of each fermentation. Thus, the information it contains would not contribute towards the prediction of variations in biomass levels between fermentations. However, since the characteristics of the fermentation is also a function of time, the batch time was considered a pertinent input. The specified network therefore had a (2-3-1) topology. Figures 7 and 8 show the performance of the neural estimator when applied to the 2 training data sets. As expected, good estimates of biomass were achieved.

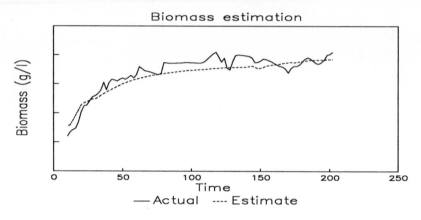

Fig.9. Biomass Estimation of Penicillin Process (Data Set 3)

OUR data from another fermentation batch was then introduced to the NNM, resulting in the estimates shown in Fig.9. It can be observed that the estimates produced by the NNM is very acceptable, and almost as good as those observed in Figs. 7 and 8. These results are very encouraging, since work on the development of a nonlinear observer to estimate the biomass concentration of the penicillin fermentation has not been as successful (Di Massimo et al, 1989). Compared to the mechanistic model based observer, relatively good estimates have been achieved without the need for corrective action from off-line biomass assays. Nevertheless, the possibility of introducing off-line biomass data, to improve the performance of the neural estimator, is presently under investigation.

3.1.3 Estimation of product composition in a high purity distillation. Distillation columns, especially those with high purity products, can exhibit highly nonlinear dynamics, resulting in controllability problems. These difficulties may be exacerbated by the measurement delays due to the use of on-line composition analysers. The column being considered here is an industrial demethaniser, where the control objective is to regulate the composition of the high purity top product stream by varying reflux flow rate. Apart from top product composition, which is subject to an analyser delay of 20 mins., all other process variables are available at 5 mins. intervals. Like the bioreactor systems discussed above, the aim is to use fast secondary measurements, here, column overheads vapour temperature and reflux flow rate, to provide an estimate of a slow primary measurement (top product composition) every 5 mins. Since column vapour temperature can be overly sensitive to disturbances which do not necessarily affect product composition, the use of a tray liquid temperature would be preferable. However, this choice of secondary variable was dictated by its availability at the time of the tests.

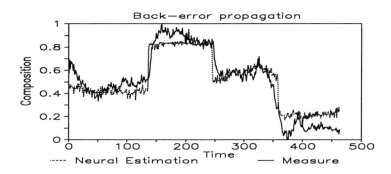

Fig.10. Neural Network Estimator Applied to High Purity Column (Back-error Propagation)

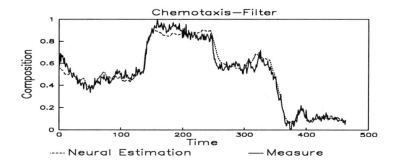

Fig.11. Neural Network Estimator Applied to High Purity Column (Chemotaxis Algorithm)

The neural estimator was based on a (2-9-9-1) network. First, the weights of the network were determined using the back-error propagation technique. It can be observed from Fig. 10, that the estimates were rather poor and estimator performance was inconsistent. The chemotaxis algorithm was then used. Additionally, 1st-order low-pass filters were associated with each neuron and the filter constants were determined simultaneously with network weights. The resulting NNM produced the results shown in Fig. 11. Clearly, much improved estimates have been achieved, thus highlighting the advantage of introducing dynamics into the network, and the power of the chemotaxis algorithm.

3.2. Inferential control via ANNs.

With the availability of 'fast' and accurate product quality estimates, the option of closed loop 'inferential' control instantly becomes feasible. The effectiveness of such a strategy has been demonstrated by Guilandoust et al (1987, 1988), where adaptive linear algorithms were used to provide inferred estimates of the controlled output for feedback control. Here, the practicality of an NNM based inferential control scheme is explored via nonlinear simulation.

The process under consideration is a 10 stage pilot plant column, installed at the University of Alberta, Canada. It separates a 50-50 wt.% methanol-water feed mixture which is introduced at a rate of 18.23g/s into the column on the 4th tray. Bottom product composition is measured by a gas-chromatograph which has a cycle time of 3 mins. The control objective is to use steam flow rate to regulate bottom product composition to 5 wt.% methanol, when the column is disturbed by step changes in feed flow rate. The column is modelled by a comprehensive set of dynamic heat and mass balance relationships (Simonsmeir, 1977). Both the pilot plant and the nonlinear model have been widely used by many investigators to study different advanced control schemes (eg. Morris et al, 1981), including adaptive inferential control (Guilandoust et al, 1987,1988).

The training data set consists of paired values of the input variable, ie. temperature of the liquid on tray 2 (the 2nd tray from the reboiler) and the output variable, ie. the corresponding bottom product composition. The data was collected at 3 mins. intervals, this being the cycle time of the gas chromatograph. The chemotaxis algorithm was used to determined both the weights and filter time constants of a (1-4-4-1) network.

Fixed parameter PI controllers were fine-tuned to obtain responses with minimum integral of absolute error. Comparative performances of PI feedback control and NNM based inferential control, under major disturbance conditions, were assessed by subjecting the column to a sequence of step disturbances in feed flow rate, viz. a 10% decrease from steady state followed by a 10% increase back to steady state. As reported in Guilandoust et al (1987,1988), the responses of bottom product composition and tray liquid temperatures, exhibit quite different gains and time-constants, depending on the direction of inputs. Thus, the NNM must be able to characterise these nonlinear effects in order to provide accurate composition estimates. Moreover, for the inferential control technique to be practicable, the NNM is required to provide composition estimates at a rate faster than that obtainable from the gas chromatograph. This is achieved by introducing into the NNM, tray 2 liquid temperatures sampled every 0.5 mins. Although the NNM had been trained on data collected at 3 mins. intervals, the use of data obtained at a faster rate is permissible because all that is required is a consistent data set.

The inferential controlled response, using a PI controller (K_c=2.2 and T_I=20), together with composition estimates, are shown in Fig. 12. It can be observed that although the estimate and actual composition compare favourably, there is a difference between the two values. This is because the neural estimator is operating in the open loop, ie. the estimates are not corrected by feedback of measured composition. Thus, if the estimates are used for control, offsets between the actual process output and the desired value will occur. However, offset free inferential control can be achieved by treating the elimination of estimation errors as a control problem. Here, whenever a new composition value is available, ie. every 3 mins., the estimation error is calculated and used to correct subsequent estimates. This technique is based on the Internal Model Control (IMC) strategy of Garcia and Morari (1982). The success of this modification is demonstrated in Fig.12, where it may be observed that it is the actual composition that is at setpoint.

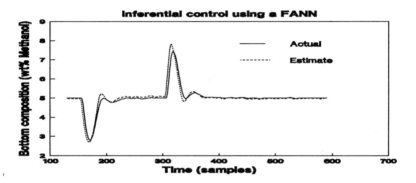

Fig.12 Inferential Control using a Neural Network

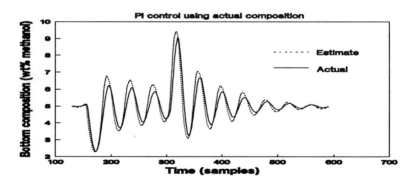

Fig.13 Control using analyser delayed value.

Figure 13 demonstrates the effect of using the actual (analyser delayed) composition values for control. The oscillatory responses observed are a direct consequence of using the same control settings as in the previous case. Clearly these parameters are unsuitable for a feedback signal which suffers from analyser delays. Reducing the proportional gain to 1.57 resulted in the response shown in Fig. 14, where the response shown in Fig. 12 has also been superimposed. Although a much improved performance has been achieved, comparison with the inferential controlled response will show that there is an increase in peak overshoot of more 1.0 wt.% methanol.

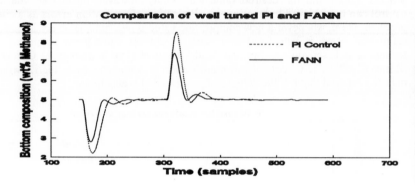

Fig.14 Detuned control using analyser delayed value

The performance of the NNM based inferential control scheme is clearly better. Using the output of the neural estimator for feedback control may be regarded as implicitly providing deadtime compensation in the closed loop. This then permits the use of higher gain control. Moreover, as changes in feed flow rate affect tray 2 temperature before bottom product composition, the estimates will contain information about the impending effects of the disturbance. As a result, disturbance rejection responses are superior to that obtained using conventional control.

4. CONCLUDING REMARKS

In this contribution, the concept of artificial neural networks was introduced. Additionally, two different neural network paradigms were discussed and their performances evaluated. Compared to the popular back-error propagation, the chemotaxis algorithm was found to be more flexible and easier to implement. The applicability of neural networks to solving some, currently difficult, process engineering problems was then explored.

Firstly, NNMs were used as process estimators. Of particular interest is the ability of the neural estimators to provide 'fast' inferences of important, but 'difficult to measure', process outputs, from other easily measured variables. Applications to data obtained from industrial processes reveal that given an appropriate topology, the network could be trained to characterise the behaviour of all the systems considered: viz. industrial continuous and fed-batch fermenters, and a commercial scale high purity distillation column. ANNs therefore exhibit potential as 'soft-sensors', ie. sensors based on software rather than hardware (Tham et al, 1989). Next, it was demonstrated that significant improvements in process regulation can be achieved, if the estimates produced by the neural estimators were used as feedback signals for control. This is possible because the use of secondary variables means that the effects of load disturbances could be anticipated in a feedforward sense.

The results presented are evidence that ANNs can be a valuable tool for alleviating many current process engineering problems. However, it is stressed that the field is still very much in its infancy and many questions still have to be answered. Determining the 'optimum' network topology is one example. Currently, *ad hoc* procedures based on 'gut-feeling' are used. This arbitrary facet of an otherwise promising philosophy is a potential area of active research. A formalised technique for choosing the appropriate network topology is desirable. There also appears to be no established methodology for determining the stability of ANNs. This is perhaps the most important issue that has to be addressed before the full potentials of ANN methodologies can be realised on-line. Nevertheless, given the resources and effort that are currently being infused into both academic and commercial research in this area, it is predicted that within the decade, neural networks will have established itself as a valuable tool for solving process engineering problems.

5. ACKNOWLEDGEMENTS

The support of the Dept. of Chemical and Process Engnrg., Uni. of Newcastle upon Tyne; Smith Kline Beechams; ICI Engnrg.; ICI Bioproducts; Dr. David Peel and Dr C. Kambhampati, are gratefully acknowledged.

6. REFERENCES

Bavarian, B. (1988). 'Introduction to neural networks for intelligent control', IEEE Control Systems Magazine, April, pp3-7.

Birky, G.J. and McAvoy, T.J. (1989). 'A neural net to learn the design of distillation controls', Preprints IFAC Symp. Dycord+89, Maastricht, The Netherlands, Aug. 21-23, pp205-213

Bhat N., Minderman, P., McAvoy, T. and Wang, N. (1989a). 'Modelling Chemical Process Systems via Neural Computation', Proc. 3rd Int. Symp. 'Control for Profit', Newcastle-upon-Tyne.

Bhat N., Minderman, P. and McAvoy, T.J. (1989b). 'Use of neural nets for Modelling of Chemical Process Systems', Preprints IFAC Symp. Dycord+89, Maastricht, The Netherlands, Aug. 21-23, pp147-153

Bremermann, H.J. and Anderson, R.W. (1989). 'An alternative to Back-Propagation: a simple rule for synaptic modification for neural net training and memory', Internal Report, Dept. of Mathematics, Uni. of California, Berkeley.

Clarke, D.W. and Gawthrop, P.J. (1979). 'Self-tuning Control'. Proc.IEE, 126, No.6, pp 633-640.

Crick, F. (1989). 'The recent excitement about neural networks', Nature, Vol. 337, 12, pp129-132

Cybenko, G. (1989). 'Continuous value neural networks with two hidden layers are sufficient, Internal report, Dept. of Comp. Sci. Tufts Univ. Medford.

Di Massimo, C., Saunders, A.C.G., Morris, A.J. and Montague, G.A. (1989). 'Non-linear estimation and control of Mycelial fermentations', ACC, Pittsburgh, USA, pp.1994-1999.

Di Massimo, C., Willis, M.J., Montague, G.A. Kambhampati, C., Hofland, A.G., Tham, M.T. and Morris, A.J. (1990). 'On the applicability of neural networks in chemical process control', To be presented at AIChE Annual Meeting, Chicago.

Economou C.G. and Morari, M. (1986) 'Internal Model Control, Pt. 5, Extension to Nonlinear Systems.' Ind. Eng. Chem. Process Des. Dev., 25, pp 403-411.

Garcia, C. and Morari, M. (1982). 'Internal Model Control, Pt. 1, A unifying review and some new results', Ind. Eng. Chem. Process Des. Dev., 21, pp 308.

Guilandoust, M.T., Morris, A.J. and Tham, M.T. (1987). 'Adaptive Inferential Control'. Proc.IEE, Vol 134, Pt.D.

Guilandoust, M.T., Morris, A.J. and Tham, M.T. (1988). 'An adaptive estimation algorithm for inferential control', Ind. Eng.Chem. and Res., 27, pp 1658-1664.

Holden, A.V. (1976). Models of the stochastic activity of neurones, Springer Verlag.

Hoskins, J.C. and Himmelblau (1988). 'Artificial Neural Network models of knowledge representation in Chemical Engineering', Comput. Chem. Engng, 12, 9/10, pp881-890.

Kirkpatrick, S., Gelatt, C.D. and Vecchi, M.P. (1983) 'Optimisation by simulated annealing', Science, 220, pp. 671- 690.

Lant, P.A., Willis, M.J., Montague, G.A., Tham, M.T. and Morris, A.J. (1990). 'A Comparison of Adaptive Estimation with Neural based techniques for Bioprocess Application', Preprints ACC, San Deigo.pp 2173-2178.

Lippmann, R.P. (1987). 'An Introduction to Computing with Neural Nets', IEEE ASSP Magazine, April.

Ljung, L. and Soderstrom, T. (1983). Theory and Practice of Recursive Identification', MIT Press.

McAvoy, T. (1990). 'Personal Communication'.

Metropolis, N., Rosenbluth, A., Rosenbluth, M., Teller, A. and Teller, E. (1953) J. Chem. Phys. 21, pp 1087.

Montague, G.A., Hofland, A.G., Lant, P.A., Di Massimo, C., Saunders, A., Tham, M.T. and Morris, A.J. (1989). 'Model based estimation and control: Adaptive filtering, Nonlinear observers and Neural Networks', Proc. 3rd Int. Symp. 'Control for Profit', Newcastle-upon-Tyne.

Morris, A.J., Nazer, Y., Wood, R.K. and Lieuson, H. (1981). 'Evaluation of self-tuning controllers for distillation column control', IFAC Conf. Digital Computer App. to Process Control, Ed. Isermann and Haltenecker, Dusseldorf, Germany, pp345-354.

Press W.H., Flannery, B.P., Teukolsky, S.A. and Vetterling, W.T. (1988). Numerical Recipes, Cambridge University Press.

Psaltis, D., Sideris, A. and Yamamura, A.A. (1988). 'A multilayered neural network controller', IEEE Control Systems Magazine, April, pp17-21.

Rumelhart, D.E., Hinton, G.E. and Williams, R.J. (1986). 'Learning representations by back-propagating errors', Nature, 323, pp 533-536.

Rumelhart, D.E. and McClelland, J.L. (1986). Parallel Distributed Processing: Explorations in the Microstructure of Cognition. Vol.1: Foundations, MIT Press, Cambridge.

Sbarbaro, D. (1989). 'Neural nets and nonlinear system identification', Control Engineering Report 89.9., Uni. Glasgow.

Simonsmeir, U.F. (1977) 'Modelling of a nonlinear binary distillation column' , MSc. Thesis, Univ. of Alberta, Edmonton, Canada

Terzuolo, C.A., McKeen, T.A., Poppele, R.E. and Rosenthal, N.P. (1969). 'Impulse trains, coding and decoding'. In Systems analysis to neurophysiological problems, Ed. Terzuolo, University of Minnesota, Minneapolis, pp86-91.

Tham, M.T., Morris, A.J. and Montague, G.A. (1989) 'Soft sensing: A solution to the problem of measurement delays', Chem. Eng. Res. and Des., 67, 6, pp 547-554.

Willis, M.J. (1990). 'Adaptive systems in chemical process control', Ph.D. Thesis in preparation, University of Newcastle

Chapter 8

Parallel processing architecture for real-time control

P. J. Fleming

1 INTRODUCTION

Following the major impact made by inexpensive microprocessors on digital controller implementation, the emergence of low-cost parallel processing devices, such as the Inmos transputer, has stimulated control engineers to investigate their application in embedded systems. The main advantages of parallel processing in real-time control are perceived to be:

- Speed

- Complexity

- Reliability, and

- Natural representation of real-time events.

Digital controllers typically perform real-time control, simulation, filtering and identification within a short sample interval together with other tasks such as event logging, data and I/O checking, etc. As sample times become shorter and control applications become more complex, in an increasing number of applications the general-purpose microprocessor is unable to execute the necessary operations in the required time. The potential speedup offered by a parallel processing system, therefore, suggests a solution to both the speed and complexity problem.

Also, at first sight, a parallel processing system, consisting of a number of PEs (processing elements), is likely to lead to reduced reliability. However, the flexibility of the system, its connectivity and ability to reconfigure, afford an opportunity for alternative system architecture designs to improve reliability.

Further, recognising that concurrent operations are naturally occurring phenomena in real-time control systems, the use of parallel programming software enables the software designer to more clearly express the variety of sequential and parallel tasks to be undertaken by a digital controller.

In this Chapter we study

- *Architectures*
- *Algorithms,* and
- *Applications*

for parallel processing in real-time control.

Parallel processing architectures are classified in the next Section. A range of architectures is described, and comment is made on the relevance of each architecture for real-time control. In the field of parallel processing, in general, this is not a typical application area. Its special features, due to its real-time nature, are the requirement to perform critical operations in a short sample time (of the order of milliseconds) and the relatively small scale of operations (small numbers of tasks and modest task size).

While little work has been carried out to date on developing new control algorithms specifically for parallel implementation (for a notable exception, see [1]), we report on a variety of ways in which sequential algorithms have been mapped onto parallel architectures. Issues range from load balancing on medium-grain architectures to new engineering of algorithms for systolic, or fine-grain, implementation.

The Chapter concludes with a look at some advantages and disadvantages of parallel processing applications. Functional and algorithmic approaches to parallelism are described and the problem of matching the algorithm to the architecture is highlighted.

2 ARCHITECTURES

2.1 General Classification

A general parallel processing system is composed of several processing elements (PEs) which can operate concurrently, communicating with each other when necessary. Parallel architectures are classified according to a number of different criteria. One of the most widely used was introduced by Flynn[2], who considered the traditional von Neumann model as a single stream of instructions operating on a single stream of data (SISD). According to Flynn's taxonomy parallel architectures are classified as (see Fig.1):

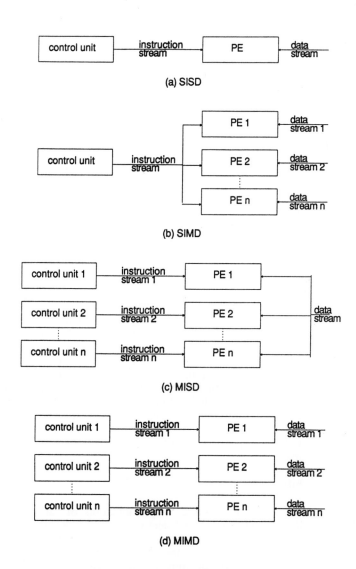

Fig.1 Flynn's classification

i)   Single instruction stream, multiple data stream (SIMD).
     The same instruction is broadcast to all PEs which will execute this instruction simultaneously on different data. Array processors are an example of this architecture.

ii) Multiple instruction stream, single data stream (MISD).
     Several processors simultaneously execute different instructions on a single data stream; a typical example is a pipeline system.

iii) Multiple instruction stream, multiple data stream (MIMD).
     This architecture consists of several independent processors, each capable of executing different instructions on different data. The processors are interconnected in some fashion to allow for interprocessor communication and synchronisation. A variety of topologies exist for the interconnections. The transputer is an example of a MIMD architecture.

(As we shall shortly see, however, while this classification is useful, it is by no means exhaustive.)

Parallel architectures also differ both in respect of the processing power of their PEs and the degree of interconnectivity between them. This leads to issues such as task granularity, which is a measure of the size of the tasks that can be effectively executed by the PEs of a specific architecture. PEs of fine-grain architectures are characterised by having limited functionality and a wide bandwidth for local data communication. On the other hand, PEs of coarse- or medium-grain architectures are more general-purpose, and the interprocessor communication bandwidth is narrower (i.e. processors are not as tightly coupled as in fine-grain architectures). In general, currently available SIMD architectures are fine-grained, with individual tasks consisting of a single operation, whilst MIMD architectures are usually medium- or coarse-grained.

2.2 SIMD Architectures

The issues involved in the parallel implementation of an algorithm are directly dependent on the target architecture, the choice of which should itself be a function of the problem under consideration, as different problems display different levels of parallelism to be exploited. Most SIMD architectures are well suited for implementing algorithms which can be expressed as a set of iterative operations on uniformly structured data, such as array operations within the "for" loops common in sequential software. Clearly, matrix-based control laws are suitable candidates for SIMD implementation; take, for example, the regulator structure

$$z(k+1) = F \ z(k) + G \ y(k),$$
$$u(k+1) = H \ z(k+1),$$

where z(k) is the regulator, y(k) is the plant sensor output vector, u(k) is the plant control vector and F,G and H are constant matrices.

SIMD implementations tend to be easier to realise than MIMD ones as the parallelism to be exploited is a direct consequence of the regular structure of the algorithm and issues such as synchronisation and task scheduling do not exist. On the other hand, MIMD machines can, in principle, deal with a wider range of problems but the control engineer must play a direct and fundamental rôle in successfully extracting the potential parallelism of the problem and in evaluating the trade-offs involved in parallel processing. These topics are covered later in the Chapter.

2.3 MISD Architectures

MISD or pipeline machines partition the overall problem into elementary tasks which are allocated to individual PEs in a pipeline. Processing is characterised by lock-step dataflow in which each preceding PE communicates input data to the succeeding PE in the pipeline (see Fig.2). Once the pipeline has been filled, each cycle produces a new result, irrespective of the number of stages in the pipeline. The machine will inevitably run at the speed of the slowest PE, thus requiring careful and efficient problem partitioning. MISD machines perform badly on data-dependent operations.

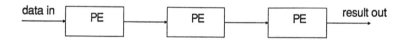

Fig.2 Pipeline configuration

Overall, the latency interval, i.e. the length of time for a piece of input data to be processed by all the stages in the pipeline, inhibits the use of this architecture for real-time control applications, where control law execution must be completed in a short time interval.

2.4 MIMD Machines

2.4.1 General

MIMD machines are deserving of special consideration due to their flexibility and ability to operate on unstructured and unpredictable operations and data. While they offer versatility to parallel computing they are also a difficult architecture class with which to work.

Performance benefits strongly depend on the R/C ratio, where R is the length of a run-time quantum and C is the length of communications overhead produced by that quantum [3].

This ratio expresses how much communication overhead is associated with each computation: clearly a high R/C ratio is desirable. The concept of task granularity can be viewed in terms of R. When R is large, it is a coarse-grain task implementation; when R is small, it is fine-grain. Although large grains may ignore potential parallelism, partitioning a problem into the finest possible granularity does not necessarily lead to the fastest solution, as maximum parallelism also has the maximum overhead, particularly due to increased communication requirements. Therefore, when partitioning the application across PEs , the designers must choose an algorithm granularity that balances useful parallel computation against communication and other overheads.

2.4.2 MIMD system topologies

The MIMD machine need not be connected in any specific way; example topologies are given in Fig.3.

The shared bus configuration is typically a low-cost, low-bandwidth solution, capable of supporting a small number of processors which are likely to be general-purpose microprocessors. As processors are added to the system, both interprocessor and processor-memory bandwidths are degraded, resulting in extended "idle" times for each processor as they wait to gain access to the bus.

While the bus interconnection offers the simplest solution, it has the highest possible contention. Conversely, the crossbar configuration offers the least contention, but has the highest complexity. This complexity is associated with contention problems arising from two or more accesses made to the same memory, for example. Sophisticated techniques are available to reduce allocation through careful allocation of data and shared program code.

The ring topology is based on point-to-point connections (avoiding bus contention) in which a transmitting PE places a message on the loop and it is repeated by each receiver until it returns to the transmitter. Inevitably, a delay is introduced at each mode while the interface repeats the incoming message. Bandwidth does not necessarily decrease as it does for buses when they are heavily loaded: the ring behaves as a pipeline with a short cycle time and long delay.

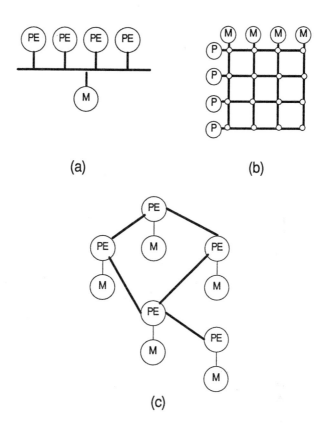

(a)   (b)

(c)

Fig.3 MIMD processor-memory configurations:
(a) Shared bus; (b) Crossbar; (c) Point-to-point.

2.4.3 The Inmos transputer

The point-to-point configuration is supported by the Inmos transputer which has four link interface units per PE to facilitate interprocessor communication [4],[5].

These links permit the transputer to be configured as arrays of processors, Fig.4, thus avoiding the potential communication bottleneck of a single-bus system, the complexity of the crossbar configuration and the delays associated with the ring topology. Further, the transputer supports many other interconnection topologies such as the pipeline and tree (see [4],[5]).

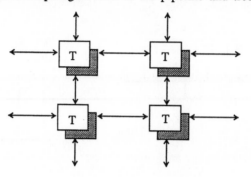

Fig.4 Array of transputers

We will consider transputer implementations of real-time controllers later in the Chapter and also study the performance of a transputer-based processor farm configuration, see Fig.5. In the processor farm, one transputer acts as a scheduler and allocates tasks dynamically to available workers (also transputers) in the chain.

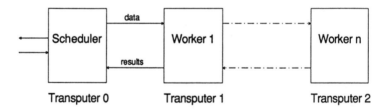

Fig.5 Transputer-based processor farm configuration

2.4.4 Task allocation

There are two main approaches to allocating tasks to processors. In static allocation, the association of a group of tasks with a processor is resolved before running time and remains fixed throughout the execution, whereas in dynamic allocation, tasks are allocated to processors at running time according to certain criteria, such as processor availability, intertask dependencies and task priorities. Whatever method is used, a clear appreciation is required of the overheads and parallelism/communication trade-offs already mentioned.

Dynamic allocation offers the greater potential for optimum processor utilization, but it also incurs a performance penalty associated with scheduling software overheads and increased communication requirements which may prove unacceptable in some real-time applications.

2.5 Other Architectures

Parallel architectures are not necessarily programmable. Some are algorithm-oriented and have specific function assigned to their PEs, a typical example being systolic array structures [6]. These are arrays of individual processing cells interconnected in a nearest neighbour fashion to form a regular lattice. The processors operate synchronously, controlled by a global clock. Most of the processors perform the same basic operation and data flows along the lattice in a highly pipelined mode, communicating with the outside world at the boundary cells only, Systolic structures are well suited to highly structured algorithms where multiple operations are performed in a repetitive manner, such as matrix operations, convolution and other signal processing applications. Fig.6 illustrates how a 2*2 matrix multiplication might be achieved using this architecture.

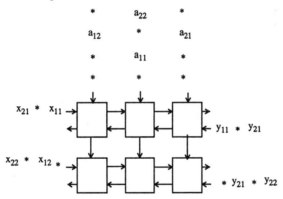

* indicates "don't care"

Multiplication of Two 2nd-Order Matrices

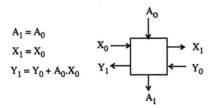

$$A_1 = A_0$$
$$X_1 = X_0$$
$$Y_1 = Y_0 + A_0.X_0$$

Systolic Cell Structure

Fig.6 Systolic matrix multiplication, order 2

An important variant of the systolic array architecture is the wavefront array processor [7], in which the required function is distributed in exactly the same way over an identical array of processors, but, unlike its systolic counterpart, the operation of the wavefront array is not synchronous. Each processor is controlled locally and an operation is executed once the necessary input data is available and the previous output data have been delivered to the appropriate neighbouring processors.

PACE (Programmable Adaptive Control Engine) is an alternative general-purpose parallel architecture whose inception was driven by the same aims associated with systolic arrays with the additional requirement of being able to support algorithm that do not map into arrays with a regular dataflow topology [8]. PACE PEs are VLSI-oriented cellular automata with medium-grain complexity, which could, perhaps, be classified as MIMD machines. Each PE can be configured to a range of basic control-oriented functions and is linked to its nearest neighbours by a regular set of programmable communication links (see Fig.7).

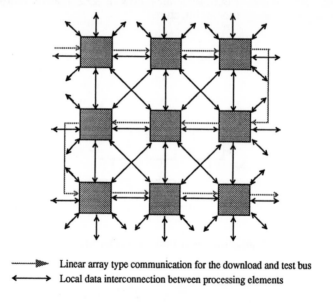

⋯⋯▶ Linear array type communication for the download and test bus
◀────▶ Local data interconnection between processing elements

Fig.7 PACE chip

To conclude this Section we remark that artificial neural networks represent a fascinating architectural alternative and are treated fully elsewhere.

3 ALGORITHMS

3.1 Parallelization of Sequential Real-Time Control Software

In [9] Shaffer reports on the implementation of a turbojet engine control program on a multiprocessor system. The concurrent program is obtained by analyzing the original sequential (FORTRAN) code for potential concurrency. This is made possible by the development of a set of tools which perform a global, hierarchical, data flow analysis on FORTRAN code in order to determine the data dependencies between code segments having sizes of the order of functions and procedures.

This particular sequential program consists of 64 control procedures (in addition to sequencing procedures and utility routines) which are used as the basic task structure for the parallel implementation. In order to determine the potential speed-up achievable by a parallel implementation it is necessary to determine the execution times of each code segment. Once the execution times for the tasks are determined and a computation graph for the program obtained with the assistance of dataflow analysis tools, the maximum speed-up achievable (ignoring communication overheads) is computed by dividing the total execution time by the length of the critical path in the computation graph [10]. In [9], for example, a potential speed-up of 5.28 was identified.

Because the program has a fixed number of tasks with fixed iteration rates and the tasks have little variation in execution times, a static assignment of tasks to processors was considered. For scheduling purposes a list-scheduling algorithm based on the critical-path method [11] was used. While this algorithm can eventually produce a schedule as much as twice as long as an optimal schedule [11], it was found to produce optimal or near-optimal results for the example considered. The schedule assumed no interprocessor communication and synchronization overheads. Simulations indicated that communication and contention overheads were not a problem for this application - the large-grain dataflow approach to parallelism extraction is likely to have contributed to this.

This approach is particularly interesting as it illustrates that the automated transformation of sequential code to concurrent software via a coarse-grain dataflow analysis can generate an efficient parallel implementation. Similar procedures may be applicable to the parallelization of a variety of real-time control programs where iterative control tasks with well-bounded execution times are performed.

There are other commercial tools (e.g. ASPAR) which are of considerable assistance in converting sequential code to run effectively on parallel machines.

3.2 Control Law Mapping

A pilot study to investigate the feasibility of mapping an existing aircraft flight control law, the Versatile AutoPilot (VAP), see Fig.8, onto a transputer based parallel processing system is described in [12]. With static allocation in mind, three different strategies were employed for parallelism extraction and evaluated with respect to general efficiency.

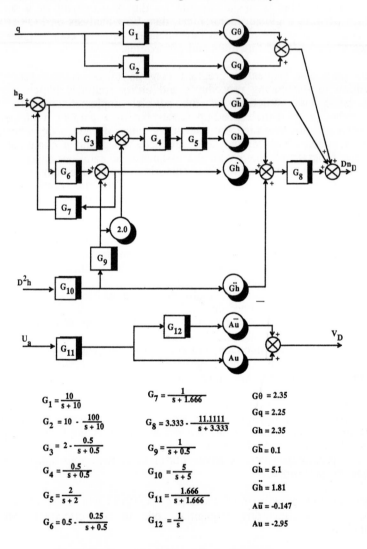

$$G_1 = \frac{10}{s+10}$$

$$G_2 = 10 - \frac{100}{s+10}$$

$$G_3 = 2 - \frac{0.5}{s+0.5}$$

$$G_4 = \frac{0.5}{s+0.5}$$

$$G_5 = \frac{2}{s+2}$$

$$G_6 = 0.5 - \frac{0.25}{s+0.5}$$

$$G_7 = \frac{1}{s+1.666}$$

$$G_8 = 3.333 - \frac{11.1111}{s+3.333}$$

$$G_9 = \frac{1}{s+0.5}$$

$$G_{10} = \frac{5}{s+5}$$

$$G_{11} = \frac{1.666}{s+1.666}$$

$$G_{12} = \frac{1}{s}$$

$G\theta = 2.35$

$Gq = 2.25$

$Gh = 2.35$

$G\bar{h} = 0.1$

$G\dot{h} = 5.1$

$G\ddot{h} = 1.81$

$A\bar{u} = -0.147$

$Au = -2.95$

Fig.8 VAP control law block diagram

In the *parallel branches* approach, the original VAP block diagram was converted into a parallel network of Laplace transfer-functions. Then, each of these parallel paths was expanded into partial fractions and converted to the discrete-time domain, thus reducing the controller to a sum of discrete functions. The result is a network of 37 independent difference equations, which were then combined to form the control signals (Fig.9).

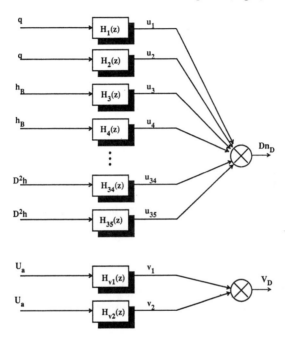

Fig.9 VAP control law: parallel branches network

In the *heuristic* approach, the discrete equivalent of each transfer function block in the original VAP control law was computed. Even though the original structure consists of a collection of sequential blocks, implicit parallelism was extracted through observation, by inspecting the dependencies of blocks along the various paths in Fig.8. Five independent groups of tasks with no common factors were extracted (see Fig.10). No further partitioning was feasible because of the constraints enforced by sequentialism within the paths.

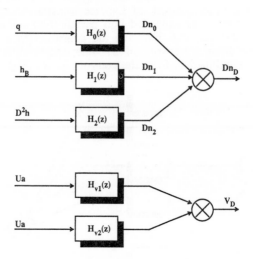

Fig.10 VAP control law: heuristic approach

In the *hybrid* approach the heuristic and parallel branches strategies were combined. First, the heuristic technique was applied to initially decompose the problem. Then, the parallel branches approach was employed to split the critical sequential paths of the controller into a set of shorter parallel paths that can be executed concurrently. (In this case, one particular path was found to be critically long for real-time implementation.)

All methods have the virtue of minimizing the communication between task groups, as essentially this only occurs during the initial distribution of data and the final addition of terms to form the output. The parallel branches approach attempts to maximize parallelism at the expense of introducing common factors between the tasks allocated to different processors. In contrast, the heuristic approach involves no wasted effort, but accepts the inherent sequentialism of the initial structure, consequently limiting the number of processors that may be used. The hybrid approach combines the best features of the two methods and, for the VAP controller case, offers the best solution.

3.3 Digital Filter-Related Approaches

Several authors have recently been looking for digital filter and controller structures suitable for implementation on SIMD architectures. For example, Ju [13] introduced four parallel computation structures for 1-D and 2-D IIR (Infinite Impulse Response) digital filters which are suitable for implementation on array processors, and Rogers [14] uses a technique called

Double-Look-Ahead computation to develop a controller structure which is claimed to be suitable for systolic arrays.

The ability to quantify the potential parallelism of a computation structure was one of the advantages of the Factored-State Variable Description (FSVD) introduced by Mullis and Roberts [15]. This notation has been used as the basis for the generation of different parallel implementations for the VAP control laws targeted at distinct MIMD and SIMD parallel architectures [16]. The FSVD approach supports the search for parallelism at a low level (add/multiply/accumulate, etc,) and, while our first impressions are that this is not well matched to MIMD implementations, it does offer a potentially attractive algorithm design method for SIMD, systolic and PACE architectures.

3.4 Systolic Algorithms

Systolic arrays have been widely applied in signal processing and many systolic algorithms have been devised to implement matrix operations such as multiplication, back-substitution, orthogonal decomposition, etc. The goals of these algorithms have been, principally, to optimise performance and PE utilisation.

More recently, there has been considerable research effort devoted to the generation of systolic Kalman filter algorithms. For a detailed overview and an insight into the ways in which algorithms can be re-engineered into the systolic array format, the reader is referred to [17]. Although intended for systolic array implementation, systolic algorithms are not confined to use on this architecture and may hold a key to successful parallel algorithm implementation on a variety of parallel machines. However, initial attempts to map systolic Kalman filter algorithms onto transputers have met with mixed success [18]. Difficulties arise from mapping fine-grain algorithms onto medium-grain architectures and from inefficiencies in the underlying systolic algorithms. Recent attempts have been more successful.

Megson [19] has identified key mathematical techniques required in H-infinity design and implemented parallel solutions, employing algorithmic parallelism, on a network of transputers. A common idea in his fine-grain solutions for singular value decompositions, Riccati equations and multivariable frequency response evaluations is that of unrolling the nested loops of a sequential program in space (processors) and time. While his efforts are directed at developing a hardware accelerator for Computer Aided Control System Design, by approaching real-time operation speeds his accelerator is capable of on-line analysis, thereby creating opportunities for more sophisticated controllers which would have been infeasible without the power of parallel processing.

3.5 Graphical Mapping

The nature of the PACE architecture suggests a radical alternative to algorithm mapping in view of its affinity with the block diagram representation of a controller. To conclude this Section, we illustrate how a simple controller described by

$$u(k) = -b*u(k-1) + K*(x(k) + a*x(k-1)),$$

may be realised on PACE (Fig.11) and draw attention to its resemblance to a conventional block diagram description. These novel mapping ideas are currently receiving close study.

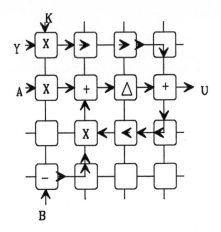

Fig.11 Sampled-data controller implemented in PACE

4 APPLICATIONS

4.1 General

The Chapter finishes with a look at applications in a few selected areas. To further investigate parallel processing applications in real-time control the reader might begin by referring to [5], [20] and [21].

4.2 Robotics

Robot control functions range through a number of levels: from decision making, path planning, and coordination at the top level to joint angle control at the bottom level. The computational requirements of high speed, high bandwidth, adaptive systems makes this area ripe for exploitation by parallel processing. Indeed, the variety of computational tasks suggests the use of a mix of architectures of differing granularity.

Mirab and Gawthrop [22] review work on the application of parallel processing for calculation of the dynamic equations of robotic manipulators. Jones and co-workers [23],[24] report on the use of transputers in this respect and suggest a granularity mismatch, this particular problem being more suited to a fine-grain architecture. Their work is further aggravated by the use of a processor farm topology for which they propose hardware improvements (see later). Daniel and Sharkey [25] draw attention specifically to the heavy computational demands of force control and to the need for a controller which is capable of switching easily between different layers in the control hierarchy. It is argued that latency is a key factor in the determination of a suitable transputer-based system architecture and they advocate their "Virtual Bus" solution.

4.3 Motor control

Until recently, the DC motor has predominated in high performance applications where a fast change of torque is required. The computing load demanded by AC machines has prohibited their application in this domain. Jones et al [26] and Asher and Sumner [27] have investigated whether transputer-based systems can provide sufficient real-time control computing power for the AC induction motor to be an attractive alternative to DC machines. Different control schemes based on the application of functional decomposition are described in [27]. The relatively slow interprocessor communication of the transputer, however, limits performance although its ease of implementation affords the designer valuable insight into the potential of parallelism. It is inferred that a parallel processing scheme is likely to yield a viable solution - perhaps the new generation of transputers with planned order of magnitude faster link communications will fulfil this promise.

4.4 Implementation issues

The control system design package, MATLAB, has been integrated with a Transputer Development System and new tools developed to automate the implementation of control laws on transputer systems of different sizes and topologies, and to simulate and evaluate strategies, by displaying, on-line, task allocation, processor activity and performance data [28]. The important point to note here is that the different strategies are tested on the actual hardware, thus avoiding simulation inaccuracies associated with imperfect knowledge of system behaviour (e.g. task switching, communications). As a result, static and dynamic task allocation strategies have been studied closely.

Fig.12 illustrates the system performance resulting from application of these strategies to implement the VAP control law described earlier. In its current realisation the processor farm approach (dynamic task allocation) displays an inferior performance when compared with the static approach. Following [23], this result was expected and is well understood; implementing the scheduler in software presents a formidable overhead in real-time control systems, where individual tasks are relatively short. Communications overhead is another significant component and is exacerbated when the linear array is long. No further speedup can be obtained for more than 5 workers in this case.

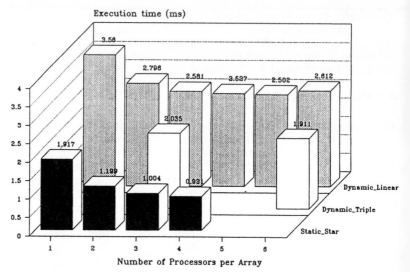

Transputers T414-15 were used
Link speed at 20 Mbits/s

Fig.12 Performance analysis: dynamic v static task allocation

The extended version of the farm, which uses three chains of workers rather than one, offers an improvement in performance, reducing execution time significantly. In this case the scheduler is able to allocate tasks to each line in parallel. Other work, involving buffering of tasks in the Worker PEs, has led to a further improvement in performance.

For this example, the static allocation approach exhibits the best performance. This strategy, has the virtue of minimising communication between task groups since this only takes place during the initial distribution of data and the final computation to form the output values.

Entwistle [29] has produced a hardware prototype of a processor farm scheduler and demonstrated that this is an effective means of significantly improving processor farm performance. Besides computational speedup issues, topology choice may also be influenced by other issues such as fault tolerance and hardware uniformity.

4.5 Fault Tolerant Systems

Clearly, a parallel processing system has great potential for fault-tolerance. However, it must be recognised that such a system will tend to be less reliable than a uniprocessor system since it generally has more elements. It only becomes more reliable if it can detect a fault and take corrective action, possibly by circumventing the defective sub-system and reconfiguring its software.

The critical design issue is redundancy management. Static redundancy techniques identify the fault source and mask its effect. This involves substantial physical redundancy and relatively simple redundancy management. On the other hand, the use of dynamic redundancy, in which the error is detected and tasks reallocated and rescheduled, entails a considerable management overhead which impacts directly on overall system performance.

The requirements of the aerospace industry, demanding a system failure probability of less than 10^{-10} per hour for flight-critical functions in advanced passenger aircraft, have driven developments in this area. Walter et al [30] advocate the physical partitioning of operating system and fault tolerance functions (Operations Controller, OC) from application tasks (Application Processor, AP). Their system consists of nodes containing an OC and an AP, where the OCs are connected by dedicated serial broadcast buses. The OCs form the heart of the system, freeing the APs to service their individual applications. This philosophy attempts to satisfy the competing objectives of system performance and system reliability through the use of high-speed data-driven hardware-based OCs.

Thompson and Fleming [31] use existing fault tolerant techniques to evolve an operationally fault tolerant transputer-based architecture suitable for gas turbine engine control. A system topology, constrained by the dual-lane configuration of gas turbine engine controllers, is devised in a way in which the majority of faults are detected, located and masked by means of a three-way vote, consistent with the conventional triplex approach. They draw attention to limitations of the present transputer generation in devising their scheme.

5 CONCLUDING REMARKS

The nature of advances in VLSI technology have resulted in increased computing power generally being made more available through parallel processing architectures of different types rather than increased clock rate in uniprocessor systems. Despite the development of faster processors, the real attraction of parallel processing to system designers is its scalability to meet increasing demands. There is a plethora of control engineering application areas. To date, much work in the area has been concerned with the efficient extraction and exploitation of concurrency. There is also a belief that the cost of parallel processing elements may become insignificant, thus encouraging their profligate use in addressing problems of growing complexity. In view of the constraints of *hard* real-time control engineering, it is felt that each approach is valid and that much depends on whether the advantage being sought is speed or complexity or both. Finally, despite the lack of enthusiasm for parallel processing expressed in Defence Standard 00-55 on "Requirements for the procurement of safety critical software in defence equipment", it is felt that its use in pursuit of high-integrity and/or maintenance-free systems merits continuing close examination.

REFERENCES

1. Minbashian B and Warwick K: "Flexible parallel control" *Proc UK IT 1990 Conference,* 1990, pp 117-124.

2. Flynn MF: "Some computer organisations and their effectiveness", *IEEE Trans Comput,* 1972, C-21, pp 948-960.

3. Stone HS, 1987, *High Performance Computer Architectures,* Addison-Wesley.

4. Harp, G (ed): *Transputer Applications,* Pitman, 1989.

5. Fleming PJ (ed): *Parallel Processing in Control - the Transputer and other Architectures,* Peter Peregrinus, 1988.

6. Kung HT: Why systolic architectures?, *IEEE Computer,* 1982, vol 15, pp 37-46.

7. Kung S-Y: On supercomputing with systolic/wavefront array processors, *Proc IEEE,* 1984, vol 72, pp 867-884.

8. Spray AJC, Jones S and Fleming PJ: PACE - an architecture for implementing irregularly structured functions in regularly structured arrays, *Proc IFIP Workshop on Parallel Architectures on Silicon,* Grenoble, France, 1989.

9. Shaffer PL: Experience with implementation of a turbojet engine control program on a multiprocessor, *Proc IEEE American Control Conference,* 1989, pp 2715-2720.

10. Even G: *Graph algorithms,* Computer Science Press, 1979.

11. Coffman Jr EG: *Computer and job shop scheduling theory*, Wiley, 1976.

12. Garcia Nocetti F, Thompson HA, De Oliveira MCF, Jones CM and Fleming PJ: "Implementation of a transputer-based flight controller", *Proc IEE, Part D,* vol 137, no 3, 1990, pp 130-136.

13. Ju C-J: Parallel algorithms for multidimensional recursive digital filters *Proc IEEE Int Conf on Computer Design: VLSI in Computers and Processors,* 1987, pp 391-395.

14. Rogers E and Li Y: Parallel realisations of real-time controllers within a feedback environment, *Proc 12th IMACS World Congress on Scientific Computing,* Paris, 1988, pp 272-274.

15. Mullis CT and Roberts RA: Synthesis of minimum round-off noise fixed-point digital filters, *IEEE Trans Circuits and Systems,* 1976, vol CAS-23, pp 551-562.

16. De Oliveira MCF: *CAD Tools for Digital Control,* PhD Dissertation, University College of North Wales, 1990.

17. Gaston FMF and Irwin GW: Systolic Kalman Filtering - An Overview, *Proc IEE, Part D, 1990, vol 137,* pp 235-244.

18. Lawrie DI, Gaston FMF, Fleming PJ and Irwin GW: "A systolic array approach to Kalman filtering using transputers", *IMACS Annals on Computing and Applied Mathematics,* Vol 5, Section 5 - Optimization, Decision Making and Control Problems, ed Borne P, Tzafestas SG, Breedveld P and Dauphin-Tanguy, G, 1989.

19. Megson GM: Transputer arrays and computer-aided control system design, *Proc IEE, Part D,* 1990, vol 137, pp 197-210.

20. *Proc IEE, Part D,* 1990, Vol 137, Issue 4, 1990, Special Issue on Parallel Processing for Real-Time Control.

21. IEE Colloquium Digests 1987/20 and 1990/050.

22. Mirab H and Gawthrop PJ: Transputers for robot control, *2nd International Transputer Conference,* Antwerp, BIRA, 1989.

23. Jones DI and Entwistle PM: Parallel computation of an algorithm in robotic control, *Proc IEE Conf Control 88,* 1988, pp 438-443.

24. Da Fonseca, Entwistle PM and Jones DI: A transputer based processor farm for real-time control applications, *Proc 2nd Int Conf on Applications of Transputers*, Southampton, UK, 1990, pp 140-147.

25. Daniel RW and Sharkey PM: The transputer control of a Puma 560 robot via the virtual bus, *Proc IEE, Part D*, 1990, vol 137, pp 245-252.

26. Jones DI and Fleming PJ: "Control applications of transputers", Chapter 7 in *Parallel Processing in Control - the Transputer and other Architectures*, Peter Peregrinus, 1988.

27. Asher GM and Sumner M: Parallelism and the transputer for real time high performance control of ac induction motors, *Proc IEE, Part D*, 1990, vol 137, pp 179-188.

28. Garcia Nocetti F and Fleming PJ: "Implementation of digital controllers on a transputer-based system", *Proc 2nd Int Conf on Applications of Transputers*, Southampton, UK, 1990, pp 135-139.

29. Entwistle PM: *Parallel processing for real-time control*, PhD Dissertation, University College of North Wales, 1990.

30. Walter CJ, Kieckhafer RM and Finn AM: MAFT: A multicomputer architecture for fault-tolerance in real-time control systems *Proc IEEE Real-Time Systems Symposium 1985*, pp 133-140.

31. Thompson HA and Fleming PJ: Fault Tolerant Transputer-Based Controller Configurations for Gas Turbine Engines, *Proc IEE, Part D*, 1990, vol 137, pp 253-260.

Chapter 9

Overview of artificial intelligence tools

P. W. H. Chung, R. Aylett, D. Bental, R. Inder and T. Lydiard

Introduction

With the advent of artificial intelligence (AI) techniques and with the increased interest in applying the new technology to a wide variety of problems, there is a proliferation of software tools marketed for developing knowledge based systems (KBSs). These tools offer different functionalities and their prices range from several hundred to thousands of pounds. One could easily be bewildered by what is available. Furthermore, the simple distinction between PC based expert system shells and hybrid toolkits for engineering workstations is becoming less meaningful due to more efficient implementation of software and to the increasing processing speed and memory capacity of new versions of PC. There are tools that run on high-end PCs that offer similar flexibility and power to those that run on workstations. Tools that run on multi-platforms are also available.

There are many factors that influence the selection of a tool for a particular project. For example, machine availability, supplier credibility, etc. These factors, though important, are not considered in this paper. The primary concern of this paper is to look at the AI aspects of tools and see how they influence tool selection. The objective is, therefore, threefold. First, it describes the AI features that are found in KBS tools. Second, it considers the problem of mapping application characteristics to these tool features. Third, it describes three representative tools that implement some of these features.

2 AI Features

The AI features of a KBS development tool that are considered here are those related to knowledge representation and inference. Issues relating to human computer interface and development environments are not addressed. In the rest of this section we will describe three kinds of representation and inference mechanisms: rules, a number of approaches to handling uncertainty, and objects.

2.1 Rules

Rule-based programming is closely associated with KBSs because many of the early KBSs were implemented in rules. However, it would be wrong to regard KBS and rule-based system as being synonymous. As we shall see later, KBSs can be implemented using other formalisms too. There are a range of rule-based programming tools available. Rule-based programming is also supported within the major KBS development systems.

A rule has the general form

```
IF   these conditions are true
THEN these are the consequences
```

It relates a set of conditions to a set of consequences. A rule-based programming tool must also provide a means of describing facts of some kind—what the system currently believes to be true—in the same format as the conditions and consequences.

As a simple example, let us consider the following two statements:

```
Socrates is a person
Every person is mortal
```

The goal is to represent this information in some unambiguous format so that the computer can manipulate and derive implicit information like `Socrates is mortal`.

The statement about Socrates can be expressed as a fact, and the generalisation about people can be encoded as a rule, as follows:-

```
person(socrates)
If person(X) THEN mortal(X)
```

In this rule, X is said to be a *variable*. Variables can stand for anything, although with the restriction that for any possible application of a rule, no variable can be associated with more than one value. Thus because the fact `person(socrates)` matches the condition part of the rule—provided X is interpreted as `socrates`—the inference engine can infer the fact `mortal(socrates)`.

Because the conclusions from one rule can relate to the conditions of another rule, it allows sets of rules to be used in combinations, or *chained*. There are two modes of combining the inferences from sets of rules: *goal directed* and *data driven*. In the goal directed mode, inference is initiated by asking the system to prove a goal—e.g. `mortal(socrates)`. The goal matches the consequence part of the rule, therefore the system *backward chains* trying to establish `person(socrates)` and it succeeds. In the data driven mode, the system is allowed to deduce whatever follows from a given collection of facts. Whenever all the conditions of a rule are satisfied the consequence is asserted into the knowledge base. If the new facts mean that all the conditions of a rule are now satisfied, that rule is itself evaluated, and its conclusions in turn are added to the database.

Let us consider a less trivial example using rule-based programming. Figure 1 shows a map with five regions on it. The task is to colour this map using three colours (in this case red, green and yellow) so that no two adjacent regions have the same colour. Instead of devising an algorithm for solving the problem, we can write down the problem's constraints as rules and let the system search for solutions that

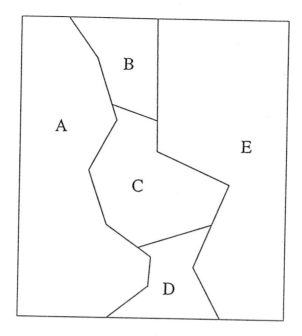

Figure 1: Map

satisfy those constraints. The following is a complete working program, which can be used in either the goal directed or data driven mode, that generates all possible solutions to the problem.

The facts

colour(red)	*Red is a colour....*
colour(green)	*....so is green....*
colour(yellow)	*...and so is yellow.*

The rules

rule 1:   *Only allow two different colours next to each other*

IF	colour(X)	*IF X is a colour....*
AND	colour(Y)	*...and so is Y....*
AND	X ≠ Y	*...and they are different.*
THEN	good-neighbours(X,Y).	*then X and Y are good neighbours.*

rule 2:   *The map is OK if all neighbours are satisfactory*

IF	good-neighbours(A,B)	*IF every pair....*
AND	good-neighbours(A,C)	*...of adjacent regions...*
AND	good-neighbours(A,D)	*...is coloured...*
AND	good-neighbours(B,C)	*in a satisfactory way.*
AND	good-neighbours(C,D)	
AND	good-neighbours(B,E)	
AND	good-neighbours(C,E)	
AND	good-neighbours(D,E)	
THEN	colour-map(A,B,C,D,E).	*....then the map is OK*

There is a superficial similarity between rules and **IF/THEN** statement found in a procedural language. However, they are very different. An **IF** statement in, for instance, Pascal will only be executed when the control of the program reaches that statement. Therefore, it is necessary for the programmer to consider when the statement will be reached and what values will then be held in the variables it accesses. Within a rule-based system, in contrast, execution does not proceed sequentially through the program. A rule is used not when it is encountered but when it's conditions are satisfied or its conclusions are relevant. The inference engine actively looks for facts in the knowledge base that will satisfy the condition parts of the rules. Furthermore, it searches for different ways of satisfying the same rule. In the map colouring example the use of rule 1 will conclude that red can be next to green, red can be next to yellow and so on.

However, control is still a very important issue in rule-based programming. Consider writing a program for playing noughts and crosses. You would have a set of rules for determining the winning moves; a set of rules for stopping the opponent from winning, a set of of rules for setting up forks, etc. A rule for determining the winning position in a row would be something like:

```
IF    row R column C is empty
AND   row R column C2 is x
AND   row R column C3 is x
AND   C2 ≠ C3
THEN  make row R column C an x
```

It is important for the system to recognise that the set of winning rules have higher priority than the other sets of rules. For example, consider the following situation in a game:

The next player has two options, to complete his own line and win the game, or to block his opponent. It is clear that the system should not just make an arbitrary choice from the rules that are currently firable. It should choose to win rather than to stop the opponent from winning.

Some systems provide very few control facilities, in which case the user has to include within rules conditions which pertain to the state of the rule based system. Other systems allows the users to assign numerical priorities to rules. More sophisticated systems allow the user much greater control of the way in which rules are queued for execution. Finally, it is possible to structure a system to include *meta*-rules—i.e. rules which reason primarily about which rules should be fired next.

For more information on rule-based programming see [3].

2.2 Handling Uncertainty

One of the main reasons for considering AI techniques is to deal with problem domains in which there is uncertainty. AI systems offer a range of techniques for dealing with the different sorts of uncertainty that may be encountered. At the highest level these techniques can be separated into two groups. Some techniques support the system in reasoning about one possibility at a time, and aim to prevent interference between them. With the other class of techniques, the system reasons about a single composite state which simultaneously embodies a quantitative representation of every alternative under consideration.

2.2.1 Numeric representations of uncertainty

Numeric uncertainty mechanisms score assertions according to the extent to which they are believed to hold. Most methods score from 'definitely false' through 'possibly false', 'unknown' and 'possibly true' to 'definitely true'. In general, a certainty is assigned to each rule and to each input fact. As inferencing proceeds, suitable scores are associated with the system's conclusions, and these can be used to order them in order to select the most appropriate or likely.

The certainty assigned to the conclusion of a rule will depend on the certainty assigned to the rule and on the certainties of the facts matching the rule's premises. A number of different schemes have been suggested, differing in the basis on which the numbers are derived (i.e. what they mean) and the way in which they are combined. Sometimes a fact may be given two scores: one for the effect of its presence and one for the negative effect of its absence.

The mechanisms that have been proposed include:-

Bayesian probability: Systems based on Bayes' rule are closest to statistical theory. For Bayes' rule to be effective, all factors must be independent, and prior probabilities of premises should be known. These conditions often cannot be met. It is possible to use subjective assessments (i.e. guesses!) of probabilities instead, but these take away any theoretical justification.

Confidence factors: Confidence factors, of the kind used in EMYCIN, are subjective and do not assume independence. They can be used where statistical probabilities are not available but subjective estimates of probabilities can be obtained. Where statistical probabilities are known and factors are independent, confidence factors are less reliable than Bayesian methods. In a deep tree, many insignificant confidence factors will combine to give significant results, which may not be what is wanted. Small differences in confidence factor are not significant. Confidence factors can usefully distinguish between very likely and very unlikely hypotheses, but they will not reliably pick the best of two very likely hypotheses.

Fuzzy logic: Fuzzy logic is used to express the degree to which an item belongs to a particular class. The factors can be combined to express the extent to which an item belongs to a combination of classes.

It is often backward chaining systems that use numeric uncertainty representations. Forward chaining systems tend to neglect uncertainty altogether or to use truth maintenance. Most systems do not allow the user to reason explicitly about the uncertainty of a rule premise. Some exceptions to this may be made for special cases such as unknown, true or false.

Schemes based on probabilities have a sound theoretical base: the numbers to be manipulated have precise definitions and the ways of combining them can be given a principled justification. However, this mathematics assumes that the various factors being combined are statistically independent, and in general this is highly questionable assumption. In contrast, schemes based on levels of confidence lack any rigorous underpinning. They can be used to produce systems with a high level of performance, and analysis of such systems suggests that the precise values of the numeric factors is generally not significant. However, the lack of a firm theoretical foundation suggests that the results of such systems must be evaluated carefully.

2.2.2   Truth Maintenance

Truth maintenance facility is concerned with maintaining the consistence of the knowledge base. It's job is to keep track of current "beliefs", given a set of justifications and assumptions. As a system carries out its inference it modifies its knowledge base by asserting and deleting information reflecting the current model of the world. Since some parts of the model are constructed from other parts, there will be dependencies present between the assertions from which the parts of the model are built. Changes in one part of the model will have repercussions in other parts. Sometimes it is desirable to represent explicitly the dependencies between assertions and the parts that cause those assertions to be made. Whenever some information is deleted from the knowledge base because it is no longer true, all other parts that are supported by it should also be deleted, thus keeping the knowledge base consistent.

For example, due to assumption **A** the system concluded **B**. Making use of this new information the system further concluded **C**. At a later point the system realised that it is no longer reasonable to assume that **A** is true and deleted it. A truth maintenance system would detect that **B** and **C** should also be deleted because they are dependent on **A** being true.

For more information on truth maintenance see [10], [11].

2.2.3   Hypothetical Reasoning

Most KBS development systems support only one *context* (sometimes also called *viewpoint* or *world*), i.e. a knowledge base in one of these systems reflects only one particular situation of the world at any one time. Sometimes it is desirable to make assumptions about what data are true or what decisions should be taken, and then explore the results of those assumptions simultaneously.

Consider the scenario where you want to explore the consequences of implementing two different sets of policies. They may be different maintenance polices for a process plant or they may be economic policies proposed by the Conservative or Labour parties before the next general election. A system that supports hypothetical reasoning will start with a common description of the world and then create two new contexts where the alternatives can be explored separately (see Figure 2).

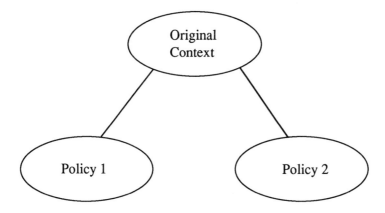

Figure 2: Context Hierarchy

Each context, besides having its own specific information, inherits all of the information from the original description. This avoids duplicating the deduction of information that is common to the child contexts. Inference is performed in them and the intermediate results and the final conclusions can be compared easily If the investigation of a third set of policies is desirable then a third context can be created, again inheriting all the information that is common to the other two contexts. There may be many branches in the context inheritance trees and the tree can grow to many levels deep. Rules can be defined to detect inconsistent contexts to prevent wasteful computation performed in them.

For more information on possible worlds see [6], [7], [8], [9].

2.3 Objects

The basic idea behind *objects* is to provide a way of grouping information together and to provide a way for the objects to communicate with one another. Because of the long and diverse history of the development of object-oriented programming, the term is not very well defined. The commonly accepted characteristics of an object system are

- to represent physical things or concepts through the *class*, *sub-class* and *instance* hierarchy of *objects*.

- to combine data and procedures of individual objects as single entities, i.e. an object should be able to store and process information.

- to invoke computation through objects sending messages to one another.

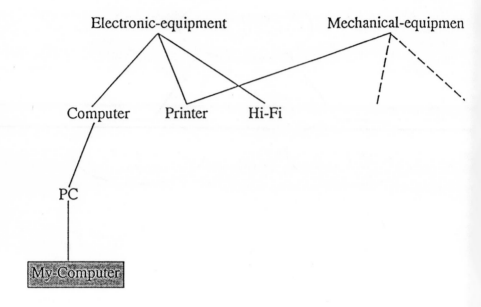

Figure 3: Object Hierarchy

As a simple example, the statements about Socrates and person may be represented as objects as follow:

```
Person                  Socrates
    Attributes              Attributes
        Mortal:  yes            Instance of:  person
        . . . . .               Address:
        . . . . .               . . . . .
```

In this example, `Socrates` is declared as an *instance of* `Person` and it automatically inherits all of the *attributes* of `Person`. Therefore, an object system can infer that Socrates is mortal.

The ideas of specialisation and inheritance are very important in object-oriented programming. They enables the creation of objects that are *almost like* other objects with a few incremental changes and it reduces the need to specify redundant information and simplifies updating and modification. Figure 3 shows a more complex object hierarchy representing electronic equipment and mechanical equipment in different levels of details. One of the branches of the hierarchy shows that *PC* is sub-class of *Computer* and it in turn is sub-class of *Electronic-Equipment*. Since *PC* is a sub-sub-class of *Electronic-Equipment* it will inherit by default of the properties that belong to an electronic equipment, eg it is fragile, its power supply should be 240 volts and so on. The definitions of the class *Computers* or *PC* can over write properties or values that are not appropriate and can add new properties that are specific to them but are not applicable to electronic equipments in general.

Computation in an object system is activated by objects sending *messages* to one another. Therefore, some of the attributes of an object may be procedures (often referred to as *methods*) defining the actions that need to be carried out in response to certain messages.

Object-oriented programming provides a convenient and modular way of describing physical things and concepts. A methodology for designing and implementing object-oriented systems consists of the following basic activities:

- select objects to represent real-world physical objects, and mental concepts.

- decide for each kind of object what local information it should hold.

- decide what the behaviour of each object will be

  − what kind of messages it should respond to.

  − what it should do when it receives each kind of message.

For more information on objects see [12], [24], [21], [22], [23].

2.4 Summary

Research in AI has developed a variety of knowledge representation and inference techniques. This section highlighted some of them, namely rules, truth maintenance, hypothetical reasoning and objects. They are essentially very different but complements one another. They deal with different aspects of reasoning: goal directed reasoning, data driven reasoning, truth maintenance, hypothetical reasoning, default reasoning. Knowledge can be represented as rules or structured objects.

KBS development tools typically incorporate one or more of these techniques. In order to select an appropriate tool for a project it is essential to characterise the application and to consider how its AI features map onto these features. This is the concern of the next section.

3 Mapping applications to tools

The general problem of tool selection is to map the requirements of the application to the type of tool features already discussed. This raises the questions of when and how to uncover the application's requirements, and of what features we should be looking for. Since requirements analysis is a well-established branch of conventional computing, it seems sensible to see if the conventional approach has anything to offer here.

3.1   The conventional approach

Conventional applications development attempts to postpone the issue of tool selection to as late a stage as possible. Development proceeds through an analysis phase, in which the problem to be solved is examined and a detailed specification is produced. This specification then forms the input to the design stage in which first a high-level design is produced, and then a more detailed design in which data structures and algorithms are selected. For instance, the detailed design might incorporate a requirement for linked lists and an insertion sort.

On the basis of the detailed design, it should be possible to make a fairly reliable selection of tool or language, since the vocabulary of data-structures and algorithms is close to the vocabulary used to describe implementation tools. Once the tool is chosen, implementation can begin. The whole process of development is sometimes described as a *waterfall*, since in theory once a stage is completed the developer never returns to it: a complete analysis forms the input to a complete design which acts as the template for implementation.

Even for conventional development, the fact that the tool choice is made so late poses problems. What if you get to implementation and find there is no feasible tool? In general terms, implementation constraints need to be incorporated into the start of the whole process, when the application is selected and its scope is determined. So the developer must have something in mind. Moreover, project organisation in the real world requires that the resources a project will need be costed before it ever gets going.

Two points thus emerge: firstly, that the more that is known about detailed design, the more likely it is that an appropriate tool will be selected. But secondly, that some kind of choice has to be made early on, at least in general terms. So tool selection may not be a once-and-for-all decision, but a refinement process in which the developer homes in on a range of tools and gradually narrows his or her choice down.

For knowledge-based systems, there is of course an additional constraint, which is that development usually involves rapid prototyping. Moreover KBS developers rarely throw away the completed prototype in order to reimplement a 'live' system, but are far more likely to keep developing it incrementally. Thus the prototyping tool may also be the implementation tool, and the choice has to be made early, with minimal analysis. There is therefore a strong requirement for a quick global characterisation of an application which maps onto the features offered by tools.

3.2   Selection by application type?

An interesting approach to this is the work of those who try to categorise applications by the kind of task involved. Some examples of such tasks might be: *diagnosis, monitoring, assessment, repair, planning.* A number of research groups are active in this area, notably that around Chandrasekaran at Ohio State University, and that of Breuker, Wielinga and others in the University of Amsterdam who were major partners in the development of the KADS methodology for KBS construction.

If it were possible to develop a taxonomy or classification for applications based on *tasks* which could be related to *tools*, then the problem of selection would be considerably simplified: the task an application is performing should be determinable early on and easily. We would like to be able to say something like: 'If the task is diagnosis, then we should be using backward-chaining rules', in other words move from the task category to the bundle of appropriate design techniques, which in turn map onto tool features.

Unfortunately life is not so simple. Real applications are often a *mixture* of tasks, as the research groups mentioned above both point out. For instance we may want to *assess* an electronic component, if it's not functioning correctly *diagnose* the fault, and to *generate* a plan to repair it.

There is also a more fundamental objection: the task an application performs may not have a decisive effect on the design techniques it requires. Thus two classic medical diagnosis systems—MYCIN for bacterial blood infections, and CENTAUR for obstructive airways diseases—used quite different techniques: MYCIN backward-chaining rules, and CENTAUR frames of prototype diseases with rules embedded within them. This in spite of the fact that they both performed the same task, diagnosis, in similar domains.

It appears therefore that extracting the kind of application features needed to match tool features requires more than a suitable label for the application. Essentially we need to establish the 'shape' of the design: the key design techniques which will most impact the choice of tool. In other words we are seeking *critical factors* in determining the design.

3.3   Tool selection by critical factor analysis

The method we are proposing runs something like this:

1. Examine the proposed application for critical factors.

2. Use these to select from the currently available set of AI design techniques those that look most appropriate. This requires a knowledge of available techniques and the advantages and disadvantages of each.

3. Map the chosen set of techniques onto the tools which best support them.

It is however important to qualify this checklist. Firstly, we should take into account the lesson from the conventional approach: that it is not necessary to look at *every* available tool initially. The overall size and complexity of a knowledge-based application will normally rule out whole classes of tools, leaving us with a short-list within which more individual critical factors can act as selectors.

Secondly, it must be recognised that most tools will cope with a given application: **with more or less effort** from the implementor, and **to a greater or lesser extent.** Tool and application are, as already argued, interdependent: if the problem doesn't fit the tool, it can usually be cut down to size.

Thirdly, given that early choices are less reliable choices, it is far better to overestimate the power and scope of the required tool than underestimate. As a sweeping generalisation, a large workstation-based AI toolkit will give the implementor more freedom and constrain the scope of the application less. This is just an AI version of the well-known equipment-bid heuristic: always ask for a bit more than you think you need.

3.4   Examples of critical factors

Here we will examine a selection of critical factors: note that they are only a subset of a much greater number that one could consider. Those who feel the need for a more complete view of critical factors should consult references [16], [17] and [18], since these workers have put substantial effort into methods of choosing AI design techniques for an application. Our subset will consist of: deep versus shallow reasoning; enumerated versus constructed solutions; the confidence one can have in the solution; single versus multiple solutions; and—very briefly—some of the factors relating specifically to real-time KBS's.

3.4.1   Deep versus shallow reasoning

Shallow, and deep—or model-based—reasoning represent alternative approaches to a large number of AI applications. To illustrate the difference, let us consider diagnosis of faults on asynchronous computer terminals.

A shallow approach would seek to represent known—or probable—connections between the observed symptoms, possible causes of those symptoms and tests which could confirm the causes. Rules would usually be sufficient to do this:

```
IF 50% of terminal characters are incorrect
THEN test for terminal parity set incorrectly
```

A deep approach would have to represent far more:

* The internal structure of the system—comms line, UART, terminal, host processor.

* The normal behaviour of each of these components

* Simulation of the expected behaviour with a particular fault and comparison with the observed symptoms

* Determination of fault-discriminating tests

Not only is far more knowledge being represented in the deep model, but the knowledge contains far more structure. For this reason it is unlikely that rules alone will provide a very satisfactory representation, and a simple rule-based shell will probably prove extremely constricting.

No judgement is implied here about which approach is the more suitable: this will be influenced by the overall aims of the system, who is to use it, how fast it is to work and how flexible it must be. Some very successful systems have taken a shallow approach, and indeed it is arguable that when an organisation gets started in knowledge-based applications it may be very sensible one to take. What is certain however, is that this initial choice has a major impact on the scale and flexibility of tool required. Indeed, many of the factors that follow need not be considered at all if a shallow approach is sufficient.

3.4.2   *Enumerated versus constructed solutions*

In some knowledge-based applications, there may only be a finite set of answers to problems. If this set is enumerable—that is, small enough to be represented explicitly in the system—then a number of simple techniques are feasible. For example, goal-driven reasoning, in which each possible answer is selected in turn for the system to confirm or disprove, can be applied. It may be possible to produce a system with one rule for each possible solution. Many diagnosis problems have this characteristic—one reason why this area has proved relatively straightforward. But it would be wrong to conclude that all diagnosis is so simple: for example, the research system INTERNIST attacked the problem of *multiple* disease diagnosis, where the tendency for patients to present with symptoms of several disorders produced far more combinations than could be enumerated practically.

In the same way, configuration is an area in which solutions must usually be constructed: though there may be cases where sufficiently few components are involved to make the answers enumerable. This is also true of other application areas involving synthesis, such as planning. Here goal-driven reasoning is usually impractical, while it may be necessary to represent many partial solutions at the same time—Plan A so far, Plan B so far—as well as constraints and consequences. These factors suggest the use of objects, with dynamic creation, and data-driven reasoning.

3.4.3   *Confidence in the solution*

There are at least three reasons why it may not be possible for a system to arrive at a conclusion with 100% confidence. One is that information it requires is missing, another that it is forced to deal with unreliable information, a third that there may be no straightforward way of evaluating its interpretation. We will look at the implications of each—briefly—in turn.

There are many applications in which some knowledge is unobtainable, or very expensive to obtain. Consider for example, the problem of diagnosing faults in a satellite. Some information may only be obtainable by sending an astronaut up to carry out tests: one would not wish to do this just on the off-chance. Different problems may arise where time is important: an industrial process may collapse irretrievably if tests are prolonged, a patient may die while cell cultures to identify an infection precisely are being grown. Finally, it may be risky or undesirable to perform certain tests—as in invasive surgical investigation in medical domains.

Broadly speaking, data-driven reasoning copes with missing knowledge better than goal-driven reasoning. If the system is pursuing a goal for which evidence is unavailable, then that goal is left in an indeterminate state. Reasoning from data means that the maximum will be extracted from knowledge the system does have, while it will not attempt to reason from the missing knowledge.

A further implication of missing information may be the need to represent its absence. A system can do this by incorporating an 'unknown' attribute, or sometimes a 0 certainty factor. Three-valued logic is an extension of this to allow automatic reasoning with *true, false* and *unknown* values. However if it is necessary to assume values for missing data, the system will need support for defaults, and probably for default reasoning. If long chains of reasoning with defaults are likely, then truth maintenance may also be a requirement because of the risk involved.

The ability to handle unreliable information is a much-publicised feature of expert systems like MYCIN and PROSPECTOR. One source of unreliability is the need for human estimates, as in those systems. It is also possible that data may be 'noisy' in some domains where much of it comes through sensor devices. Finally, defaults, as already mentioned above, may be seen as unreliable measures too.

The normal requirement with unreliable pieces of information is some way of measuring the amount of confidence the system has in each. Methods of dealing with uncertainty usually boil down to one of the methods described in Section 2.2: confidence factors, Bayesian statistics and fuzzy logic. All have their advantages and disadvantages: likelihood ratios may produce good results in spite of their ad-hoc nature, Bayesian statistics may frequently represent an overkill, or be applied when necessary criteria, such as independent measures of probabilities, are not met. It is interesting to note that most large AI tool kits do not provide any form of numerical uncertainty handling, but leave the developer to deal with the problem in a domain dependent way.

Finally, in some domains it may be difficult for the system to evaluate its interpretation. A particular area in which this problem arises is that of data fusion, where knowledge from different sources—say sonar, vision, and manipulators—must be combined. In this case the system may need to be able to meta-reason in order to justify its conclusions. This would also require a model-based approach. Additionally, if mistakes are expensive—only one mission can be sent up to repair the satellite, there is only time for one medication if the patient is not to die—the system may need to produce multiple solutions, with measures of confidence in each.

3.4.4   Single versus multiple solutions

We have already seen that there may be domains in which multiple hypotheses must be maintained. This normally implies that a large number of elements are involved in reasoning at any one time, suggesting the use of objects rather than mere variables to represent knowledge. It may be possible to follow each hypotheses through to a conclusion in turn, but if not, the system must support a breadth-first approach in which each hypothesis in turn can be expanded a step at a time.

Where long chains of mutually exclusive hypotheses must be maintained because it is difficult to choose between them at an early stage, more elaborate facilities may be required. These would usually take the form of 'worlds' or 'viewpoints', and are both computationally expensive and a good indicator that a large toolkit is required.

3.4.5   Real time factors

The issues involved in real-time KBS's really require an article to themselves, so only a short summary is provided here. Monitoring and process control are typical areas in which such systems are developed, and the real-time constraints may fall in a very wide range—from say a two-and-a-half hour blast furnace run to a four second heart monitoring response.

Some of the requirements of a KBS in this area are common to any real-time application: for example good data capture facilities, or at least the ability to integrate tightly with a conventional data capture system. A tool with direct access to programming languages is often necessary, while extensive use of dynamic data structures which have to be tidied by a garbage collector—usually at an inconvenient moment—are frequently to be avoided.

Other issues are particular to KBS's. For instance, the system will probably have to be able to respond to arbitrary events, which argues against a goal-driven approach where data not relevant to the current goal would just be ignored. Data-driven reasoning is likely to be preferable.

The KBS must also be able to cope with knowledge and inferences whose status changes over time: an old piece of knowledge may be invalidated by a new one, and in this case all the inferences based on the older knowledge must also be updated. There are a number of techniques that can be applied here: the simplest is the use of recency to perform conflict resolution in a forward-chaining production rule system.

However it may be necessary for the system to carry out explicit time-stamping, and in this case the ability to support structured data-types is required so that value and time can be associated. More powerful than this would be the use of truth maintenance to manage knowledge dependencies; it would be essential to check on the computational power required before this technique was used where real-time constraints are very tight.

Finally, a real-time KBS may need to be able to choose between pursuing new information or following existing inferences. In general, new information will be more reliable, but there may be important exceptions: for instance if a system is monitoring an area in which a fire has broken out, there is a strong probability that sensors will have been damaged and that older readings should be preferred over newer ones. This suggests a requirement for control reasoning, possibly through an agenda.

3.5 Summary

In summary, possibly the most important initial target is to be in the correct ball-park. Once there, more detailed consideration of the type of critical factors discussed above can help the developer home in on an appropriate tool—always remembering that tools and problems interact. In the end, the final choice may not be based AI factors at all, but on what hardware is available, what skills already exist, or on company policy. All the more important that the shortlist is based on tools of appropriate power and flexibility.

For further information see [1], [14], [25], [13], [4], [5], [16], [17], [18].

4   An Overview of Tools

This section aims to give a brief overview of the range of A.I. features available within three knowledge based system development environments and the extent to which these features have been implemented. The tools selected illustrate the differing complexity between tools having superficially similar architectures with Xi Plus representing a simple rule-based shell; ART–IM representing a more complex pattern-matching tool with object-oriented programming capability; and ART representing a highly complex hybrid toolkit development environment incorporating a worlds mechanism. The differing complexity of the tools is reflected by their different hardware requirements.

The AI features of knowledge representation and knowledge base control described in an earlier section are outlined for each tool, and additional information given on their help and debugging facilities, user interface, and external interface.

4.1   Xi Plus

4.1.1   Background

The Xi Plus expert system shell was designed to run on IBM-compatible personal computers, and has recently been ported to ICL and IBM mainframes, Unix machines and DEC's VAX minicomputers. Originally implemented in PROLOG, it has been re-written in C which has improved its speed of execution and integration capabilities to other PC software. It is a largely menu-driven shell but previous programming experience is useful. It has proved to be a popular pc-based expert system shell, being used in banking and finance, engineering, manufacturing, medical, oil industry and many more.

4.1.2   Knowledge Representation

Rules are the main form of knowledge representation. There are two types of rule, the backward-chaining IF-THEN rule and the forward-chaining WHEN-THEN demon. The rules are made up of an identifier/relation/value triple, either using one of the pre-defined relations or by declaring new ones. Pattern-matching rules can also be written, matching on information held in an internal database of facts. These facts can be used to structure identifiers into classes. Membership of a class denoted by the 'is a' relation and attributes of the identifier is denoted by the 'of' connector.

Although the pattern-matching and class membership are limited they do provide a clear mechanism for structuring knowledge and the creation of more general rules. This prevents the knowledge base becoming too verbose and thus difficult to maintain.

4.1.3   Knowledge Base Control

There are two inference mechanisms available within Xi Plus. These are forward and backward chaining. Knowledge bases can contain a mixture of forward and backward chaining rules.

The rules are used in the order in which they appear in the knowledge base. An agenda is maintained of the tasks which need to be done to derive a conclusion or fact. Items on the agenda are dealt with in order of recency, with the tasks most recently added to the agenda being dealt with first. Inferencing stops when no items are left on the agenda.

The programmer has very limited control over the behaviour of the knowledge base by controlling the position of the rules within the knowledge base, and the conditions and consequences of the rules.

4.1.4   Help and Debugging Facilities

Xi Plus provides limited help and debugging facilities to knowledge base developers. Two dictionaries are associated with each knowledge base. These contain entries relevant to the knowledge base such as a list of identifiers, their relations and assertions; and entries relevant to system building. The dictionaries are available at most points in the development system and are context-related.

The Xi Plus manual suggests that a considerable amount of validation can be carried out by the expert simply reading the rules to ensure their correctness and provides guidelines to follow in terms of validating your knowledge base. However some debugging facilities are provided by the shell itself. These include a WHY facility which causes the rules that led to a particular question to be displayed, and rule traces which present detailed information of the Xi Plus reasoning process for that knowledge base. These facilities are adequate for the type of application developed using this software.

4.1.5   User Interface

There are a number of default forms which can be used to obtain input from the user. These were very easy to use and could be customised in terms of size, colour and position of text. The user interface is limited but effective.

4.1.6   External Interfaces

Very little is provided in the way of access to other commonly used file formats. A READ function is provided to ASCII, DIF, SYLK and WKS files. The source code is provided together with guidelines on how to code up other functions such as WRITE. Good access is provided to other languages such as C, BASIC and ASSEMBLER through a user program interface and there is a built-in facility for executing DOS commands.

Access to data held in other software is provided primarily through a high level interface which can call large user programs and other software products such as spreadsheets, databases and word processors directly from the knowledge base. This can be achieved either by loading the program into memory alongside Xi Plus or by rolling Xi Plus out to disk to make space for the called program.

4.1.7   Xi Plus—Summary

Xi Plus provides facilities for a rule-based programming style of system development with knowledge represented as simple pattern-matching rules and facts. There is limited knowledge base control available although both forward and backward chaining inference are provided. Help and debugging facilities are restricted to dictionaries and traces. Easy access is provided to other PC software products, user programs and programming languages.

4.2   ART–IM

4.2.1   Background

ART–IM (Automated Reasoning Tool for Information Management) is a new product which has been designed specifically to support knowledge based systems development and delivery on PCs and mainframes, conforming to IBM SAA standards. There are also workstation versions for DEC, HP, IBM, SUN and APOLLO. It is implemented in C and there is strong emphasis placed on its ability to be embedded within large existing applications. It offers a range of AI programming styles in an interactive menu-based environment which allows easy monitoring of knowledge-base development or execution via an integrated network of menus and windows. ART–IM is currently being used for knowledge-based systems in a variety of domains, including financial and auditing systems, real-time monitoring, diagnosis and control, engineering design support and operations optimisation.

4.2.2   Knowledge Representation

Although primarily a forward-chaining rule-based system, ART–IM provides a variety of methods of knowledge representation such as facts, schemata, rules, and objects. A mixture of these can be used in a knowledge base. Relations are used to connect a schema to one or more other schemata. Declarative informative is held in facts and schemata, and procedural knowledge is held in rules and functions. ART–IM provides two pre-defined inheritance relations; the *is-a* and the *instance-of* relations. In addition to the pre-defined inheritance relations, non-inheritance relations can be defined by the user.

ART–IM is a rule-based programming tool, supporting an extensive pattern-matching language which is invoked by patterns held within the rules. These rules become active whenever the patterns are matched by information held within the ART–IM memory, causing procedural code to be executed. ART–IM provides an easy-to-use procedural language together with a wide variety of pre-defined functions. Additional functions can be defined using ART–IM procedural language or the C programming language. Object-oriented programming is also available.

4.2.3   Knowledge Base Control

Essentially ART–IM is a forward-chaining system but backward-chaining can be implemented easily. The flow of control within the knowledge base is designed to be opportunistic with each rule coded in such a way that it will be invoked only when the LHS pattern matches information currently contained in memory. An agenda is maintained of rules whose conditions have been matched. The order in which rules are fired is based on the result of the most recent action, leading to a depth-first exploration of the possibilities.

There are a number of mechanisms available to the programmer to influence the knowledge base control. These include the use of control facts—conditions which make the firing of the rule dependent upon the state of the expert system itself—meta-rules—rules affecting the order of firing of other rules—and salience which is a numerical priority which can be associated with a rule.

4.2.4 Help and Debugging Facilities

An extensive hypertext-style context-sensitive help system is provided within the studio. This is divided into three sections; help using the studio itself; help with the ART–IM language; and help with the user interface toolkit. Help is provided either as an on-line tutorial session for new users or as a series of reference cards for more experienced users, with an index which refers to both.

The ART–IM studio provides an interactive debugging environment, with menu-driven facilities for controlling and monitoring applications during execution. An extensive network of browsers is provided for editing and debugging. This can be used to browse schemata, rules and facts and colour coding of the source definition indicates the current status of that object. Trace points can be set for individual or entire classes of objects such as schemata, rules and facts, and the agenda and rule activations can also be traced.

4.2.5 User Interface

A specific user interface toolkit has been incorporated which provides a series of functions for the development of pull-down menus, boxes, push-button type controls etc. operating in a windows environment. A number of default constructs are available. The system itself does not provide any graphics facilities, but it is intended to be used with a graphics package which can be purchased separately.

4.2.6 External Interfaces

ART–IM can call or be called by other C routines easily and data can be exchanged between ART–IM and C in a number of ways. Calls to DOS are also made easily. A generic integration facility is provided which allows the format of external data records to be defined and mapping functions used to obtain the data.

4.2.7 ART–IM—Summary

ART–IM is a very powerful tool incorporating a high degree of sophistication. It supports a range of knowledge representations with pattern-matching rules based around facts and schemata, and object-oriented programming with message passing between objects. A number of schema relations are provided. Inference can be forward or backward chaining and mechanisms for influencing the flow of control within the knowledge base are available. Extensive help and debugging facilities are provided. A good end-user interface can be developed and generic interfacing to external data is available.

4.3 ART

4.3.1 Background

Belonging to the same family of products as ART–IM is ART (Automated Reasoning Tool). ART is a well-established hybrid toolkit first released in March 1985. It is implemented in LISP and runs on workstations only. It has been used mainly by Research and Development groups for developing large knowledge based systems.

ART incorporates all of the features previously seen in ART–IM and many more. These differences will be made clear throughout the overview.

4.3.2   Knowledge Representation

The knowledge representation and the majority of the syntax of ART and ART–IM are identical, with representation as rules, schemata and facts. However it is common to force the programmer to program in the underlying LISP system directly as well as using the higher level language of ART rules. Object-oriented programming within ART is more extensive than in ART–IM, including both object-oriented and access-oriented programming; qualifiers to be attached to the messages to determine the order of execution of actions on an object; and messages to be defined having the same name but attached to and acting differently upon a number of objects.

ART also contains a more extensive set of pre-defined relations, and both inheritance and non-inheritance relations can be user-defined.

However the main difference between ART and ART–IM lies in the fact that ART possesses a powerful viewpoint mechanism. The viewpoint mechanism provides a means of carrying out hypothetical reasoning or "what-if" analysis by enabling contradictory possibilities to be explored. This has not been implemented in ART–IM but this is probably a restriction of the development platform.

4.3.3   Knowledge Base Control

ART is a forward-chaining system, with backward-chaining is also available. In both ART and ART–IM, backward chaining is achieved within an essentially forward chaining system by means of goal facts. These identify a particular proposition pattern as a goal, and its presence directs the normal forward-chaining mechanism to select rules on the basis of their relevance to this goal. Unlike ART–IM where the user must explicitly generate the goal fact in the action part of a rule, ART will generate a goal fact for a proposition whenever facts with that pattern would contribute to the matching of a rule. This mechanism gives true goal-directed (backward chaining) behaviour integrated smoothly within a data-directed (forward chaining) system.

The same knowledge base control features are available here as for ART–IM, that is meta-rules, control facts and salience.

4.3.4   Help and Debugging Facilities

The help and debugging facilities are more extensive than in ART–IM, providing a graphical representation of the knowledge base. However the selectable text system and programmable hypertext system used within ART–IM are not available.

4.3.5   User Interface

The user interface facilities within ART are good, with the usual range of menus, boxes etc. An integral graphics package called ARTIST (ART Imagery Synthesis

Tool) is included. ARTIST can be used to create animated graphics, windows, menus etc and thus build an intelligent interface.

4.3.6 External Interfaces

Until recently external interfacing has not been seen as important since the fact and schema system provide an internal database. However Release 3.00 of ART will incorporate automatic generation of SQL queries and interface to LOTUS 1-2-3.

4.3.7 ART—Summary

ART is a very sophisticated development environment, having a variety of knowledge representations which have been implemented more fully than ART–IM, and a viewpoint mechanism. A number of schemata relations have been provided and new inheritance and non-inheritance relations can be defined. Inference can be forward or backward chaining and mechanisms for influencing the flow of control within the knowledge base are available. Extensive help and debugging facilities are provided. A good end-user interface can be developed, incorporating graphics. Automatic SQL queries can be generated and access is provided to LOTUS 1-2-3 spreadsheet files.

4.4 Summary

It is clear from the brief overviews given above that although all of these tools share the same principal architecture, namely pattern-matching rules, there are significant differences between them. This is seen most clearly when looking at the structuring of the internal database used in pattern-matching. The fact system of Xi Plus is primitive when compared to the schema system and relations of ART–IM, which is itself only a subset of the schema system and relations found in ART. Other features such as knowledge base control, help and debugging and user interface capabilities show increased complexity with increased sophistication of knowledge representation.

However this pattern does not necessarily follow with respect to integration facilities. Complex internal database structures have provided an alternative to using external data sources such as database or spreadsheet packages and led to the development of stand-alone knowledge based systems. Where there no internal database, or a very simple one, integration with external data sources has been seen as essential. Similarly for tools with a simple knowledge representation language integration with an external language has been considered important to greatly extend the functionality of that tool. Tools having a rich knowledge representation language have had less need for this functionality. This pattern has been changing recently with more and more tools providing access to external languages and data sources so that knowledge base components can be better integrated with conventional applications and routines.

Table 1 gives a brief comparison of the tools in terms of the range of features they possess. As can be clearly seen from the table, the more sophisticated the software, the bigger machine that is required to run it, and the greater the cost.

	Xi Plus	ART–IM	ART
price (approx)	£2000	£5000	£12000
hardware	PC	PC + 2MB	workstation
representation	rules facts	rules facts objects	rules facts objects hypothetical reasoning
control	limited	good	good
debugging	limited	good	extensive
user interface	limited	good	extensive
external interface	product programmable	generic	some

Table 1: Comparison of Tools

Further information on these tools can be found in references [2], [15], [20], [19] available from AIAI, University of Edinburgh, 80 South Bridge, Edinburgh EH1 1HN, Tel. 031-225-4464.

Acknowledgements

The work forming the basis for this article was carried out at AIAI under contract to the European Space Operations Centre and under the AI Support for Engineers Project, funded by the Computing Facilities Committee of the Science and Engineering Research Council as part of their Engineers Applications Support Environment (EASE) Programme.

References

[1] J. Breuker, B. Wielinga, P. de Greef, R. de Hoog, M. van Someren, J. Wiele-
maker, J. Billaut, M. Davoodi, and S. Hayward. Model-driven Knowledge
Aquisition: Interpreatation Models. Deliverable Task A1, Esprit Project 1098,
University of Amsterdam, STL, 1987.

[2] Jason Brown. Product Evaluation : Xi Plus Version 3.0. *KEG*, (127), 1990.

[3] Lee Brownston, Robert Farrell, Elaine Kant, and Nancy Martin. *Programming Expert Systems in OPS5 - An Introduction to Rule-Based Programming.*
Addison Wesley, 1985.

[4] B. Chandrasekaran. Generic Tasks in Knowledge-based Reasoning: High Level
Building Blocks for Expert System Design. *IEEE Expert*, pages 23 – 30, Fall
1986.

[5] B. Chandrasekaran. Generic Tasks as Building Blocks for Knowledge-based
Systems: the diagnosis and routine-design examples. *Knowledge Engineering
Review*, 3(3):183 – 219, 1988.

[6] J. de Kleer. Choices Without Backtracking. *Proceedings of AAAI-84*, pages
79 – 85, 1984.

[7] J. de Kleer. An Assumption-based Truth Maintenance System. *Artificial
Intelligence*, 28:127 – 162, 1986.

[8] J. de Kleer. Extending the ATMS. *Artificial Intelligence*, 28:163 – 196, 1986.

[9] J. de Kleer. Problem Solving With The ATMS. *Artificial Intelligence*, 28:197
– 224, 1986.

[10] J. Doyle. A Truth Maintenance System. *Artificial Intelligence*, 12:231 – 272,
1979.

[11] J. Doyle. The Ins and Outs of Reason Maintenance. *Proceedings of IJCAI-8*,
pages 349 – 351, 1983.

[12] A. Goldberg and D. Robson. *SMALLTALK-80*. Addison Wesley, 1983.

[13] F. Hayes-Roth, D. Waterman, and D. Lenat (eds). *Building Expert Systems.*
Addison-Wesley, 1983.

[14] F. R. Hickman, J. L. Killin, L. Land, T. Mulhall, D. Porter, and R. M. Tay-
lor. *Analysis for Knowledge-based Systems - a practical guide to the KADS
methodology.* Ellis Horwood, 1989.

[15] Robert Inder. The State Of The ART. *AIAI-TR-41*, June 1988. Also published
in Expert System Applications, (ed. Sunil Vadera), Sigma Press 1989.

[16] P. Kline and S. Dolins. Choosing Architectures for Expert Systems. Technical
Report RADC-TR-85-192, Rome Air Development Center, 1985.

[17] P. Kline and S. Dolins. Problem features that influence teh design of expert systems. *Proceedings of American AI Association*, pages 956 – 962, 1986.

[18] P. Kline and S. Dolins. *Designing expert systems: A guide to selecting implementation techniques.* John Wiley and Sons, 1989.

[19] Terri Lydiard. PC-Based Expert System Shells: A Survey of Their External Interfaces. *AIAI-TR-80*, May 1990. also published in BUG Technical Report for Software Developers Vol. 1, No. 1, and AIRING No. 9, Jan 1990.

[20] Terri Lydiard. Product Evaluation : ART-IM Version 1.5. *AIAI-TR-79*, May 1990.

[21] OOPSLA. *Proceedings OOPSLA Conference - 1986.* ACM Press, 1986.

[22] OOPSLA. *Proceedings OOPSLA Conference - 1987.* ACM Press, 1987.

[23] OOPSLA. *Proceedings OOPSLA Conference - 1988.* ACM Press, 1988.

[24] Mark Stefik and Daniel G. Bobrow. Object-Oriented Programming: Themes and Variations. *The AI Magazine*, 6(4), Winter 1986.

[25] B. Wielinga and N. Shadbolt. Conceptualisation of a Knowledge Engineering Workbench. Deliverable Del 1.4, Esprit Project P2576, University of Amsterdam, 1990.

Chapter 10

Application of fuzzy logic to control and estimation problems

B. Postlethwaite

1.   INTRODUCTION

Several commercial applications of fuzzy logic to control problems
already exist, with the most obvious being that of cement kiln control.
However, since I expect that other speakers will be discussing these
applications, this chapter concentrates on application studies carried
out within the Chemical Engineering Department at Strathclyde University.

The second section of this chapter describes application studies using a
fermenter problem. Both rule-based and relational models were
investigated and it was found that both could produce very good results.

The third section of the chapter describes the early stages of work on a
project to apply relational modelling techniques to the control of a
real industrial process.

2.   APPLICATION TO FERMENTATION PROBLEMS

Processes involving the large-scale culture of micro-organisms, or
fermentations, are important and becoming more so as the biological
sciences advance. Traditionally fermentation was associated with the
food and drink industries, but now is of major importance in the
production of drugs and other medical materials. In the future, it is
probable that genetically engineered organisms will be used in the
production of many substances which are currently manufactured, at high
energy cost, by the conventional chemical industry.

The control of fermentations has always been problematic. This is not
really surprising since effective control requires providing the correct
environment for many millions of micro-organisms all at different stages
in their life cycle. Temperature and pH are important environmental
variables in a fermentation, and both are affected by the microorganisms
themselves, but probably more important are the concentrations of the
various compounds within the fermentation broth. This broth not only
includes the micro-organisms and water but also substances which are
added such as substrates, nutrients, anti-foam agents, pH regulators,
etc., as well as substances which are produced by the organisms
themselves. Changes in the fermentation environment may inhibit micro-
organism growth and/or may reduce, or stop, the production of desired
compounds. The control problem is further complicated by the fact that
many of the important environmental variables cannot be directly
measured on-line.

For these reasons, most fermentations are manually controlled, and the operators of these processes usually have a good idea of how their charges will behave under most operating conditions. The object of the work described in this section was to investigate whether the 'process understanding' of the operators of fermentation processes could be reproduced as qualitative models within a fuzzy framework.

2.1   Description of the Problems

At an early stage in the work it was decided to base the initial investigations on a standard mathematical simulation of a process rather than on a real fermentation. The primary reason for this decision was the problems in obtaining data from real processes.

The simulation chosen was that used by Takamatsu et al[1], and represented a fed-batch fermenter used for the production of Bakers Yeast. A fed-batch fermenter begins operation with a small volume of cells, substrate and nutrients, which is gradually increased as the fermentation proceeds by the addition of fresh feed. The rate at which this fresh feed is added is an important variable which can be used to manipulate the conditions in the fermenter. The model used is expressed by the equations

$$\frac{d(VX)}{dt} = g\ VX + a_1\ Y_{X/e}\ V_e\ VX$$

$$\frac{d(VS)}{dt} = F\ S_o - g\ VX/Y - mVX - a_2 \pi\ e/Y_{e/s}\ VX$$

$$\frac{d(VCe)}{dt} = a_2\ \pi\ e\ VX - a_1\ Ve\ VX$$

$$\frac{d(VP)}{dt} = K_1\ VX + K_2\ g\ VX$$

$$\frac{dV}{dt} = F$$

$$\alpha = \frac{dX}{dt}\ /X$$

where   X   =   concentration of biomass $(g.1^{-1})$
S   =   concentration of substrate $(g.1^{-1})$
P   =   concentration of inhibiting substance $(g.1^{-1})$
E   =   concentration of ethanol $(g.1^{-1})$
V   =   working liquid volume (1)
π_e =   specific production rate of ethanol (hr^{-1})
=   0.155 + 0.123 log S
V_e =   specific growth rate produced by consumption of substrate (hr^{-1})
=   0.138 - 0.062P + 0.0028/(S-0.28)

$$g = \text{specific growth rate produced by consumption of substrate (hr}^{-1})$$

$$= g_{max} \, S/(K_s + S)(1+ P^2)$$

$$a_1 = 0, \, a_2 = 1 \text{ for } S > 0.28$$

$$a_1 = 1, \, a_2 = 0 \text{ for } S \leqslant 0.28$$

$$K_1 = 0.0023, \, K_2 = 0.0070, \, K_s = 0.025, \, m = 0.03, \, Y = 0.5$$

$$g_{max} = 0.42, \, Y_{x/e} = 0.48, \, Y_{e/s} = 0.51$$

The control objective for this fermentation is to maximise the production of biomass, and this can only be achieved if cell growth rate is made to follow a precise trajectory. Operation away from this trajectory will lead to some of the substrate being used for the production of ethanol rather than biomass, and/or excess production of inhibitor. A major problem in achieving this growth rate control is that, in real fermenters, it is rather difficult to directly measure growth rate on-line.

A useful test of the applicability of fuzzy logic to fermentation problems was therefore felt to be the production of an estimator for the apparent specific growth rate of cells. To provide data for estimator development the simulation model was run with three different constant feed rates over a simulated sixteen-hour period. A further sixteen-hour run with a linearly increasing feed rate was also carried out to provide extra test data.

2.2 Generation of fuzzy reference sets

The first step in the construction of any fuzzy model is the generation of appropriate reference sets used to link real-world values to fuzzy qualitative terms. In this work, it was decided that all the required reference sets would be defined with triangular membership functions. The triangular functions were chosen because they could be easily defined and easily incorporated into computer code. Initially, non-overlapped membership fuctions (see Figure 1a) were used, but these were soon replaced by fully-overlapped functions (Figure 1b) which proved to have the advantages of easier definition and a smoother transition between adjacent reference sets.

Two methods were used to fix the numerical values which marked the boundaries of the reference sets. The first method of 'educated guess-work' was used to generate one batch of reference sets for the rule-based estimator and two for the relational model. The second method, which involved dividing each variables range into sub-intervals such that equal numbers of observations fell within each sub-interval, was used to generate a further group of reference sets for the relational model.

.3 The rule-based model

The development of an effective rule-based estimator was found to require process of trial-and-error. Initially, the variables considered to ost affect the apparent specific growth rate were the substrate,

inhibitor and cell concentrations, and using these variables the
following set of rules was stipulated:

1.   If S is ZERO then α is ZERO
2.   If P is LARGE then α is ZERO
3.   If P is MEDIUM and (X is MEDIUM or LARGE) and
     (S is SMALL or ZERO) then α is SMALL
4.   If (P is SMALL or ZERO)) and S is SMALL then α is MEDIUM
5.   If S is LARGE then α is LARGE

When run using the data provided by the simulation experiments at the
lowest and highest constant feedrates, the rule-based estimator produced
the results summarised in Tables I and II. Table I shows the estimator
performing very badly, and the reason for this can be discovered by
examining Figure 2. Substrate concentration rises to a peak after one
hour and then rapidly falls away to a very low value as the small feed
rate becomes unable to replace the substrate consumed by the growing
cells. After three hours, the substrate concentration is close to zero,
but in spite of this a high growth rate is maintained. This is because
the cells switch from producing to consuming ethanol. This eventuality
was not allowed for in the original rule-base. Figure 2 also shows cell
growth even at very low values of substrate and ethanol concentration,
and in this phase the growth rate seems to be limited by the concentration of inhibitor. This effect indicated that some additional modification to the rule-base was required. Also, the second trial, summarised
in Table II, indicated that the high dilution rates occurring at the
start of high flowrate runs seriously reduced the apparent specific
growth rate.

As a result of the observations listed above, the initial rule-base was
modified to give:

1.   If S is ZERO and (E is ZERO or SMALL) then α is SMALL
2.   If P is LARGE then α is ZERO
3.   If S is ZERO and (E is MEDIUM or LARGE) then α is MEDIUM
4.   If (D is SMALL or ZERO) and S is SMALL then α is MEDIUM
5.   If P is MEDIUM then α is SMALL
6.   If S is LARGE then α is LARGE
7.   If X is SMALL and D is LARGE then α is SMALL
8.   If S is MEDIUM then α is MEDIUM.

Again, the rule-base was tested against the simulation results, and
subsequently modified and retested iteratively until an acceptable
performance was obtained. This process required around seven major
modification steps and several more minor changes. The final rule base
is given below:

1.   If (S is not (ZERO) or E is not (ZERO)) and P is LARGE then
     α is SMALL
2.   If (S is not (ZERO) or E is not (ZERO)) and P is MEDIUM then
     α is MEDIUM
3.   If (S is not (ZERO) or E is not (ZERO)) and (P is ZERO or
     SMALL) then α is LARGE
4.   If P is LARGE then α is ZERO
5.   If D is LARGE then α is NEGATIVE LARGE
6.   If D is MEDIUM then α is ZERO

7.   If P is MEDIUM then α is SMALL.

As you will see, the cell concentration, X, is no longer included in
the final rule-set as its inclusion did not seem to improve the
estimator's performance. It also appears that, for as long as they are
not zero, the magnitudes of the substrate and ethanol concentrations are
not important and that the growth rate is regulated by the inhibitor
concentration. High dilution rates also appear to have a major effect
on the growth rate.

Figures 3, 4 and 5 show the performance of the final rule-base for each
of the sets of the development data, and Figure 6 shows its performance
using the test data set. Overall, the performance of the estimates is
very good with a mean deviation between the predicted and actual growth
rates of 0.023 hrs^{-1} and a mean percentage deviation of 29.8%. The
poorest fit occurs in the data represented in Figure 3 between four and
six hours into the fermentation. The mismatch between predicted and
actual growth ratio occurs when both ethanol and substrate concentrations were close to zero, and it was not possible to find a simple rule
to represent this area which did not seriously unbalance the rule base.

The effects of another source of deviation can be seen in Figures 4,5
and 6, although most noticeable in Figure 5 between three and five hours
into the fermentation. The kink in the predicted line was found to be
caused by rule 3 and, in particular, the combination

(P is ZERO or SMALL)

The problem is caused by the method chosen to represent the OR
combination, in this case by taking the maximum grade of truth of the
two conditions. Between three and five hours the inhibitor concentration
moves between the zero and small regions. In making this transition
there is a dip in the degree of truth of the condition (P is zero or
small) and, as a result of this dip, the degree of truth of the rule
and hence its result, a large growth rate, is also reduced. An
alternative method of composition based on probabilistic expressions
was tried in an effort to reduce this problem, but it was found that
the overall performance of the estimator was significantly reduced,
suggesting that the rule-base is sensitive to the method of fuzzy
composition.

The computational requirements of the rule-based model were minimal and
the program, which was initially developed using FORTRAN on an IBM XT,
now runs for demonstration purposes on an AMSTRAD PCW coded in BASIC.

The main problem with rule-based modelling was found to be the length
of time required to develop the rules. The trial-and-error development
process required the attentions of someone with a good process knowledge
and a familiarity with the fuzzy modelling technique.

2.4   The relational model

Since the development of the relational model followed that of the rule-
based, what is perhaps the most difficult stage in this type of modelling,
structural identification, had already been completed. All that was
required was to identify a relational matrix which linked the four

input variables (the substrate, ethanol and inhibitor concentrations and the dilution rate) to the single output, the apparent specific growth rate.

The identification algorithms described by Czogala and Pedrycz[2] and Pedrycz[3] were applied to the data and the best performing model was obtained from the second method. Briefly, the Pedrycz method operates in the following way:

The initial relational matrix is set to zero

i.e. $R_o = 0$

Each I/O data set is processed in turn to identify elements in the array according to

$$R_k = \max(U_{1_k} \times U_{2_k} \times U_{3_k} \times U_{4_k} \times Y_k, R_{k-1})$$

where $U_{1_k} \dots U_{4_k}$ are matrices containing memberships of the reference sets for the four input variable of data set k

Y_k is a matrix containing the membership of the reference sets for the output variable for data set k.

The operator X denotes the cartesian product and in this work the individual results of this are taken to be the products of the appropriate membership values.

Although the Pedrycz method gave the best results it was found that when the same reference sets as the rule-based model were used, the identified relational model's performance was considerably inferior (with an overall mean error of 0.034 hrs^{-1} as opposed to 0.023 hrs^{-1}). Modifying the fuzzy reference sets improved the relational model's fit and dropped the mean prediction error to 0.028 hrs^{-1}.

In an effort to further improve the relational model, a self-learning algorithm similar to that described by XU & LU[4], was applied. The self-learning algorithm differs from the identification algorithm in that it makes multiple passes through the input/output data and modifies the relational array in such a way as to reduce the differences between the predicted and simulated outputs. Symbolically, the modified XU & LU method is as follows; the starting point is a relational matrix which has been previously identified using the Pedrycz method

$$\therefore \quad R_o \neq 0$$

This matrix is then modified by the self-learning algorithm, which makes repeated passes through the I/O data until convergence is achieved.

During each pass, the matrix is modified by every set of I/O data according to:

$$R_k(s,i,j,l,m) = \begin{cases} a_s d_{s_k} + (1-a_s)R_{k-1} \ (s,i,j,l,m), \text{ if the entry was used to make a prediction} \\ R_{k-1} \ (s,i,j,l,m) \quad \text{otherwise} \end{cases}$$

d_{s_k} is defined as

$$d_{s_k} = U_{1_k}(i) * U_{2_k}(j) * U_{3_k}(1) * U_{4_k}(m) * Y(s)$$

where * represents a fuzzy AND combination.

a_s , the learning coefficient is defined as

$$a_s = h \, \beta_s / \mathcal{E}_k /$$

where   h = tuning constant

β_s = relative contribution factor = $Y'(s)^2$

$\mathcal{E}_k$ = prediction error = $y_k - y'_k$

The use of the self-learning algorithm produced a relational model with a predictive performance which was equal to that of the rule-based equivalent, even when the original reference sets were used.

Further experiments were carried out to examine how the identification and self-learning algorithms responded to noise in the input/output data.   It was found that the algorithm's sensitivity to noise was a function of the reference sets used, but that with the correct choice of reference sets very high levels of noise could be tolerated.

In all cases, it was found that, once the relational model structure had been set up, the identification and self-learning algorithms, running on an IBM AT, produced models from the input/output data sets in a matter of seconds.   The actual coding required to create the relational structure was, however, found to be more complicated than that for a rule-based model.

3.   APPLICATION TO A PRODUCTION LINE PROBLEM

The work described in this section is an industrially based project which is supported by the Science and Engineering Research Council (Grant Ref GR/F5734.2) and the company concerned.   The work is at an early stage, and the project described here is intended as a learning exercise for the research staff involved.

3.1   Description of the Problem

The principal product of the company who are   partially supporting the project, is a very thin-walled hollow casing.   This casing is extruded from a gel and for most of the subsequent process is handled as a continuous length and transported by conveyer belts and rollers.

A part of the process involves the casing being immersed in a chemical treatment bath.   The arrangement of the bath is shown in Figure 7. The casing arrives at the bath on a variable speed conveyer belt and is distributed into the bath by a fixed speed oscillating arm.   The surface on to which the casing falls at the bottom of the bath is a fixed speed conveyor belt which moves the distributed casing down the bath , away from the feed point.   The casing is removed from the bath by a set of nip rollers.

The length of time the casing spends in this treatment bath is
considered to have important consequences for downstream operations,
and either inadequate or excess treatment times can cause problems.
Currently the treatment time is controlled manually. The average
treatment time is inferred by the operaters from the position of the
leading edge of the casing within the bath , and this position is
controlled by altering either the take-off or feed speeds.

The company were investigating a method of automating this position
control by means of limit switches to detect the casing position. This
would obviously lead to oscillation between the limit positions and it
was suggested that a model which could continuously predict the casing
leading-edge position within the bath could be used instead of, or as a
supplement to, the limit switches. The production of such a model would
not be a trivial exercise, since the packing density of the casing in
the bath varies non-linearly (and sometimes discontinuously!) with the
feed and take-off speeds, and the casing itself may shrink or stretch.

3.2   Obtaining the Data

The only directly measurable variables which were likely to affect the
leading edge position were the feed and take-off speeds and casing
diameter. Discussions with the operators, and direct observation,
revealed that significant diameter changes only occurred when the
product specification was changed. To simplify the construction of the
model it was decided, therefore, to construct a model for one particular
specification of casing and to use only the feed and take-off speeds as
input measurements.

To gather the data required for model identification, there are two
methods. The first is to record actual operating data, and the second
method is to deliberately carry out experiments, in this case by
altering feed and take-off speeds. The use of operating data has the
significant advantage of not requiring the process to be disturbed, but
does have the disadvantages of no guarantee of full coverage of operating
regimes and no record of external disturbances to the process. After
discussion with the process operators it was decided that the second
method; of direct experimentation, was most suitable.

The first stage in devising a set of experiments was to establish normal
operating ranges for take-off and feed speeds, and this was done by
talking to several operators and observing the operation of the process
lines. A program of experiments was then constructed which covered the
whole range of feasible operating conditions, and this required eighteen
experiments. During each experiment the position of the casing leading
edge was recorded over a period of at least forty minutes.

3.3   Modelling

Examination of the data produced by the experiments revealed that the
leading edge position changed at a constant rate within each experiment,
and this indicated to us that the actual position of the edge could be
ignored as an input variable to any model. For relational modelling of
the treatment bath   five potential model structures were therefore

evaluated:

a) Feed and Take-off speed to rate of change of position
b) Feed speed and speed difference to rate of change of position
c) Take-off speed and speed difference to rate of change of position
d) Feed and Take-off speeds and speed difference to rate of change
    of position
e) Speed difference to rate of change of position.

The results of the evaluation are shown in Table III, and it is clear
that the best performance is achieved with structure (d). The results
for this structure are shown in more detail in Table IV. From these
results it can be seen that several experiments contribute very large
deviations to the overall total. Investigation revealed that in most
cases the experiments which produced the largest deviations had been
subject to external upsets, ranging from line failures to someone
manually re-arranging the casing in the bath! These experiments will
be repeated and hopefully results from the final model will be available
for presentation at the school in September.

4.   Conclusions

The work carried out at Strathclyde has confirmed, in our minds at
least, that fuzzy logic has a real part to play in the modelling of
complex or ill-defined systems. It has been demonstrated that rule-
based and relational systems can be made to represent the sort of
processes occurring in fermentation, and that relational modelling is
easily applied to real industrial problems.

On the question of whether rule-based, or relational modelling, is best
it has been our experience that rule-based modelling brings the modeller
closer to the problem and that the resultant models are easier to
understand, but that relational models are very much quicker to develop.
The choice of which type of fuzzy model to use is therefore very
dependent on the application.

References

1.   Takamutsu, T., Shioya, S., Okada, Y. and Kanda, H. Biotechnology
     and Bioengineering, 27(1985), pp 1675-1686.

2.   Czogala, E. and Pedrycz, W.   Fuzzy Sets and Systems, 6(1981),
     pp 73-83.

3.   Pedrycz, W.   Fuzzy Sets and Systems, 13 (1984), pp 153-167.

4.   Xu, C.W. and Lu, Y.Z.   IEEE Tran. on Systems, Man and
     Cybernetics, SMC-17(4), 1987, pp 683-689.

TABLE I - Results for a Rule-based Model at a Low Feed Rate

Time (hr)	4.0	6.0	8.0	10.0	12.0	14.0	16.0
Estimated	0	0	0	0	0	0	0
Actual	0.26	0.20	0.061	0.039	0.03	0.02	0.014

TABLE II - Results for a Rule-based Model at a High Feed Rate

Time (hr)	4.0	6.0	8.0	10.0	12.0	14.0	16.0
Estimated	0.29	0.30	0.30	0.051	0.033	0	0
Actual	0.22	0.28	0.30	0.23	0.074	0.051	0.03

TABLE III - Comparison of Structure for Treatment Batch Model

	Structure				
	a	b	c	d	e
Mean deviation (cm.min^{-1})	0.14	0.20	0.31	0.086	0.32

TABLE IV - Full Results for Structure (d)

Feed Speed (ft.min⁻¹)	Take-off Speed (ft.min⁻¹)	Actual Change (cm.min⁻¹)	Predicted Change (cm.min⁻¹)	Deviation (cm.min⁻¹)
87	103	-0.38	-0.29	0.09
84	108	-0.35	-0.47	0.13
89	112	-0.71	-0.39	0.32
87	99	-0.29	-0.13	0.16
86	104	-0.36	-0.45	0.09
100	100	0.73	0.73	0
75	106	-1.25	-1.25	0
102	106	0.27	0.26	0.01
90	102	0.13	-0.14	0.27
90	105	-0.08	-0.27	0.19
96	90	0.81	0.81	0
75	90	-0.50	-0.54	0.04
85	95	0	-0.09	0.09
75	95	-0.54	-0.54	0
74	100	-1.27	-1.27	0
105	100	0.95	0.95	0
95	100	0.43	0.41	0.02
95	106	0.17	0.03	0.14
106	105	0.75	0.75	0

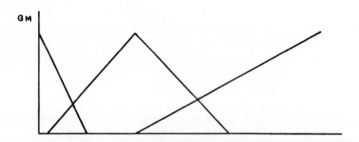

FIG. 1a. – NON – OVERLAPPED MEMBERSHIP FUNCTIONS.

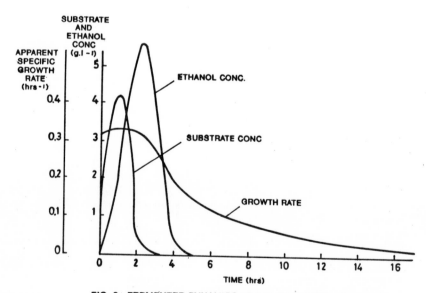

FIG. 1b. OVERLAPPED MEMBERSHIP FUNCTIONS.

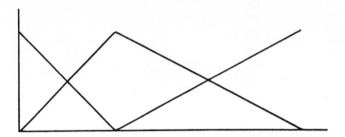

FIG. 2. FERMENTER DYNAMICS AT A LOW CONSTANT FEEDRATE

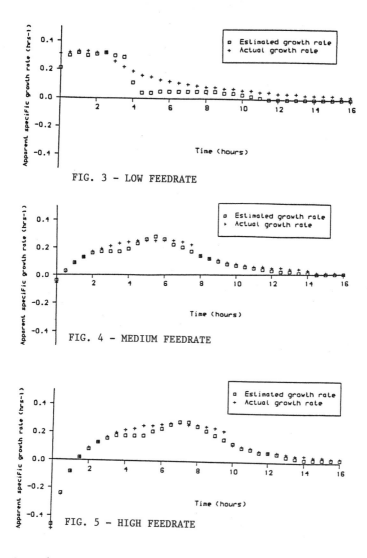

FIG. 3 - LOW FEEDRATE

FIG. 4 - MEDIUM FEEDRATE

FIG. 5 - HIGH FEEDRATE

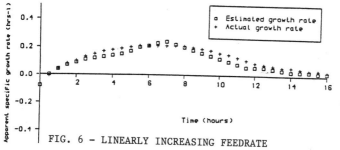

FIG. 6 - LINEARLY INCREASING FEEDRATE

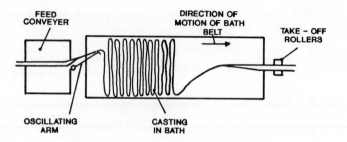

FIG. 7. ARRANGEMENT OF TREATMENT BATH.

Chapter 11

Real-time knowledge-based systems in fermentation supervisory control

M. Aynsley, D. Peel, A. G. Hofland, G. A. Montague and A. J. Morris

Summary. In this paper the issues involved with the design and implementation of real-time knowledge based systems (RTKBS) are reviewed. These will be demonstrated with reference to a RTKBS approach for the improved supervision and control of fermentation plant. The system is composed of three elements; a supervisory knowledge base, a scheduling knowledge base and an on-line relational database. The supervisor is responsible for monitoring and controlling individual fermenters and is instructed when to initiate or terminate a fermentation by commands issued by the scheduler, which aims to maximise plant-wide productivity. The system also performs sensor validation, fault detection/ fault diagnosis and incorporates relevant expertise and experience drawn from both the process engineering domain and the control engineering domain. The database provides a centralised store of information which can be retrieved on-line by both knowledge bases.

1. INTRODUCTION

There is presently a very strong interest in the application of Knowledge Based Systems (KBS) in the process industries, most of which are concerned with monitoring and fault diagnosis. Systems that are in regular, day to day operation are, however, still uncommon. A major reason for this lies in the difficulty of validating KBS code and the lack of integration between KBS and conventional real time control systems, discussed in a subsequent section. Of the systems which have been installed, most have used one or more of the many general expert system shells or development environments such as KEE, ART, etc., or written directly in a symbolic language such as LISP or Prolog. More recently, a small number of companies have produced packages targetted specifically for application in the real-time domain such as G2 from the GENSYM Corporation, Moore et al [3,4]. Another good example is the MUSE toolkit from Cambridge Consultants [12].

1.1 Conventional Techniques versus Knowledge Based Systems

What is it that KBS and RTKBS techniques can provide that cannot be provided by conventional computer based programming systems ?

This is not easy to answer. There are certainly many similarities between rule based systems and well programmed conventional systems. Rules resemble programming logic's; the class-instance structure of frame based systems is a natural way in which to describe function blocks in a conventional system. In addition, a functional overlap exists for certain types of monitoring and diagnosis applications. Differences do, however, exist with respect to both functionality and operator interface. One of the major functional differences lies in the rule set. Fragmentary heuristic knowledge, relating, say, fault symptoms with causes, can be easily expressed and chained together through the inference engine to imitate operator reasoning. However, systems based purely on heuristic operator knowledge expressed in terms of rules have many problems. It is difficult to acquire consistent knowledge and the knowledge acquired only applies to a chosen specific process. This becomes invalid as soon as any process changes occur. Such a system also inherits operator misconceptions and cannot provide solutions for unanticipated problems that operators have no solution for. These problems may be overcome by the use of a 'deeper' (model based) knowledge based representation in terms of either first principles physical/chemical knowledge of the process, or in terms of the way a process responds to given stimuli (cf. a transfer function approach in conventional systems).

A further powerful concept typically associated with KBS is object oriented programming which allows the encapsulation of data and associated program code in the form of structured objects or schemas and also allows inheritance of properties from superior classes in a (user-defined) class hierarchy. In addition, generic expressions can be constructed which are applicable to all members of a given class. In conventional programming approaches however, program code is written for each individual member of the class. The use of symbolic variables and symbolic manipulation is another feature associated with KBS and the multiple window, interactive browsing, natural language expressions and explanations of knowledge based systems are much more advanced and easier to use than in most conventional systems.

The motives behind a move towards knowledge based systems techniques mainly arise from the complexity of today's and future processing operations and the need for safe, effective economic operation on versatile plants responding to ever changing market demands. It is here, that significant attention is being directed towards the provision of better aids for process operators and production management.

1.2 Real-Time Knowledge Based Systems

RTKBS can provide novel solutions to many problems encountered in the operation of time critical processes. Chantler [1], Stephanopoulos and

Stephanopoulos [2] and Moore et al [3,4] have discussed the basic requirements of RTKBS which are now becoming well established in a wide range of applications such as medicine, finance and process control [5].

Real-time process control applications demand special requirements from knowledge based systems. The important issues for real-time operation have been outlined in a number of reviews [1,5] and can be briefly summarised as follows:

1. Non-monotonicity: reasoning on collected data is dynamic and data is not entirely durable. Its validity decays with time or ceases to be valid due to changing conditions and events.

2. Guaranteed response times: reasoning under time constraints where the system must produce a response to meet prespecified deadlines even if data is missing or uncertain.

3. Asynchronous events and focus of attention: unscheduled events may occur in an unpredictable manner. When a significant event occurs the system must focus its resources on achieving important goals.

4. Temporal reasoning: the ability to reason about past, present and future events, eg rates of change and time series functions such as average and standard deviation.

5. Continuous operation: incremental garbage collection is important to preserve continuous real-time operation.

1.3 System Integration

The integration of knowledge based software environments with conventional process control system software and hardware can be achieved in several ways. Most popular are those based upon Interfaced Systems, Embedded Systems and Totally Integrated Systems [13].

In an Interfaced approach, the KBS is an optional add-on to a conventional system. They usually have the same man-machine interface and a well defined communications interface. An advantage lies in the separate development of the KBS and conventional system and in use the KBS will not interfere with the speed of the on-line control system. Redundancy will almost certainly be a feature of these systems, however.

In the Embedded approach, the KBS is contained in a separate module that is actually embedded within the conventional system. The module maybe entirely software that is executed on the conventional system processor, or executed in additional processor hardware. Here the data communications part of the Interfaced approach is eliminated. This can be advantageous.

The Totally Integrated approach forms the basis for Real-time knowledge based control system, with conventional and KBS techniques being completely merged. Here a common knowledge base is a key element. A natural basis for the knowledge base is a hierarchical object-oriented description of the process together with all its interconnections, control systems and specifications. It is important to understand that this is not necessarily a return to centralised approaches since different reasoning agencies could be implemented on different processors in a distributed system with a distributed knowledge base. It is only seen as a completely unified system through the various operator, engineer and management interfaces. Systems of this type will not be available in the near future although one or two systems are attempting to adopt some of the principles involved.

2. A KBS APPROACH FOR IMPROVED SUPERVISORY CONTROL OF A FERMENTATION PLANT

The ability to control a highly non-linear and time variant fermentation process is of considerable importance to the biotechnological industries which are continually striving to obtain higher yields and improved uniformity of production. Many industrial fermentations are operated in a fed-batch mode using a pre-defined (open loop) substrate feeding regime based on years of empirical development. Experienced operators continually monitor the process and hold microbial growth to an "ideal" trajectory using heuristics and process knowledge to make adjustments to the feeding strategy in order to compensate for variations between batches. These modifications can be quite significant since even a small increase in product yield can considerably affect process profitability by making more efficient use of carbon substrate.

With most fermentation processes, growth, product formation and substrate concentration are not amenable to direct measurement but may be inferred using a number of indirect techniques eg mass balancing [7], off-gas analysis [8] or ammonia addition rate [9]. This has enabled the successful application of closed loop algorithmic control to many fermentations, but such schemes are generally inflexible to unexpected changes in the process and rely heavily on the accuracy of sensor measurements. In contrast, knowledge based systems can be designed to cope with uncertainty and allow the coupling of quantitative information with the qualitative or symbolic expressions (in the form of heuristics) used by humans so as to reproduce the actions of an experienced process operator. They can therefore be used as an intelligent, on-line assistant to the process operator or, with extra knowledge, as a supervisor in running and maintaining fermentations under optimal conditions.

On a plant-wide perspective, the scheduling of process operations is also traditionally undertaken manually by experienced personnel using a trial and error approach with a planning board. This also appears to be a potential area for the application of a KBS [10]. In the particular fermentation installation described in this paper, the preferential harvesting of fermentations out of their initiated sequence to maximise productivity, while ensuring this does not result in lengthy down-times in other process units, could yield a very significant improvement in the economics of production.

An integrated system for improved supervisory control and scheduling of fermentation processes is proposed using a KBS approach. The system will comprise a fermentation supervisory knowledge base and a plant scheduling knowledge base, both of which will be linked to an on-line relational database to provide a maximum level of integrity and intelligence in a real-time environment.

2.1 Fermentation Processes

The basic aim of any fermentation process is to achieve high productivity while also maximising the product yield. The method by which this is achieved is clearly dependent upon the type of fermentation under study, but essentially requires the continuous availability of a balanced supply of nutrients (carbon, nitrogen, etc.) and the maintenance of environmental parameters (temperature, pH, etc.) at optimal levels for product synthesis.

In this study two distinct fermentation processes are considered in order to develop RTKBS methodologies; a fed-batch Penicillin fermentation and a fed-batch Bakers Yeast fermentation. These fermentations are carried out in 20 litre and 6 litre fully instrumented laboratory fermenters, which are shown schematically in figure 1. Industrial fermentations are carried out in 100-200m^3 fermenters.

The fed-batch Penicillin fermentation consists of essentially two distinct phases; a fast growth phase during which a high concentration of physiologically active cells are generated, followed by a slower production phase during which the antibiotic is produced. It is essential in this fermentation to maintain mould growth to an ideal trajectory from an early stage since overfeeding can inhibit product formation through catabolite repression, whilst underfeeding can result in an irrevocable loss of synthetic ability or even cellular death. This fermentation is also particularly prone to contamination problems owing to the relatively slow growth of the mould and aeration problems arising from the complex rheology and high viscosity of mycelial broths. Qi et al [14] have reported the application of an expert system to the penicillin fermentation which achieved intelligent aeration / agitation and supervisory control on an industrial plant.

In the case of the fed-batch Bakers Yeast fermentation it is the organism itself which is the final product. These fungi are relatively easier to cultivate in that they grow rapidly and display a fairly well understood metabolic switch from oxidative to fermentative growth. The control objective here is to push the specific growth rate as high as possible using an exponential feeding regime while minimising ethanol formation which is produced as a response to the Crabtree effect or a saturated respiratory capacity. In practice, this means maintaining the specific growth rate between 0.2 - 0.25 hr^{-1}. Wang et al [9,15] have previously developed a control algorithm for this fermentation which was subsequently incorporated as part of an expert system control strategy by Cooney et al [6].

3. PROJECT DEVELOPMENT

3.1 Hardware Environment

The hardware environment which has been developed for the real-time industrial implementations of advanced control algorithms at Newcastle is shown in figure 2. The structure is composed of a number of standard industrial process control and signal processing devices which provide direct interfacing to the process under study. These devices are then linked by an RS422/RS232 serial connection to a local control computer which is typically an IBM PS/2 (or AT). This is in turn linked to a supervisory computer, in this case a SUN 3/60 workstation, via a high speed Ethernet connection.

The hardware architecture described above represents a safe, yet flexible communication structure which is generally acceptable to industry. The process control and signal processing devices are from the TCS (Turnbull Control Systems) range which support a fairly rigourous communications protocol which minimises errors in communication and which allows a remote computer to monitor process variables and to update controller settings or process inputs (outputs from the signal processor). These devices are linked via a multi-drop serial highway to the local control computer which is responsible for managing communications between the supervisory computer to the TCS devices and vice-versa. In passing process data to the supervisory controller, the local computer may also carry out some simple data conditioning tasks such as filtering or more complex "soft-sensing" which will be discussed later.

3.2 Software Environment

The G2 Real-time Expert System was used for system development. The concept of real-time is represented within the system in terms of update intervals which direct G2 to collect values for variables at regular time intervals; validity intervals which specify the length of time the current value of a variable remains relevant, and rule scanning intervals which inform the inference engine how often to invoke any given rule. Data which is currently valid, can be reasoned with directly or can be analysed with past data using statistical features. It is also possible to import functions written in 'C' or Fortran which can be used to carry out complex numerical calculations. G2 uses rules which are written in a very expressive English-like language and has an icon based graphical interface to create knowledge frames (ie an object-orientated approach). The system also supports arithmetic and symbolic expressions and has a built-in simulation facility which can be used in the 'background' while the actual process is being controlled in real-time.

3.3 Knowledge Based System for Fermentation Supervisory Control

Bio-SCAN (Supervision Control ANalysis) is a RTKBS which has been designed to provide a general purpose framework for the monitoring and supervisory control of a range of fermentation processes. Internally, the system incorporates knowledge of operating strategies (eg feeding regimes, process set-points) and expected behaviours to enable rapid detection of any process faults. When faults occur, the system attempts to diagnose the cause of the problem and will offer recovery advice to process operators. In addition to knowledge encoded within Bio-SCAN, the utility of the system has been extended by interfacing to conventional algorithmic methods of analysing and controlling fermentations. A toolkit of on-line modules has been developed to incorporate a number of features into the overall control strategy such as simulation and prediction, statistical evaluation and estimation algorithms. The architecture of Bio-SCAN is presented in figure 3 and further details concerning the development of the system can be found in Aynsley et al [27]. The basic philosophy behind the development of Bio-SCAN has been to make the solutions as generic as possible (applicable across a broad spectrum of fermentations) and to provide the system with as much (high quality) information as possible. This led to the development of a database system for on-line interrogation by Bio-SCAN.

Each of the fermentation processes under study is defined by different operating philosophies which therefore require specific knowledge (rulesets) for optimal supervisory control. These "supervisory rulesets" are used to govern the general operation of the fermentation by identifying growth or production phases and determining which rulesets are applicable to a given phase (ie supervisory rulesets function as meta rules). The supervisor is responsible for feed scheduling, or on-line modifications to the schedule in response to changes in the process ie faults. Specific rulesets are also necessary in order to assess and respond to the metabolic state of a process organism in any given fermentation (ie detect "metabolic faults"), but for the diagnosis of hardware faults, it is possible to use many generic-type rules for all fermentations under Bio-SCAN control. As a simple example we can write:

For any fermenter,

IF the value of the pH sensor connected to the fermenter is greater than the pH set point of the fermenter (+ 0.1)
THEN there is evidence of a fault.

The diagnostic knowledge base has been structured into a number of discrete rulesets and meta rules again determine which ruleset should be accessed next. The decision to invoke a particular set of rules is based upon a comparison of the current raw, or processed, data with that permitted or expected in the current phase of the fermentation. This ensures that knowledge can be focused in response to the occurrence of specific events.

Once a fault has been detected the operator is informed of the problem on a message board and additional rulesets are invoked in an attempt to establish the nature of the fault. A list of possible causes is then presented to the operator together with advice on how to correct the fault, or confirm a diagnosis (eg contamination) if Bio-SCAN cannot solve the problem automatically. This is possible if the fermentation is sufficiently overdetermined, since the expert system capitalises on redundancies to test for data consistency and error identification. The source of these redundancies are usually balances or load cells, although recently soft-sensing techniques have been used to reduce the need for hardware redundancy [16].

Since structured, generic rulesets have been used in the development of the system, coupled with an object-orientated approach to the description of the fermentation process, it is hoped that much of the knowledge base will be generally applicable across a wide range of fermentation processes. Setpoints and control profiles could possibly be loaded from a suitably structured input file and process specific knowledge can be incorporated into the existing modular framework relatively easily. Integration with the rest of the knowledge base however, would require some further work.

3.4 Integration with Conventional Software

Whilst the knowledge base described above is expected to be capable of adequately supervising fermentation processes under most circumstances, the utility of the system can be greatly extended by interfacing to conventional real-time algorithmic methods of analysing and controlling fermentations. For this reason a toolkit of on-line modules is being developed that will incorporate the following features into the overall control strategy:

(a) Measured signal conditioning, screening and interrogation to place confidence bounds around data. This is essential for robust applications of KBS computations

(b) Simulation using process models or imported subroutines in addition to the use of the G2 simulator.

(c) Identification of process model parameters using on-line recursive parameter estimation algorithms.

(d) Estimation of hidden states using 'soft sensors' (software estimation schemes). This will provide for increased process observability, analytical redundancy of process measurements and elimination of performance restrictions due to long on-line or off-line assay times. Feedback of estimates of difficult to measure variables such as biomass should lead to improved fermentation supervision and control.

(e) Prediction of future process outputs given pre-specified open-loop feeding regimes, and use of adaptive predictive control to achieve closed-loop profiling of fermentation states, eg Generalised Predictive Control.

(f) Continuous assessment of process observability and controllability. This will be achieved by analysis of the on-line identified process models using well researched linear analysis routines, eg a software link with Matlab and its toolboxes.

(g) On-line optimisation using on-line identified process models that capture the essential non-linear structure of the fermentation. Constrained optimisation is applied to a pseudo-steady state' extraction of the identified model and the 'optimal' environmental control applied.

(h) Continuous statistical process control to provide interactive assessment of overall fermentation performance against prespecified specifications.

(i) Neural Network identification of non-linear process models and hidden state estimates [17,18].

These modules can be linked to the Bio-SCAN software using the G2 Standard Interface which can run on any network that supports ICP, Gensym's Intelligent Communications Protocol, or interfaced directly if they are written in 'C' or Fortran.

Bio-SCAN will therefore process raw data from the plant directly and evaluate the actions/conclusions suggested from algorithms running outside the system in real-time in order to determine the performance and future course of a fermentation.

3.5 Knowledge Based Systems for Scheduling Operations

In the process industries generally, commercial scheduling software is very little used, often considered to lack the flexibility and level of detail required for day-to-day plant operation [19]. This may be due to the nature of the predominantly algorithmic methods used in these packages (eg mixed integer linear programming) which may fail to converge in a reasonable period of time or require oversimplifications to be made in defining the problem. Moreover, no allowance is made for constraint relaxation which may be the only method of generating a feasible solution under certain circumstances. The idea of using a KBS approach is attractive in that these systems are well suited to chaining through rules and constraints that govern the heuristic approach used on most plants. This may well achieve the speed and flexibility required, albeit at the expense of the near optimal solutions provided by the algorithmic methods [20].

The industrial fermentation installation considered in this paper is a single product plant comprising several production vessels with capacities in excess of 100,000 litres together with numerous storage facilities and a range of smaller seed vessels. Once a seed vessel has been inoculated, the length of the batch can be manipulated to a certain degree during the first few hours, but then becomes committed to transfer its culture at a fixed time and a production vessel must be available. Production batches then typically run for around 200 hours before harvesting and recovery of product. In order to achieve maximum plant efficiency, production vessels must be utilised in such a way as to ensure high potency broths are always available at regular intervals so that downstream processing facilities are continuously supplied. In theory this simply requires an orderly sequence of operations involving seed inoculations, growth of seed, transfer of culture to production vessels and subsequent growth and product formation. In practise however, the ideal schedule may not be realised owing to "upsets" caused by factors such as contaminations of seed or production vessels or maintenance requirements. The problem is then compounded in that there are different sizes of both seed and production vessels and there may be constraints imposed on where a seed vessel can transfer its culture. This can result in lengthy downtimes for production units if an existing schedule cannot be changed by redirection of previously committed seed cultures.

Further disturbances to the "orderly" harvesting of batches arises as a consequence of the inherent batch to batch variability in production rate. At any one time several batches on the plant may have achieved a sufficient titre to make them candidates for harvesting. However, it is often found that total plant productivity can be improved by harvesting a vessel out of its inoculated sequence. For this reason an on-line forecaster has been developed to identify poor performing batches based on off-line titre information. One method of forecasting is based on the classification of historical titre profiles and identification of the current batch type to predict future behaviour. An alternative strategy is to employ a curve-fitting approach to a number of possible model structures. Whatever strategy is used, the forecaster seeks to identify which fermenters should be dispatched to downstream processing as fast as possible and which should be left to run-on. The scheduler must then decide if harvesting one fermenter out of sequence is workable and economically feasible with regard to the current schedule in operation.

The (simplified) problem description outlined above is not of the conventional flow or job-shop type described in the literature [21] and is essentially one of on-line rescheduling. A solution to the problem using a KBS approach is being developed which combines a model of the plant with a module which will use rule-based heuristics to examine operating strategies. This does not, however preclude the use of algorithmic methods if a mixed approach is found to be needed. The model is being designed to incorporate detailed knowledge of plant structure and operation and will be used to test what-if scenarios by process operators in a manner similar to the system proposed by Bernstein et al [22]. An "intelligent" user interface will allow operators to easily change constraints or operating conditions and examine the effects. The knowledge base will be particularly useful in analysing the feasibility of the harvesting sequence suggested by the on-line forecaster, and in training operator personnel. System output will be in the form of text messages which can then be manually transferred to the plant planning board or processed to provide a traditional Gantt type representation.

3.6 Fermentation Database System

The important problems to be tackled when developing fermentation databases are not merely how to collect large volumes of different types of data, but also how to validate it before storage and then extract meaningful information.

The types of fermentation data which are usually collected and stored have been reviewed by Carleysmith [23] and are summarised in Table 1. In addition to these, information could also be held concerning characteristic trajectories of key variables with their associated standard deviations as an aid to process evaluation and fault detection by Bio-SCAN. For the scheduling knowledge base the database would be required to maintain a record of the current plant status with expected completion times of process units (based on the current schedule in operation). Information concerning the maintenance requirements of equipment and vessels could also be incorporated [24], coupled with manpower availability and stock levels of replacement equipment and raw materials.

From a user-standpoint the database must also be simple to interrogate, update and view data, and must be flexible in design. Provision for report generation and the statistical analysis of data to establish the relationships between variables would also be useful.

The system chosen to develop our database was Ingres by Relational Technology Inc. which operates a powerful relational database management system [25]. Ingres proved simple to design and update via its forms-based-interfaces and supports a powerful query language (SQL) based on virtually any combination of criteria. SQL can also be embedded in external host code such as C which proved important in establishing the link with the scheduling and supervisory knowledge bases.

4. OVERALL SYSTEM OPERATION

The supervisory RTKBS, Bio-SCAN, has been designed to oversee the operation of a range of (potentially different) fermentation processes simultaneously, by providing a permanent, consistent level of "expert" supervision and monitoring When a seed or production fermentation is to be initiated, requests will initially be made to the database for retrieval of operating conditions and feeding regimes for the strain of organism and mode of operation specified by the scheduler. Once a fermenter is running, data from the process is received by Bio-SCAN at regular intervals and is analysed with respect to both expected and recent values (there is provision for limited short-term storage of data within the RTKBS), and for deviations from "optimal" behaviour. In checking for data consistency, the supervisor also validates the data before it is passed to the database for permanent storage. During the course of a run, requests may also be made for retrieval of eg a standard profile of alkali addition or CO_2 evolution to evaluate fermenter performance. When faults are detected and diagnosed, text messages will be sent to the database specifying the nature of the fault and the action taken Should a contamination occur, a message is also sent to the scheduler which will then pass back an instruction to stop feeding and terminate the run when an available slot in downstream processing becomes available.

The scheduler interrogates the database to ascertain the plant status and the current schedule in operation and periodically instructs the forecaster to recommend the next fermentation to be harvested. To accomplish this, the forecaster will itself interrogate the database for off-line titre information. The scheduling knowledge base instructs the supervisory knowledge base which fermenter is to be harvested and manual shut-down and transfer procedures would then be completed by process operators. In evaluating the feasibility of schedules, the scheduling KBS retrieves information on plant maintenance requirements and on the availability of both labour and equipment (perhaps using a link to an inventory control database). The scheduler will also direct the initiation of seed fermentations and specify transfer times to production vessels to ensure that production can maintained. Once a batch has been completed, data gathered during the course of the run is integrated into standard profiles and abstractable data such as the specific production rate are derived. The complete data set associated with the run is then transferred to a mass storage medium and catalogued, the architecture of the proposed system is presented in figure 4.

5. RESULTS

Since the 1 Km fibre optic Ethernet link between the fermentation unit and the SUN workstations running Bio-SCAN has only recently been established, results are presented using off-line data from industrial fed-batch penicillin fermentations.

Figure 5 compares the typical CO_2 profiles observed in two "standard" industrial fed-batch penicillin fermentations with those of two "abnormal" runs. For proprietary reasons the abscissa scaling in this figure has been omitted. One rule which will detect any abnormality in the fermentation is of the general form:

> IF the CO_2 production rate or rate of change of CO_2 production is greater or less than that expected
> THEN there is evidence of a fault.

Clearly this rule must be expanded to incorporate the limits at which the rule will fire, how these limits could change during the course of a fermentation and perhaps the probability of a process fault. The CO_2 must also be reconciled with other process measurements such as the oxygen uptake rate and dissolved oxygen concentration before diagnostic rulesets are subsequently invoked. In the contaminated fermentation shown in figure 4, Bio-SCAN quickly detected the increased CO_2 production rate early in the run and since this reading was found to be reconcilable with other measurements and no other abnormalities in the operation of the fermentation could be detected, the system concluded that a contamination had most likely occurred and informed the operator after 17 hours. It is interesting to note that this contamination was detected by the actual process operators after 75 hours when laboratory analysis identified the presence of a yeast and terminated the fermentation. Had the fermentation been terminated earlier a considerable saving in substrate feed costs would have been realised.

In the case of the second abnormal fermentation shown in figure 5, Bio-SCAN detected an atypical fall in the CO_2 measurement after 160 hours which was not concomitant with any mini-harvests. As all other operational parameters appeared normal, the system invoked a ruleset which established from balance measurements that substrate flow into the vessel was below normal. The operator was then instructed to investigate the cause of this problem (eg a blocked line or pump failure). In a real situation the operator could inform Bio-SCAN once the problem was corrected using the intelligent end-user interface. Supervisory rules would then modify the feeding strategy in an attempt to bring microbial growth back onto a predefined trajectory and recover the productivity of the fermentation.

The supervisory KB was also tested and validated against a mechanistic model of the penicillin fermentation into which faults had been introduced (11). Bio-SCAN is currently being used to supervise a number of fed-batch and continuous Bakers Yeast fermentations. The scheduling KB is still undergoing development involving close consultations with experienced scheduling personnel at the site of our industrial collaborators. The links between the supervisory control and scheduling KB's and between the KBs and the database have now been established and are described in detail (26).

6. CONCLUSIONS

This chapter has dealt with some of the issues involved with the application of real-time knowledge based systems. To demonstrate the potential utility of using this approach, a system has been designed for the improved supervisory control of fermentation plant. The system is composed of three elements: a supervisor , a scheduler and relational data-base system. The supervisor is responsible for individual batch performance and aims to improve yields and reduce variability using a blend of integrated technologies such as process control, estimation and simulation. The scheduler employs an on-line titre forecaster and is designed to ensure the most efficient use of production facilities, to maximise plant throughput to downstream processing. Both of these knowledge bases have on-line access to the database which serves to maintain a centralised store of process information. Although we currently at an intermediate stage in the project, the potential benefits of the proposed system appear quite significant. In large scale, established fermentation processes such as penicillin production, or in smaller scale value-added fermentations such as vaccine production, even a small increase in fermenter or plant productivity will realise major savings.

7. ACKNOWLEDGEMENTS

The authors would like to thank Beecham Pharmaceuticals plc. and Gensym Corporation for support and valuable assistance. We also acknowledge financial support provided by the SERC.

8. REFERENCES

1. Chantler, M. J. (1988). "Real Time Aspects of Expert Systems in Process Control". In "Expert Systems in Process Control", IEE Colloquium, March 1988.
2. Stephanopoulos G. and Stephanopoulos G. (1986)."Artificial Intelligence in the Development and Design of Biochemical Processes". Trends in Biotechnology p.241-248.
3. Moore, R. L., Hawkinson, L. B., Levin, M., Hofman, A.G., Matthews, B. L. and David, M. H. (1987). "Expert Systems Methodology For Real-Time Process Control". Pre-prints of 10th World Congress on Automatic Control,Munich, FRG, July 27-31.
4. Moore, R. (1988). "The G2 Real-Time Expert System for Process Control". International Symposium on Advanced Process Supervision and Real-Time Knowledge-Based Control, Newcastle-upon-Tyne, England, U.K., Nov. 17th.
5. Laffey, T. J., Cox, P. A., Schmidt, J. L., Kao, S. M. and Read, J. Y. (1988). "Real-Time Knowledge-Based Systems". AI Magazine 9, 27-48.
6. Cooney, C. L., O'Conner, G. M. and Sanchez-Riera, F. (1988). "An Expert System For Intelligent Supervisory Control of Fermentation Processes". Preprints of 8th International Biotech. Symp., Paris, July 1988.

7. Cooney, C. L., Wang, H. Y. and Wang D.I.C. (1977) "Computer-aided material balancing for predicting biological parameters". Biotech. Bioeng. **19**, 55-66.
8. Calam, C.T. and Ismail, B.A. (1980). "Investigation of factors in the optimisation of penicillin production". J. Appl. Chem. Biotech. **30**, 249-262.
9. Wang, H. Y., Cooney, C. L. and Wang, D.I.C. (1977) "Computer-aided Bakers Yeast fermentation" Biotech. Bioeng. **19**, 67-86.
10. Hofmeister, M., Halasz, L. and Rippin, D.W.T.(1989)."Knowledge Based Tools for Batch Processing Systems". Comp. Chem. Eng. 13, 1255-1261.
11. Aynsley, M. (1988). "Modelling and Simulation of Mycelial Growth in Submerged Culture With Application to the Fed-Batch Penicillin Fermentation". PhD Thesis University of Newcastle-Upon- Tyne, England.
12. Reynolds, D., (1988), "MUSE: A toolkit for embedded real-time AI", in Blackboard Systems, R. Engelmore and T. Morgan (Eds.), Addison Wesley.
13. Arzen, K-E., (1989), "Knowledge-based control systems - aspects on the unification of conventional control systems and knowledge-based systems", Proc. ACC, Pittsburgh, 2233-2238.
14. Qi, C., Wang, S-Q and Wang, J-C. (1988). "Application of Expert System to the Operation and Control of Industrial Antibiotic Fermentation Process". Pre-prints of 4th International Congress on "Computer Applications in Fermentation Technology" Cambridge, U.K. Sept. 25-29.
15. Wang, H-Y. Cooney, C.L. and Wang, D.I.C. (1979). "Computer control of Bakers Yeast production". Biotech. Bioeng **21**, 975-995.
16. Guilandoust, M.T., Morris, A.J. and Tham, M.T. (1988), "An Adaptive Estimation Algorithm for Inferential Control", Ind. Eng. Chem. and Research, Vol 27, 9, pp 1658-1664.
17. Lant, P.A., Willis, M.J., Montague, G.A., Tham, M.T. and Morris, A.J., (1990). "A Comparison of Adaptive Estimation with Neural Based Techniques for Bio-process Application", Proc. ACC, San Diego, USA, pp 2173-2178.
18. Willis, M.J., Di Massimo, C., Montague, G.A., Tham, M.T. and Morris, A.J., (1990). "Solving Process Engineering Problems using Artificial Neural Networks", IEE Vacation School on Knowledge-Based Systems for Process Control, University of Strathclyde, September 1990.
19. D.T.I Report, (1989). "Batch Process Scheduling Computer Software". The R&D Clearing House.
20. Bruno, G., Elia, A. and Laface, P. (1986). "A Rule Based System to Schedule Production". IEEE Computer 32, 32-40.
21. Ku, H-M, Rajagopalan, D., and Karimi, I. (1987) "Scheduling in Batch Processes", Chem. Eng. Prog., August, 35-66.
22. Bernstein, G., Carlson, E.C. and Felder, R.M. (1989). "Development of a Simulation-Based Decision Support System for a Multipurpose Pharmaceutical Plant". AIChE Annual Meeting, San Francisco, CA, November.
23. Carleysmith, S.W. (1988). "Data Handling for Fermentation Development - An Industrial Approach". Preprints, 4th Int. Cong., "Computer Applications in Fermentation Technology", Cambridge, U.K., September.

24. Flynn, D.S. (1982). "Instrumentation for Fermentation Processes". Proc. 1st IFAC Conf., "Modelling and Control of Biotechnical Processes" Helsinki, Finland.

25. Codd, E.F. (1970). "A Relational Model of Data for Large Shared Data Banks". Comm. ACM 13, 377-387.

26. Aynsley, M., Hofland, A.G., Montague, G.A., Peel, D. and Morris A.J. (1990). "A Real-time Knowledge Based System for the Operation of a Fermentation Plant". Proc. ACC, San Diego, USA, pp 1992-1997.

27. Aynsley, M., Peel, D. and Morris, A.J. (1989), "A Real-time Knowledge Based System for Fermentation Control", Proc. ACC, Pittsburgh, USA, pp 2239-2244.

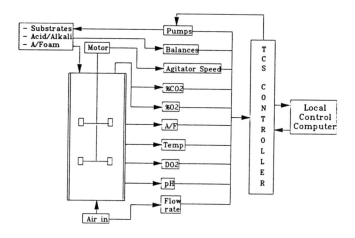

Figure 1. Schematic representation of the fermenter configuration and instrumentation.

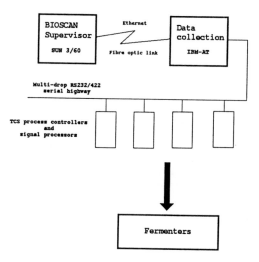

Figure 2. Hardware architecture for the supervisory control of fermentation processes.

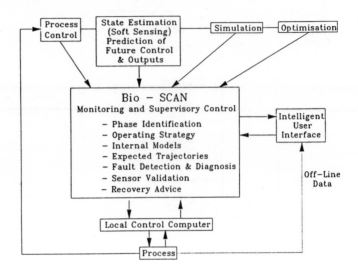

Figure 3. Bio-SCAN supervisory architecture.

Table 1. Examples of Data Required for Collection and Storage.

On-Line	Off-Line	Set-up	Abstracted
Temperature	Biomass conc.	Run-no.	spec. growth rate
Agitation	Product titre	Ferm Identity no.	spec. prod'n rate
Aeration	Viscosity	Inoc/Harvest time	max. product conc
Pressure	Nutrient conc.	Strain of organism	yield
pH	Precusror conc	Growth medium	Model fits with
DO_2	Enzyme activity	Incubation cond's	parameters
%CO_2 prod	Sediment volume	Feeds & feedrates	
%O_2 uptake		Sample schedule	
Balances		Text comments	

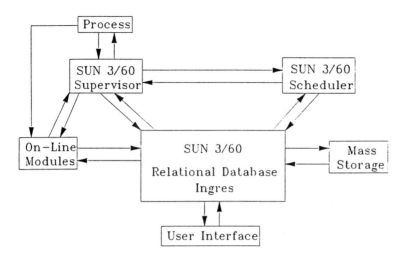

Figure 4. System configuration.

Penicillin Fermentations

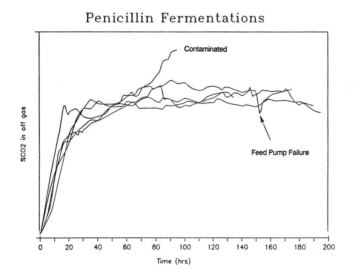

Figure 5. Comparison of the profiles of CO_2 evolution in normal and abnormal penicillin fermentations.

Chapter 12

Machine-learned rule-based control

M. E. Bain

1   Introduction

Machine-learned rule-based control differs from more typical approaches to the engineering of controllers for physical systems in the following respect. In traditional control theory, a mathematical model of the system is constructed and then analysed in order to synthesise a control method. This approach is clearly deductive. A machine-learning approach to the synthesis of controllers aims to inductively acquire control knowledge, thereby avoiding the necessity of constructing a mathematical model of the system. In applications where systems are very complex, or insufficient knowledge is available, the construction of such a model may be impossible, and traditional methods therefore inappropriate. It is for these applications that an inductive approach promises solutions.

The laboratory problem studied in the work reported below is the control of an unstable mechanical system, the inverted pendulum, or as it is referred to in the remainder of this paper, the "pole-and-cart". A diagram of the pole-and-cart system is given in Figure 1. This system has been extensively analysed in the literature on control (e.g. [3, 5]), and therefore the equations of motion and control solutions are widely available. However, the aim of the work reported here is the development of inductive or more specifically "machine learning" methods which are, as far as possible, generic. This requires that the physical system to be controlled is treated as a black box. Control knowledge is to be learned from experience by the machine.

The definition of machine learning underlying the work reported here is that of Michie [9], namely :

> [a machine learning] system [is one which] uses sample data (training set) to generate an updated basis for improved performance on subsequent data *and* can communicate its updates in explicit symbolic form.

This criterion is somewhat stronger than that usually assumed in the field, since it requires that learned knowledge be communicable to other intelligent agents.

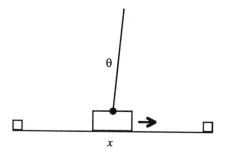

Figure 1: Pole-and-cart system.

A symbolic language in which learned knowledge may be expressed [1] is required to satisfy the second part of the adopted criterion. One such language is that of "production rules". These rules are of the general form

if   *condition*   then   *action*

In the context of controlling the pole-and-cart system the condition part of such rules will consist of tests on one or more of the state variables, while the action part dictates the control action to be applied. Typically with rule-based methods only a small number of discrete control actions are allowed. Where there are only two control actions, e.g. applying a force of fixed magnitude in opposite directions, this is known as "bang-bang" control. Unless indicated to the contrary it is the bang-bang method which is used throughout the work reported in the rest of this paper.

2   Background

Having restricted the range of methods of interest to those fitting the strict criteria of machine-learned rule-based control given above some previous work in this area will be discussed. Those methods selected are based on the BOXES algorithm of Michie and Chambers [11] which dates from the 1960s. Firstly, the original work on BOXES will be reviewed. The discussion is then brought up to date with a survey of further work based on this system in the last few years.

---

[1] Under this restriction approaches within the connectionist or neural-network paradigms are excluded from this discussion since they do not usually satisfy the explainability criterion, although some work has been done on the interpretation of learned networks in symbolic languages, e.g. [6, 7]

2.1   Michie and Chambers' BOXES

The original report by Michie and Chambers [11] on the development of their BOXES algorithm describes an application of a machine learning technique devised for simple games (e.g. noughts-and-crosses, small Nim, etc.) to the pole-and-cart problem.

2.1.1   Origins in game-playing

BOXES originated in work on game-playing automata. The idea behind it is that an automaton is built with a number of "boxes". In an automaton designed for a particular task these boxes will correspond to discrete states of the task. For example, in the game of noughts-and-crosses there is a state for each board position. Positions equivalent by symmetry are covered by the same state. Each box is equipped with its individual learning agent or "demon" which learns how to play from its assigned board position. In this way the automaton learns how to play the whole game by learning what to do in each board position of the game.

2.1.2   Optimality considerations

The learning mechanism used is categorised as "reinforcement learning", and is based on rewarding the box demons for making moves with successful outcomes. A consequence of this basic method, which makes a move in order to maximise its expected outcome based on the outcomes of previous moves, is that the performance of the automaton may level out at sub-optimal local maxima. In the original paper, this is demonstrated with a simple example from the game of Nim. The authors note that an optimal learning mechanism based on the reinforcement of move probabilities is not possible in general, but may for some practical applications be approximated. As they explained in the original report,

> ... it can pay to make a move which is, on the evidence, inferior, in order to collect *more evidence* as to whether it really is inferior.

Using this insight to improve the algorithm, a bias towards experimentation was incorporated into the process of move selection. This was implemented by means of a technique termed the "target" method. Essentially, the target method augments the learning mechanism in order to maximise the optimistic rather than the expected outcome of a move. This optimistic outcome is calculated with respect to the current global performance of the system.

2.1.3   BOXES applied to the pole-and-cart

The choice of an adaptive-control problem for the application of a game-learning technique might seem unlikely. However, the problem of learning to control the pole-and-cart, when viewed as a "game against nature", can be constrained to fit the BOXES method in the following way.

The boxes corresponded to "states" of the pole-and-cart system. These are defined by partitioning the system variables into a small number of ranges. The imits of any box are then the maximum and minimum values of one such range or each of the system variables. For example, the thresholds used to partition the ole angle (θ) variable were $-12, -6, -1, 1, 6, 12$ degrees, giving 5 ranges. Values ess than -12 or greater than 12 degrees are designated failure states, where the ystem is deemed to be out of control. Each system variable is partitioned in a imilar manner. With four system variables, i.e. cart position, cart velocity, pole ngle and pole angular velocity, the total number of boxes was $5 \times 3 \times 5 \times 3 = 225$.

The moves from each box were restricted, under a bang-bang control regime, to force of fixed magnitude applied to either left or right. The outcomes of moves vere measured in terms of a performance value based on a weighted average of the uration between making a move and system failure. A system failure occurred vhen any of the state variables exceeded the pre-defined maximum or minimum artition thresholds.

The pole-and-cart system used in this application was a computer simulation mplementing the equations of motion defining its behaviour. The behaviour of this imulator was tuned to closely resemble the characteristics of a physical system. In he original work, the simulator and the BOXES program ran on separate computers onnected by a high-speed link. The authors reported a set of experiments in which range of durations for balancing the pole were recorded. In one case this was quivalent to over an an hour of real-time control.

.2 Extensions and a comparative study

ince the original report covered in the previous section, several extensions of the pplication of BOXES to the pole-and-cart problem have been published. Chambers nd Michie [4] extended the algorithm to allow human cooperation on the task. From heir experiments they concluded firstly that a machine trained by a human could utperform its trainer when the human's errors were "averaged out". (Some recent ork in this area using a different machine learning technique is reported in the aper by Michie, Bain and Hayes-Michie in this volume.) Secondly, human-machine ooperation on an "interactive learning" basis did result in a performance increase ver a number of trials.

To date several studies on the application of BOXES with a physical pole-and-art have been undertaken (e.g. [2, 13]). Although the general conclusion has been nat performance levels of the learned control strategies were below those obtained ith simulators, nonetheless performance improvement over the course of a number f training runs was achieved.

In 1988 Claude Sammut [14], working at the Turing Institute, compared a number f machine learning algorithms, including BOXES, applied to the control of a pole-nd-cart simulator. His detailed results may be summarised as concluding that though BOXES required more trials before learning to control the system for the equired period (equivalent to 200 seconds of real time), it proved to be clearly more bust than the other algorithms when an asymmetry [2] was introduced into the

---

[2]The simulation was changed so that the force applied to the left was halved from 10 to 5 ewtons while the force applied to the right remained at 10 Newtons.

simulation.

Also in this study Sammut combined the reinforcement learning method of BOXES with an inductive decision tree algorithm, C4 [12]. This joint metho enabled the learned rule embedded in BOXES, when expressed as a decision tree, to explain its control decisions. With this last extension, the learning system can sat isfy the second part of the adopted criterion for machine learning, i.e. that update knowledge be communicable to external intelligent agents.

2.3   A successful application

Issues which make the pole-and-cart system worth studying from the point of view of developing generic machine learning solutions occur in important real-world prob lems. Dynamic instability, the influence of unpredictable factors which change ove time, etc. are as liable to occur in such problems as in the pole-and-cart. One suc case is space craft attitude control, as reported by Sammut and Michie [15] in recent study. The authors undertook a trial of rule-based control methods applie to a black-box simulation of an orbiting space vehicle supplied by the commercia client.

The task was defined as three-axis rigid body attitude control. The space craf simulator output consisted of six state variables, namely pitch, roll and yaw, an the three body rates ω_x, ω_y and ω_z. Three control inputs were expected, namely th torques applied by firing thrusters aligned to the body axes.

In previous experiments on the pole-and-cart simulator multiple runs of BOXE had been averaged to produce a master set of boxes. One such "master decisio array" was then simplified to produce a rule of identical structure to that derive from a qualitative model by Makarovic [8]. Based on this experience, the author developed a control rule which successfully completed the task, which as defined b the client required that the system be driven from its initial state to a specified fina state and maintained in that state. This solution was then improved by replacing th bang-bang strategy with one in which a range of discrete control actions (thruste torques) were available to permit more sensitive control. This reduced the amount o fuel used to complete the task, an important consideration for orbiting space craft The final rule compared favourably with the client's own solution derived with th benefit of knowledge of the differential equations within the simulator.

3   Learning to control the 2-pole system

In the remainder of this paper results are reported for extensions of the BOXE method applied to a more complex problem, namely controlling a second pole or top of the first in the pole-and-cart system. This will be referred to as the 2-pol system, and is illustrated in Figure 2. The pole-and-cart problem was known to be readily generalised by adding $1, 2, \ldots, n$ poles each on top of the next in ar infinite sequence of ascending complexity [3]. In addition, the deductive, qualitativ modelling approach of Makarovic [8] which had given a solution to the pole-and cart was extended by its author for a 2-pole system, also under bang-bang contro

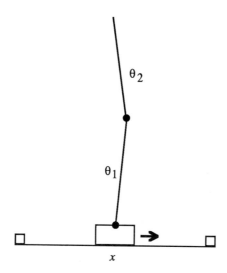

Figure 2: The 2-pole system.

However, this appeared to be stretching the bounds of applicability of the author's method, i.e. the problem was approaching the "ultra-complex" [10]. It was decided to set up an experiment to see if an extended version of BOXES could learn to control the system.

3.1   Experiment 1: 2-pole BOXES

The 2-pole system used was a computer simulation. Output from this simulator consisted of the six state variables: cart position (x) and velocity ($\dot{x}$); lower pole angle (θ_1) and angular velocity ($\dot{\theta}_1$); and upper pole angle (θ_2) and angular velocity ($\dot{\theta}_2$). The control regime was bang-bang, with in this case an applied force of ± 1 N.

Adding two variables for the angle and angular velocity of the second pole expands the dimensionality of the state-space from four for the pole-and-cart to six. It is desirable therefore to minimise the number of partitions on each variable in order to minimise the number of boxes required. Following Makarovic [8], two partitions were defined for cart position and three for every other variable. This gave a total of $2 \times 3^5 = 486$ boxes. The partition thresholds are shown in Figure 3. The equations of motion used as a simulator to model the 2-pole system were adapted from those published by Makarovic in the same report. Friction, slop, noise, etc. were ignored. Simulator constants are given in Figure 3. The Euler method of updating the state vector was used, with a time interval of 0.005 seconds. Pole angles were measured relative to the vertical, clockwise positive. Cart position was measured from the centre of the track, right-hand side positive.

Length of track: 4.8 m.   Force of motor: 1 N.
Sampling rate: 200 Hz.   Mass of cart: 1.0 kg.
Length of poles: 1.0 m (upper); 1.0 m or 0.98 m (lower).
Mass of poles: 0.1 kg (upper); 0.1 kg or 0.098 kg (lower).

x	(cart position)	$0, \pm2.4$ m
$\dot{x}$	(cart velocity)	$\pm0.1, \pm\infty$ m s^{-1}
θ_1	(lower pole angle)	$\pm0.017, \pm0.2$ radians
$\dot{\theta}_1$	(lower pole angular velocity)	$\pm0.05, \pm\infty$ radians s^{-1}
θ_2	(upper pole angle)	$\pm0.00007, \pm0.2$ radians
$\dot{\theta}_2$	(upper pole angular velocity)	$\pm0.007, \pm\infty$ radians s^{-1}

Number of boxes : $2 \times 3 \times 3 \times 3 \times 3 \times 3 = 486$

Figure 3: 2-pole BOXES : simulator constants and variable partitions.

3.1.1   Method

The experiment consisted of a training phase followed by a testing phase. In the training phase, a single run of the BOXES program is made up of number of trials. Each trial starts with the simulator variables randomly initialised within the training range, shown in Figure 4. A trial ends in failure when the simulator is judged to be out of control. This occurs when the value of one or more simulator variables is above the maximum or below the minimum partition thresholds on those variables. If this happens the BOXES algorithm updates its decision settings in each box and a new trial is initiated. Alternatively, if the 2-pole system does not enter a failure state before a user-defined "cutoff" point, here set to 100 seconds or 20000 decision cycles, the run terminates and the number of trials taken to reach the cutoff is recorded as a measure of speed of learning. The decision settings in each of the 486 boxes are also saved.

The testing phase measures the performance attained by the decision settings learned by BOXES. This is done by combining the output of several runs into a single "master array". The actual setting of a box in this master array is determined by majority vote for a "push left" or a "push right" action from the settings recorded after each of the runs. In this instance, 32 replicate runs of BOXES produced the decision settings used to compile the master array. The master array was loaded into a runtime (i.e. non-learning) version of BOXES. This was then tested over 20 trials, recording the "lifetime" (duration of balancing the poles) of each. As before, a trial lasts until either the lifetime reaches the 100 seconds cutoff point or the 2-pole system enters a failure state. Two measures of performance were saved: mean lifetime over 20 trials; and number of trials out of 20 in which the cutoff point was reached. The complete train and test cycle is summarised in Figure 4.

	Training ranges	Testing ranges
x	−1.0 to 1.0 m	−1.0 to 1.0 m
$\dot{x}$	−0.1 to 0.1 m s^{-1}	0.0 m s^{-1}
θ_1	−0.001 to 0.001 radians	−0.001 to 0.001 radians
$\dot{\theta}_1$	−0.01 to 0.01 radians s^{-1}	0.0 radians s^{-1}
θ_2	−0.00001 to 0.00001 radians	−0.00001 to 0.00001 radians
$\dot{\theta}_2$	−0.001 to 0.001 radians s^{-1}	0.0 radians s^{-1}

Train and test cycle :
1. Train BOXES to 100 second cutoff for 32 replicates storing final settings;
2. Construct "master array" from majority votes in each box;
3. Test master array up to 100 second cutoff for 20 random starts.

Figure 4: 2-pole BOXES: experimental method.

Pole-dimension ratios (*lower* : *upper*)	Training performance (a)	Test performance (b)	(c)
100 : 100	305.5	53.4	26/80
98 : 100	314.7	58.2	28/80
Overall Means	310.1	55.8	54/160

Results :
  (a) BOXES - number of learning attempts before first 100 second
      success (means of 32 trials);
  (b) BOXES master array - runtime performance in seconds (means
      of 20 trials);
  (c) BOXES master array - number of 100 second successes out
      of 20 trials.

Figure 5: 2-pole BOXES: summary of experimental results.

3.1.2   Results

The results are summarised in Figure 5. Two versions of the 2-pole simulator were employed in the experiment. In one version, both poles were of identical length and mass. In the other, these dimensions were reduced by 2 % for the lower pole, maintaining the same density. No significant differences were observed between the two variants either in training or test performances. Therefore results for both are included in Figure 5, indicated respectively 100 : 100 and 98 : 100 for the ratio *lower* : *upper*, as replicates in the overall averages and totals.

For the second variant of the experimental task an additional action, "do nothing", was added to the BOXES algorithm. This is of interest since in many applications, such as that of satellite attitude-control mentioned above, conservation of energy resources is an important consideration, so the ability to "coast" is desirable. This modified version gave results similar to those for the bang-bang BOXES shown in the top half of Figure 5. The overall means and totals, for eight separate learning runs, were as follows :

    (a) BOXES - number of learning attempts before first 100 second
        success (means of 32 trials) = 367.9;
    (b) BOXES master array - runtime performance in seconds (means
        of 20 trials) = 60.5;
    (c) BOXES master array - number of 100 second successes out
        of 20 trials = 51/160.

The slight increase in learning time (from 310.1 to 367.9 trials) is acceptable since in raising the number of decision options from 2 to 3 the amount of entropy to be overcome during training is also correspondingly increased. This is an interesting result since it opens a route to the investigation of learning with control methods more sophisticated than bang-bang, a topic briefly discussed further in Section 4.

3.1.3   Discussion

The first point to be made is that the BOXES algorithm when applied to the 2-pole problem manages to learn up to the 100 second cutoff within a mean of 310.1 trials (367.9 trials with an extra "do nothing" action), over 8 separate learning runs. By comparison, in his 1988 study Sammut [14] recorded a learning time for the single-pole BOXES of 225 trials, a mean value taken over 5 separate learning runs. Given the greater number of boxes in the 2-pole configuration (486) compared to the single-pole problem (162), the increase in learning time recorded for the 2-pole variant is not as great as might have been expected. This suggests that not all boxes are required for a solution with "reasonable" performance, i.e. up to criterion. In fact, typically less than 50 % of all boxes were visited in a learning run.

Secondly, the question of performance measurement presents some difficulties. In Michie and Chambers original paper [11], some performance graphs were given in which values of *merit*, a figure computed by the BOXES algorithm, were plotted against the number of learning trials. Essentially, merit is a weighted average of the duration of balancing the poles over the sequence of trials in a learning run. Increased merit is interpreted as increased performance. To anticipate some results given below, note that values of merit have also been recorded as part of the measurement of the Incremental Freezing variant of BOXES. In Sammut's comparative study [14], performance of a set of boxes was gauged by the number of "successes" out of twenty runtime trials, a success being recorded when the poles were balanced for 100 seconds, the cutoff criterion. The results for the present study are given both in terms of the number of successes, and the mean lifetime (up to the cutoff value) of the twenty runtime trials. The performance on these measures was 55.8 seconds with 54/160 successes (60.5 seconds with 51/160 successes with an extra "do nothing" action), over eight separate test runs. Sammut reports, for two replicates only, success rates of 6/20 and 14/20. Taken together, these results may be interpreted to suggest, in common with Sammut, that although some solutions are learned which perform well, in general the method is not sufficiently robust to guarantee that a good set of boxes will result from any training session.

Lastly, a comparative study of the performance of BOXES with a hand-crafted decision rule published by Makarovic [8] was carried out. The results may be summarised as showing performance of 98.8 seconds with 193/200 successes over ten separate test runs for the rule. This can be compared to the 55.8 seconds with 54/160 successes over eight separate test runs for BOXES. The clear conclusion is that under the learning regime described, BOXES solutions do not perform as well as the Makarovic rule, although since the latter does not always keep the poles balanced for the standard 100 second criterion, it too suffers from a lack of robustness.

In the final section of this paper, a new method, "Incremental Freezing", is described. Experimental results for a new algorithm which implements this method, IF-BOXES, are given. It is concluded that the new method demonstrates one way in which BOXES may be improved, at least as applied to the 2-pole problem.

3.2   Experiment 2: Incremental Freezing

In the experiment reported above on the application of BOXES to the 2-pole problem, it was found that under the bang-bang control regime typically around 5% of the boxes comprising a master array displayed what appeared to be a decisive preference by majority vote for a left setting over right, or vice versa. This observation was the starting-point for the "Incremental Freezing" variant of BOXES, named IF-BOXES , which implements a form of incremental learning.

An incremental learning approach is based on the idea of learning a partial solution to the problem which is then used to guide the subsequent learning of a more complete solution, thereby speeding convergence. Usually the method is iterated until a pre-defined level of performance is attained. The IF-BOXES method differs in some respects to the typical definition of an incremental learning method (e.g. [1]). Nonetheless the principle is the same.

3.2.1   Method

In the case of IF-BOXES applied to the 2-pole problem, the method is based on the construction of a master array from a number of replicate learning runs of the basic 2-pole BOXES algorithm.

However, a new criterion which distinguishes "decisive" boxes and "freezes" their setting is introduced to augment the simple majority voting of box settings previously used in the construction of the master array. This extension from the majority vote scheme is designed to incorporate a measure of the depth of experience of a particular box (how often the box has been entered during a number of learning runs) and the degree to which one action setting is preferred over the other. The form of the decisiveness criterion used was determined by prior experimentation; the details are shown in the bottom half of Figure 6. Informally, the "lifetime" of a box is the weighted average of expected balancing duration following entry to that box. Likewise, the "usage" of a box is a weighted average of the number of times that box was previously entered during a learning run. For the exact definitions of lifetime and usage the reader is referred to the original BOXES paper [11]. Note that the minimum decisive vote from a learning run of 20 replicates is 14 to 6 in favour of a particular action, according to the current criterion.

It is the frozen boxes which constitute the partial solution at each cycle of the incremental learning process. Any boxes which are not decisive are set in the master array, as before, by the normal majority vote method, or by random choice in the event of equal preference.

Once constructed, the master decision array was used to initialise the box settings for the next training cycle. During learning, IF-BOXES cannot change the settings in any frozen boxes, although otherwise the trial-and-error method proceeds as previously described BOXES. The incremental training and test procedure was run for a total of five cycles in the current experimental configuration, with two replicates in this initial study. At each cycle, the cutoff duration was doubled, with the aim of raising the general performance level of the resulting solution and possibly visiting different areas of the state-space to increase the "quality" of the experience gained during training. To anticipate a point in the discussion, this latter goal was not necessarily achieved due to the occurrence of oscillations between boxes.

The details of the IF-BOXES training and test cycle are given in Figure 6. Note that the box partitions, and the training and testing ranges, were identical to those used in the first experiment, as shown in Figures 3 and 4 respectively.

In the remainder of this section the results of the initial experimental work with IF-BOXES applied to the 2-pole problem are given and discussed. A comparison between this learned solution and an deductively-derived control rule is also given, together with a rule induced from a trace of an IF-BOXES master array balancing the poles.

3.2.2   Results

The results for 2-pole IF-BOXES given here are for 2 replicates of 20 runs in each of 5 cycles, which makes a total of 200 training runs. The same number of runtime tests was carried out to determine the performance of the learned solutions.

With regard to performance results from the training phase, it should first be noted that at each cycle of the incremental process the cutoff duration is doubled. Training performance was measured on two counts, namely the number of learning trials required before the cutoff was reached at each cycle, and a new measure – the number of boxes frozen following each cycle. These results are given in Figure 7.

The number of learning trials taken to reach cutoff on the first cycle, where the cutoff is 100 seconds, was higher at 383.2 than that of 310.1 obtained for the non-incremental 2-pole BOXES, shown in Figure 5. However, the latter result is the mean of 256 (8 × 32) replicate training runs, whereas the IF-BOXES figure is the mean of 40 (2 × 20). Results from a variant of IF-BOXES in which all non-decisive boxes were randomly initialised gave a result of 321.1 from 100 (5 × 20) replicate training runs.

Of more interest is the profile of the changing number of learning trials taken to reach an exponentially increasing cutoff. After peaking at 439.4 on the second cycle where the cutoff is 200 seconds, by the fifth cycle where the cutoff is 1600 seconds

Incremental Freezing

Training cycle :
1. Randomly initialise box settings to left or right
2. Set cutoff = 100 seconds
3. For 5 cycles
   a. Run 20 replicates of IF-BOXES to cutoff and store final settings
   b. Construct master array and mark boxes which satisfy **decisiveness criterion** as frozen
   c. Initialise box settings to those of master array and double duration of cutoff

Test cycle :
1. Test master array stored after each cycle up to 2× final cutoff duration for 20 random starts

Decisiveness criterion for freezing box settings :

For each action compared to the other, if
   mean decilog lifetimes difference ≥ 5, and
   mean decilog usages difference ≥ 5, and
   votes ratio ≥ 2,
then freeze box setting to the preferred action.

Note :
(i) means for each box are from 20 sets of stored boxes
(ii) decilog(x) is $10 \times log_{10}(x)$ rounded to the nearest integer
(iii) votes for each action in box_i counted as number of sets of stored boxes in which box_i is set to that action

Figure 6: 2-pole IF-BOXES: experimental method.

Cycle	Cutoff (seconds)	Training performance	
		(a)	(b)
1	100	383.2	27.0
2	200	439.4	46.5
3	400	430.1	57.0
4	800	77.1	60.5
5	1600	26.1	63.5

Results :
(a) IF-BOXES - number of learning attempts before cycle cutoff
reached (overall means from 2 replicates of 20 trials);
(b) IF-BOXES master array - number of frozen boxes after each
cycle (means of 2 replicates).

Figure 7: 2-pole IF-BOXES: Training performance.

it has fallen to 26.1. In fact, on this final cycle the cutoff was reached within ten or less learning trials in 14 out of the 40 replicate training runs.

As the number of cycles completed increases, fewer of the remaining boxes are frozen at each step. Despite this, the partial solution which the frozen boxes represent rises from a mean of 27.0 or 5.5% of the total of 486 boxes after the first cycle to 63.5 or 13.1% of the total after the fifth cycle.

Taken together the results for training performance suggest convergence of the incremental learning process. The next step is to review the runtime performance of the learned solutions as stored in the master array following each cycle.

Once again, two measures were chosen for the assessment of the runtime (i.e. non-learning) performance of the master arrays of boxes. These were mean duration in seconds of balancing the poles, and the number of successes scored, where a success is continuous balancing for a pre-defined period from a randomly chosen starting state. The results are summarised in Figure 8. The overall mean duration of runtime tests of the master array following the first cycle was 48.0 seconds, which is slightly below that of 55.8 obtained in the non-incremental experiment, although as pointed out above the latter value was obtained from many more replicates.

Runtime testing for master arrays from all cycles was carried out up to a pre-defined cutoff duration of 3200 seconds. This was chosen by doubling the cutoff duration applied on the final training cycle of the incremental process, and is equivalent to just under an hour of balancing (53.33 minutes). It is therefore not surprising to find that after the first cycle the master array did not achieve any successes (continuous balancing up to the cutoff), which is also in line with the results from experiment 1, with the non-incremental 2-pole BOXES.

Two major points emerge from the results of runtime testing. They apply both to the measures of runtime duration and number of successes. Firstly, an improvement in performance was recorded over the five incremental cycles. The mean duration of

Cycle	Cutoff (seconds)	Test performance	
		(a)	(b)
1	3200	48.0	0/40
2	3200	506.9	0/40
3	3200	1977.9	19/40
4	3200	676.1	3/40
5	3200	2535.1	27/40

Results :
  (a) IF-BOXES master array - runtime performance in seconds
      (overall means from 2 replicates of 20 trials);
  (b) IF-BOXES master array - number of 3200 second successes
      in 40 runtime trials.

Figure 8: 2-pole IF-BOXES: Test performance.

balancing increased by from 48.0 seconds after the first cycle to 2535.1 seconds (over 42 minutes) after the fifth cycle. In the majority of the runtime tests (27/40), the cutoff duration was reached. Recall that this was twice as long as the cutoff applied in the final incremental cycle of the training phase. In fact, one of the two replicate master arrays constructed after the final incremental cycle performed perfectly on both measures, i.e. it recorded a mean runtime performance of 3200 seconds thereby scoring 20/20 successes.

Secondly, the performance increase was not monotonic. After rising following each of the first three cycles, on the next cycle performance dropped back almost to the level of cycle two before peaking at the fifth cycle.

A third measure of performance, merit, which is computed as part of the BOXES learning algorithm, was also recorded. Merit was defined informally above as a weighted average of the duration of balancing the poles over the sequence of trials in a learning run. In Figure 9 the mean value of merit at the end of the last learning trial is plotted for each of the five cycles.

Lastly, as for the experiment with the non-incremental version of 2-pole BOXES, the runtime performance of the inductively constructed rules was compared to that of the deductively derived rule of Makarovic [8]. The overall mean runtime duration in seconds of the latter rule was 1183.0. This figure was obtained from 5 replicates of 20 runtime trials. The proportion of 3200 second successes in these runtime trials was 7/100. By way of comparison, the mean runtime duration obtained for the inductively-constructed rule after the third IF-BOXES cycle was 1977.9 seconds, with the proportion of 3200 second successes being 19/40. Although this level of performance fell on the subsequent cycle, the Makarovic rule was again out-performed after completion of the fifth IF-BOXES cycle.

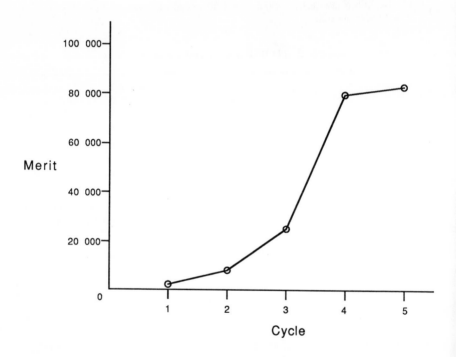

Figure 9: 2-pole IF-BOXES: Mean value of merit after each cycle.

3.2.3 Discussion

The results given in the previous section for the performance of the 2-pole IF-BOXES system are promising, although much work remains to be done. It can be concluded that performance improved over the course of the incremental learning process. It is also clear that performance is liable to fall between one incremental cycle and the next, i.e. that the performance improvement is non-monotonic. From the training results shown in Figure 7, it would appear that the incremental learning process was converging on a solution. To determine whether this effect is genuine would require further iterations of the training phase. High performance was recorded on the runtime testing summarised in Figure 8, with a maximum score obtained for one of the replicate master arrays. More replicates would be needed to determine whether this result is robust.

The results for merit, as shown in the graph in Figure 9, are of interest since they, unlike the other performance tests, form a part of the BOXES algorithm. Merit may be thought of as BOXES "level of aspiration". During learning merit is continually updated relative to the current global performance of the algorithm. Since calculating merit involves a pronounced smoothing of the durations of successive learning trials, this tends to reduce the effect of extremely bad or good periods of balancing on the final result. For this reason it is encouraging that the numbers obtained show a steady monotonic performance improvement.

As indicated above, the performance of the Makarovic rule was surpassed by that of IF-BOXES when the results were compared. However, the IF-BOXES rules' performance included very short balancing durations as well as durations consistently up to the cutoff, although the latter were in the majority (67.5%) after the final incremental cycle. These performance scores suggest that the learned rules form imperfect solutions. For example, a potentially infinite balancing duration may occur if an oscillation is set up between two or more boxes. This "cycling-in-the-stack" behaviour has been observed in preliminary investigations with a graphical interface connected to the IF-BOXES system controlling the 2-pole simulator. Since the BOXES algorithm is designed to learn to avoid failure rather than optimise its control strategy such oscillations constitute "desirable" behaviour. Oscillations of this type, it should be noted, might not last for very long in any physical system due to the influence of factors such as noise on sensors and perturbations from external influences.

It is probable that an algorithm which learned to exploit such cycles would perform well on the pole-balancing task. However, the possibility of getting into cycles for a trial-and-error learner such as any current variant of BOXES carries the risk of failing to adequately cover all areas of the problem space during the training period. This would result in an apparently good solution being "brittle", i.e. liable to very bad performance when the controller is in state-space regions for which learned rules are incorrect.

One way of trying to overcome this problem would be to change the training strategy used by IF-BOXES. The current approach in which starting states are randomly initialised within a pre-defined range appears to be inadequate. This could be amended so that all areas of the state-space (i.e. all boxes) were used to

if $\dot{\theta}_1 \geq threshold_{\dot{\theta}_1}$ then   push right   else
if $\dot{\theta}_1 < -threshold_{\dot{\theta}_1}$ then   push left   else
  if $\theta_1 \geq threshold_{\theta_1}$ then   push right   else
  if $\theta_1 < -threshold_{\theta_1}$ then   push left   else
    if $\dot{\theta}_2 \geq threshold_{\dot{\theta}_2}$ then   push left   else
    if $\dot{\theta}_2 < -threshold_{\dot{\theta}_2}$ then   push right   else
      if $\theta_2 \geq threshold_{\theta_2}$ then   push left   else
      if $\theta_2 < -threshold_{\theta_2}$ then   push right   else
        if $\dot{x} \geq threshold_{\dot{x}}$ then   push left   else
        if $\dot{x} < -threshold_{\dot{x}}$ then   push right   else
          if $x \geq 0$ then   push left   else   push right.

Figure 10: Control rule for 2-pole balancing (after Makarovic).

provide the starting states. Furthermore, termination of the training phase could be altered to depend not only on reaching a cutoff period but also on ensuring, for example, that all boxes had been visited sufficiently often.

The IF-BOXES method might be improved by experimentation with some of BOXES internal parameters, or with different settings for the Incremental Freezing criterion. These could include fixing decisiveness relative to current number of frozen boxes, or "unfreezing" boxes if performance drops during the learning process. It would also be invaluable to investigate the effect of adding various levels of noise and other discontinuities to the simulator to model real-world effects and gauge corresponding performance changes in the learned solutions.

3.2.4   A machine-learned rule-based controller

Finally, having presented results for particular techniques of machine learning applied to control, it is appropriate to briefly discuss the issue of the rules which comprise these inductively constructed controllers. The case for rule-based control of both the pole-and-cart and the 2-pole systems has been made by Makarovic [8]. A rule derived by that author for the latter system appears in Figure 10. Experimental results given above show that the performance of this rule was surpassed by IF-BOXES. In an initial investigation, the method developed by Sammut [14] of coupling reinforcement learning (BOXES) with decision-tree induction (C4) for generating explanatory rules of pole-and-cart control was applied to the IF-BOXES system.

The method used differed slightly from that of Sammut, since one of the IF-BOXES master arrays was run in test mode to generate a trace, which was then used as input to an updated version of the decision-tree induction system, C4.5. This trace consisted of a list of records of the form

< state-vector, control-action >

---

if $\theta_2 > 8.7 \times 10^{-5}$ **and** $\dot{\theta}_2 > -0.007$ **then** push left **else**
if $\dot{\theta}_2 > 0.007$ **then** push left **else**
if $\theta_2 \leq 8.7 \times 10^{-5}$ **and** $\dot{\theta}_2 \leq 0.007$ **then** push right **else**
if $\dot{\theta}_2 \leq -0.007$ **then** push right.

Default : push right.

Evaluation on test data (3334 items):
Tested 3334, errors 41 (1.2%).

Figure 11: Control rule induced from runtime IF-BOXES trace (50 seconds).

---

where the state-vector contained the values of the state-variables $x, \dot{x}, \theta_1, \dot{\theta}_1, \theta_2, \dot{\theta}_2$, and the control-action was either "push left" or "push right". Each record may be thought of as an instantaneous snap-shot of the simulator and the action being applied by the controller. The master array was run to produce a trace containing 10000 records, corresponding to 50 seconds balancing duration. This trace was split into two sets of examples in the ratio 2 : 1. The larger of these sets provided the training examples from which the rule shown in Figure 11 was induced. The remaining set of examples was used as a test set to measure the accuracy of induced rule.

It must be emphasised that this rule does *not* represent a complete description of the functionality of the IF-BOXES master array. Rather it is a description of the behaviour of this master array over a (relatively short) period of balancing the poles. Nevertheless it is sufficient to illustrate some interesting points regarding this behaviour.

Firstly, the structure of the IF-BOXES derived rule is compatible with that of the Makarovic rule. This is satisfactory since although its author gave no formal proof or empirical validation, the Makarovic rule appears to be approximately correct. The fact that it does not balance the poles indefinitely may be due to the fact that the thresholds must be re-adjusted for different implementations of the simulation equations, or that the rule is incomplete and cannot control the simulator in particular pathological states.

Secondly, the particular structure of the rule reflects the behavioural trace from which it was induced. The rule is only explicitly concerned with detecting the position and movement of the upper pole (θ_2 and $\dot{\theta}_2$), since these are the only state variables occurring in the condition parts of the rule. The applied force ("push left" or "push right") which appears in the action parts of the rule corrects the position and movement of the upper pole towards the vertical.

The rule is clearly incomplete since it does not cover all possible states of the 2-pole system. However, upon examination of the records in the trace, it is apparent that only the upper pole variables determined those particular control decisions, since the lower pole was more or less upright and stable and the cart was practically immobile near the centre of the track.

Generating a control rule from traces of the behaviour of an observed controller is an interesting method explored both in Sammut's work and in the paper by Michie, Bain and Hayes-Michie in this volume. It should be noted, however, that the trace of control behaviour from which the rule in Figure 11 was induced comprised less than 2% of the total 3200 second balancing time in a single runtime trial. Clearly, therefore, to use this method to generate a more complete set of rules demands a more comprehensive training method. Despite this limitation, as a method of constructing or as an aid to "debugging" controllers the potential benefits of this "learning-by-watching" method are considerable.

Since the boxes of the master array are equivalent to a set of pattern-based rules, a direct translation to the production rule formalism, for example, would be possible. However, a set of 486 production rules, each with up to six tests in condition part, does not meet the requirement set out at the beginning of this paper that rules be user-comprehensible. Some work on reducing the complexity of representing a set of boxes as a set of rules has been attempted, but this is of a preliminary nature and has not been automated.

4   Conclusion

The results presented above constitute a revival and extension of methods first designed and implemented over two decades ago. The successful application of variants of the BOXES algorithm has been surprising to some, since the technique appears to be so simple. In fact, this simplicity is perhaps the key to its success and has facilitated extensions where required. It is obvious, however, that the work completed so far is only the beginning. There is much which remains to be done, and by way of conclusion a short list of possible topics for further investigation is given below.

On an important practical point, all the results given here have been empirical and in the nature of a preliminary study. Whether the system to be controlled is a simulator or a physical device, any real-world application of these techniques would require greater certifiability. Either a standardised empirical testing procedure or formal proofs would be needed.

In terms of developing improved algorithms which implement machine-learned rule-based control, several starting points have emerged from the work reported above. Within a BOXES-type framework, there is clearly a need to be able to exploit additional actions (e.g. the null action). This allows considerations of the cost of different control actions to play a part in the learning process. For instance, weight might be added to boxes whose setting is the null action. This weighting factor could be related to the ratio of the cost of failure to the cost of applying unit force.

Weights could also be added to boxes in favoured (e.g. more stable) regions of the state-space. This opens a route to incorporating optimisation of the control strategy as a goal during learning, rather than merely avoiding failure.

BOXES benefits from a large amount of implicit background knowledge about the "black-box" to be controlled, most noticeably in the partitioning of the state-space to form the boxes. Automation of this task, which currently is left to the user, would be desirable.

A general point regarding the development of new techniques is that the 6-dimensional state-space of the 2-pole system is difficult to represent in any graphic form. Use of a much simpler problem like the "hill-and-hovercraft" where there are only two state variables necessary for successful control might be useful here. With only two dimensions, the control surface could be easily inspected during the learning process. This problem has the additional advantage that since it is much simpler, learning is faster, permitting a greater variety of possible techniques to be implemented and tested.

With regard to the findings of Michie, Bain and Hayes-Michie elsewhere in this volume, a replication and development of the Chambers and Michie [4] version of BOXES in which a human cooperated with the machine-learning algorithm on the pole-balancing task would be of interest in the area of skill acquisition and transfer.

Over the last few years, many points of reference between this type of work and other methods, within and beyond Machine Learning have been established. The techniques described in this paper are still some way from many real-world applications of much greater difficulty even than trying to balance two jointed poles mounted upright on a cart running up and down a linear track. Nevertheless, the fact that this type of adaptive control has been shown to have a measure of success, together with the promise of automatically constructing "knowledgeable" descriptive rules of a controller's functionality, justify the further investigation of inductive machine learning in this area.

Acknowledgement Thanks are due to: Professor Donald Michie, who directed this work and originally suggested the "incremental freezing" method; Dr Stephen Muggleton, for his comments on this paper; and Dr Andrew Hay of the National Engineering Laboratory (NEL) for his interest in the application of machine learning methods in control. Funding support was received in part from Wespace, Inc. and in part from a consortium of NEL, British Aerospace and Apple Computer (Europe).

References

[1] M. Bain and S. H. Muggleton. Non-monotonic learning. In J. E. Hayes-Michie and E. Tyugu, editors, *Machine Intelligence 12*. Oxford University Press, Oxford, 1990.

[2] I. Bridge and M. Whyte. Controlling the inverted pendulum. Unpublished report, Cranfield Institute of Technology, 1988.

[3] R. H. Cannon. *Dynamics of physical systems*. McGraw-Hill, Inc., 1967.

[4] R. A. Chambers and D. Michie. Man-machine co-operation on a learning task. In R. Parslow, R. Prowse, and R. Elliott-Green, editors, *Computer Graphics: Techniques and Applications*, pages 79 – 186. Plenum Publishing, London, 1969.

[5] E. Eastwood. Control theory and the engineer. *Proc. IEE*, 115(1):203 – 211, 1968.

[6] S. Gallant. Example-based knowledge engineering with conectionist expert systems. In *IEEE Midcon, August 30 - September 1*. Dallas, Texas, 1988.

[7] I. Kononenko. Interpretation of neural networks decisions. In *Proceedings of IASTED Internat. Conf. on Expert Systems and Applications*. Zurich, 1989.

[8] A. Makarovic. A qualitative way of solving the pole-balancing problem. In J. E. Hayes-Michie and E. Tyugu, editors, *Machine Intelligence 12*. Oxford University Press, Oxford, 1990.

[9] D. Michie. Machine learning in the next five years. In D. Sleeman, editor, *Proceedings of the Third Working Session on Learning*, pages 107 – 122, London, 1988. Pitman.

[10] D. Michie and I. Bratko. Ideas on knowledge synthesis stemming from the kbbkn endgame. *Journal of the International Computer Chess Association*, 10(1):3 – 13, 1987.

[11] D. Michie and R. A. Chambers. Boxes : an experiment in adaptive control. In E. Dale and D. Michie, editors, *Machine Intelligence 2*, pages 137 – 152. Edinburgh University Press, Edinburgh, 1968.

[12] J. R. Quinlan, P. J. Compton, K. A. Horn, and L. Lazarus. Inductive knowledge acquisition : a case study. In *Proceedings of the Second Australian Conference on Applications of Expert Systems*, pages 183 – 204, New South Wales Institute of Technology, Sydney, 1986.

[13] D. W. Russell, S. J. Rees, and J. Boyes. A microsystem for control of real-life situations. In *Proc. Conf. on Information Sciences and Systems*. Johns Hopkins University, Baltimore, MD, 1977.

[14] C. Sammut. Experimental results from an evaluation of algorithms that learn to control dynamic systems. In J. Laird, editor, *Proceedings of the Fifth International Conference on Machine Learning*, pages 437 – 443, Los Altos, 1988. Morgan Kaufmann.

[15] C. Sammut and D. Michie. Controlling a 'black-box'simulation of a space craft. Technical Report TIRM-89-039, The Turing Institute, Glasgow, 1989.

Chapter 13

Expert systems for self-tuning control

K. J. Hunt and G. R. Worship

1 INTRODUCTION

The application of self-tuning control can in certain process control problems lead to improvements in economic, safety and control performance. However, the components of a self-tuning controller are more complex than conventional loop controllers and require considerable knowledge of a variety of advanced algorithmic techniques.

In addition, as much detailed process specific knowledge as possible must be built into the self-tuner in order to select good design parameters for a given application.

We identify a two-way knowledge threshold which must be crossed before self-tuning control can be used and fully exploited on industrial processes.

This paper examines the components of the knowledge threshold present for self-tuning controllers and considers some possible solutions. The use of expert systems to lower the knowledge threshold is discussed with reference to a prototype system.

2 BACKGROUND

The majority of loop controllers currently operating in the process industries are of the PID (Proportional Integral Derivative) form. These controllers have three free parameters which must be chosen in such a way that satisfactory control performance is achieved. The conventional approach to the tuning of PID controllers is simply a trial-and-error method whereby the plant engineer successively refines the controller settings based on a subjective view of the resulting plant performance. Alternatively, the controller parameters can be determined using step response analysis or the application of long established tuning rules, such as those of Ziegler and Nichols (Ziegler and Nichols, 1942). In either case the success of the tuning procedure relies upon the wealth of process knowledge and experience of the plant operators and engineers.

In the majority of cases controllers tuned using these techniques can operate in service for many years without problems. The functional simplicity of PID controllers means that they can be operated in a straightforward manner. In a small number of "difficult" loops, however, the tuning procedure can be difficult and very time consuming. On these loops the controller performance can be poor.

A further complicating factor is the commonly occurring source of uncertainty resulting from the variation of plant dynamics with time. These variations can result from non-linearities, ageing or other reasons. Frequently, the performance of a PID controller will seriously deteriorate in the face of such plant variations.

These considerations have led to the emergence in recent years of industrial PID controllers having some form of automatic tuning capability. The auto-tuning mechanism in these devices is frequently based upon an automated open-loop step response analysis. Alternatively, portable self-tuning devices employing advanced methods can be used to determine the tuning parameters of a range of standard PID controllers (Gawthrop and Nomikos, 1990). In addition to the initial tuning of PID controllers, auto-tuners have the potential to be re-tuned at some later stage should the performance deteriorate.

There remains a small class of critical process control loops which the basic PID algorithm fails to control satisfactorily. This problem often appears in loops with long time delays, high order lags, or some other dynamic complexity.

In order to provide control of processes incorporating such complicated dynamics, control science has developed advanced algorithms which employ models of the process. These advanced algorithms can give more accurate control which can lead to economic and safety improvements.

In contrast to the three parameters of the PID controller, these newer methods involve a relatively high number of design variables. This precludes manual approaches to the proper adjustment of these algorithms. In contrast to PID controllers, these advanced algorithms require a mathematical model of the plant in order to synthesise a controller. Without a mathematical model of reasonable accuracy the performance these algorithms can be severely degraded. The generation of an accurate process model is therefore essential if any improvement in control performance is to be achieved.

To produce an accurate process model requires the adoption of a suitable model structure (appropriate order, inclusion of time delays etc.) and the subsequent estimation (or identification) of the model parameters.

For a process with time-invariant dynamics, the advanced algorithm will now produce the specified control performance. In the event of changes in the plant dynamics, the advanced algorithm will, like PID, suffer degradation in performance as the plant characteristics deviate from the assumed model.

For such plant changes, the model parameters approximating the plant dynamics will change with time or plant conditions. In some cases, it is also possible for the model structure suitable for plant identification to change. These factors introduce uncertainty to the model of the plant used to synthesise the controller which, in turn, introduces variability to the control performance.

For the PID algorithm, or the advanced algorithms considered so far, such variability in control performance is undesirable. In advanced algorithms, the variability is due to the controller synthesis procedure employing an assumed plant model which is different to the actual plant.

As any real process will exhibit changing characteristics, the preservation of control performance throughout the operating range of a process is an important criterion.

Control science offers many ways of tackling this problem. Methods available range from qualitative modelling and fuzzy control, which assume that a model of numerical accuracy cannot be produced, through robust control techniques, where control performance is designed to be maintained throughout a specified range of model parameters, to adaptive control schemes. Adaptive control aims to maintain control performance over a range of plant characteristics by tracking and compensating for changes in the process. Self-tuning control is an adaptive scheme in which the selection of model structure, the parameter estimation and the controller synthesis stages are automated.

3   SELF-TUNING CONTROL

As mentioned above, the basic idea in self-tuning control is to automate the procedures of process modelling and identification, and controller synthesis. A detailed background to self-tuning control, and other forms of adaptive control, is given in Åström and Wittenmark (Åström and Wittenmark, 1989). A block diagram of a self-tuning controller is shown in Figure 1. In the modelling stage a linear transfer-function of fixed structure is normally taken *a priori* as a plant model. The unknown parameters of this model are estimated on-line using a recursive estimation method. Many different estimation schemes can be used. Many of these techniques are variants of the basic recursive least-squares algorithm.

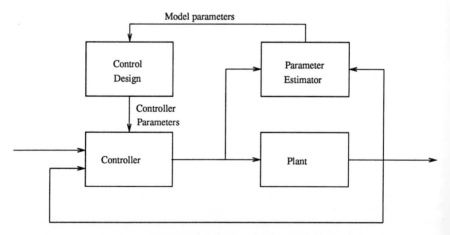

Figure 1: Self-tuning Control

The estimated parameters are passed to the controller synthesis stage and used as the basis of the control design. Again, a range of control design algorithms can be used. These designs differ primarily in the specifications of closed-loop performance, and in the associated user design parameter interface.

A particular self-tuning controller can be configured using different combinations of estimation methods and design methods. It should be noted that in practice continuous adaptation is rarely used. Many strategies for adaptation can be used. Some of these include:

- Auto-tuning - adaptation is used at the beginning of a control session and then switched off.

- Periodic retuning - adaptation is switched on periodically. In this mode parameter estimation can be performed continuously if desired; the controller synthesis algorithm is only periodically activated when significant plant variations are detected.

- Continuous adaptation - only used in special cases.

As mentioned above, different combinations of estimation methods and design methods can be used to configure a self-tuner. One can conceive of a very general self-tuning control instrument which comprises a collection of algorithms for estimation, control and supervision. A natural step is to enhance the numerical algorithms by constructing an expert system containing a number of knowledge sources, each one being specific to a particular identification, control or supervision algorithm. This is the basic idea behind Expert Control (Åström et al., 1986), or Knowledge Based Control (Årzén, 1987; Årzén, 1989). Each knowledge source has information on the characteristics of specific algorithms. Moreover, a higher level knowledge source can be utilised. This has knowledge about when to use each particular algorithm (a meta-knowledge source). The expert system uses the meta-knowledge and the specific knowledge sources to orchestrate the overall operation of the self-tuner.

Expert systems have also been used for the configuration and on-line use of self-tuners (Sanoff and Wellstead, 1985) and for the configuration of identification algorithms (Betta and Linkens, 1988).

4 CONFIGURING AND OPERATING A SELF-TUNING CONTROL SYSTEM

Self-tuning control offers the opportunity to employ advanced controller synthesis techniques, incorporating process models, enabling the control of the "difficult" control loops which cannot be adequately controlled by PID control. Further, self-tuning controllers aim to track plant changes using parameter identification techniques so as to maintain control performance during changes in the process during operation.

Advanced control synthesis procedures require a reliable model of the process to be controlled because the control performance is degraded by model inaccuracies. It is essential therefore that a self-tuner is set-up and maintained so as to produce a reliable model for use in control synthesis.

The successful configuration and maintenance of a self-tuning controller is a much more complex task than the tuning of a PID control loop and involves many other considerations. The procedure is outlined as follows.

4.1   System Identification

The choice of an appropriate identification method relies upon knowledge of the properties of each method under consideration, insight into the characteristics of the process to be controlled, and experience in the practical reconciliation of these two factors. The on-line use of recursive identification can be separated into two distinct phases: initialisation and run-time. Each of these phases requires the selection of a range of parameters which have a critical effect on the algorithm performance.

4.1.1   Initialisation

Before applying a self-tuner the model structure must be chosen. This choice will depend primarily on process knowledge and in particular on the nature of the disturbances to which the process is likely to be subjected. Key issues are whether the process is subject to constant offsets or drifting disturbances. The next important choice is the order of the model. Selection of model order will determine the number of parameters to be estimated. This choice relies on knowledge of process dynamics. Typically, a second order model will capture the essential information content in a range of process control applications.

If more complex dynamics are apparent, however, this order may have to be increased. Another issue relates to knowledge of the process time delay. This information can be obtained from the operators or by performing simple open loop step tests. Knowledge of the likely variations in time delay has a direct effect on the selection of the number of model parameters to be estimated. If the time delay is likely to vary widely (flow problems, for example), or if the time delay is highly uncertain, then the number of estimated parameters in the transfer-function numerator will have to be increased.

When the model structure has been selected the next stage is to select an appropriate identification method. This will require a detailed understanding of available system identification techniques. This choice will in part be dictated by the assumed model structure; certain methods are specific to certain models. A further issue is the nature of expected process disturbances. The signal to noise ratio of the disturbance, and whether the disturbance is stochastic or deterministic in nature are important questions. Choice of a suitable identification method therefore relies upon an appropriate synthesis of process and algorithmic knowledge.

Having selected an identification algorithm initial values for it's design values must be chosen. If prior information on the plant dynamics is available then this can be used as the basis of the initial model parameter estimates. Otherwise default values can be used. A second important choice is the initial gain of the estimation scheme. This is related to prior knowledge of plant dynamics. If such knowledge is scarce then a higher initial value for this gain is appropriate in order to speed convergence of the estimates. The third major choice in the identification algorithm is the so-called forgetting factor. This is a scalar variable which effectively determines the memory length of the estimation scheme. The greater our uncertainty (or the smaller our confidence) about the parameter estimates the shorter we would like this memory to be so that old data is discarded more quickly.

4.1.2   Run-time

The selection or adaptation of identification parameters during a run-time experiment depends upon monitoring the estimator performance. As mentioned above, an appropriate value for the forgetting factor depends upon our confidence in the current estimates. It follows that we would like the forgetting factor to adapt as the plant parameter estimates evolve; if the estimation is converging to better estimates then our confidence increases and so the memory length should be increased. A related issue is the estimator gain. If the estimates are becoming accurate and information rich data is still available then it is known that the estimator gain will tend to a small value.

Knowledge of the likely variations in the plant dynamics with time will help in the determination of a strategy to address the above issues. If the plant dynamics have changed then two possibilities are either to decrease the estimator memory length, or to increase the gain (the two approaches in fact amount to the same thing). If the plant is subject to infrequent and sudden dynamic variations then it may be more appropriate to completely re-initialise the parameter estimation.

4.2   Control Design

The choice of a control design algorithm is dictated by the available specifications on closed-loop performance. In process control situations performance specifications are frequently given in terms of transparent time domain concepts such as rise-time or maximum permissable overshoot. These specifications are some⁺imes complemented by frequency domain stability concepts including gain and phase margins. Unfortunately, many control algorithms used in self-tuners do not have performance related user variables which can be neatly expressed in terms with which plant engineers are familiar. This problem can sometimes be addressed in methods using reference models (including pole/zero assignment methods) where the dynamical modes of the reference model are directly related to closed-loop bandwidth (and therefore to time-domain measures).

The problem is more apparent in high performance self-tuners based upon optimal control designs or multi-step prediction. In these methods the performance measures and design variables as understood by the self-tuning expert must be reconciled with the more traditional closed-loop specifications. As with the choice of identification algorithm, the selection of a suitable control synthesis technique relies upon an appropriate synthesis of process and algorithmic knowledge.

When a control algorithm whose performance related variables can be satisfactorily matched to the closed-loop performance specifications has been selected, those variables can then be set up in such a way that the specifications are met as closely as possible. It is often worthwhile selecting initial values for the controller design parameters which are rather conservative (i.e. lead to a reduced closed-loop bandwidth) since the uncertainty in the estimates will be higher in this phase. This will help to maintain stability as the estimates converge.

4.3   On-line Use

Monitoring is required to ensure the proper on-line operation of the self-tuner. The most important factor is the performance of the parameter estimator. Certain parameters in the estimator act as estimation performance indicators. These indicators help in deciding when to re-initialise the estimator and, crucially, when the estimated parameters should be used by the control algorithm to update the controller. As discussed above, the estimation performance indicators also help in the selection of values for the forgetting factor. A variety of techniques, both automatic and heuristic, can be applied for this purpose. This issue clearly relies upon a deep understanding of the system identification algorithm area.

The control performance must also be monitored to ensure that the closed-loop specifications are met. The initially conservative control parameters can be altered to tighten up closed-loop performance as better estimates are obtained. These parameters may also be fine-tuned on-line by observing the control performance. This clearly requires insight into, and detailed algorithmic knowledge of, the physical properties of the control algorithm being used.

5   THE KNOWLEDGE THRESHOLD

The setting up and use of a self-tuner, as discussed in the preceding section, clearly relies upon a two-way flow of ideas between plant engineers and the self-tuning control expert. The detailed process knowledge which plant engineers have is usually the result of many years experience on the plant. This knowledge must be used to the full in order to select the best possible configuration for the self-tuner. The self-tuning control expert's knowledge is also usually the result of many years of study in this area.

The configuration and operation of a self-tuning system requires a suitable synthesis of plant specific information and algorithmic knowledge relevant to the self-tuner. The knowledge involved has two parts:

1. General process knowledge required to use plant information (plant order, time delays, non-linearities, actuator characteristics etc.) for the selection of

    (a) suitable control algorithms and identification schemes, and

    (b) suitable performance related design parameters for the specific algorithms chosen.

2. Algorithmic knowledge relating to the characteristics of identification methods and controller synthesis techniques.

Thus, hindering the successful employment of a self-tuning controller on a specific plant is a two-way knowledge threshold. This threshold is represented in Figure 2.

On one side of the threshold is the plant engineer or plant operator who has the detailed process knowledge required as the basis of performance specifications and algorithm configuration, but has little knowledge of the algorithms themselves.

On the other side of the threshold is the self-tuning expert who has command of the algorithms required to produce a self-tuner but limited knowledge of the process.

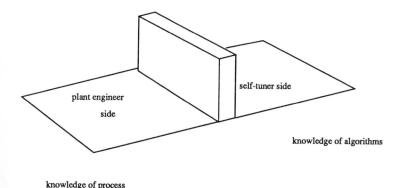

Figure 2: The Knowledge Threshold

6   REDUCING THE KNOWLEDGE THRESHOLD

In order to make self-tuning control fully available to the difficult loops described earlier and thus achieve the potential of the technique a means of reducing, or ideally eliminating, the two-way knowledge threshold of Figure 2 is required.

Simple consideration of Figure 2 reveals that the threshold should be tackled from both sides.

6.1   The Plant Engineer

As described earlier, the plant engineer possesses the necessary process knowledge so as to define the performance required from a controller and set parameters of the algorithms. The engineer does not have knowledge of the algorithms or the relationship between the process knowledge and parameter values.

An increase of the current engineers' knowledge to encompass these skills, or the selective recruitment of better qualified engineers would breach the threshold and allow confident exploitation of the self-tuner.

This step has implications for education, training and recruitment. As such, this option is relevant to the medium or longer term.

6.2   The Self-tuner

From Figure 2 it can be seen that if process knowledge is made available then an automatic configuration for the self-tuner algorithms can be achieved. This requires communication with the plant engineer to establish general plant information and performance specifications during configuration, and problem areas during operation.

One way in which to achieve this and thus breach the knowledge threshold from the self-tuning expert side is to employ expert systems technology. The use of expert system techniques in this application is discussed in the following section.

7   AN EXPERT SYSTEM FOR SELF-TUNING CONTROL

An expert system provides a means of overcoming the knowledge threshold. The expert system performs the specialised roles of configuration and operation as described in Section 4. The expert system thus mimics a self-tuning control expert in liasing with the plant engineer to establish general information and performance criteria. The expert system then applies the knowledge upon which it is based to the plant engineer's information to derive algorithm parameters, on-line changes, and so on.

A well developed expert system should allow the plant engineer to express information in familiar form and also allow questioning of the system to receive justification or explanation of decisions or questions.

An expert system can be developed quickly and inexpensively using an expert system toolkit. Expert system toolkits, while often restricted in terms of representation or inference, provide a fast prototyping route to a developer. In the self-tuning area, the development of an expert system prototype will allow demonstration of the potential of the self-tuning technology while limiting the need for retraining.

8   THE MASTER SYSTEM

A prototype of a self-tuning system employing expert system technology has been created (Worship, 1989). The system is known as MASTER (Monitoring and Advice on Self-Tuning with an ExpeRt).

The MASTER expert system components tackled the configuration of the self-tuning system and also performance monitoring of the complete system. The knowledge base developed was designed so as to demonstrate the utility of the approach for a range of possible problems.

MASTER's experts were produced using a commercially available expert system toolkit. This allowed representation of knowledge as frames, demons and rules. Rules were used in backward chaining inference and demons operated during forward chaining. The MASTER configuration expert employed backward chaining to force selection of identification and control routines, and their appropriate parameters. This strategy was appropriate due to the ability to control the order of queries to the user.

The MASTER run-time expert system employed demons so that a data value outwith an acceptable range could generate an assertion provoking remedial action as soon as it appeared. This removed the need for repeated and computationally expensive backward chaining tests for unacceptable values.

The MASTER system demonstrated that expert systems do offer an effective means of reducing, and ultimately overcoming, the self-tuning control knowledge threshold. A further conclusion of the work was that an expert system development toolkit allowed rapid development and refinement of a knowledge base.

9   CONCLUSIONS

Work on the MASTER prototype system has shown the potential results of combining self-tuning control and expert systems technology. Such a combination can offer a short term solution to the problems presented by the self-tuning control knowledge threshold. The use of a development toolkit enhances the productivity of development although subsequent implementation may be achieved using a procedural language.

With such a prototype, the benefits of self-tuning control can be released to the plant engineer in a transparent fashion without the requirement for extensive additional training. To an organisation considering the use of self-tuning control in its production, such a prototype offers relatively easy investigation of the technique.

For medium to long term solutions, the retraining or selective recruitment of staff offers the most effective means of ensuring the confident employment of self-tuning control or, indeed, any other advanced control strategy.

However due to the economic implications of retraining or selective recruitment, the investigation of a new strategy generally cannot be achieved by this method. In such cases, expert systems offer a route to the investigation without great expense.

References

Årzén, K. E. (1987). *Realization of expert system based feedback control.* PhD thesis, Department of Automatic Control, Lund Institute of Technology.

Årzén, K. E. (1989). An architecture for expert system based feedback control. *Automatica*, 25:813–827.

Åström, K. J., Anton, J. J., and Årzén, K. E. (1986). Expert control. *Automatica*, 22:277–286.

Åström, K. J. and Wittenmark, B. (1989). *Adaptive Control.* Addison-Wesley, Reading, Mass.

Betta, A. and Linkens, D. A. (1988). EASI (Expert Advisor for System Identification): A prototype package for linear and non-linear systems. In *Proc. IEE Conf. Control '88, Oxford, England.*

Gawthrop, P. J. and Nomikos, P. E. (1990). Automatic tuning of commercial PID controllers for single-loop and multiloop applications. *IEEE Control Systems Magazine*, 10:34–42.

Sanoff, S. P. and Wellstead, P. E. (1985). Expert identification and control. In *Proc. IFAC Symposium on Identification and System Parameter Estimation, York, England.*

Worship, G. R. (1989). Development of a self-tuning controller demonstration system incorporating an expert system monitor and advisor. M. Eng thesis, Department of Electrical and Electronic Engineering, Heriot-Watt University.

Ziegler, J. G. and Nichols, N. B. (1942). Optimum settings for automatic controllers. *Trans. ASME*, 64:759–768.

Chapter 14

Case studies in condition monitoring

R. Milne

1.1 INTRODUCTION

In this paper, we summarise a number of systems developed by Intelligent Applications, primarily in heavy industry. Most of the systems have the characteristic that they are focussed on diagnostics that are on-line to the plant. That is, they are running continuously; receiving data, trying to reach conclusions and giving you output.

We will focus on what the applications are and the benefit of the application, without discussing how they were actually implemented internally.

This paper discusses some of the applications we have developed in the mechanical and process area.

1.2 DATA INTERPRETATION

The problems we are interested in are as follows. Assume there is a massive amount of data, and by itself that data is useless. Now normally that data is from an on-line data acquisition system, the system is constantly bringing in a set of information, presented on a panel or mimic diagram. The data itself is useless, but it is very valuable to get an interpretation. You really want to know whether a light is on or off, and whether to turn on pump seven or shut off pump seven.

Right now most companies are dependant on a very expensive person to do that interpretation and that person works shifts, that person has good good days and bad days. That person has varying degrees of knowledge. Normally, because that person is very good at it, there are many other things for him to do, so you need to have some way to free him up for the hard problems. It is clearly a waste of his time to do the simple, routine, easy problems. So the whole concept of what you would like to achieve is, replace that person with a computer programme.

Now a computer programme can be fairly complicated or it may be fairly simple, but the fundamental goal in all of these is to take the person out of the decision loop for the routine ordinary decision, and let the computer do that same task. We just happen to use expert systems as a programming technology to let us achieve this. This is a very efficient way to build this type of system. It is quicker to build, and it is easier to work with. So that is the fundamental task - automatic data interpretation.

2.1   ANNIE

The applications are divided by the type of data that is present. We will discuss firstly the *Annie* product area which deals with simple analog measurements. Things that are a dial or a gauge, that have a simple number, or a digital output to tell you if something is on or off. Later we will discuss the *Violet* work where it is not simple data, but a full spectrum of information that it is looking at. The idea fundamentally here is that the data coming in is just simple data, and that is all you need to deal with. *Annie* is the foundation product that is used to interface to the process equipment, and interfaces into the diagnostic part to build complete systems with.

Imagine a diesel engine with a number of parameters that are normal, high or low. The point is with an on-line diagnostic system, you can either look at all of these measurements and decide what it means or you could just read the one line conclusion from the expert system. What *Annie* does is provide the extra functionality needed to take the expert system itself and hook it directly to the plant, whatever that might be. So every time new data comes in, the diagnostic process is run and a simple summary comes out, which is really what you want to know.

2.2 BRITISH STEEL, RAVENSCRAIG

Turning to applications, we are developing a system at British Steel Ravenscraig, which is a very large scale system on the VAX. What it is we are trying to do is monitor the entire steel making process as part of the steel works and identify both the faults they have now, and predicting faults that are going to occur in the future.

There is a bucket of molten iron (over 300 tons in this case) from the blast furnaces, and it is poured into a large vessel. That vessel is turned upright and an oxygen lance comes down and blasts it with oxygen. The oxygen combines with the carbon, producing carbon monoxide waste gas, which results in very purified iron. This is called basic oxygen steelmaking (BOS), it fits between the blast furnace, producing the molten iron and the mills where they roll it all out in the tubes and plates and beams of various sorts.

The system we are developing monitors all the gas extraction that comes off the system. If anything goes wrong it affects the process, but it also leaves severe safety problems and severe performance problems.

You could imagine that with a violent reaction such as this action, there is a lot of damage that can happen very quickly. We want to detect problems as quickly as possible. The system is currently installed at Ravenscraig. It is not for use by the computer department, but by the hard hat engineers, using the system in a hard hat environment.

Primarily, what we are trying to identify is what needs to be fixed and when. The customers are the engineering maintenance staff. They want to know what do I fix now, what do I fix in the future. Ideally they want various degrees of information. So the senior managers are able to look and see complex faults and make complex decisions about what has to be fixed and when, for example if there is a short shutdown. On the other hand, there are junior staff who want to be able to look at a display and see a fault indicated, such as gas analyser faulty, and go and fix it right away. The value is that they can look at, and then go and fix the gas analyser, and get it done without having to get senior managers to step in and make lots of checks.

This is not an experimental system. This is one of the largest real time expert systems in the UK now. It is the state of the art, in that there are very few system like this installed and working. There is some uncertainty whether it will actually work 100%. The intention is that it will be a day to day usage system and not a toy or a research tool.

The system is quite complicated and one of the things to recognise in large systems is that the expert system is only a small portion of the total system. The data acquisition is standard British Steel. All the equipment was already in place when we added the expert system, there was no added data acquisition and no special requirements. All we have done was fitted in with what they had already, which is very important as it is becoming quite common. That's what *Annie* lets us do.

One of the other tasks is to store tremendous amounts of data in databases. The system accumulates about 500 mega bytes of data a month. One of the main problems they have is that they have never actually seen properly many of the faults. If the control cone clog up or one of the drains clogs up they haven't known exactly what happens to the system, they have never had the data logging before.

With regard to some of the problems in developing rules, the experts on the steel making process know some of the rules, but they have never really actually tried them. On the other hand, there are a lot of things they just don't know about, and the idea is that we are going to capture all the data and all the process parameters as it runs. As faults occur, we are going to tag the data noting those faults and then we can go back over the data and work out what the data tells us that the rules should be according to this fault data. We are amassing a tremendous amount of data that no one has ever looked at before, but now with the technology we have been talking about, it would be quite straight forward to go through.

There are two primary outputs of the system. The scheduler ties into their own databases such as the production database and gives them a schedule. For example, if there is a two hour shut-down or a two week shut-down, what would be repaired first. Then a report that ties into the standard plant reporting system - integrated into their terminals that are spread throughout the plant to tell them what the faults are. Expert systems are just a small part of the total system. It is mostly standard databases, standard data acquisition, tieing into the plant schedule and tieing into the standard reporting terminals.

The top level fault display is made up of histogram bans. The bars show for each part of the equipment how many faults are actually in that area. For example, the control cone. To control the air flow a large cone is moved up and down. One thing that we can look at over a period of time is the build-up of particles on the outside of the cone. It gradually gets materials sticking to it and that clogs it up. What we can do is trend over time how high the cone is and look at its average position. As it gets built up we have to keep it further and further open each time. We can then trend on how long until the cone is fully open, at which point it has lost control and can only close in the one direction. At that point you have to fix it and so we can now forecast how many days until you have to fix it.

and so we can now forecast how many days until you have to fix it.

2.3   BRITISH STEEL, SCUNTHORPE

That's for a large scale application - let's look at the same steel process but now something more common.   At British Steel, Scunthorpe, we have installed a diagnostic system for their programmable logic controllers (PLC).   Many companies have systems sequenced and controlled by a PLC with a large number of safety interlocks.   What we have done here is implement an expert system that follows the sequence of the PLC and at each step of the way checks for faults, and if anything goes wrong, tells them instantly.

It was mentioned before that they get carbon monoxide off the process which is a very good fuel and what they normally do is just burn it, but it is wasted energy. Where the expert system sits, is called the slag yard sub station. All the slag (molten waste that comes off that process) is poured out there, and on a windy day when we are here commissioning the system, the molten slag is cooling in the air and then blowing all over our computer keyboard.   Again it is not an office environment, it is a hard hat area.   You have to be in protective clothing to get anywhere near some of the equipment.

What we do is monitor all the valve movements to control between the gas going to the flare stacks and the gas holder. The pipes - 5ft in diameter, valves over 10ft in diameter, it is a fairly large process system. It is controlled by a programmable logic controller.   Our system follows the operator as he pushes the buttons to start the blow process, to charge the vessel, and to actually start the process up.   The system watches all the valve movements happen.   The benefit they give is to increase gas recovery.   The problem is fairly easy to see, right now the operator up in the control room notices that he has selected to recover gas but the recovery hasn't happened.   But the engineering manager has to fix it, and he is working around the plant fixing things and checking things, doing his rounds and he may not know about the problem for a long time. By the time he knows there is a problem, it really is to late to work out what is going on because the PLC has gone into a fail safe state.

Our system on the other hand is constantly watching the steps, if the operator pushes the button and for example: A large goggle valve is open when the operator pushes the button ten minutes before gas collection, our system will tell the engineering manager instantly that the valve is open.   He can then get on the radio and send a lad around to close the valve quickly.   Or if the water dump tank dumps as a safety action it might take hours to fill up.   We can bring it to his attention the moment it dumps, and then he can send someone around to fill it up and get immediate gas recovery.   So it is a very rapid fault diagnosis and in this case we are actually able to anticipate what is going to go wrong by checking things ahead of time. This system is now in and working. It has been installed since August 1990, and they are starting to expand it quite considerably because it is working so successfully for them.

There is another simple example of data interpretations: one can look at the data, or you can look at the expert system. Given the state of the PLC, and your job is to look at that quickly and work out what is wrong.   Or you can look at the display of the expert system. It might   say that the water seal check valve level is below normal, but the operator has selected to collect gas, and won't be able to. The engineering manager can now sent someone around to fill the water tank.   A big difference in looking at all that data and just looking at the answer.

3.1 VIOLET

Lets turn to another area now, heavy machinery.   This area has some important characteristics.   One of the things about the process industry is that every process and every machine is a little bit different.   Rotating machinery tends not to have that characteristic, in that they are more standard.   We have done a lot of very successful work in the machinery areas, where you are trying to look at a pump or compressor and try and determine when do I fix it, when is it going to break down and what is wrong with it? We use*Violet* in a very similar concept to *Annie*, it provides an interface between the data acquisition system and the diagnostic expert system, it provides all the functionality you need to deal with the data (in this case with vibration spectrum from spectrum analysis).

We are interested in large pumps, compressor, fans. The question we want to know is when does this machine need to be fixed? Slightly different from the process work, where you are trying to identify faults. Now we are looking for predictive maintenance to detect faults early enough, where you can repair it in time. It can be a fairly complex test unless you have the right training. *Violet* is the foundation for all of our vibration work, it knows not only about expert systems but also how to tie into vibration based data acquisition system and how to process data such as spectrum data.

One of the areas we are most active in is the area of hand held vibration data collection. In this case of a refrigeration compressor, what a user can do is walk around with a hand-held vibration collector, checking each bearing, and each gearbox along the way. After every six hours of walking on the plant they will collect over 600 vibration signatures. They now down load that to a PC database. They now have 600 vibration signatures to check and see what problems there are. It requires an experienced person to do it and it requires a very long time. What we are trying to do is automate that very quickly.

For example, consider the vibration we can see where the engine and compressor vibration are, and they are a little higher than they should be, which indicates that they should be tightened up a bit. The tail rotor vibration is fine, they have no tail rotor problems. The overall balance is okay, but the balance of blades is a bit higher than it should be, they need to rebalance the rotor blades. That is what can be learned by looking at the spectrum. We need to know; where the vibrations occur, what the faults are and what the patterns are. With experience that is easy, without experience you haven't a hope. Rather than look at the spectrum, *Violet* can recommend you ground the aircraft, because there is high 1 and 2 x vibration. Simple interpretation instead of lots of complex data to look at.

3.2 AMETHYST

One of our main activities in this area is a product called **Amethyst**: **Amethyst** was developed by IA for a company in the USA called IRD Mechanalysis, who are the world wide leader for hand held vibration data collectors. Unlike many of the systems we have described before that were custom built systems, this is a standard application. Many companies buy exactly the same application for the same problems. In fact, **Amethyst** in it's first year sold over 150 copies, so it's one of the most widely circulated expert systems in the engineering area at this point. The 150 copies were sold to engineers in hard hats, that don't know anything about computers, all they want to know is the answer. They want to know whether their pump is okay. One of the important things is that the diagnosis is based on a rotating shaft, and shaft diagnostics are fundamentally the same whether it is air or water, or if it is something else going around them. So **Amethyst** is a standard product because it's a standard diagnostic task.

What **Amethyst** does is take all those vibration signatures, and after 600 of them are collected there might be 20 points in alarm. Normally **Amethyst** will look at 4 or 5 vibration signatures for each possible fault, it looks at both ends of the shaft, it looks at the horizontal and axial vibrations. A hundred spectrum will take you well over 4 hours, but **Amethyst** can analyse them in about 5 minutes. So there are tremendous time savings, not to mention skill saving. The only thing **Amethyst** needs to know is a bit about the machine; where the bearing frequencies are, where the gear frequencies are, where the blade frequencies are and what is the fundamental speed of the machine?

The end user fills in a table which describes what type of machine it is, if it is a pump or a compressor, a bit about the frequencies like the RPM, the bearing and gears and a bit about the configuration. So when **Amethyst** needs the axial vibration it knows where to find it in the data base. That is a very simple description of the machine. **Amethyst** then takes all the vibration signatures that have been collected and automatically scans the database. Again the choice is to look at the spectrum and apply your configuration knowledge, or let **Amethyst** scan through all the points in alarm, loading up the vibration data and then run the expert system rules, looking for the most common problems.

These include twenty faults such as: inbalance, misalignment, looseness, general gear problems and general bearing problems.

Eighty percent of the day to day machinery problems are covered by **Amethyst**. There are some very difficult faults, but we set those aside. We pick a standard core which is reliable and that is what we have automated. So the experts are still needed, but in the routine cases they are now freed up and available.

A four hour task now takes only five minutes.

The conclusion screen is a simple lsit of faults. For example: the magnetic frequency range is exceeded, they used the magnet transducer mount, and they shouldn't have because it is unreliable for the high frequency vibration signatures. They do not have the axial measurement which means they don not have enough information for part of the fault diagnosis. There is a bad bearing problem and the machine is not balanced properly. That is what they want to know. **Amethyst** again can do this very quickly with no skill requirement and that is what the benefit is, lower skill, less time.

3.3   ON-LINE VIOLET

One more application which is very similar to **Amethyst**: In some of the larger plants you want the diagnosis to run constantly, on-line, 24 hours a day. We developed a system at Exxon Chemicals where we tie into their standard machinery protection system. As the main equipment runs, it pulls in the data needed to identify any faults. The important thing is, if the plant shutdown should occur, they can't restart the machine until they know it is okay.

If the plant trips they can't restart the plant until they have been checked with the machinery expert, who might be home in bed, to make sure it is okay. After a long time delay they can restart for the plant, not to mention the hassle for the poor engineer. He is one of the few people, that has enough expertise to go and look at the data and tell them if there is any serious faults or not. Instead of using a hand-held data collector, the data acquisition is permanently wired and scanned by a computer every few minutes.

Every couple of minutes the system scans this data. The engineer only looks at it once or twice a day. The real value is lost because no one is there to look at the data.

What we now have is a system sitting in his office displaying a little box for each machine showing overall health of the system. One of the key ideas is that the operators can look at this display and instead of ringing the person up they just check it and if the computer says everything is okay, they know it is all right to turn the plant back on. All they have to do is hit a key and see exactly what the fault is. For example: it might say the turbine is alright but there is a bit of misalignment and a bit of looseness on the compressor and on the screen is the basic suggested actions to take.

This system has been in use at Exxon since January 1990. They have not given the system to the operators yet, because

This system has been in use at Exxon since January 1990. They have not given the system to the operators yet, because they are testing it thoroughly. One of the disadvantages of a project this scale is that faults on the big machine do not occur too often, so it takes a while to test and verify it.

One of the important aspects is the engineer at Exxon is computer literate and he is now developing the expert system diagnostics himself. We built the initial system, developed the initial diagnosis, and did all the integration as needed. He has now taken over improving the diagnosis. So it is not just a specialist technology, but something any machinery expert who is computer literate can pick up on.

There was two machinery examples, both on-line and off-line. A very successful area just now. Consistently we are able to build reliable systems.

4.1   CONCLUSION

In this talk we have illustrated a number of practical expert system applications both in the process industry, where they have process data, or PLC data and also in the rotating machinery area both on-line and off-line. Practically, these systems are a good idea. The systems that were discussed are working, people are getting benefits from them. Normally the benefits come from allowing the company to use lower skilled people and saving diagnostic time.

Strategically, you can see this direction is necessary. The data interpretation has to be automated. Most companies do not have enough people, if they do have the people, they are to busy. So sooner or later you are going to automate that interpretation task. Given it's a clear direction in the future, you obviously need to get started now.

Chapter 15

COGSYS—the real-time expert system builder

R. Shaw

1.1   INTRODUCTION

Successful collaborative research projects are rare, but examples of the endeavour resulting in a viable product are even rarer. However, COGSYS is one of these.

COGSYS is unusual in two other respects. Firstly the product which has emerged from the 6 year collaborative initiative is in the challenging technology of realtime knowledge-based systems, and is designed for the competitive world of industry and commerce. Secondly, the technical specification was developed almost wholly by the members of the collaborative COGSYS Club themselves.

1.1.1   Background

Realtime knowledge-based processing is an important but difficult area for expert systems. The absence of suitably robust proprietary products in 1984 stimulated early research work, supported at that time by a group of 25 major organisations under the Alvey research project called RESCU - Realtime Expert Systems Club of Users, (Leitch and Dulieu, 1987).

The RESCU project was sucessfully completed in 1987, and led to the formation of a second club, this time to develop COGSYS (COGnitive SYStem), as the commercial outcome of RESCU. The 35 Club members, who have provided all the financial backing for the COGSYS project, include firms in computing (IBM, DEC, Ferranti), automation (GEC, ABB Kent, Turnbull), energy (British Coal, British Gas, CEGB, British Nuclear Fuels), food (Whitbread, Heinz), chemicals (ICI, Kodak) and oil (BP, Shell). Possible competition has proved no barrier to sucessful collaboration within the Club.

2.1   COGSYS -THE REQUIREMENT

As an environment for building expert systems, COGSYS provides the framework and functions for the configuration of realtime reasoning systems for a wide variety of applications. COGSYS can be employed in monitoring realtime process systems, intepreting financial data, managing critical resource situations, controlling systems at a supervisory level, and regulating complex communication networks.

COGSYS faces two fundamental problems inherent in the operation of realtine expert systems. One is the conflict between the need to process chains of rules without interuption and the opposing requirement of being able to redirect attention immediately in response to some realtime event.

The other challenge relates to the continuous and inconclusive nature of realtime processing, which can generate large amounts of data and swamp available storage unless care is taken over memory management. COGSYS, being specifically designed for realtime applications, has overcome these difficulties while still using conventional hardware.

2.1.1   Specification

The Technical Sub Committee of the COGSYS Club steered the design of the product from User Requirement through to final testing. The key elements in COGSYS were specified as:

-Simple configuration/build procedure,
-DEC VAX hardware initially, but design for portability,
-Flexible external interfaces with multi-COGSYS networking ,
-Choice of knowledge representations, eg rules, frames etc,
-Modular knowledge base with consistency protection,
-Full forward and backward chaining facilities,
-Temporal windows,
-Time dependent reasoning with propagation of confidence factors,
-Multi-level "hard" and "soft" interrupts,
-Facilities for user written software,
-Fast C-based runtime environment,
-Quality Assurance design to international standards,
-Product support for at least 10 years.

3.1   COGSYS SYSTEM STRUCTURE

The COGSYS product comprises two linked sub-systems, a Generator System, and a Runtime System, (Fig 1).
The Generator System which is written mainly in POP-11 and uses a subset of the POPLOG environment (Sloman, 1983), allows the user to create and refine a COGSYS system tailored to the specific application.

The output of this generation process is a set of files ready for loading into the Runtime System. The latter contains all the components for connection to and servicing of the on-line application.

3.1.1   Development options

COGSYS will be used by a variety of organisation whose range of needs has been anticipated. Among these are:

  -Development with the Generator System mounted on one multi-user machine, or across several machines, allowing flexibility in team size or composition,
  -Mounting of the Generator and Runtime systems on the same or different computers,
  -Use of external software routines by which knowledge represention alternatives can be extended,
  -Special device handlers for unusual I/O requirements, eg data pre-processing equipment.

4.1   THE COGSYS GENERATION PROCESS

Whatever the application configuration, the COGSYS generation process is the same and involves three tasks:

  -Building the knowledge base using the Knowledge Representation Language, KRL, (Morgan, 1990a),
  -Configuring the interfaces for the Runtime System by defining the General Purpose Interface, GPI,
  -Choosing the required debug and diagnostic options.

To ensure secure policing of changes to the operational system, it is neccesary to use the Generator System for all modifications to the Runtime System.

4.1.1   Compiling and Linking

In the Generator System, (Fig 2), the KRL is input via a special editor, checked for syntax, and finally compiled into Knowledge Object (KOB) files. The KOB files are combined by the COGSYS Linker to form a set of K-code files. The Linker also uses information from the configuration of the GPI to define the application-specific data areas through which the knowledge base communicates with the users of the realtime process, (Fig 3).

Two other Linker functions are respectively, a "make" facility to insert new KOB file versions without a full recompilation, and a configuration log which records the structure of each individual Runtime System. User-written "library" files can also be included at both source and object levels, (Morgan, 1990b).

5.1   KNOWLEDGE REPRESENTATION

5.1.1   Entities

The knowledge base of a COGSYS application is defined using KRL. KRL has a block-structured form similar to Pascal or Ada and contains a number of options which can be set to a default state if not required.

The basic data units about which COGSYS reasons are Cognitive Entities which may relate to external data or be the result of inferences. They are defined in the KRL from a number of pre-specified types (eg. numbers, strings, booleans), and structures can be created as complex as the application requires, for example, arrays of entities, aggregates of different types, or frame-like structures.

Entities are used in several ways:

    -Full entities receive values by assignment, without justification, eg. time references,
    -Constant entities have an initial undeletable value,
    -External entities map onto points in the GPI to provide communication to and from the knowledge base.

An important use of COGSYS entities is their definition as values relating to different points in time, eg. a series of past values, or values up to a given expiry age. The entity updating process loses values lying outside the defined "temporal window", and all values are stamped with real time and date.

5.1.2   KRL Structure

KRL for an application comprises a number of modules arranged as files in the host operating system, and each module contains several blocks. The first module has a mandatory block which defines general knowledge-base parameters, eg. the initial start-up activity, and the inheritance paths to be used.

There are four other kinds of block:

    -Demons, triggered by an event or data pattern,
    -Activities, containing sequences of actions,
    -Rule sets, for inferring entity values,
    -KRL functions of three types, which are called with arguments and return values.

Blocks are allocated priority levels and zone identifiers. On starting a new higher priority activity which shares a zone held by an existing lower priority activity, the latter is generally aborted. Entities are claimed and released by activities as required.

A variety of confidence propagation mechanisms cán be provided by the user, eg. Shafer-Dempster, Bayesian etc, but the default scheme simply combines the certainties of the condition and the expression using fuzzy logic.

6.1   THE GENERAL PURPOSE INTERFACE (GPI)

Each COGSYS application generation requires the configuration of the GPI. The communication functions of the GPI are grouped into higher level (upper ISO 7 layers), and lower level (physical and link layers). Menu-based editors support the configuration process and provide a form-filling format which adapts to the type of edited data. The communication facilities provided with COGSYS can be augmented by user-written or purchased software.

GPI configuration data is held in files which:

-Identify all I/O requirements,
-Define the treatment of all data Points,
-Identify the external Device handlers,
-Specify the I/O scan loading ,
-Detail all I/O Points.

Points are record structures which contain either dynamic input/output data from Devices, or static configuration data. Groups of points, which are input or output together on a periodic or on demand basis, are a Scan Group. The value of any Point can be held as a time-series of defined length (trending). Points are time-stamped and can be accessed in the KRL. Time-stamping is definable to a millisecond resolution, and records the time when the value finally appeared in the Runtime system, not its original time of collection.

6.1.1   Debug and Diagnostic Options

The COGSYS Generator contains a number of optional features which can be activated by the user. These include the extent of KRL rule checking and a range of debug, trace and diagnostic facilities such as tracing various types of KBS activity like inferencing or scheduling, defining break points at which to suspend an activity for inspection, and single-stepping.

7.1   THE RUNTIME SYSTEM

The final compiled and linked output of the generation process is loaded into the COGSYS Runtime System as a set of K-code files. The task of the Runtime System is to perform realtime knowledge-based processing using the knowledge base and the information arriving from the external world, and to provide appropriate responses.

The two key modules of the Runtime System are the Knowledge-Based System (KBS), and the communication module, GPI, both of which are supported by a Runtime Kernel for realtime control, (Fig 4). The KBS contains the application knowledge base in the compiled K-code form of KRL, which is effectivly interpreted by the KBS inference process, the results being held in the KBS data store. Dynamic memory management is provided to create and reclaim records as required. (Morgan, 1990c)

7.1.1   Interrupts

Although COGSYS operates in realtime, this has two degrees of immediacy; hard realtime, where the system must respond within a defined period of time; and soft realtime when processing is required at a minimum average rate. To be able to react to both of these constraints, COGSYS has two kinds of interrupt; hard and soft.

Hard interrrupts are ones which suspend the KBS while urgent processing is carried out elsewhere, and they are typically used for low-level data transfers with the external interfaces.

On the other hand, because a set of inference steps may take a significant time in computer terms, soft interrupts are synchronous with the KBS and take place at convenient boundaries in the reasoning process to make their data transfers to and from the KBS data store. Soft interrupts are stored and the table is tested every few cycles of the inference process. These interrupts comprise:

-Signals; information from the GPI to the KBS,
-Demons; indications of some change in a value relevant to the KBS,
-Events; message transfers between the subprocesses.

7.1.2   Action Blocks

In a realtime knowledge-based system, unstructured interrruption of the reasoning process can have dire consequences. COGSYS overcomes this problem by enclosing the reasoning activities in an Action Block which lays claim to the KBS data-store entities it needs, (Fig 5).

Changes are restricted to within the block until it terminates, when the entities are freed and the results published. Depending on the nature of any interruption of the block activity, it can either be resumed or aborted without damage.

COGSYS Action Blocks, which perform sequential operations on entities in the KBS data store, are scheduled at 4 levels:

-User activation of blocks, or activation by demons,
-Pre-declared usage of entities by two or more activities,
-Checks on the use of data items to exclude simultaneous access,
-Mechanisms to support concurrent activities in a single computer.

Certain sanity checks are imposed on KBS activites to detect execution errors, the result of these checks ranging from simple error messages to total abortion of the activity.

7.1.3 Inferencing

Both backward and forward chaining mechanisms are provided in COGSYS. If the value of a referenced entity is not known it becomes the current goal for backward chaining. Forward chaining is invoked by a "Consequences" function which defines a limit to the length of chaining.

There are also "All-infer" and "All-consequences" options which continue to infer until a "significantly different" conclusion is reached. All inferred values have a time-stamp indicating the time at which the value became valid for KBS purposes. COGSYS provides built-in default conflict-resolution strategies.

Explanation facilities in the COGSYS reasoning process are synthesised out of fragments of "canned" text from the KRL together with the justification links in the KBS datastore.

8.1 REAL-TIME OPERATION

The normal start-up mode is a "cold start" which is also used after an orderly shut-down. To economically carry over selected data between successive system runs, values of identified data can be saved at regular intervals, or on KBS command.

Control over the realtime operation is provided by the Runtime Kernel. System operation is cyclic, consisting of the execution of a number of instructions by the KBS, the stimulation of an activity as a result of a soft interrupt flag, and the setting/resetting of the soft interrupt flags and KBS-related timers. The Kernel also contains the code to handle hard interrupts.

8.1.1   Watch-dog timers

The COGSYS Kernel supports a number of watch-dog timers which are attached to critical activities. The timers are set/reset by the sub-processes concerned (eg. the KBS) and if a watch-dog times out, it generates a hard interrupt which could result in an attempted restart or in the limit, the close-down of the whole system. As an alternative or addition to the sub-process watch-dogs, I/O device handlers may also incorporate device-specific watch-dog timers.

8.1.2   Other Facilities

Included in the COGSYS Runtime System is a Record/Replay facility. Selected data points from the GPI are stored together with relevant timing information, to allow a sequence of events to be reproduced for debugging purposes or external event investigation.

8.1.3   Configuration options

COGSYS Runtime Systems can be configured for a variety of applications in a very flexible way. A system can be distributed across several computers linked via a local area network and using appropriate interfaces on each Runtime system. In this case the total data-gathering and knowledge-based processing load is shared between the computers with only high-level data transfer between them.

Alternatively, several independent COGSYS Runtime systems may share the same processor effectively in parallel. Each system's GPI permits communication with the knowledge bases, external data or front-end processors as required.

9.1   COGSYS APPLICATIONS

Two early applications of COGSYS are at the Midlands Research Station of British Gas plc and the Wantage Research Establishment of CMB plc (was Metal Box).

The objective of the British Gas application (T.P. Williams and R. Kraft, 1989) is to enable staff, less skilled than the present British Gas research team, to efficiently operate a complex chemical plant. The installation is a synthesis gas production plant where COGSYS will provide alarm handling and analysis, give advice on plant efficiency and condition monitoring, provide control loop optimisation at a supervisory level, and offer context-sensitive animated text of relevant operating procedures.

At CMB the application is on a multi-unit plastics moulding machine making laminated plastics bottles. The objective of COGSYS here is to continuously derive the best controlling function from the complex relationship between the variables which control bottle weight. As well as the control task, COGSYS will provide alarm interpretation and response guidance for the operators.

10.1   THE FUTURE OF COGSYS

At first sight, collaborative support for a commercial product amy seem strange. But the 35 members of the COGSYS Club have minimised the risk by sharing the cost of developing COGSYS, and they have had the major say in the specification of the system.

However, the Club is not the right vehicle toexploit COGSYS in the international market place, so it has set up COGSYS Ltd whose function is to hold the rights, and exploit and support the COGSYS technology while at the same time protecting Club member's essential interests. Public release of COGSYS is expected after the middle of 1990.

11.1   ACKNOWLEDGEMENTS

The author wishes to thank Tony Morgan of SD-Scicon who produced the bulk of the material for this paper.

COGSYS itself is the result of the loyal support of the many members of both the RESCU and COGSYS Clubs. However, special acknowledgement is due to the SD-Scicon development team, led by Ryllan Kraft, the Club Technical Sub-Committee chaired by Derek Irving, the Club Steering Committee chaired by Dick Peebles, who has also led the Club through the whole development period, and finally Digital Equipment Corporation who generously provided the Club's computing resources.

12.1   REFERENCES

RESCU Revisited: A Review of a Practical Expert System
R.R. Leitch and M.R. Dulieu 1987
Pcoceedings of Expert Systems 87, Brighton, UK.

POPLOG-   a   Multi-purpose,   Multi-language   Development
Environment
A. Sloman 1983
Cognitive Studies Programme, University of Sussex, UK,
1983.

Knowledge Representation for Real Time Applications
T. Morgan 1990a
Submitted to ECAI '90

Developing Real Time Expert Systems in COGSYS
T. Morgan 1990b
Submitted to AAAI '90

The Control of Processing in Real Time Knowledge-based
Systems
T. Morgan 1990c
Submitted to AAAI '90

COGSYS: An Expert System for Process Control
T.P. Williams and R. Kraft 1989
Proceedings of the Fifth International Expert Systems
Conference, London, UK.

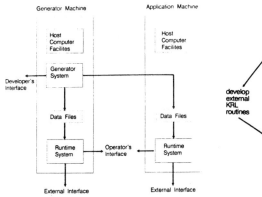

FIG 1 OVERALL COGSYS SYSTEM

FIG 3 THE COGSYS GENERATION PROCESS

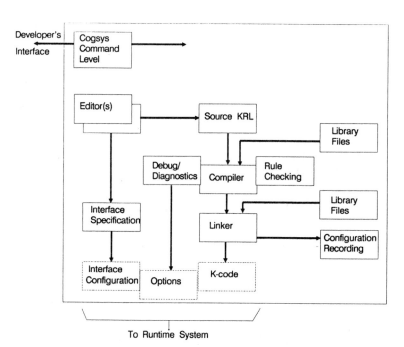

FIG 2 COGSYS GENERATOR SYSTEM

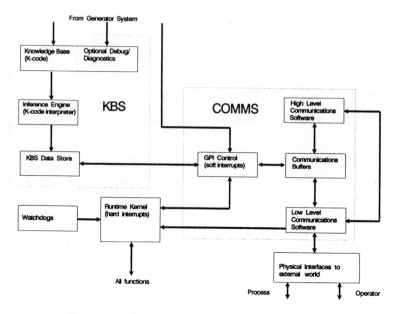

Fig 4   COGSYS RUNTIME SYSTEM

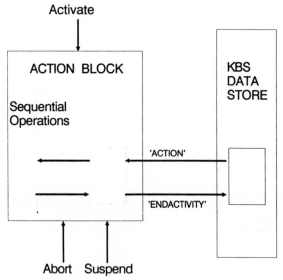

FIG 5   ACTION BLOCK PROTECTION

Chapter 16

Application of COGSYS to a small gas-processing plant

T. P. Williams

27.1   INTRODUCTION

This paper describes the application of COGSYS to a small gas processing plant at the British Gas Midlands Research Station, Solihull. COGSYS (for COGnitive SYStem), is a new real-time expert system which is particularly suited to industrial process control. It was specified and developed within a collaborative group of some 35 major companies and has been made commercially available through the formation of a new company, COGSYS Ltd.

Previous papers (Refs. 1 & 2) have given an overview of the COGSYS design including some features of the system-building facilities within the Generator software and a description of the Run-time system. This paper describes one of the first applications of COGSYS which has been used to provide alarm handling and analysis; give advice on plant efficiency; provide control loop optimisation and analyse trends for condition monitoring and operational guidance. In addition, operating procedure advice is given by text animation.

27.2   THE OBJECTIVES

The objectives were to provide a decision support facility for process engineers and show that less skilled caretaker staff may in future safely and efficiently operate complex chemical plant. The British Gas application is a small gas synthesis plant which provides gas for research activities and is operated by skilled R&D staff.

The application of COGSYS to a plant takes place in two stages. First come the problem definitions, knowledge acquisition and knowledge representation culminating in the production of KRL code (a new COGSYS knowledge representation language) using the facilities of the COGSYS development system, the Generator. Also the Generator is used to configure the required interfaces for the Run-time system. The end product of this stage is a number of compact files ready for loading into the Run-time system. The second stage involves the Run-time system which does not contain all of the system-building facilities provided within the Generator, but does provide the necessary support for final commissioning and operational use.

The first phase of the British Gas project, therefore, involved problem definition. The gas synthesis plant should be able to operate with as little supervision as possible for periods of around 6 months. The rationale behind this is that highly trained process engineers should be able to devote their main efforts to the research plants which the gas synthesis plant feeds. The main problem identified by process engineers concerned difficulties encountered when operating the plant under automatic control out of normal working hours. At night and over the weekend the plant is left under the supervision of caretaker shift technicians whose responsibility it is to telephone the on-call staff member when an alarm occurs on the plant. It had proved difficult for the process engineer to assess the information over the phone as the shift technician was often unable to describe the situation accurately and comprehensively. This led to unnecessary callouts when the plant may have been left running and tended the next day since it is governed by a series of staged shutdown levels, some of which are more critical than others.

As a result of this initial analysis it was decided to build a system capable of providing a decision support capability to both skilled chemical engineers and less skilled caretaker staff. In addition the system should be able to reason within sometimes quite tight time constraints. In particular, it was expected that although many of the system functions take place as regular 'background' activities, the system should be able to respond to higher priority events without violating the reasoning associated with the background activities. The main functions to be provided under the decision support heading were identified as alarm analysis, condition monitoring, intelligent procedures and optimal control. These functions covered the range of tasks commonly undertaken in typical gas processing environments, and as such provided a realistic and challenging test for a real-time expert system language.

27.3   KNOWLEDGE ACQUISITION

The next stage of the project was to begin knowledge acquisition. An initial survey of the various techniques found it to be a highly contentious subject which some believe is one of the most serious hurdles to be overcome in any expert systems project. There are numerous methods for knowledge acquisition such as induction, repertory grids, questionaires, essays, interviews, observation and prototyping.

Not all of these techniques are applicable in all situations. The first objective was to decide which of these methods was suitable for our application. Induction and repertory grids were immediately discounted. Induction requires a complete set of training examples and this was seen as a major hurdle since it would be very difficult to provide such a set for a real-time system. The other problem with induction was that COGSYS is not restricted to simple production rules as its means of knowledge representation. The repertory grid technique, which is essentially a method for getting the expert to organise his/her model of a problem, also suffers from this second drawback. In addition it is more suited to fairly superficial classification problems unlike the British Gas application which is based upon a 'deep' understanding of the process using physical and chemical laws.

Questionaires and essays were considered as likely candidates to begin the whole process. However, in hindsight it could have been forseen that the experts would find it difficult to divulge any information in this unsupervised fashion as their main commitments are normally elsewhere on plant operations. More interactive techniques were therefore adopted based on interviews, observation and a limited prototype.

Initial interviews were fairly informal and unstructured,

allowing the application developers to gain a first insight into the details of the process and the required functionality of the expert system. This technique also allowed both parties to gain a common understanding of the objectives of the project before going on to more detailed and structured interviews. In total about 30 interviews took place lasting between 1-2 hrs each as well as a period of observation, when the application developers were seconded to a shift team during a one week plant startup. Establishing a good working relationship with the operators proved useful for gaining more detailed information on plant problems. The interviews, involving 2 interviewers and 2 experts, were recorded and written notes were obtained though complete transcriptions were avoided. Towards the end of this period a series of detailed designs were produced for each task and agreed with the relevant expert.

As a further means of gaining operator feedback, a preliminary PC-based prototype alarm system was installed. This system used a limited pattern-matching technique to give auxiliary plant data to the operator in the event of alarms being triggered. This approach proved to have several benefits for a relatively small outlay in effort and cost. Plant management, the experts and operators could all see some positive results from discussions on alarm handling; the PC system promoted feedback from the operators on both plant data, leading to new alarm handling rules, and also alarm display; the PC installation enabled the communications highway and serial links to be proved early in the project.

27.4   KNOWLEDGE REPRESENTATION

Our application required the design of an overall knowledge representation scheme which could be used equally well for alarm analysis, procedures, optimal control and condition monitoring. Further criteria for this scheme were that the design should model as closely as possible the actual chemical process and also, it should allow the detailed design of separate modules in relative isolation. COGSYS facilitates this with its modular structure and import/export declarations between modules. In this way various levels of scoping are definable within the KRL which are used to produce cohesive modules with restricted interaction between them.

It was found necessary to break the overall design into two parts, concentrating on the two design criteria separately. Two structures have been developed which allow the representation of plant specific and abstract knowledge. The first is a static representation based upon the connectivity between the various chemical process routes and as such is highly plant specific (Fig. 1). However, the concept of the design is readily portable to similar chemical process plants. This model of the process is a highly structured hierarchy which forces the partitioning of plant data, such as sensor readings and alarm signals and sections of declarative knowledge into separate modules. However, the structure is flexible enough to allow further subdivisions into progressively more detailed modules.

The term static has been applied to this model since it has been assumed that the nature of the chemical process and the physical layout of the plant will not change significantly

th time. This means that the various sensor readings and
larm signals can be allocated places in the hierarchy
epending upon their physical location in the plant.
ometimes ambiguities occured; for instance should a
rticular flow reading be associated with the outlet of the
mp or the inlet of the evaporator which is fed by the pump ?

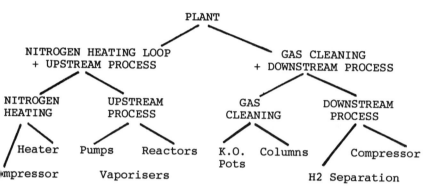

Figure 1 : Physical Knowledge Structure

ch conflicts were resolved by the process engineers. If it
oved impossible to identify the reading with either area of
e plant, since the sensor may have been located half-way
ong a 20 metre length of pipe, then a "connector" plant item
s created as an means of identifying the signal with both of
e physical process units. For simple analogue and digital
gnals this was a trivial process. However, the sensor
lues and actuator signals associated with the 15 discrete
ntrollers were paired up into 15 controller modules rather
an allocating them to separate physical process units. In
is way a closer representation of the plant is achieved
lowing a form of reasoning which models the actual
eraction of the process engineer with the plant.

The same arguments were used to partition low level procedural and declarative knowledge, such as which procedure to show in the procedures module when a particular part of the process is being brought online at startup. In general, sensor values and other variables can be thought of as internal and external attributes of a module. Internal attributes, such as raw sensor values, have a scoping local to the module whereas external attributes, such as processed readings, can be seen by all other modules higher in the hierarchy in the same branch. This has important consequences in terms of runtime efficiency and debugging. It leads to faster reasoning and also easier debugging since the possible search space has been restricted at the outset.

The second data structure is of a more abstract nature and allows the partitioning of the high level tasks according to the different levels of plant operational state, such as fully operational, partially shutdown etc. An eight-layered model was devised which is defined by the default sensor readings, such as alarm values and valve states, in each state (Fig. 2). This allowed the high level tasks to be split into generic and more plant specific modules. For instance, within the alarm analysis module much of the reasoning is equally applicable in any state of the plant. However, the initial alarm filtering depends on which alarms are expected and this is achieved by placing the filtering at subtasks within each abstract level. The consequence of this approach is that large parts of the design and code within this data structure will be directly transferable to other plant for which similar tasks are appropriate.

KNOWLEDGE/DATA UNITS

P	1.	Fully	ALARMS	OPTIMAL CONTROL	....
L		Operational	1	1	
A					
N	2.	1st Level	ALARMS	OPTIMAL CONTROL	....
T		Shutdown	2	2	
		¦	¦	¦	
S	¦	¦	¦	¦	
T	¦	¦	¦	¦	
A	¦	¦	¦	¦	
T	¦	¦	¦	¦	
E	8.	Fully	ALARMS	OPTIMAL CONTROL	....
		Shutdown	8	8	

Figure 2 :   Abstract Knowledge Structure

In terms of actual data representation COGSYS supports a wide variety of types, both primitive and user definable. In addition these types may be combined into structures of the desired degree of complexity. In this way one can implement frames which may involve inheritance if desired, though this was not required in the British Gas application. The combination of structured data types and flexible rules was found to cope well with representing operator heuristics combined with deeper physical process knowledge. In addition, the same data structures were shared by several of the high-level tasks. Complex structured frames were used extensively for condition monitoring and optimal control. Symbolic data types are also allowed and helped make the KRL very readable and easy to debug.

Since most real-time applications will have several tasks running concurrently, it is extremely important that any real-time expert system is able to handle data flow in a controlled and well structured way. COGSYS employs a blackboard approach to the use of common data which may be plant data or conclusions resulting from one piece of inferencing and used elsewhere within the system (Ref. 3). In the form of a transaction, data is only placed on the blackboard after the successful completion of an inferencing activity. If, at a later time, plant sensor data is found to be inaccurate or uncertain, then COGSYS has a facility to retract all conclusions from inferencing based on that data and this provides truth maintenance as normally defined. There are also facilities to provide mutual exclusion zones within the blackboard to prevent conflicting hypotheses overwriting common data and COGSYS has the ability to recognise and resolve deadlock situations.

27.5   APPLICATION TASKS

27.5.1 Alarm analysis

Besides offering a whole range of built-in reasoning strategies, COGSYS also has the facility to reason with uncertain data. The alarm analysis task makes extensive use of this facility as a method for propagating strengths of belief in particular lines of reasoning. Basically, the alarm analysis task is driven by active alarms and abnormal trends. When an alarm signal is received by COGSYS dynamic causal links are formed depending upon the strengths of the connections in a predefined causal net. Link strengths can be estimated in a number of ways, depending upon the known possible causes and consequences of an event. Simple dependencies arise between digital signals but the situation becomes more complicated when abnormal trends are considered as one must know how 'abnormal' a trend is. COGSYS provides a 'certainty' data type to facilitate such calculations.

27.5.2 Condition monitoring

The condition monitoring module has been divided into four tasks; predicting component lifetimes, analysing long-term process trends, interpreting off-line chemical analyses and predicting operational problems on a hydrogen separation unit which is part of the process. The plant must run continuously for 6 months or more and any unscheduled shutdowns can have serious consequences. COGSYS has therefore been used to monitor the operational lifetime of plant equipment (compressors, pumps etc.) and to advise at each plant turnround as to whether a particular component needs replacing or servicing. Trended data, some of which will be entered by the operator, will be used to identify problems on the plant before they become serious. This will involve analysing parameters such as maximum deviation from normal, averages and maximum rate of change to highlight abnormal performance. Results from off-line gas chromatography can be entered into the system and COGSYS will interpret these to indicate the level of gas quality in the product and if necessary give advice on changes in operating conditions to overcome any deviations from the required gas composition. There are tight operating conditions for the hydrogen separation unit and a rule base has been defined for these and installed in COGSYS to ensure that the complex relationships between flow, pressure and temperature are correctly maintained.

Condition monitoring makes extensive use of the temporal reasoning facilities available in COGSYS. At the highest level COGSYS provides built-in data types to represent instances an durations in addition to special operators and functions. Thi has allowed the construction of the following types of rules (ir pseudo-KRL) :

```
RULE  Calculate_elapsed_time
        elapsed_time IS  NOW() - installation_date
ENDRULE
RULE Component_status
 IF elapsed_time < expected_life THEN
        status IS OK
 ELSE
        status IS EXPIRED
 ENDIF
ENDRULE
```

In the above example 'status', 'elapsed_time' and 'installation_date' are instances of COGSYS variables, called cognitive entities (COGs for short). COGS are used to hold data, goals and hypotheses, any of which can be trended. Built-in functions are provided to reason with such data. The procedural aspects of the KRL are based around what are called activities which access data held on a blackboard as COGs. Priorities and zones can be defined for separate activities so that potential conflicts do not arise when accessing the blackboard.

27.5.3 Optimal control

Implementation of an optimal control scheme within COGSYS has been carried out on a nitrogen heating loop which provides heat to three separate process units with varying heat loads and controlling this heat balance can prove difficult for less skilled operators. A design has been produced which enables the operator to use one of three alternative control optimisation schemes, each implemented by COGSYS via the existing 3-term (PID) controllers (Ref. 4). First, manual single loop tuning can be carried out based on conventional open or closed loop tuning procedures (Ref. 5) or with additional heuristic rules which the expert control engineer would use. This latter method is based on the operator's assessment of a previous response to some plant disturbance which has either been logged as a trend by COGSYS or has been recorded on strip chart. It has a fuzzy logic approach where initially the operator matches the logged trend to one of nine expected responses (Ref. 6) and then provides a grading (1 - 5) to adjust the overshoot or settling time. The grading of the operator (eg. 2 = would_accept_larger_overshoot) is translated by the expert system into a controller coefficient adjustment (increase controller gain or decrease proportional band by X%) (Ref. 7). This will result in the calculation of PID parameters which the operator can then enter into the relevant controller.

Alternatively, the operator can adopt an auto-tuning scheme. In order to implement auto-tuning, a sub-optimal PID controller based on the pole placement technique has been used (Ref. 8). No attempt is made to provide on-line system identification and known dynamic models of the process are assumed explicitly. The approach is therefore auto-tuning rather than self-tuning. COGSYS exports the known plant operating conditions and the plant disturbances, such as wind speed, to external FORTRAN code which uses the process models to obtain a balanced simulation of the plant. The relevant process unit model is then linearised, transformed into Laplace, frequency domain, form and reduced by Levy complex fit algorithm into a second order linear model. The prefered response selected by the operator enables COGSYS to calculate the required damping ratio and natural frequency of the desired total system (process with controller). These are fed to external FORTRAN code to enable the pole placement design to be carried out, calculating modified PID controller settings to achieve the required response. These new settings can then be automatically entered into the plant controller in an auto-tuning mode.

A third scheme goes beyond single loop tuning and can optimise the control of the complete nitrogen heating process. This is done within COGSYS by minimising a linear quadratic cost function for the plant (Ref. 9) which contains elements of both operational objectives, such as minimising the temperature variance of gas entering a reactor, and economic objectives, such as minimising gas fuel flow to a heater. A Kalman filter design has been added to reduce the effect of signal noise and to estimate some unmeasured variables. External FORTRAN code is used for the Kalman filter and parameter estimation and this is linked to COGSYS. COGSYS calculates LQG control outputs which can drive the plant via the existing controllers. These existing controllers can have output limits associated with them and may still be used to generate alarm information etc. COGSYS will also be used to advise the operator on the choice of economic and operational weightings within the LQG cost function.

27.5.4 Procedures

The purpose of the procedures module within COGSYS is that of a context-sensitive operating manual. The plant operating procedures are held in the module and a request from the operator to view the procedures will result in the display of only that part which is relevant to the current status of the plant. There are different levels of detail which can be selected within the procedures module depending on whether an overview or detailed sequenced instructions are required. Also, some checkpoints have been installed in COGSYS to stop display of additional procedures until either automatic plant interlocks are proved in the correct state or in some instances the operator confirms checks have been done manually. The expert system serves to enhance the safety of the plant and cannot override plant interlocks. In the event of computer failure, a watchdog facility within the COGSYS system provides transfer to automatic control on conventional equipment.

For our application, zone groups and priorities were defined taking into account the fact that optimal control and procedures are mutually exclusive tasks. However, alarm analysis and condition monitoring may potentially conflict with each other at runtime and with each of the other two tasks. Since the main objective of the application was to provide decision support in terms of immediate process problems, the priorities were assigned in descending order as alarm analysis, condition monitoring, procedures and optimal control.

27.6   CONCLUSIONS

Expert systems technology can now be integrated into computer control schemes to provide useful reasoning with changing plant data, leading to improved supervisory computer control or decision support to the human operator.

A new real-time expert system, COGSYS, has been developed for application on industrial process control problems. The new Knowledge Representation Language, KRL, has been used to construct a knowledge base and install an advisory system for alarm analysis, condition monitoring, optimal control and procedures on a small gas-processing plant at the British Gas Midlands Research Station.

The benefits of COGSYS are seen as being developed specifically for real-time applications and running on proven, relatively low-cost industrial hardware. The Knowledge Representation Language is easy to structure and program and has many novel features to ensure consistent reasoning within time constraints.

In anticipation of a wide commercial market for this product, a new company, COGSYS Ltd., has been formed and following test site assessments and pre- releases of software to the collaborative Club members who funded the development, the COGSYS expert system will be on sale during 1990.

27.7   ACKNOWLEDGEMENTS

The author wishes to thank the management of British Gas plc for permission to publish this paper. Acknowledgement is also given to the development teams in both SD-Scicon Ltd. and British Gas for work on the design and application of COGSYS.

27.8   REFERENCES

1. WILLIAMS T.P. & KRAFT R.

   COGSYS : An Expert System for Process Control.

   5th International Expert Systems Conf. London, June 1989.

2. DAVISON S.J. & KRAFT R.

   COGSYS : Real-time Decision Support for Process Control

   Expert Systems '90. London, Sept., 1990.

3. ENGELMORE R.S. & MORGAN A.J.

   Blackboard Systems. Addison-Wesley, 1988.

4. BRIGHTWELL A. & KATEBI M.R.

   Application of an Optimal Control Scheme to a Small Gas-processing Plant.

   IEE Colloq. C9. London, March, 1989.

5. SHINSKEY F.G.

   Process Control Systems

   2nd Edition. McGraw-Hill. NY. 1979.

6. JONES A.H.

   Design of Adaptive Digital Setpoint Tracking PI Controllers Incorporating Expert Tuners for Multivariable Plants.

   IFAC Conference. April, 1989.

7. LEWIN D.R. & MORARI M.

   ROBEX: An Expert System for Robust Control Synthesis.

   Comput. Chem. Eng., Vol.12, No.12. 1988.

8. WELLSTEAD P.E., EDMUNDS J.M., PRAGER D. & ZANKER P.

   Self-tuning Pole-Zero Assignment Regulators.

   Int.J.Control. Vol.30. No.1. 1979.

9. GRIMBLE M.J.

   Implicit and Explicit LQG Self-tuning Controllers.

   Automatica. Vol.20. No.5. 1984.

Chapter 17

Expert system issues for multivariable control

D. H. Owens and F. Ahmed

1. INTRODUCTION

Control theory has developed over the past two to three decades and provides a powerful collection of concepts, algorithms and theorems for simulation, computation, analysis and design based on an assumed available model of process dynamics. More generally, a model plus a description of the known uncertainty is assumed to be available. This field of knowledge covers a wide range of areas including feedback, feedforward, predictive and adaptive control for both single-input-single-output (SISO) and multi-input-multi-output (MIMO) systems in the time and frequency domain descriptions [1]-[5]. The field has a relatively large mathematical content due to the need for modelling from data or physical principles and the formulation of control algorithms as mathematical operations on data. Hence a practitioner of the subject needs a wide training in areas of instrumentation, computing, computation, modelling, data analysis, the mathematics of control algorithms and experience of their application and the choice of method to suit the application in hand. The limited time available in university courses and the pressure of industrial demands inevitably have lead to a situation where this training is, in general, superficial. The relative success of simple PID controllers designed by trial and error has, in many people's opinion, reduced the incentive for industry to bridge this "training gap". As a consequence the application of many of the developed techniques has been patchy and, in some cases, non-existent despite the great potential that the research presents for improvements in performance, safety, efficiency and reductions in the off-line design time.

In effect, the expertise in recent developments in control systems design resides in specialist (academic?) researchers and practitioners of the field and it is a natural idea to consider how this expertise can be captured for the use of the wider academic and industrial user. The question of how this can be done is the subject of this chapter. The mechanism for achieving a realisation is that of a knowledge-based or expert computer aided design (CAD) facility. The reader is referred to a previous publication in the area [6] for an indication of the possible approaches to the problem and to [7] for considerations in the related area of real-time control.

The purpose of this chapter is to explore the issues of expert systems development for computer aided control systems design (CACSD) from the point of view of the theoretical underpinning of the area and its consequences for the possible form of system to be developed. The approach is not unique but represents an important attempt to bridge the long standing gap between theory and practice using a knowledge based approach.

Specific issues addressed include the following:

(1) What are the essential ingredients of an expert CACSD facility?

(2) What form do the rules of CACSD take?

(3) Where do the rules come from?

(4) Are rules generally valid or do we need rules describing the situation where other rules can be applied?

(5) How can we describe uncertainty in CACSD rules?

(6) What is the potential for the approach and what are its limitations?

In the following sections an approach currently being developed at the University of Exeter with the support of the Science and Engineering Research Council is outlined. Emphasis is placed on the issues rather than the details of rules, software etc. In particular, a general model based approach to rule generation is proposed as a natural extension of the way classical control systems have been implicitly designed to avoid the difficulty in the unfortunate non-generalizability of applications specific design knowledge.

2. STRUCTURE AND NEEDS OF EXPERT CACSD

In this section we discuss some of the basic issues of CACSD from the point of view of the needs of expert systems and the essential mathematical structure of the reasoning and consequent rule-base. One of the important conclusions of the section is the essential structure of an expert CACSD facility as a realisation of the expert designers ability to manage graphical data and representations and coordinate the use of computational algorithms to investigate possibilities, eliminate others and compute the final control form.

To fully capitalize on and further develop CACSD in an expert systems context, it is necessary to recognise the ultimate need to make available to the user:

(1) The theoretical tools and algorithms of control theoretical based design methodologies,

(2) the experience of experts in question formulation and algorithm management, and

(3) a mechanism for sharing experience of the design process.

The computing environment should be such that:

(4) only natural language and the traditional and well-known semi-mathematical language of classical SISO design is used,

(5) the system is compatible with a wide range of user experience, and

(6) a capability of providing guidance, advice, computational tools and options is incorporated.

Some of these requirements are essentially software related issues that are not within the brief of this chapter. We shall concentrate on specific issues of rule generation within the description of the expert systems facility as given in Fig. 1 which represents the essential components and interconnections in the system.

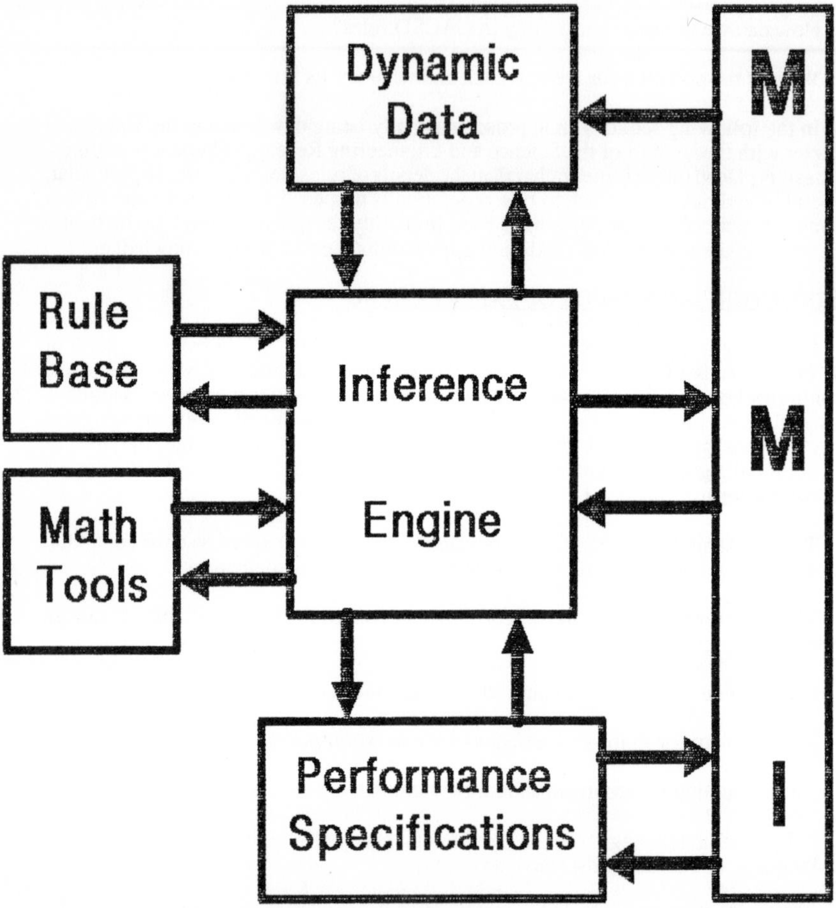

Fig 1. Expert System Structure for CACSD

The system contains a number of blocks with particular relevance to the CACSD problem. These are:

(a) dynamic data manipulation and creation,

(b) performance specification and manipulation,

(c) a man machine interface,

(d) a rule base,

(e) computational tools and other algorithmic support and

(f) an inference engine.

These are discussed further below in general terms.

The essence of the system is the mapping of data on the system dynamics and the performance requirements into the selection of a control configuration and the selection of a control structure and parameters. There is considerable flexibility in practice in the choice of descriptions of these quantities but the principle is still the same. For example, system data in the form of a model in state space, transfer function or input-output data record form can be envisaged. This is not really a problem as they are theoretically equivalent and the inclusion of computational routines can enable any form to be converted into any other.

System performance requirements can be divided into

(a) those that are applications specific and

(b) those that are of a general form and amenable to general statements and analysis.

The first of these will require the use of user experience and applications specific knowledge whilst the second may be amenable to generally applicable statements and hence made available for all to use. In this category lie the typical requirements of bandwidth, response speeds, rise-times, overshoots and steady state characteristics in each control loop and the general form and magnitude of the interaction in the various loops in the process. This list is not exhaustive but the point is made that such general requirements exist and relate strongly to the needs of industrial controllers specifications.

Of course, in practice, there is the strong possibility that the specifications and the achievable performance are not compatible with the available choice of control structures and parameter choices due to unquantified and/or unquantifiable constraints or requirements. These could include nonlinearities, known but unmodelled system characteristics or simple constraints on control magnitudes or rates. There is hence a need for the system to strongly interact with a user through an interface to resolve ambiguities, relax constraints, seek confirmation of the acceptability of a proposed control structure change, correct inadequate reasoning in the expert system and check on the final acceptability of the design etc. This interface should satisfy all the normal requirements of a good interface including the following attributes:

(1) An ease of representation of system characteristics and easy interchangeability of the various representation to suit the situation at hand,

(2) the use of the familiar natural language of classical control to describe input-output quantities, specifications etc. even if they are not the natural language of the underlying computations used in the system,

(3) the possibility of use by users of a variety of backgrounds and experience and hence an ability to hide "irrelevant" data and other quantities from the user if the user is not able to usefully respond,

(4) a capability of providing guidance, advice and tentative designs in cases where systems dynamics are sufficiently simple as to make this a possibility,

(5) a capability of explaining the reasoning behind any recommendation etc.

This list can be extended but the above gives the flavour of the requirements.

The central core of the expert system is the rule base and the inference engine that manipulates the rules. It is this that will govern the success of the system as a whole and great care must be put into their design and theoretical underpinnings. The need for a computational support package is evident from the following discussion.

The form of the rule base is rather different from that in applications in other areas where expert systems have been successful. More precisely, CACSD is based on principles that are not empirical in nature and if they are the rules do not easily generalise to other situations. In the SISO case the design procedures are mathematical in nature in the sense that a mathematical description of the process is used, most of the quantities of interest have a mathematical definition and are the consequence of mathematical calculations. A moment's reflection should convince the reader that the majority of rules relating to CACSD in this case are:

(1) rules related to the management of algorithms and

(2) rules arising from the general results and theorems of control theory

The need for a computational support module is self evident as, in order to replicate the decision making of an expert design engineer, the system will need to contain rules which invoke algorithms, choose between algorithms, use algorithms to provide data for assessing the relevance of rules to a particular situation etc. That is the system will have to acknowledge that an expert designer is an expert in the use of algorithms and pattern recognition in the results of such algorithms in the construction of the control structure and parameters. It is worthwhile indicating the form of reasoning that is typified by the following rules:

(a) The system step response looks like a first (resp. second) order response so it could be useful to approximate the system for the purposes of design by a first (resp. second) order system.

(b) A first (resp. second) order system is an adequate representation of the process for the purpose of control systems design provided that the desired closed loop bandwidth is less than..........

(c) If the system is first order with gain k and time constant T then the proportional unity negative feedback controller producing a closed-loop control with time constant T'is given by the formula $K=(T-T')/kT'$.

(d) The system contains a time delay so either phase compensation is required or a predictor control scheme will be necessary.

(e) The system is approximately second order and is extremely underdamped so rate feedback will help to improve performance of the system.

(f) The roots of the system characteristic polynomial all have negative real parts so the system is stable.

(g) The system has right half plane zeros so control difficulties can be expected unless the zeros have magnitude much greater than.........

(h) The system contains a pure integrator and hence integral compensation may not be necessary.

Of course the list is much longer than the above representative list but it is not the purpose of this chapter to be exhaustive. Note however in the SISO case that the rules are many due to the relative simplicity of the situation, the availability of a large number of theoretical analyses of situations of practical interest (ie. low order transfer function models such as first and second order models) and the abundance of graphical design rules arising out of Nyquist and root-loci considerations. These rules relate observed (approximate) system/plant characteristics in the time and frequency domain to control difficulties, control structures and the systematic selection of control parameters. For example, examination of the pole-zero plot of the system (or an approximating model) can reveal dominant system behaviours and suggest compensation networks based on control pole and zero position selection using the topology of the plot and root-locus rules. The use of approximate relationships between the pole zero plot and the expected transient performance can then be invoked together with the trend rules suggesting the improved accuracy of the predictions as gain increases and an approximate way of thinking that gets the designer into the right ballpark before final parameter tuning using simulation and graphical inspection of, say, closed-loop step responses.

The SISO case is rich with structure and hence rich with rules for systematic and successful design in most cases of practical interest. The MIMO case is however a more difficult case! This is discussed in the next section and used to present a conceptual approach to expert systems design that has the potential to take best advantage of the current state of theoretical knowledge.

3. A PHILOSOPHY FOR EXPERT SYSTEMS DEVELOPMENT

In the MIMO case it is the authors' opinion that we cannot rely on the development of empirical knowledge for the enhancement of any conceivable expert CACSD facililty for there does not appear to be any degree of generalisation in the empirical knowledge typically gained in practice. This can be underlined by the observation that over the past two decades there appear to be few (if any) MIMO design rules of general validity arising out of experimental or plant experience.

A further problem is that, although much of the formal theory of SISO systems can be extended to the MIMO case, the general topologically based rules of classical control can only be partially generalised to the multivariable case by the manipulation of, for example, characteristic loci or root-loci [2], [3]. The power of these approaches is however relatively weak as they are stability based and stability is easily seen to be independent of similarity input-output transformations and hence the form of the system transient characteristics. Indeed it can be easily shown that for example, any stable pole-zero plot can represent a system with excellent transient characteristics but can also correspond to a system with arbitrarily appalling behaviour. In effect, topologically based methods and rules appear to break down in the MIMO case because of the weaker link between pole-zero and related stability descriptions and the transient performance of the closed-loop system. More simply the problem is due to the general increase in complexity and richness of potential dynamic characteristics in the MIMO case and our inability to describe this complexity in a classical rule-based form.

The obvious question to ask, given this observation, is "how can we generate a useful rule base in this situation?". Note that any answer to this question will also apply to the SISO case and could be of value in SISO expert systems development or enhancement.

It seems clear that the general core of the rule-base must rest on rules generated theoretically. That is, rules obtained from the theorems of control theory of the form:

IF A(i), i=1,N THEN B(j), j=1,M

where A(i) denotes a property or relationship and B(j) denotes a consequent conclusion.

Rules are required for:

(1) Data manipulation and modelling including model selection and model reduction.

(2) Model analysis for information extraction, structure probing, identification of control problems and limitations.

(3) Feasibility tests for control structure and complexity selection and the testing of the feasibility of the selection for the attainment of the given performance and robustness requirements.

(4) Advisory functions for control structure suitability, control structure ranking and potential improvements.

(5) Control systems design using algorithm management and optimisation.

(6) Decision making to release the user, where possible, from the need for detailed understanding whilst retaining control over strategic decision making.

It is not clear that there exists sufficient theory of the correct form to realise the above. This could be the spur for the creation of theory as rule generators and indicators of the validity of rules. For our purposes here, it is sufficient to concentrate on the nature of the theoretical rules to be used and generated.

A study of the SISO case indicated the presence of two types of rule:

(1) General (EXACT) systems theoretical rules and

(2) specific (FUZZY) design rules

The systems theoretical rules are many and can be typified by the following:

(a) A linear system is stable if, and only if (iff), all of the eigenvalues of the system A matrix have strictly negative real parts.

(b)   A system is minimum phase if all roots of the system zero polynomial have strictly negative real parts.

(c)   If the first nonzero system Markov parameter is nonsingular then the system is uniform rank.

(d)   If the system transfer function matrix (TFM) is diagonal then the design reduces to independent SISO designs.

(e)   The orders of the infinite zeros of the generic root-locus of the system are equal to the Kronecker indices of the system.

(f)   If any infinite zero has order greater than two then stability cannot be achieved by high gain feedback.

(g)   If the rank of the system controllability matrix is full then full pole allocation is attainable by full state feedback.

(h)   If the rank of the system observability matrix is full then an observer can be designed to realise a state feedback policy in terms of output feedback.

The list is obviously very long and can be specialised to suit the users expertise and preference.

It is important to note at this stage however the general rule that exact theoretical treatment of complex, high order SISO and MIMO systems leads to controls of a complexity similar to that of the plant and complex rules that, in the main, do not add to understanding for the average control engineer. If this were the real state of affairs then creation of a generally useful expert design facility would be impossible. Fortunately this is not the case as can be seen by an analysis of the underlying philosophy of SISO CACSD and its methodology.

SISO design methods are based on a number of ingredients:

(1)   The generally available computational and graphical exact tools of simulation, Nyquist theory,..........,

(2)   trend rules and rules of thumb based on qualitative analysis of, say, root-locus plots and

(3)   design rules that are based on approximate "canonical" plant models such as first and second order systems for which one can derive.

    a)   rules relation plant model parameters to control problems, control structures and required performance.

    b)   control structures parameterised in terms of closed loop performance.

The exact methods of (1) are the mainstay of the approach guaranteeing generality and precision in the calculations whilst the methods of (2) provide trend rules to guide tuning of parameters etc.

The real success of the SISO design theory is however due to (3) and the physical fact that engineering systems have been designed in such a manner to ensure that systems dynamics are frequently dominated by only one or two modes. This enables the design engineer to explicitly or implicity approximate the system by the choice of one of the canonical models as representative of the systems dynamics. It is then possible to quickly identify control problems and the required structure to compensate for these problems and estimate control parameter settings for final tuning during simulation or commissioning studies. To illustrate the truth in these statements the reader is referred to any text on classical control where first and second order systems are central to the teaching programme (and hence familiar to all control engineers) and for which detailed formulae and rules are available for designing controls to achieve almost any performance objective envisaged in practice.

Although rather idealised, this picture of SISO design captures much of the essence of the approach and underlines the fact that,

"together with a small number of exact results for special cases, the success of SISO design in relating control structure to plant dynamics in the open loop to produce predictable closed loop performance lies in the use of model based approximation methods".

It is worthwhile expressing this in a form suitable for interpretation for expert systems applications as follows,

"a crucial observation of SISO design methodologies is the use of approximate models to generate feasibility, structure and parameter selection rules for higher order and more complex systems and the successful application of the results to such systems by coping with the error using techniques such as gain and phase margin rules and simulation assessment and tuning".

This model base for the generation of rules is a fundamental observation that is, in the authors' opinion, one of the keys to the solution of the problem of this chapter. Note that a system may be modelled in a variety of ways depending on plant dynamics, performance requirements and the situation or question under consideration.

The natural conclusion of the above discussion is that, if MIMO expert design is feasible, it will need substantial theoretical support to generate rules by the construction of,

(1)   A model data base of model structures (parallelling the canonical structures of SISO control) with each model being of maximal simplicity for the purpose of answering a given question and possessing the property that the question can be answered for this model.

(2)   Rules relating design questions to the best of the models suitable for the analysis of such questions.

(3)   Computational procedures for the construction of the relevant approximate model from the model base for a given process of interest.

In order to reflect the approximations involved it is necessary to have available,

(4)   quantitative error characterization and error assessment rules to assess the validity of a rule generated from a given approximate model for our original process.

In this format the need to understand the nature and implications of errors is clearly vital and, as a consequence, there is a need to include errors in the form and expression of the rules. Typical rules are expected to take the form, for example,

(a) MODEL MA YIELDS THE PERFORMANCE PA USING THE CONTROL K

indicating the parameterization of the controller in terms of the model and performance specifications and

(b) THE CONTROL K BASED ON THE MODEL MA OF THE PLANT M WITH ERROR CHARACTERIZATION E WILL PRODUCE THE PERFORMANCE P WITH ERROR ECL

expressing the success that the controller will have in solving the control problem for the original process.

The above typical rule has been selected to illustrate the strong connection between the problem of expert CACSD and the theory of robust control and approximation theory [8], [9] and illustrated by the familiar INA [2] design technique. Clearly the use of a model need not be aimed at the control selection but rather at the feasibility of or need for a particular control scheme or the ranking of options in, say, loop pairing [10].

The richness of the theory of robust control approximation and sensitivity methods indicates a good resource of methods if expressed in the correct form and it may be that little needs to be done in these areas other than apply the ideas to rule generation. This will need attention to be given to the problem of the model base underlying the algorithmic aspects of the system. At the current time the MIMO case is relatively underdeveloped in that the only canonical MIMO models known to the author are as follows:

(1) A square diagonal plant model representing a situation of no loop interaction.

(Note: this approximate model is central to the INA design method with errors represented by the Gershgorin circles)

(2) The MIMO generalizations of the notions of first and second order systems [2] introduced by the author.

(3) The idea of dyadic systems [2] for the modelling of plant with substantial modal content.

There is no simple and applicable model containing time delays that is amenable to analysis except for the situation where the delays occur only on the output measurements when the MIMO generalisation of the classical Smith predictor can be attempted (as the delay essentially disappears from the designer's consideration).

4. SUMMARY AND CONCLUSIONS

The discussion in this chapter has highlighted some of the issues related to the off-line design of SISO and MIMO control systems. Particular emphasis has been placed on the issues concerning the transfer of the expertise implicit in control theoretical knowledge into the design environment for general use by industrial design engineers. It is noted that considerable insight is obtained by the analysis of the procedures (both implicit and explicit) of classical SISO design. In particular the procedures are seen to be model intensive and based on the interplay between exact stability theory and the use of canonical approximate models to generate controller parameterizations in terms of the plant dominant characteristics and desired closed-loop performance. Exact stability theory provides the precision necessary for confident applications whilst the models provide the insight necessary for effective design and the translation of frequency domain representations into estimates of transient performance.

It has been argued that this approach can enable the creation of a rule base for MIMO CACSD but that it is imperative that effort is put into the creation of a model "data-base" parallelling that of SISO methods and that the error in using models as reasoning tools is incorporated into the rule-base as part of the reasoning. This will require the development of new theoretical tools and the application of the ideas of robust control and approximation theory in an imaginative way.

A prototype facility based on the above considerations is currently under development at the University of Exeter using Prolog and Matlab and its toolboxes.

5. ACKNOWLEDGEMENT

The work described in this chapter is supported by the Science and Engineering Research Council under contract number GR/E/79781.

6. REFERENCES

[1]   G. F. Franklin, J. D. Powell and A. Emami-Naeini: "Feedback control of dynamic systems", Addison-Wesley, 1986.

[2]   D. H Owens: "Feedback and multivariable systems", Peter Peregrinus Ltd., 1978.

[3]   J. O'Reilly: "Multivariable control for industrial applications", Peter Peregrinus Ltd., 1987.

[4]   D. H. Owens: "Multivariable and optimal systems", Academic Press, London, 1981.

[5]   R. E. Skelton: "Dynamic systems control", John Wiley & Sons, New York, 1988.

[6]   G. K. H. Pang and A. G. J. MacFarlane: "An expert systems approach to CAD of multivariable systems", Springer-Verlag, Lecture Notes in Control & Information Sciences 89, 1987.

[7]   K. E. Arzen: "Realization of expert systems based feedback control", Dept. Automatic Control, Lund Institute of Technology, Sweden, LUTFD2/(TFRT-1029)/1-199/(1987).

[8]   D. H. Owens and A. Chotai: "Robust controller design for linear dynamical systems using approximate models", Proc. IEE(D), 1983, 130, pp45-57.

[9]   J. Lunze "Robust multivariable feedback control", Prentice-Hall series in Systems and Control Engineering, New York and London, 1988, 235pp.

[10] D. H. Owens: "A loop tuning condition for process control using steady state step response data", C-TAT, 1985, pp267-274.

Chapter 18

Design of LQG and H∞ multivariable robust controllers for process control applications

M. J. Grimble

Abstract

The computation of H_∞ and LQG optimal controllers is considered for process control applications. There are many process control problems where significant uncertanties exist in the system models which therefore require robust control designs.

A simple solution for the optimal H_∞ robust design problem is considered and the relationship to super-optimal solutions is discussed. For special types of weighted plant model the main H_∞ equations to be solved are shown to be decoupled so that the calculations are similar to the scalar case. This situation is shown to arise when a mixed-sensitivity cost-function is selected and the plant has an interaction structure typical of many hot or cold rolling mill gauge control applications. A simplified design procedure is also introduced which further simplifies the calculations of the optimal controller and enables standard eigenvector/eigenvalue algorithms to be employed in solving the equations. The procedures are illustrated using a multivariable metal processing control design example.

1. Introduction

Robust control design procedures enable good performance to be maintained even though significant modelling errors exist in the system description. If a system has disturbance rejection robustness the output will not be unduly influeneced by the presence of disturbances. However, stability robustness is the most important requirement since the final closed-loop design should be stable despite modelling errors.

The importance of the H_∞ robust design approach has been recognized since the early work of Zames (1981 [1],[2]) and Zames and Francis (1981[3]). Although much of the current work on this subject is following the new state-space methods (Doyle, Glover, Khargonekar and Francis, 1988[4]), the development of the polynomial systems approach is continuing. The solution of H_∞ control problem by polynomial systems method was first proposed by Kwakernaak (1984[5], 1986[6]) and recently new approaches have emerged using this mathematical setting (Kwakernaak, 1988[7]). The polynomial system description is particularly appropriate in adaptive systems which are now finding wide application in process control systems.

A procedure for solving scalar H_∞ control problems by embedding them within related LQG (Linear Quadratic Gaussian) problems has recently been established (Grimble, 1986[8], 1987[9], [10]). This approach has been extended to the multivariable case (Grimble, 1987[11], 1988[12]). The solution for the multivariable problem is in polynomial matrix form and provides simple expressions for both the controller and the sensitivity matrices. However, the computational procedures are not straighforward. The objective in the following is to consider a restricted class of process control problems which do lead to simple numerical algorithms for the multivariable case. The motivation for considering this type of system stemmed from several metal processing rolling problems which were found to have this structure. Systems having the same type of structure are referred to as having a *canonical* or *standard* industrial model.

Because of the special structure of the system model it is possible to obtain the *super optimal* solution, where all the singular values of the cost-function are minimised, not only the H_∞ norm which involves the maximum singular value only. This problem was considered by Young (1986 [21]) and by Postlethwaite et. al. (1989 [22]). Although stability robustness results are not improved by this device it is likely that other measures of performance in a process control system will be enhanced. For example, disturbance rejection properties will be enhanced.

Knowledge based systems and expert systems techniques provide a useful support mechanism for the control system designer when using CAD techniques. Both the LQG and H_∞ design procedures can be formalized so that a set of design rules and guidelines can be established. This will considerably simplify the use of such design procedures and ensure certain robustness criteria are met.

The polynomial system models are introduced in §2 and the solution to the general multivariable problem is summarized in §3. Attention turns to the special system structure in §4. The plant and weighting models are assumed to be presented in what might be termed a a semi-Smith form. The equations which determine the H_∞ controller are evaluated using this canonical model and are summarized in Theorem 4.3.

The main equations to be solved involve diagonal matrices and hence the so called 'Lambda iteration' stage of the calculations reduces to r (plant r-square) independent computations, using the software already developed for scalar systems. That such a solution provides super-optimal designs is explained in §4.6. A multivariable beam mill design problem is presented in example 4.1. Finally, a simplified design procedure is discussed in §5 which ensures the equations simplify even further and is related to the recent coprime factorization loop-shaping design procedure of McFarlane and Glover (1990, [23]). A simple eigen-problem provides the solution for the optimal controller in this case, even when the cost-function is of mixed sensitivity form. This has the advantage that iterations are not required on the minimum value of the cost index.

2.   System Description

The discrete-time multivariable, linear, time-invariant system of interest is shown in Fig. 1. This is the type of mulitvariable plant model used in self-tuning process control systems which are normally identified in ARMAX form. The system is represented in a matrix fraction description as:

Plant	:	$W = A^{-1}B$	(1)
Input Disturbance	:	$W_d = A^{-1}C_d$	(2)
Reference	:	$W_r = A^{-1}E_r$	(3)
Controller	:	$C_o = C_{od}^{-1}C_{on}$	(4)

The r-output and m-input system equations become:

lant output equation:

$$y(t) = A(z^{-1})^{-1}(B(z^{-1})u(t) + C_d(z^{-1})\xi(t)) \tag{5}$$

ontroller input:

$$e_0(t) = r(t) - y(t) \tag{6}$$

eference generation:

$$r(t) = A(z^{-1})^{-1}E_r(z^{-1})\zeta(t) \tag{7}$$

'he various subsystems are assumed to be free of unstable hidden modes and are
represented by a left coprime matrix fraction decomposition:

$$[W \quad W_d \quad W_r] = A^{-1}[B \quad C_d \quad E_r] \tag{8}$$

The white driving noise sources $\{\xi(t)\}$ and $\{\zeta(t)\}$ are assumed to be zero-mean and
statistically independent. The covariances for these signals are without loss of
generality taken to be the identity. The reference is of course null in regulating
ontrol problems.

The adjoint of the polynomial matrix $A(z^{-1})$ is denoted by $A^*(z^{-1}) = A^T(z)$.
The spaces $P^{rxm}(z^{-1})$ and $R^{rxm}(z^{-1})$ are those of the rxm matrices,
with polynomial or transfer-function elements, respectively. A square polynomial
matrix $D(z^{-1})$ will be called (strictly) Hurwitz if all of its zeros are (strictly) within
the Unit-circle of the z-plane.

.1 *Sensitivity, complementary and control sensitivity matrices*

The robustness of the control design depends upon the sensitivity matrices and the
stochastic regulating properties depend upon the power spectra of signals.

The output and input *sensitivity* and *complementary sensitivity* matrices
are defined, respectively, as:

$$S_r = (I_r + WC_0)^{-1}, \qquad S_m = (I_m + C_0W)^{-1} \tag{9}$$

and

$$T_r = I_r - S_r = WC_0S_r, \quad T_m = I_m - S_m = C_0WS_m = C_0S_rW \tag{10}$$

and the **control sensitivity** matrix is defined as:

$$M = C_0S_r = S_mC_0.$$

These matrices determine the disturbance rejection and reference tracking properties
of the control system. The different sensitivity matrices determine the robustness, at
the input or output of the system, to model uncertainties.

These matrices determine the spectra and spectral factors of the following signals:
ontroller input:

$$e_0 = r - y = S_r(r-d) \tag{12}$$

$$\Phi_{e_0e_0} = S_r\Phi_{cc}S_r^* = Y_{e_0}Y_{e_0}^* \tag{13}$$

where Φ_{cc} denotes the total noise spectrum $\Phi_{cc} = \Phi_{rr} + \Phi_{dd}$.

Control signal:

$$u = C_oS_r(r-d) = M(r-d) \tag{14}$$

$$\Phi_{uu} = M\Phi_{cc}M^* = Y_uY_u^*. \tag{15}$$

Undisturbed plant output:

$$m = Wu = WC_oS_r(r-d) = WM(r-d) \tag{16}$$

$$\Phi_{mm} = T_r\Phi_{cc}T_r^*.$$

The total noise spectrum Φ_{cc} may be spectrally factored into the form:

$$Y_fY_f^* = \Phi_{cc}$$

where $Y_f = A^{-1}D_f$ and D_f is defined in the Theorem 3.1 to follow.

3.   LQG and H_∞ Problem and Solutions

The most popular multivariable control design method is probably the LQG design approach which has found wide application in aerospace and marine systems but is still relatively intried in the chemical process industries. The design rules can be embedded in an expert systems framework to determine the selection of the Q_c and R_c weighting matrices.

The LQG problem (Kučera, 1979[13]) will now be presented. The LQG cost-function to be minimised is defined as:

$$J = \frac{1}{2\pi j} \oint_{|z|=1} (\text{trace}\{Q_c\Phi_{e_oe_o}\} + \text{trace}\{R_c\Phi_{uu}\}) \frac{dz}{z} \tag{17}$$

The weightings $Q_c = H_q^*H_q$ and $R_c = H_r^*H_r$ are assumed to be positive definite on the unit-circle of the z-plane. The weightings H_q and H_r can be dynamic and have the following polynomial matrix representations:

$$H_q = B_qA_q^{-1} \quad \text{and} \quad H_r = B_rA_r^{-1} \tag{18}$$

where $A_q(0) \underset{=}{\Delta} I_r$, $A_r(0) \underset{=}{\Delta} I_m$ and A_q, A_r are strictly Hurwitz. The design of the LQG controller depends upon the selection of the disturbance models and the choice of error Q and control R dynamic weighting functions. In process control applications the weightings can be parameterized to simplify the choice of weighting functions. If the control weighting becomes small the speed of response of the system is increased and the tracking errors are reduced.

The right coprime decomposition of the system $A_q^{-1}A^{-1}B$ is defined using:

$$A_q^{-1}A^{-1}B = B_1A_1^{-1} \ \varepsilon \ R^{rxm}(z^{-1}) \tag{19}$$

and similarly write: $A_r^{-1}A_1 = A_{1o}A_{ro}^{-1} \ \varepsilon \ R^{mxm}(z^{-1})$ (20)

and define: $A_c = A_rA_{1o} = A_1A_{ro} \ \varepsilon \ P^{mxm}(z^{-1})$.

Theorem 3.1: LQG Stochastic Optimal Controller

Consider the system shown in Fig. 1 and assume that the cost-function (17) is to be minimized. Define the strictly Hurwitz spectral factors D_c *and* D_f *using:*

$$D_c^* D_c = A_{ro}^* B_1^* B_q^* B_q B_1 A_{ro} + A_{1o}^* B_r^* B_r A_{1o} \tag{21}$$

$$D_f D_f^* = E_r E_r^* + C_d C_d^*. \tag{22}$$

The following diophantine equations must be solved for the minimal degree solution (H_o, G_o, F_o) *with respect to* $F_o \in P^{mxr}(z^{-1})$:

$$D_c^* z^{-g} G_o + F_o A_2 = A_{ro}^* B_1^* B_q^* B_q D_2 z^{-g} \tag{23}$$

$$D_c^* z^{-g} H_o - F_o B_2 = A_{1o}^* B_r^* B_r D_3 z^{-g} \tag{24}$$

The following right coprime decompositions are defined:

$$A_2 D_2^{-1} = D_f^{-1} A A_q \in R^{rxr}(z^{-1}) \tag{25}$$

$$B_2 D_3^{-1} = D_f^{-1} B A_r \in R^{rxm}(z^{-1}). \tag{26}$$

The scalar $g > 0$ *is the smallest positive integer which ensures the above equations (23) and (24) are polynomials in* z^{-1}.

Controller:

$$C_o = (H_o D_3^{-1} A_r^{-1})^{-1} G_o D_2^{-1} A_q^{-1} \tag{27}$$

Implied equation:

$$G_o D_2^{-1} B_1 A_{ro} + H_o D_3^{-1} A_{1o} = D_c \tag{28}$$

Minimum cost:

$$J_{min} = \frac{1}{2\pi j} \oint (\text{trace}\{F_o^* D_c^{-1} D_c^{*-1} F_o\}$$

$$+ \text{trace } \{Y_f^* A_q^{*-1} B_q^* (I_r - B_q B_1 A_{ro} D_c^{-1} D_c^{*-1} A_{ro}^* B_1^* B_q^*) B_q A_q^{-1} Y_f\}) \frac{dz}{z} \tag{29}$$

Input sensitivity matrix:

$$S_m = A_r A_{1o} D_c^{-1} H_o D_3^{-1} A_r^{-1} \tag{30}$$

Control sensitivity matrix:

$$M = A_r A_{1o} D_c^{-1} G_o D_2^{-1} A_q^{-1} \tag{31}$$

and the remaining sensitivity matrices follow as:

$$T_m = MW, \quad T_r = WM, \quad S_r = I_r - T_r. \tag{32}$$

•

Proof: Grimble (1986[14]), Grimble and Johnson (1989[19]).

•

The optimal controller would be realized using state-space models by a Kalman filter and a constant LQ feedback control matrix. The above form of the LQG solution is less well known but is particularly useful when adaptive features must be included. In many process control applications the plant model is not known and must be identified in polynomial system form. An adaptive controller can then be constructed using the *Certainty Equivalence Principle*.

3.1 Relationship between the H_∞ and LQG problems

The H_∞ control philosophy can be motivated by the LQG poynomial system results. The link will now be investigated, since the objective is to consider robust design procedures and these require the use of H_∞ indices.

The **LQG cost-index** may be written (using (18)) in the form:

$$J = \frac{1}{2\pi j} \oint_{|z|=1} \text{trace}\{X(z^{-1})\} \, \frac{dz}{z}$$

where

$$X(z^{-1}) \underset{=}{\Delta} Y_{e_0}^* Q_c Y_{e_0} + Y_u^* R_c Y_u \quad (Y_{e_0} \underset{=}{\Delta} S_r Y_f, \ Y_u \underset{=}{\Delta} MY_f) \tag{33}$$

$$= Y_f^*(S_r^* Q_c S_r + M^* R_c M) Y_f \tag{34}$$

The motivation for constructing a H_∞ criterion is similar to that which produces the LQG cost-index. The H_∞ *criterion* may therefore be defined as:

$$J_\infty = \| X \|_\infty = \sup_{|z|=1} \{ \| X(z^{-1}) \|_2 \} \tag{35}$$

where $\| X(z^{-1}) \|_2 \underset{=}{\Delta} \sigma_{max}\{X(z^{-1})\}$ denotes the spectral norm of the complex matrix $X(z^{-1})$. The selection of the cost-function weighting elements is discussed in Grimble and Biss (1988, [15]).

3.2 Auxiliary problem linking the LQG and H_∞ problems

The H_∞ problem to be solved is embedded within an LQG problem whose solution is known from the preceeding results. The auxiliary lemma which links the two problems is presented below. This result is valuable in providing a useful connection between the LQG stochastic optimal control solutions and the recent robust design procedures.

Lemma 3.1:

Consider the auxiliary problem of minimizing:

$$J = \frac{1}{2\pi j} \oint_{|z|=1} \text{trace}\{X(z^{-1})\Sigma(z^{-1})\} \, \frac{dz}{z} \tag{36}$$

with respect to all stabilizing compensators C. Suppose that for some spectral density matrix Σ the auxiliary problem is solved by a compensator C_0, for which $X(z^{-1}) = \lambda^2 I_r$, with λ a real constant. Then C_0 also minimizes:

$$J_\infty = \| X \|_\infty = \sup_{z=1} \sigma_{max}\{X(z^{-1})\}. \tag{37}$$

•
•

Proof: Kwakernaak (1984[6], 1987[20]).

This lemma enables the following theorem to be developed. The details of the proof need not be considered here since attention will concentrate on design issues.

Theorem 3.2: H_∞ Stochastic Optimal Controller

Consider the system shown in Fig. 1 and assume that the cost index (34) is to be minimized, with cost weights (18). The spectral factors D_c and D_f are defined by (21) and (22), respectively. The optimal controller may be computed from the solution (H_1, G_1, F_1), with F_1 *of minimal degree, of the equations:*

$$D_c^* z^{-g} G_1 + D_{co} F_1 \tilde{A}_2 = A_{ro}^* B_1^* B_q^* B_q \tilde{D}_2 z^{-g} \tag{38}$$

$$D_c^* z^{-g} H_1 - D_{co} F_1 \tilde{B}_2 = A_{1o}^* B_r^* B_r \tilde{D}_3 z^{-g} \tag{39}$$

where $\tilde{A}_2, \tilde{B}_2, \tilde{D}_2$ and $\tilde{D}_3$ *satisfy the following right coprime decompositions:*

$$\tilde{A}_2 \tilde{D}_2^{-1} = F_{1s}^{-1} S D_f^{-1} A A_q \tag{40}$$

$$\tilde{B}_2 \tilde{D}_3^{-1} = F_{1s}^{-1} S D_f^{-1} B A_r \tag{41}$$

The scalar g is the smallest positive integer to make these equations polynomial in z^{-1}. *The tranfer-function matrix* $S \in R^{rxr}(z^{-1})$ *is obtained by spectral factorization using:*

$$S^* S = \Lambda^2 A - D_f^* A^{*-1} A_q^{*-1} B_q^* (I_r - B_q B_1 A_{ro} D_c^{-1} D_c^{*-1} A_{ro}^* B_1^* B_q^*) B_q A_q^{-1} A^{-1} D_f \tag{42}$$

The matrix $F_{1s} \in P^{rxr}(z^{-1})$ *is Hurwitz and satisfies:*

$$F \in F_{1s}^* F_{1s} = F_1^* F_1$$

and the spectral factor $D_{co} \in P^{mxm}(z^{-1})$ *satisfies:*

$$D_{co} D_{co}^* = D_c^* D_c. \tag{43}$$

Controller:

$$C_o = (H_1 \tilde{D}_3^{-1} A_r^{-1})^{-1} G_1 \tilde{D}_2^{-1} A_q^{-1} \tag{44}$$

Implied equation:

$$G_1 \tilde{D}_2^{-1} B_1 A_{ro} + H_1 \tilde{D}_3^{-1} A_{1o} = D_c \tag{45}$$

Optimum function and minimum cost:

$$X = \lambda^2 I_r \quad and \quad J_\infty = \lambda^2 \tag{46}$$

Input sensitivity matrix:

$$S_m = A_r A_{10} D_c^{-1} H_1 \tilde{D}_3^{-1} A_r^{-1} \tag{47}$$

Control sensitivity matrix:

$$M = A_r A_{10} D_c^{-1} G_1 \tilde{D}_2^{-1} A_q^{-1} \tag{48}$$

and the remaining sensitivity matrices satisfy (32).   •

Proof: Grimble (1988[12]).   •

Notice that the controller has a similar complexity to that in LQG design problems. It is of course normally much more complicated than the traditional PID controller, found in the process industries. However, H_∞ controllers are required to achieve many more performance and robustness objectives than are PID designs. Moreover, if the system description is restricted to that normally used for PID design and special cost weightings are introduced, then the H_∞ controller has a PID type of controller structure.

3.3. Non-minimum phase property of F_1

When constructing a numerical algorithm to solve the equations it is valuable to establish the properties of F_1 and F_{1s}.

Lemma 3.2:

Without loss of generality F_1 can be taken to be a non-Hurwitz matrix and F_{1s} can be taken as a Hurwitz matrix.   •

3.4 Physical significance of the Λ matrix:

In the proof that the equations presented in Theorem 3.2 minimize an H_∞ norm a lemma due to Kwakernaak (1984[6]) is required. This lemma shows that when an auxiliary LQG problem is solved and the Λ matrix has the special form $\Lambda = \lambda I_r$ then the H_∞ problem is also solved.

However, a solution to equations (38) to (41) may not exist which ensures Λ is a scalar times the identity : $\Lambda^T \Lambda = \lambda^2 I_r$. For the industrial problems considered in the following Λ can, however, be taken to be a diagonal matrix and Λ^2 has the form: $\Lambda^2 = \text{diag}\{\lambda_1^2, ..., \lambda_r^2\}$ where the $\{\lambda_i^2\}$ are not the same values. The significance of this solution will now be explained.

Write Λ^2 in the form $\Lambda^2 = \lambda^2 \Lambda_0^2$ where λ^2 is the largest element of λ^2 and

$$\Lambda_0^2 \underset{=}{\triangle} \text{diag}\{\lambda_1^2/\lambda^2, ..., 1, ..., \lambda_r^2/\lambda^2\}.$$

In such a case equation (42) may be written as:

$$S^*S = \lambda^2 \Lambda_0^2 - \Lambda_0 \Lambda_0^{-1} D_f^* A^{*-1} A_q^{*-1} B_q^*(.) B_q A_q^{-1} A^{-1} D_f \Lambda_0^{-1} \Lambda_0$$

or $S = S_0 \Lambda_0$ where S_0 satisfies:

$$S^*S = \lambda^2 I_r - \Lambda_0^{-1} D_f^* A^{*-1} A_q^{*-1} B_q^*(.) B_q A_q^{-1} A^{-1} D_f \Lambda_0^{-1}$$

The term SD_f^{-1} may now be written as:

$$SD_f^{-1} = S_o (D_f \Lambda_o^{-1})^{-1}.$$

Equation (42) in Theorem 3.1 may now be replaced by the expression for $S_o^* S_o$ which includes the diagonal $\lambda^2 I_r$ matrix. The solution to the *scaled* problem may be shown to be H_∞ optimal by applying Kwakernaak's lemma (1986[5]) which links the H_2 and H_∞ problems.

To understand the physical significance of the above steps note that the expression for $S_o^* S_o$ above is equivalent to the case where a system with disturbance model

$Y_f = A^{-1} D_f$ is replaced by: $\tilde{Y}_f = A^{-1} D_f \Lambda_o^{-1}$. Since all of the elements of Λ_o^2 have a magnitude less than or equal to unity the modified disturbance model elements are increased in size. In fact, each disturbance channel can be thought of as being increased until all of the singular values represented in Λ^2 reach the largest λ^2. No further increase is possible in any channel without λ^2 being exceeded. The scaled problem therefore enables the "worst case" disturbance model $\tilde{Y}_f$ to be determined.

Note that it would be straightforward to scale the disturbance model spectral factor $\tilde{Y}_f$ so that all of the singular values are equal to unity. In this case Λ_o^2 would be defined equal to Λ^2.

The scaling operation does of course modify the cost (34) as:

$$X = \tilde{Y}_f^* (S_r^* \tilde{Q}_c^* S_r + M^* R_c \tilde{M}) \tilde{Y}_f$$

since it includes the worst case disturbance model $\tilde{Y}_f$. However, notice that the basic equations (39) to (41) were assumed to have a solution in both the original and the *scaled* roller is determined by equations (40), (41), and (44) and these were not affected by the alternative way of writing $SD_f^{-1} = S_o(D_f \Lambda_o^{-1})^{-1}$.

The controller which minimizes the H_∞ norm of $\tilde{X}$ which gives: $\tilde{X}_{min} = \lambda^2 I_r$ and $\| \tilde{X}_{min} \|_\infty = \lambda^2$, is therefore the same as the controller which gives: $X_{min} = \Lambda^2$ with a maximum singular value of λ^2.

The above results may be summarized in the following lemma.

Lemma 3.2 *Worst case disturbance model and the H_∞ optimization problem*

Assume that the controller defined from the solution of the equations in Theorem 3.2, for some disturbance spectral factor Y_f gives $X_{min} = \Lambda^2$. Here Λ^2 denotes a diagonal matrix with largest element λ^2 so that $\| X_{min} \|_\infty = \lambda^2$. Then this controller minimizes the H_∞ norm of $\tilde{X}$, where $\tilde{X}$ is defined in terms of the worst case disturbance model $\tilde{Y}_f$, and $\| \tilde{X}_{min} \|_\infty = \lambda^2$. •

It therefore follows from the above results that an H_∞ controller may be generated from the equations of Theorem 3.2. for a worst-case disturbance model. This is the worst disturbance which can be dealt with by the system without exceeding the H_∞

norm bound of and can be found from $\tilde{Y}_f = Y_f \Lambda_o^{-1}$.

4.   Simplified System and Weighting Models

There are many process control plant models which have a relatively simple multivariable structure which can be exploited in the design process.   This is particularly helpful for H_∞ control law computations which are often quite complicated by whatever solution technique is employed.

To achieve a simplified design procedure the system and weighting models must have a special form. The plant will now be assumed to be square.

4.1 *Weighting definitions*

The weighting transfer-functions are defined to have the following form:

Error weighting:

$$H_q = B_q A_q^{-1} \tag{49}$$

Control weighting:

$$H_r = B_r A_r^{-1} = B_r A_{r1}^{-1} A_{12}^{-1} \tag{50}$$

where A_r is partitioned as: $A_r = A_{12} A_{r1}$ and A_{12} is defined from the plant model (there is no loss of generality in this assumption). The error and control weighting terms B_q and B_r may be assumed to be of normal full rank.   In most process control applications H_q is chosen to be an integrator to force integral action into the controller.   The filter H_r normally has a high pass characteristic ensuring that the controller rolls off at high frequencies.

4.2 *System Model*

The system model to be considered, linearized about a given operating point, has the following form:

Plant model:

$$B_q B_1 A_{ro} = N_b \Lambda_b N_i \tag{51}$$

$$B_r A_{11} = N_a \Lambda_a N_i \tag{52}$$

where A_1 is partitioned as $A_1 = A_{12} A_{11}$ and A_{12} is Hurwitz, N_a and N_b are real-orthogonal, and N_i is unimodular. It is of course an assumption that the weightings can be chosen so that N_i is common to these equations. The Λ_a and Λ_b are diagonal polynomial matrices.   The control weighting term A_{r1} and A_{11} are assumed to commute.   The control spectral factors D_c and D_{co} simplify considerably after substituting from the above equations (51) and (52).   From (21) and (43):

$$D_c = \Lambda_{dc} N_i \text{ and } D_{co} = N_i^* \Lambda_{dc} z^{-n} \tag{53}$$

where $n = \deg\{N_i\}$ and Λ_{dc} is strictly Hurwitz and satisfies:

$$\Lambda_{dc}^* \Lambda_{dc} = \Lambda_b^* \Lambda_b + \Lambda_a^* \Lambda_a \tag{54}$$

From equation (20) and the definitions of A_r and A_1, the matrices A_{ro} and A_{1o} may be defined:

$$A_r^{-1}A_1 = A_{1o}A_{ro}^{-1} = A_{r1}^{-1}A_{11}$$

so that $A_{1o} \triangleq A_{11}$ and $A_{ro} \triangleq A_{r1}$. Using (51) and (52) the plant model may be written in the form:

$$A^{-1}B = A_q B_1 A_{11}^{-1} A_{12}^{-1} = H_q^{-1}(N_b \Lambda_b \Lambda_a^{-1} N_a^{-1})H_r$$

4.3 System structure

The process control system structure resulting from the above system and weighting definitions may now be considered.

Disturbance Model:

$$N_b^{-1}B_q A_q^{-1} A^{-1} D_f = N_b^{-1} B_q D_2 A_2^{-1} = \Lambda_d \Lambda_{a2}^{-1} \tag{55}$$

where it is convenient to assume that Λ_d and Λ_{a2} are diagonal polynomial matrices $\Lambda_d = N_b^{-1}B_q D_2$ and $\Lambda_{a2} = A_2$. The matrix Λ_{a2} is assumed to include any unstable modes in the plant model Λ_a (these are then assumed to cancel when forming $\Lambda_{a2}^{-1}\Lambda_a$).

The Λ equation:

Substituting in equation (42) for the above system and weighting definitions:

$$S = S_n(\Lambda_{dc}S_d)^{-1} \tag{56}$$

where S_n and S_d are strictly Hurwitz, diagonal polynomial matrices, satisfying:

$$S_n^* S_n = \Lambda_{a2}^* \Lambda_{dc}^* \Lambda^2 \Lambda_{dc} \Lambda_{a2} - \Lambda_d^* \Lambda_a^* \Lambda_a \Lambda_d \tag{57}$$

and

$$S_d^* S_d = \Lambda_{a2}^* \Lambda_{a2} \tag{58}$$

The optimization is performed with respect to the diagonal matrix Λ^2 elements.

Plant pole spectral factor:

Let $\Lambda_{as} \triangleq S_d \Lambda_{a2}^{-1} \Lambda_a$ \hfill (59)

and note from (59) that Λ_{as} is Hurwitz and satisfies:

$$\Lambda_{as}^* \Lambda_{as} = \Lambda_a^* \Lambda_a \tag{60}$$

First weighted disturbance model:

From equations (25) and (40):

$$\tilde{A}_2 \tilde{D}_2^{-1} = F_{1s}^{-1} S D_f^{-1} A A_q = F_{1s}^{-1} S A_2 D_2^{-1}$$

Substituting from (56) and (59):

$$\tilde{A}_2 \tilde{D}_2^{-1} = S_n \Lambda_a \Lambda_{as}^{-1} F_{1s}^{-1} \Lambda_{dc}^{-1} D_2^{-1} \tag{61}$$

Cancelling common factors between Λ_a and Λ_{as}:

$$\Lambda_a \Lambda_{as}^{-1} \triangleq \Lambda_a \Lambda_{as}^{-1}$$

giving

$$\tilde{A}_2 \triangleq S_n \Lambda_a \quad \text{and} \quad \tilde{D}_2 \triangleq D_2 \Lambda_{dc} F_{1s} \Lambda_{as}. \tag{62}$$

The following result is also required based on (62) and (55):

$$N_b^{-1} B_q D_2 = \Lambda_d \Lambda_{dc} F_{1s} \Lambda_{as} \tag{63}$$

Second weighted disturbance model:

From equations (41), (56) and (59):

$$\begin{aligned} B_2 D_3^{-1} &= F_{1s}^{-1} S D_f^{-1} B A_r = F_{1s}^{-1} S_n S_d^{-1} \Lambda_{dc}^{-1} (D_f^{-1} A A_q A_q^{-1} A^{-1} B) A_r \\ &= S_n \Lambda_a \Lambda_{as}^{-1} F_{1s}^{-1} \Lambda_{dc}^{-1} D_2^{-1} B_1 A_1^{-1} A_r \end{aligned} \tag{64}$$

But from (50), (51) and (52):

$$\begin{aligned} B_1 A_1^{-1} A_r &= B_1 A_{11}^{-1} A_{r1} = B_1 A_{r1} A_{11}^{-1} \\ &= B_q^{-1} N_b \Lambda_b \Lambda_a^{-1} N_a^{-1} B_r \end{aligned} \tag{65}$$

and

$$D_2^{-1} B_1 A_1^{-1} A_r = \Lambda_d^{-1} \Lambda_b \Lambda_a^{-1} N_a^{-1} B_r$$

Substituting for this result in (64) gives:

$$\tilde{B}_2 (B_r \tilde{D}_3)^{-1} = S_n \Lambda_b \Lambda_{as}^{-1} F_{1s}^{-1} \Lambda_{dc}^{-1} \Lambda_d^{-1} N_a^{-1} \tag{66}$$

and hence

$$\tilde{B}_2 \triangleq S_n \Lambda_b \quad \text{and} \quad B_r \tilde{D}_3 \triangleq N_a \Lambda_d \Lambda_{dc} F_{1s} \Lambda_{as}. \tag{67}$$

4.4 *Solution of the linear equations*

The above choice of system and weighting models considerably simplify the equations to be solved. Substituting in equation (38):

$$D_c^* z^{-g} G_1 + D_{co} F_1 \tilde{A}_2 = A_{ro}^* B_1^* B_q^* B_q D_2 z^{-g}$$

from (53), (62) and (63):

$$N_i^* \Lambda_{dc}^* z^{-g} G_1 + N_i^* \Lambda_{dc} z^{-n} F_1 S_n \Lambda_a = N_i^* \Lambda_b^* N_b^* N_b \Lambda_d \Lambda_{dc} F_{1s} \Lambda_{as} z^{-g}$$

Defining $g_1 = g - n$, noting G_1 may be written as: $G_1 = G \Lambda_{dc}$, and multiplying by N_i^{*-1} obtain:

$$\Lambda_{dc}^* z^{-g_1} G + F_1 S_n \Lambda_a = \Lambda_b^* \Lambda_d F_{1s} \Lambda_{as} z^{-g_1} \tag{68}$$

Substituting in equation (39):

$$D_c^* z^{-g} H_1 - D_{co} F_1 B_2 = A_{1o}^* B_r^* B_r D_3 z^{-g}$$

from (52), (53) and (67);

$$N_i^* \Lambda_{dc}^* z^{-g} H_1 - N_i^* \Lambda_{dc} z^{-n} F_1 S_n \Lambda_b = N_i^* \Lambda_a^* N_a^* N_a \Lambda_d \Lambda_{dc} F_{1s} \Lambda_{as} z^{-g}$$

Noting H_1 may be written as: $H_1 = H \Lambda_{dc}$ and multiplying by N_i^{*-1} obtain:

$$\Lambda_{dc}^* z^{-g_1} H - F_1 S_n \Lambda_b = \Lambda_a^* \Lambda_d F_{1s} \Lambda_{as} z^{-g_1} \tag{69}$$

Equations (68) and (69) can be satisfied by H, G and F_1 which are diagonal matrices, since all the other matrices in the equations are diagonal. Equations (68) and (69) may be used to generate the implied equation. Multiplying (68) by Λ_b and (69) by Λ_a and adding (noting $\Lambda_a \Lambda_{as} = \Lambda_{as} \Lambda_a$) gives:

$$\Lambda_{dc}^* z^{-g_1} (H \Lambda_a + G \Lambda_b) = (\Lambda_b^* \Lambda_b + \Lambda_a^* \Lambda_a) \Lambda_d \Lambda_{as} F_{1s} z^{-g_1}$$

Substituting from (54) and multiplying Λ_{dc}^{*-1} gives:

$$H \Lambda_a + G \Lambda_b = \Lambda_{dc} \Lambda_d \Lambda_{as} F_{1s}. \tag{70}$$

4.5 *Controller and optimal solution*

The optimal controller may be computed from (44), (62):

$$C_0 = A_r \tilde{D}_3 H_1^{-1} G_1 \tilde{D}_2^{-1} A_q^{-1} = (A_r B_r^{-1}) N_a \Lambda_{as} \Lambda_{as}^{-1} H^{-1} G \Lambda_d D_2^{-1} A_q^{-1}$$

$$= (A_r B_r^{-1}) N_a H^{-1} G \Lambda_s N_b^{-1} (B_q A_q^{-1}) \tag{71}$$

where $\Lambda_s \underset{=}{\Delta} \Lambda_{as} \Lambda_{as}^{-1}$ is a polynomial matrix which is Hurwitz and depends only on the stable plant pole polynomial. The system model with this controller is shown in Fig. 2. This is redrawn in Fig. 3 after cancellation of transformations within the loop. Clearly for simulation purposes and stability analysis, a number of non-interacting loops may be considered.

The actual system is not of course decoupled, since each output and control signal, depends upon contributions from the various loops (via the transformations $H_q^{-1} N_b$ and $H_r^{-1} N_a$ in Fig. 3). However, the problem has effectively been reduced to a number of single-input, single-output, design calculations. The structural decomposition achieved should be valuable for commissioning and plant testing in addition to the computational simplifications achieved.

The function X being minimized may therefore be expressed in the form:

$$X = Y_{e_0}^* Q_c Y_{e_0} + Y_u^* R_c Y_u = Y_{e_\ell}^* Y_{e_\ell} + Y_{u_\ell}^* Y_{u_\ell} = \Phi_{e_\ell e_\ell} + \Phi_{u_\ell u_\ell}$$

where Y_{e_ℓ} and Y_{u_ℓ} are the (diagonal) spectral factors of the loop signals.

The above results may be collected within the following theorem.

Theorem 4.3: H_∞ Controller Calculation Procedure

Consider the system model described in §4.2 which has the following canonical weighted plant and disturbance models:

Plant:

$$B_q B_1 A_{ro} = N_b \Lambda_b N_i$$

$$B_r A_{11} = N_a \Lambda_a N_i, \quad A_1 = A_{12} A_{11}$$

Disturbance:

$$N_b^{-1} B_q D_2 = \Lambda_d$$

$$A_2 = \Lambda_{a2}.$$

Here A_1, B_1 satisfy (19) and A_2, D_2 satisfy (25) (D_f is defined by (22)). The matrix Λ_{as} is Hurwitz and satisfies: $\Lambda_{as}^* \Lambda_{as} = \Lambda_a^* \Lambda_a$. The matrices Λ_a and Λ_{as} are obtained by cancelling common factors from the equation:

$$\Lambda_a \Lambda_{as}^{-1} = \Lambda_a \Lambda_{as}^{-1}, \text{ and } \Lambda_s \triangleq \Lambda_{as} \Lambda_{as}^{-1}.$$

Assume that the cost-function (34) is to be minimized with the cost weights (18). The control spectral factor Λ_{dc} satisfies:

$$\Lambda_{dc}^* \Lambda_{dc} = \Lambda_b^* \Lambda_b + \Lambda_a^* \Lambda_a \tag{72}$$

The following linear equations must be solved for the minimal degree solution (H, G, F), with respect to F:

$$\Lambda_{dc}^* z^{-g} G + F S_n \Lambda_a = \Lambda_b^* \Lambda_d F_s \Lambda_{as} z^{-g} \tag{73}$$

$$\Lambda_{dc}^* z^{-g} H - F S_n \Lambda_b = \Lambda_a^* \Lambda_d F_s \Lambda_{as} z^{-g} \tag{74}$$

The scalar g is the smallest positive integer to make these equations polynomial in z^{-1}. The polynomial matrix spectral factors S_n and F_s satisfy:

$$S_n^* S_n = \Lambda_{a2}^* \Lambda_{dc}^* \Lambda^2 \Lambda_{dc} \Lambda_{a2} - \Lambda_d^* \Lambda_a^* \Lambda_a \Lambda_d \tag{75}$$

$$F_s^* F_s = F^* F \tag{76}$$

Controller:

$$C_o = H_r^{-1} N_a H^{-1} G \Lambda_s N_b^{-1} H_q \tag{77}$$

Implied equation:

$$G \Lambda_b + H \Lambda_a = \Lambda_{dc} \Lambda_d \Lambda_{as} F_s \tag{78}$$

Optimum function:

$$X_o = \Lambda^2 \text{ (constant, diagonal matrix)}$$

Input sensitivity matrix:

$$S_m = H_r^{-1} N_a (F_s^{-1} \Lambda_d^{-1} \Lambda_{dc}^{-1} H \Lambda_a \Lambda_{as}^{-1}) N_a^{-1} H_r$$

Output sensitivity matrix:

$$S_r = H_q^{-1} N_b (F_s^{-1} \Lambda_d^{-1} \Lambda_{dc}^{-1} H \Lambda_a \Lambda_{as}^{-1}) N_b^{-1} H_q$$

Control sensitivity matrix:

$$M = H_r^{-1} N_a (F_s^{-1} \Lambda_d^{-1} \Lambda_{dc}^{-1} G \Lambda_s \Lambda_a \Lambda_{as}^{-1}) N_b^{-1} H_q$$

Complementary sensitivity:

$$T_r = H_q^{-1} N_b (F_s^{-1} \Lambda_d^{-1} \Lambda_{dc}^{-1} G \Lambda_b \Lambda_{as}^{-1}) N_b^{-1} H_q.$$

●

Proof: Obtained from the preceding results and the expressions derived in Appendix 1,
4.6 *Optimality*   ●

The equations (73) and (74) are diagonal because of the assumed form of the system structure. Each of the equations may therefore be solved, as in the scalar case, for

$$\Lambda^2 = \text{diag}\{\lambda_1^2, \lambda_2^2, ..., \lambda_r^2\}.$$

The maximum singular value, or Λ^2 in Lemma 3.1, can be equated with the largest of these values of λ_i^2 (denoted by λ_0^2).

Clearly in this problem, where the loops are independent, each of the λ_i^2 may be set at the optimum levels without changing the minimum value of λ_0^2. This solution is *super-optimal* in the sense that not only the maximum singular value is minimized but all the singular values are limited and each has an equalizing solution.

Note that as indicated in §3.2, by changing the disturbance model Λ_d (equation (55)) the values of λ_i^2 may be changed without changing the controller. For example, changing Λ_d to $\Lambda_d \Lambda_n$ and replacing Λ^2 by $\Lambda^2 \Lambda_n^2$ implies $S_n \to S_n \Lambda_n$, $G \to G \Lambda_n$ and $H \to H \Lambda_n$. The controller (77) is not therefore changed by such rescaling but the singular values are changed by Λ_n. If Λ_n is chosen so that all the λ_i^2 are equal to λ_0^2 then the associated disturbance model $\Lambda_d \Lambda_n \Lambda_a^{-1}$ is a worst case disturbance. This corresponds with the situation where the disturbance in each loop is increased until all the λ_i^2 are equal to the maximum.

4.7 *Mixed sensitivity cost-function*

The mixed sensitivity cost-function considered by Kwakernaak (1985[16]) and other authors, is defined as:

$$J_\infty = \| X \|_\infty \text{ where } X \triangleq Y_f (S_r Q_c^* S_r^* + T_r P_c T_r^*) Y_f^*$$

where S_r and T_r are defined by (9) and (10), respectively. The cost-function (33) may be written in this form by writing:

$$R_c = W^* P_c W = A_r^{*-1} B_r^* B_r A_r^{-1} \quad \text{(from (18))}$$

The B_r and A_r terms are defined from the stable spectral factors of this expression.

4.8 Inherent robustness properties of H_∞ optimal control laws

There is a belief that H_∞ optimal control laws are fundamentally more robust than other design methods. However, this is not necessarily true unless careful design procedures are followed. To illustrate the problem consider equation (71) which includes the inverse of the $B_r A_r^{-1}$ weighting term. Now if the B_r weighting term is selected, as noted above, to weight the complementary sensitivity term, then B_r will depend upon N_i (see equation (51)), and the controller will include the inverse of N_i. If N_i is a square constant matrix which is nearly singular, then although this is an optimal solution it may be very sensitive to parameter variations.

This observation is not a result of unrealistic assumptions in the problem description. If say the system has a multiplicative uncertainty conventional wisdom is to minimize a cost function $J_\infty = \| \Delta G T Y_f \|_\infty^2$ and hence N_i will appear as mentioned above. Clearly if N_i is nearly singular two options are available. Input and output transformations can be used on the plant to reduce the number of inputs and outputs (Grimble and Fotakis, 1982[16]). Alternatively, a more sophisticated criterion can be introduced which will ensure N_i does not appear in the spectral factors D_c and D_{co} (equation (53)). This will then avoid the inverse of N_i in the controller. It is therefore possible to obtain good robust designs but as with competing design procedures, such as robust LQG (Athans, 1986[18]), the cost-function and system model structure must be selected carefully.

Example 4.1:   Industrial Design Problem

The block diagram of a beam rolling mill multivariable system is shown in Fig. 4. This represents conditions about a given operating point. A negative change in s_1 or s_2 corresponds to a positive increase in the outputs f_1 or f_2.

Discrete System models:

$$W(s) = \begin{bmatrix} 1 & -0.045 \\ -0.0045 & 1 \end{bmatrix} \begin{bmatrix} -342 & 0 \\ 0 & -600 \end{bmatrix} \begin{bmatrix} \dfrac{8000}{(s^2+72s+90^2)} & 0 \\ 0 & \dfrac{7830}{(s^2+71s+88^2)} \end{bmatrix}$$

$$= \begin{bmatrix} -2.736 & 0.211410 \\ 0.012312 & -4.698 \end{bmatrix} \begin{bmatrix} \dfrac{10^6}{(s^2+72s+90^2)} & 0 \\ 0 & \dfrac{10^6}{(s^2+71s+88^2)} \end{bmatrix}$$

The sampled model (sample time T = 20 millisecs) is given as:

$$W(z^{-1}) = \begin{bmatrix} -2.736 & 0.211 \\ 0.0123 & -4.698 \end{bmatrix} \begin{bmatrix} W_{11}(z^{-1}) & 0 \\ 0 & W_{22}(z^{-1}) \end{bmatrix}$$

$$W_{11}(z^{-1}) = \frac{39.53(z+1)^2 z^{-1}}{z^2 - 0.15z + 0.43} = \frac{39.53(z+1)^2 z^{-1}}{((z-0.075)^2 + 0.652^2)}$$

$$W_{22}(z^{-1}) = \frac{40.25(z+1)^2 z^{-1}}{z^2 - 0.182z + 0.43} = \frac{40.25(z+1)^2 z^{-1}}{((z-0.091)^2 + 0.648^2)}$$

The disturbance model may be represented in discrete form as:

$$W_d(z^{-1}) = \text{diag}\{W_{d11}(z^{-1}), W_{d22}(z^{-1})\}$$

where

$$W_{d11}(z^{-1}) = \frac{z(z-0.9928)}{z^2 - 1.98z + 0.9975} = \frac{z(z-0.9928)}{((z-0.991)^2 + 0.119^2)}$$

$$W_{d22}(z^{-1}) = \frac{z(z-0.9824)}{z^2 - 1.96z + 0.9962} = \frac{z(z-0.9824)}{((z-0.98)^2 + 0.1856^2)}$$

The model frequency responses are shown in Fig. 5.

System Model:

$$W = A_q^{-1} A^{-1} B = B_1 A_1^{-1} = \begin{bmatrix} -2.736 & 0.2114 \\ 0.0123 & -4.698 \end{bmatrix} \begin{bmatrix} W_{11}/(1-z^{-1}) & 0 \\ 0 & W_{22}/(1-z^{-1}) \end{bmatrix}$$

Writing $A_1 = A_{12}A_{11}$ and letting $A_{11} = (1-z^{-1})I_2$ and

$$A_{12} = \begin{bmatrix} 1-0.15z^{-1} + 0.43z^{-2} & 0 \\ 0 & 1-0.182z^{-1} + 0.43z^{-2} \end{bmatrix}$$

thus

$$B_1 = \begin{bmatrix} -108 & 8.5 \\ 0.486 & -189 \end{bmatrix} \begin{bmatrix} (1+z^{-1})^2 z^{-1} & 0 \\ 0 & (1+z^{-1})^2 z^{-1} \end{bmatrix}$$

Cost weighting functions:

$$B_q A_q^{-1} \quad \text{and} \quad B_r A_{r1}^{-1} | A_{12}^{-1}$$

To introduce integral action into the controller let $B_q = \text{diag}\{q_1, q_2\}$ and $A_q \triangleq (1-z^{-1})I_2$. To ensure the controller rolls off at high frequency let the control weighting include the sampled equivalent of $(s+10)^2$, that is $12100(z-0.8182)^2/(z+1)^2$. Thus, as in §4.7, equation (81), define:

$$B_r A_{r1}^{-1} = \begin{bmatrix} -108 & 8.5 \\ 0.486 & -189 \end{bmatrix} (1+z^{-1})^2 . 12100^2 \frac{(1-0.8182z^{-1})^2}{(1+z^{-1})^2}$$

or

$$B_r \triangleq 12100 \begin{bmatrix} -108 & 8.5 \\ 0.486 & -189 \end{bmatrix} (1-0.8182z^{-1})^2$$

and

$$A_{r1}E_1 \triangleq I_2.$$

By defining $B_r A_r^{-1}$ to include the plant transfer-function $A^{-1}B$ (excluding the delay term) the control weighting provides a complementary sensitivity costing term, as described in §4.7. The frequency response of the above control weighting term is shown in Fig. 6.

Canonical System models:

$$B_q B_1 A_{ro} = B_q B_1 A_{r1} = \begin{bmatrix} q_1 & 0 \\ 0 & q_2 \end{bmatrix} \begin{bmatrix} -108 & 8.5 \\ 0.486 & -189 \end{bmatrix} (1+z^{-1})^2 z^{-1} = N_b \Lambda_b N_i$$

and hence $N_b = I_2$, $\Lambda_b = \text{diag}\{q_1(1+z^{-1})^2 z^{-1}, q_2(1+z^{-1})^2 z^{-1}\}$,

$$N_i = \begin{bmatrix} -108 & 8.5 \\ 0.486 & -189 \end{bmatrix}$$

$$B_r A_{11} = 12100 N_i (1-0.8182z^{-1})^2 (1-z^{-1}) = N_a \Lambda_a N_i$$

and hence $N_a = I_2$, $\Lambda_a = 12100(1-0.8182z^{-1})^2(1-z^{-1})I_2$.

$$N_b^{-1}B_q A_q^{-1}A^{-1}D_f = \frac{1}{1-z^{-1}}\begin{bmatrix} q_1 & 0 \\ 0 & q_2 \end{bmatrix}\begin{bmatrix} \dfrac{z(z-0.9928)}{z^2-1.9831z+0.9975}, & 0 \\ & \\ 0 & \dfrac{z(z-0.9824)}{z^2-1.961z+0.9962} \end{bmatrix}$$

$$= \Lambda_d \Lambda_{a2}^{-1}$$

and hence

$$\Lambda_d = \begin{bmatrix} q_1(1-0.9928z^{-1}) & 0 \\ 0 & q_2(1-0.9824z^{-1}) \end{bmatrix}$$

and

$$\Lambda_{a2} = \begin{bmatrix} 1-1.9831z^{-1}+0.9975z^{-2}, & 0 \\ 0 & , 1-1.961z^{-1}+0.9962z^{-2} \end{bmatrix}(1-z^{-1})$$

By definition Λ_{as} is Hurwitz and satisfies $\Lambda_{as}^*\Lambda_{as} = \Lambda_a^*\Lambda_a$ and hence $\Lambda_{as} = \Lambda_a$ in this problem. This implies $\Lambda_a = \Lambda_{as} = I_2$ and $\Lambda_s = \Lambda_{as} = \Lambda_a$.

Equations to be solved:

The equations to be solved in Theorem 3.3 for the optimal controller may be written as:

$$\Lambda_{dc}^* z^{-g}G_m + FS_n\Lambda_a = \Lambda_b^*\Lambda_d\Lambda_a F_s z^{-g} \tag{82}$$

$$\Lambda_{dc}^* z^{-g}H_m + FS_n\Lambda_b = \Lambda_a^*\Lambda_d\Lambda_a F_s z^{-g} \tag{83}$$

where

$$\Lambda_{dc}^*\Lambda_{dc} = \Lambda_b^*\Lambda_b + \Lambda_a^*\Lambda_a \tag{84}$$

$$S_n^*S_n = \Lambda_{dc}^*\Lambda_{dc}\Lambda_{a2}^*\Lambda_{a2}\Lambda^2 - \Lambda_d^*\Lambda_d\Lambda_a^*\Lambda_a \tag{85}$$

$$C_o = H_r^{-1}H_m^{-1}G_mH_q$$

$$= A_{12}N_i^{-1}\frac{1}{12100(1-0.8182z^{-1})^2}H_m^{-1}G_m\,\mathrm{diag}\{q_1,q_2\}\frac{1}{(1-z^{-1})} \tag{86}$$

$$W = A_q B_1 A_1^{-1} = N_i(1+z^{-1})^2 z^{-1} A_{12}^{-1}$$

$$WC_o = \frac{(1+z^{-1})^2 z^{-1}}{12100(1-0.8182z^{-1})^2(1-z^{-1})} H_m^{-1} G_m \, diag\{q_1, q_2\}$$

Observe that the choice of cost weightings ensures the controller includes integral action and the loop transfer-function WC_o includes the inverse of the control lead element $12100(1-0.8182z^{-1})^2/(1+z^{-1})^2$ which ensures the loop gain falls off at high frequencies.

Results

If $q_1 = q_2 = 0.2 \times 12100$ then the computed controller matrices (to 2 decimal places) become:

$$H_m^{-1} G_m = diag \{ \frac{(2.43 - 8.1z^{-1} + 10.1z^{-2} - 5.57z^{-3} + 1.15z^{-4})}{(1 - 1.1z^{-1} - 0.4z^{-2} + 0.2z^{-3} + 0.34z^{-4})},$$

$$\frac{2.4 - 8.05z^{-1} + 10.05z^{-2} - 5.6z^{-3} + 1.15z^{-4}}{(1 - 1.1z^{-1} - 0.39z^{-2} + 0.21z^{-3} + 0.34z^{-4})} \}$$

and the computed Λ^2 matrix becomes:

$$\Lambda^2 = \begin{bmatrix} \lambda_1^2 & 0 \\ 0 & \lambda_2^2 \end{bmatrix} = 12100^2 \begin{bmatrix} 0.5538 & 0 \\ 0 & 0.5576 \end{bmatrix}.$$

The open-loop frequency responses and the step responses for the two loops are shown in Figs. 7 to 9. The sensitivity functions for the system are shown in Fig. 10. The presence of the integrator within the error weighting term ensures that the sensitivity function is small at low frequencies. The choice of the control weighting term ensures the controller gain falls at high frequency to reject measurement noise, as shown in Fig. 11.

Mismatched Conditions

In practice the controller will not include on exact inverse to the plant constant matrix. Interaction will therefore occur, as for example, in the following case:

$$G_x N_i^{-1} = \begin{bmatrix} -80 & 25 \\ 40 & -170 \end{bmatrix} \begin{bmatrix} -108 & 8.5 \\ 0.486 & -189 \end{bmatrix}^{-1} = \begin{bmatrix} 0.74 & -0.1 \\ -0.37 & 0.88 \end{bmatrix}$$

The closed-loop step responses for this case are shown in Fig. 12.

5. Simplified Design Procedure

McFarlane and Glover (1990, [23]) have developed a loop shaping design procedure which is closely related to the situation considered below. In each case the H_∞ problem is particularly simple to solve. This is particulalry appropriate in process control applications where simplified controllers and calculation procedures are necessary if they are to become widely accepted.

The solution of the H_∞ control problem is much simplified if a certain relationship exists between the weighting matrices and disturbance model (Grimble, 1988 [12]). Consider for example equations (42), (57) and (58):

$$S^*S = \Lambda^2 - (S_d^*\Lambda_{dc}^*)^{-1}(\Lambda_d^*\Lambda_a^*\Lambda_a\Lambda_d)(\Lambda_{dc}S_d)^{-1}. \tag{87}$$

Assume that the weighted disturbance model (55) $\Lambda_d\Lambda_{a2}^{-1}$ is chosen so that Λ_{a2} satisfies:

$$\Lambda_{a2}^*\Lambda_{a2} = \Lambda_a^*\Lambda_a = \Lambda_{as}^*\Lambda_{as} \text{ and from (58):}$$

$$S_d = \Lambda_{a2} = \Lambda_{as} \text{ and } \Lambda_d \triangleq \Lambda_{dc}\Lambda_\rho \tag{88}$$

where $\Lambda_\rho = \text{diag}\{\rho_1,\rho_2,..,\rho_r\}$ denote weighting scalars to be selected by the designer. In this case (87) gives:

$$S^*S = \Lambda^2 - \Lambda_\rho^2. \tag{89}$$

The matrix S is a diagonal real constant matrix:

$$S = \text{diag}\{s_1,s_2,..,s_r\}$$

where $s_i = (\lambda_i^2-\rho_i^2)^{1/2}$, i=1,2,..,r (for a solution to exist the $\lambda_i^2 > \rho_i^2$). Note from equation (56): S_n is given as $S_n = S\Lambda_{dc}S_d$.

The above procedure is equivalent to choosing the matrix Y_f in the cost-function (34) so that S reduces to a diagonal constant matrix. This implies that Y_f is treated as a weighting function as in the work of Kwakernaak (1985 [16]). The consequence of selecting the weighting function in this way is that the equations to be solved reduce to an eigenvalue/ eignvector problem which is particularly easy to solve. The disadvantage of selecting the function in this way is that the disturbance rejection properties of the system may deteriorate since normally y_f is selected based upon the stochastic models in the system. The set of $\{s_i\}$ values represent the eigenvalues to be computed.

A lemma may be used to summarize the results for this simplified design procedure.

Lemma 5.1: Simplified Design Procedure

Consider the canonical industrial system introduced in Theorem 3.3 but with the additional assumption that the disturbance model is related to the weightings by defining $\Lambda_d\Lambda_{a2}^{-1} = \Lambda_{dc}\Lambda_\rho\Lambda_{as}^{-1}$ where Λ_ρ is a diagonal constant scaling matrix. The following linear equations must be solved for the minimal degree solution (H_0, G_0,F), with respect to F:

$$\Lambda_{dc}^*z^{-g}G_0 + FS\Lambda_a = \Lambda_b^*\Lambda_\rho F_s z^{-g} \tag{90}$$

$$\Lambda_{dc}^*z^{-g}H_0 - FS\Lambda_b = \Lambda_a^*\Lambda_\rho F_s z^{-g} \tag{91}$$

where F_s is Hurwitz and satisfies $F_s^*F_s = F^*F$.

Controller:

$$C_0 = H_r^{-1} N_a H_0^{-1} G_0 N_b^{-1} H_q \tag{92}$$

Implied equations:

$$G_0 \Lambda_b + H_0 \Lambda_a = \Lambda_{dc} \Lambda_\rho F_s \tag{93}$$

Optimum function:

$$X = \Lambda^2 \tag{94}$$

Input sensitivity matrix:

$$S_m = H_r^{-1} N_a (F_s^{-1} \Lambda_\rho^{-1} \Lambda_{dc}^{-1} H_0 \Lambda_a) N_a^{-1} H_r$$

Output sensitivity matrix:

$$S_r = H_q^{-1} N_b (F_s^{-1} \Lambda_\rho^{-1} \Lambda_{dc}^{-1} H_0 \Lambda_a) N_b^{-1} H_q$$

Control sensitivity matrix:

$$M = H_r^{-1} N_a (F_s^{-1} \Lambda_\rho^{-1} \Lambda_{dc}^{-1} G_0 \Lambda_a) N_b^{-1} H_q$$

Complementary sensitivity:

$$T_r = H_q^{-1} N_b (F_s^{-1} \Lambda_\rho^{-1} \Lambda_{dc}^{-1} G_0 \Lambda_b) N_b^{-1} H_q.$$

Proof: By substituting in the results of Theorem 3.3

5.1 Computational procedure

Note the main equations to be solved (90), (91) are, because of the canonical model, diagonal. The computations are therefore similar to those involved in the scalar case. In addition, because of the assumed form of the disturbance model, the equations (90), (91) reduce to a linear eigenproblem with set of eigenvalues collected in the diagonal matrix S. Thus, the consequence of the two types of assumption is a very simple numerical calculation procedure.

6. Conclusions

A canonical industrial system model has been proposed which is representative of a reasonable class of process control problems. If the control weighting function is chosen in a particular way, as when complementary sensitivity is being costed, then the main H_∞ equations to be solved, for this class of system, are decoupled. The equations can therefore be solved by repeatedly using a scalar equation solver. This does not imply the H_∞ optimal controller is diagonal, since the controller depends both on the solution of these equations and on other terms. However, the equations which involve the most difficult calculations are decoupled.

A simple design procedure was then introduced which employed a relationship between the cost weights and disturbance model to considerably simplify the equations. This assumed relationship can be shown to be physically reasonable in some problems and leads to a set of equations which can be solved as a standard eigenproblem. Thus, Lambda iteration can be avoided when this assumption is made. The two sets of simplifications enable a class of process control multivariable problems to be solved, by standard eigen-problem software, following a very straightforward procedure.

The H_∞ robust design procedures have much to offer the process industries. However, both the theory and algorithms are relatively complicated. Expert systems techniques can be employed in CAD procedures to assist the designer and to exploit more fully the formalized design procedures. These procedures can be easily established and they include well defined design rules, particularly suitable for the application of AI methods.

Other multivariable design procedures developed for process control applications such as Dynamic Matrix Control or Generalized Predictive Control do not have good robustness properties. For example, if the system is non-minimum phase and the control weighting is small then the closed loop system will be unstable with such designs. The LQG and H_∞ design appoaches are robust in such circumstances, however, they are more computationally intensive.

Acknowledgements

We are grateful for the collaboration with Professor Huibert Kwakernaak of Twente University of Technology, The Netherlands, and for the support of the European Economic Community. We are also grateful for the support of the Science and Engineering Research Council.

References

1. Zames, G., *Feedback, optimal sensitivity and plant uncertainty via multiplicative seminorms*, IFAC Congress VIII, Kyoto, Japan, pp. 74-78, 1981.

2. Zames, G., *Feedback and optimal sensitivity : model reference transformations, multiplicative seminorms and approximate inverses*, IEEE Trans. on Auto. Control. AC-26, 2, pp. 301-320, 1981.

3. Zames, G., and B.A. Francis, *A new approach to classical frequency methods : feedback and minimax sensitivity*, CDC Conference San Diego, California, 1981.

4. Doyle, J., Glover, K., Khargonekar, P., and B. Francis, *State-space solutions to standard H_2 and H_∞ control problems*, presented at American Control Conf. Atlanta, Georgia, Vol. 2, 1691-1696, June 1988.

5. Kwakernaak, H., *A polynomial approach to minimax frequency domain optimization of multivariable systems*, I.J. Control, No. 1, pp. 117-156, 1986.

6. Kwakernaak, H., *Minimax frequency domain optimization of multivariable linear feedback systems*, IFAC World Congress, Budapest, 1984.

7. Boekhoudt, P., and H., Kwakernaak, *A polynomial approach to the H_∞ control design method*, Presented at American Control Conf. Atlanta, Georgia, Vol. 2, 1219-1224, June 1988.

8. Grimble, M.J., *Optimal H_∞ robustness and the relationship to LQG design problems*, Int. J. Control, 43, 2, pp. 351-372, 1986.

9. Grimble, M.J., *Simplification of the equations in the paper Optimal H_∞ robustness and the relationship*, Int. J. Control. Vol. 46, 5, pp. 1841-1843, 1987.

10. Grimble, M.J., H_∞ *robust controller for self-tuning control applications, Part 2 : Self-tuning robustness*, Int. J. Control. Vol. 46, No. 5. 1819-1840, 1987.

11. Grimble, M.J., *Generalized LQG and H_∞ multivariable controllers* Presented at the American Control Conf. Minneapolis, 1987.

12. Grimble, M.J., *Optimal H_∞ multivariable robust controllers and the relationship to LQG design problems*, Int. J. Control, Vol. 48, 1, pp. 33-58, 1988.

13. Kucera, V., *Discrete Linear Control*, John Wiley & Sons Ltd., Chichester, 1979.

14. Grimble, M.J., *Multivariable controllers for LQG self-tuning applications with coloured measurement noise and dynamic cost weighting*, Int. J. Systems Science, Vol. 17, No. 4, 543-557, 1986.

15. Grimble, M.J., and D. Biss, *Selection of optimal control weighting functions to achieve good H_∞ robust design*, Presented at IEE Control 88 Conf. Oxford, April 1988.

16. Kwakernaak, H., *Minimax frequency domain performance and robustness optimization of linear feedback systems'*, IEEE Trans. on Auto. Control, AC-30, 10, pp. 994-1004, 1985.

17. Grimble, M.J. and J. Fotakis, *The design of strip shape control systems for Sendzimir mills*, IEEE Trans on Auto. Contr., Vol. AC-27, No. 3, pp. 656-665, June 1982.

18. Athans, M., *A tutorial on the LQG/LTR method*, American Contr. Conf. Seattle, WA, June 1986.

19. Grimble, M.J. and Johnson, M.A., *Optimal Control and Stochastic Estimation Theory, Parts I and II* John Wiley, London, 1988.

20. Kwakernaak, H., *A polynomial approach to H_∞ optimization of control systems*, in Modelling, Robustness and Sensitivity Reduction in Control Systems, edited by R. Curtain, Series F. Computer and Systems Sciences, Vol. 34, pp. 83-94, Springer Verlag, 1986.

21. Young, N.J. *The Nevalinna-Pick problem for matrix-valued functions*, J. Operator Theory, 15-2, pp. 239-265.

22. Postlethwaite, I. Tsai, M.C. and Gu, D.W., *State space approach to discrete-time superoptimal H_∞ control problems*, Int. J. Control, Vol. 49, No. 5, pp. 247-268, 1989.

23. McFarlane, D.C. and Glover K., *Robust controller design using normalized coprime factor plant descriptions*, Springer-Verlag, 1990.

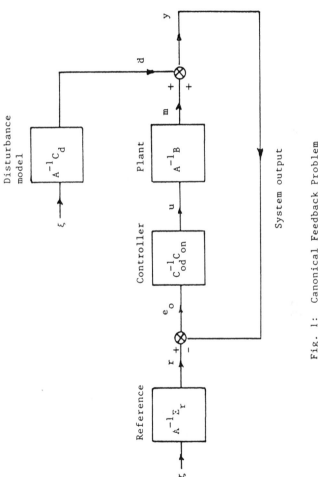

Fig. 1: Canonical Feedback Problem

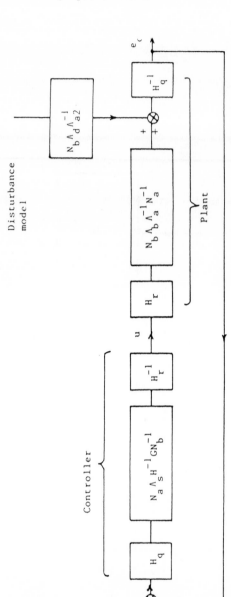

Fig. 2: System Model Using Canonical Subsystem Models

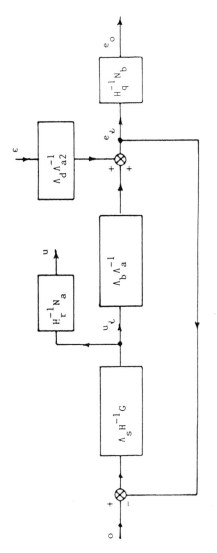

Fig. 3: Equivalent Weighted Controller and System Models

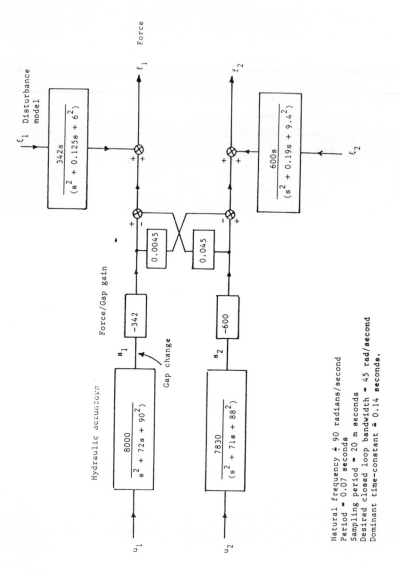

Fig. 4: Industrial Multivariable System Model

Natural frequency $\doteq$ 90 radians/second
Period = 0.07 seconds
Sampling period = 20 m seconds
Desired closed loop bandwidth = 45 rad/second
Dominant time-constant $\doteq$ 0.14 seconds.

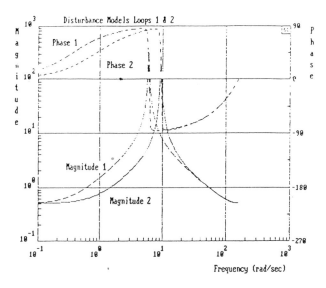

Fig. 5: <u>Disturbance Model Frequency Responses</u>

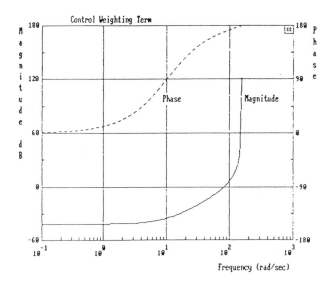

Fig. 6: <u>Frequency Response of the Control Weighting Term</u>

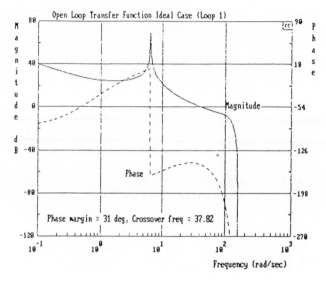

Fig. 7: <u>Open Loop Frequency Response (Loop 1)</u>

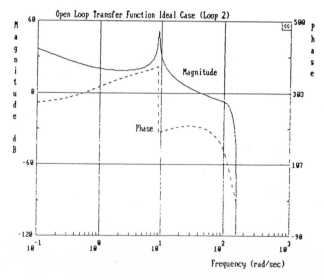

Fig. 8: <u>Open Loop Frequency Response (Loop 2)</u>

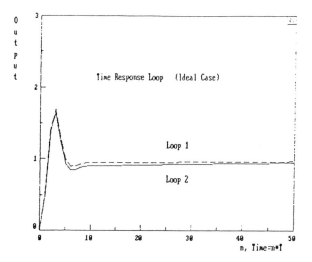

Fig. 9: The Closed-Loop Step Response
for Loops 1 and 2

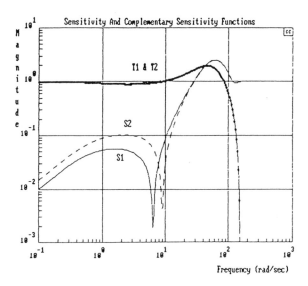

Fig. 10: Sensitivity and Complementary Sensitivity
Function Frequency Responses

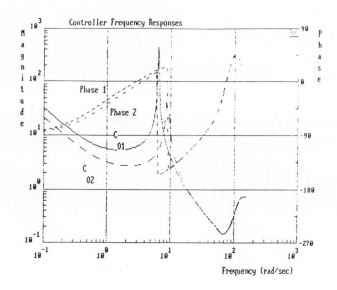

Fig. 11:   Controller Frequency Responses for
          Loops 1 and 2

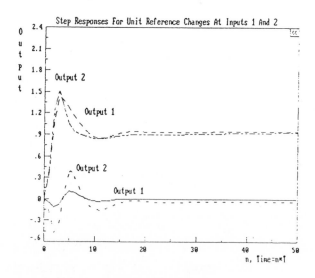

Fig.   12:   Unit Step Responses For Closed-Loop
            System Under Mismatched Conditions

Index